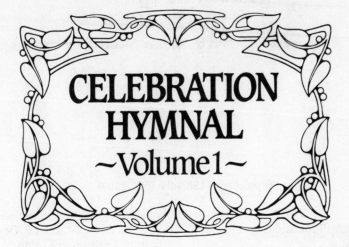

CELEBRATION HYMNAL
~Volume 1~

With Supplement

MAYHEW McCRIMMON
Great Wakering Essex England

First published in Great Britain in 1977
by
Mayhew-McCrimmon Ltd.
Great Wakering, Essex

(Supplement) ISBN 0-85597-230-0

Cum originali concordat John P. Dewis
Imprimatur Christopher Creede, V.G.

The imprimatur has been given in respect of the Supplement, the Order of
Mass only.

Compilation by Fr. Patrick Taylor, Fr. Anthony Boylan, Fr. Tim Sullivan.

Cover: Jim Bowler

Printed and bound in Great Britain by
Bemrose Printing, Confidential & Information Products, Derby

INTRODUCTORY RITES

The purpose of these rites is to make the assembled people a unified community and to prepare them to listen to God's Word and celebrate the Eucharist worthily and well.

The Introductory Rites may vary in a number of ways and on certain occasions some parts are omitted or are replaced by alternative rites.

Entrance Rite

All stand as the celebrant and ministers enter. An entrance song is sung or recited.

All make the sign of the cross with the celebrant as he says:

In the name of the Father, and of the Son, and of the Holy Spirit.
Amen.

The celebrant greets the people and all reply:

And also with you.

A few words may be said to introduce the celebration.

Then follows

Either: *The Rite of Blessing and Sprinkling Holy Water (page 5)*
Or: *One of the forms of the Penitential Rite (below).*

Penitential Rite

One of three forms is used:

1 *The celebrant invites the people to reflect in silence. All then pray together:*

I confess to almighty God,
and to you, my brothers and sisters,
that I have sinned through my own fault

All strike their breast

in my thoughts and in my words,
in what I have done,
and in what I have failed to do;
and I ask blessed Mary, ever virgin,
all the angels and saints,
and you, my brothers and sisters,
to pray for me to the Lord our God.

The celebrant says the absolution

> May almighty God have mercy on us,
> forgive us our sins,
> and bring us to everlasting life.
> > **Amen.**

The invocations, Lord, have mercy follow (below).

Or 2 *The celebrant invites the people to reflect in silence.*
He then leads them in prayer for mercy.

> Lord, we have sinned against you:
> Lord, have mercy.
> > **Lord, have mercy.**
> Lord, show us your mercy and love.
> > **And grant us your salvation.**

The celebrant says the absolution

> May almighty God have mercy on us,
> forgive us our sins,
> and bring us to everlasting life.
> > **Amen.**

The invocations, Lord, have mercy follow (below).

Or 3 *The celebrant invites the people to reflect in silence. Then he, or another minister, introduces the following petitions for mercy by proclaiming reasons for our trust in God's forgiveness:*

> . . . Lord, have mercy. **Lord, have mercy.**
> . . . Christ, have mercy. **Christ, have mercy.**
> . . . Lord, have mercy. **Lord, have mercy.**

The celebrant says the absolution:

> May almighty God have mercy on us,
> forgive us our sins,
> and bring us to everlasting life.
> > **Amen.**

The celebrant continues with the Glory to God (page 5) or, if this is omitted, the Opening Prayer (page 6).

Invocations

The invocations, Lord, have mercy, *follow unless they have already been used in one of the forms of the act of penance.*

> Lord, have mercy. **Lord, have mercy.**
> Christ, have mercy. **Christ, have mercy.**
> Lord, have mercy. **Lord, have mercy.**

The celebrant continues with the Glory to God (below) or, if this is omitted, the Opening Prayer (page 6).

Rite of Blessing and Sprinkling Holy Water

This may replace the Penitential Rite.

The water will be used to remind us of our baptism.

The celebrant invites the people to pray. After a pause for silent prayer, he blesses the water. All respond: **Amen.**

Where customary, he may also bless salt and mix it with the water. To this prayer of blessing the people respond: **Amen.**

The celebrant then sprinkles himself, his ministers and the people. Meanwhile, an appropriate song is sung.

When he returns to his place, the celebrant concludes as follows.

May almighty God cleanse us of our sins,
and through the eucharist we celebrate
make us worthy to sit at his table
in his heavenly kingdom.
    Amen.

Glory to God

On Sundays outside Advent and Lent, on solemnities and feasts and on certain other days, all sing or recite together:

Glory to God in the highest,
    and peace to his people on earth.

Lord God, heavenly King,
almighty God and Father,
    we worship you, we give you thanks,
    we praise you for your glory.

Lord Jesus Christ, only Son of the Father,
Lord God, Lamb of God,
you take away the sin of the world:
    have mercy on us;
you are seated at the right hand of the Father:
    receive our prayer.

For you alone are the Holy One,
you alone are the Lord,
you alone are the Most High,
    Jesus Christ,
    with the Holy Spirit,
    in the glory of God the Father. Amen.

Opening Prayer

The celebrant invites the people to pray. After a pause for silent prayer, he sings or says the Opening Prayer.

At the end of the prayer, all respond: **Amen.**

All sit for the first part of the Liturgy of the Word which follows.

LITURGY OF THE WORD

In the readings, explained by the homily, God speaks to his people of redemption and salvation; in the Gospels Christ is present among the faithful through his word. By sacred songs and by the Profession of Faith, they express their joy and belief. Finally, moved by this Word, they pray in the Prayer of the Faithful for the needs of the Church and for the World's salvation.

First Reading (sit)

All listen to the reading, at the end of which the reader adds:

This is the Word of the Lord. **Thanks be to God.**

Responsorial Psalm

The people join in the response to the psalm. It is customary to repeat the response after the cantor at the beginning of the psalm. The response is repeated after each verse.

Second Reading

The Psalm may be followed by a second reading, at the end of which the reader adds:

This is the Word of the Lord. **Thanks be to God.**

All stand for the proclamation of the Gospel.

The Gospel (stand)

An Alleluia or Acclamation may be sung or recited as a welcome to Christ who is present and speaking to us in the Gospel.

The deacon or priest greets the people and announces the Gospel:

The Lord be with you. **And also with you.**
A reading from the holy gospel according to *N.*
Glory to you, Lord.

At the end of the Gospel the deacon or priest adds:

This is the gospel of the Lord. **Praise to you, Lord Jesus Christ.**

On Sundays and holydays a homily is always given (sit).

If a Sacrament or other special rite is to be celebrated during the eucharist it takes place after the homily.

On Sundays and Solemnities there follows the Profession of Faith. On other days, the celebration continues with the Prayer of the Faithful (page 8). or, if this is omitted, the Liturgy of the Eucharist (page 8).

The Profession of Faith (stand)

On Sundays and Solemnities, all stand to sing or recite together:

We believe in one God,
    the Father, the Almighty,
    maker of heaven and earth,
    of all that is, seen and unseen.

We believe in one Lord, Jesus Christ,
    the only Son of God,
    eternally begotten of the Father,
    God from God, Light from Light,
    true God from true God,
    begotten, not made,
    of one Being with the Father.
    Through him all things were made.
    For us men and for our salvation
        he came down from heaven: *all bow*
    by the power of the Holy Spirit
        he became incarnate from the Virgin Mary, and was made man.

For our sake he was crucified under Pontius Pilate;
    he suffered death and was buried.
    On the third day he rose again
        in accordance with the Scriptures;
    he ascended into heaven
        and is seated at the right hand of the Father.
He will come again in glory to judge the living and the dead,
    and his kingdom will have no end.

We believe in the Holy Spirit, the Lord, the giver of life,
    who proceeds from the Father and the Son.
    With the Father and the Son he is worshipped and glorified.
    He has spoken through the Prophets.
    We believe in one holy catholic and apostolic Church.
    We acknowledge one baptism for the forgiveness of sins.
    We look for the resurrection of the dead,
        and the life of the world to come. Amen.

The Apostles' Creed, for use where permitted, e.g. children's masses.

I believe in God, the Father almighty,
    creator of heaven and earth.

I believe in Jesus Christ, his only Son, our Lord.
    He was conceived by the power of the Holy Spirit
        and born of the Virgin Mary.
    He suffered under Pontius Pilate,
        was crucified, died, and was buried.
    He descended to the dead.
    On the third day he rose again.
    He ascended into heaven,
        and is seated at the right hand of the Father.
    He will come again to judge the living and the dead.

I believe in the Holy Spirit,
    the holy catholic Church,
    the communion of saints,
    the forgiveness of sins,
    the resurrection of the body,
    and the life everlasting. Amen.

Prayer of the Faithful (stand)

The celebrant invites the people to pray.

A series of intentions are announced to the people. The celebrant and people pray for each intention silently, then aloud in these or similar words·

Lord, in your mercy: **hear our prayer.**
or:
Lord, hear us. **Lord, graciously hear us.**

To the celebrant's concluding prayer, all respond: **Amen.**

LITURGY OF THE EUCHARIST

At the Last Supper, Christ instituted the Paschal sacrifice and meal through which Christ is continually made present in the Church.

Taking bread and wine, the priest does what the Lord commanded his disciples to do in his memory.

PREPARATION OF THE ALTAR AND GIFTS (sit)

The altar is prepared. The gifts may be brought in procession. A song may be sung.

If singing is still in progress, the following prayers are said silently and the responses omitted: otherwise, the celebrant may say them in an audible voice and the people respond.

8

Holding the paten with the bread, the celebrant prays:

> Blessed are you, Lord, God of all creation.
> Through your goodness we have this bread to offer,
> which earth has given and human hands have made.
> It will become for us the bread of life.
> **Blessed be God for ever.**

The celebrant prays silently as he pours wine and a little water into the chalice. Then, holding the chalice in his hands, he prays:

> Blessed are you, Lord, God of all creation.
> Through your goodness we have this wine to offer,
> fruit of the vine and work of human hands.
> It will become our spiritual drink.
> **Blessed be God for ever.**

The celebrant prays silently as he washes his hands.
The people then stand.
The celebrant invites the people to pray:

> Pray, brethren, that my sacrifice and yours
> may be acceptable to God, the almighty Father
> **May the Lord accept the sacrifice at your hands,**
> **for the praise and glory of his name,**
> **for our good, and the good of all his Church.**

The celebrant then prays the Prayer over the Gifts, to which all respond:
> **Amen.**

THE EUCHARISTIC PRAYER

The eucharistic prayer is the great hymn of thanksgiving for the whole work of salvation.

The celebrant invites the people to lift their hearts to God in praise and thanksgiving:

> The Lord be with you.
> **And also with you.**

> Lift up your hearts.
> **We lift them up to the Lord.**

> Let us give thanks to the Lord our God.
> **It is right to give him thanks and praise.**

The celebrant continues the preface appropriate to the day. At the end, all sing or recite:

Holy, holy, holy Lord, God of power and might,
heaven and earth are full of your glory.
>Hosanna in the highest.
Blessed is he who comes in the name of the Lord.
>Hosanna in the highest.

Where customary, the people kneel.

The celebrant continues the eucharistic prayer.

At the Consecration:

The celebrant shows the consecrated host to the people. When he genuflects, all bow their heads in adoration.

The celebrant then shows the chalice to the people. When he genuflects, all bow their heads in adoration.

After the Consecration:

The deacon or celebrant sings or says:

Let us proclaim the mystery of faith:

All respond, using one of the following acclamations:

1 Christ has died,
Christ is risen,
Christ will come again.

2 Dying you destroyed our death,
rising you restored our life.
Lord Jesus, come in glory.

3 When we eat this bread and drink this cup,
we proclaim your death, Lord Jesus,
until you come in glory.

4 Lord, by your cross and resurrection
you have set us free.
You are the Saviour of the world.

The celebrant continues the Eucharistic Prayer.

Conclusion of the Eucharistic Prayer:

The celebrant takes the chalice and paten with the host and, lifting them up, sings or says:

Through him,
with him,

in him,
in the unity of the Holy Spirit,
all glory and honour is yours,
almighty Father,
for ever and ever.
Amen.

All stand.

THE COMMUNION RITE

The Lord's Prayer (stand)

The celebrant invites the people to pray with him in the prayer Jesus taught us:

**Our Father, who art in heaven,
hallowed be thy name,
Thy kingdom come.
Thy will be done on earth, as it is in heaven.
Give us this day our daily bread,
and forgive us our trespasses,
as we forgive those who trespass against us,
and lead us not into temptation,
but deliver us from evil.**

The following prayer is sometimes omitted.
At a Nuptial Mass it is replaced by the Nuptial Blessing to which all respond:
Amen.

Deliver us, Lord, from every evil,
and grant us peace in our day.
In your mercy keep us free from sin
and protect us from all anxiety
as we wait in joyful hope
for the coming of our Saviour, Jesus Christ.

**For the kingdom, the power, and the glory are yours,
now and for ever.**

Rite of Peace

The celebrant prays for peace, saying:

Lord Jesus Christ, you said to your apostles:
I leave you peace, my peace I give you.
Look not on our sins, but on the faith of your Church,
and grant us the peace and unity of your kingdom
where you live for ever and ever.
Amen.

The peace of the Lord be with you always.
And also with you.

The deacon or celebrant may then invite everyone to share with those around them a sign expressing their love and unity in the Risen Lord.

Breaking of the Bread

The celebrant breaks the host and prays silently as he places a small piece in the chalice. Meanwhile, the people sing or recite:

**Lamb of God, you take away the sins of the world:
have mercy on us.
Lamb of God, you take away the sins of the world:
have mercy on us.
Lamb of God, you take away the sins of the world:
grant us peace.**

All kneel.

Communion

Communion is the source and sign of our unity in the Church with Christ and one another.

After a brief, silent prayer, the celebrant shows the host to the people, inviting them to share in the eucharistic banquet.

To his invitation, all respond:

**Lord, I am not worthy to receive you,
but only say the word and I shall be healed.**

After the celebrant and ministers have received communion, the people come forward to receive. A communion song may be sung.

After Holy Communion (sit)

All may be seated. A period of silence may be observed or a song of praise may be sung.

As the celebrant rises, all stand. (Stand)

The celebrant invites the people to pray. After a pause for silent prayer, he sings or says the prayer after communion.

At the end of the prayer, all respond: **Amen.**

CONCLUDING RITE

If another liturgical celebration is to follow the eucharist, this rite is omitted.

Some announcements may be made.

Blessing

The celebrant greets the people:

The Lord be with you.
And also with you.

In its solemn form, the blessing below is preceded either by a prayer or by a series of invocations. The people respond to the prayer or to each invocation: **Amen.**

The celebrant then says:

May almighty God bless you,
the Father, and the Son, and the Holy Spirit.
Amen.

The deacon or celebrant dismisses the people. All respond:

Thanks be to God. Amen.

A recessional song may be sung as the celebrant and his ministers leave.

s 1

1. God gives his people strength
   if we believe in his way,
   he's swift to repay all those
   who bear the burden of the day.
   God gives his people strength.

2. God gives his people hope.
   If we but trust in his word,
   our prayers are always heard.
   He warmly welcomes
       anyone who's erred.
   God gives his people hope.

3. God gives his people love.
   If we but open wide our heart,
   he's sure to do his part;
   he's always the first to make a start.
   God gives his people love.

4. God gives his people peace.
   When sorrow fills us to the brim,
   and courage grow dim,
   he lays to rest
       our restlessness in him.
   God gives his people peace.

Medical Mission Sisters

s 2

1. I have counted the cost
       of the years that are gone,
   all the battles I lost
       and the few that I won.
   And the plans that would dawn
       that I somewhere mislaid,
   and the hopes that were born
       and the dreams that decayed.
   Still in spite of the loss
       and the labour in vain,
   still in spite of it all.
       I'll start over again,
   still in spite of it all
       I'll start over again.

2. Lord, I thought that I knew
       all the questions you'd ask,
   what you'd want me to do
       ev'ry truth, ev'ry task;
   and your word seemed so near

and your light seemed so strong
and the road seemed so clear
   that you called me along.
Still in spite of it all
   I will walk in your way,
still in spite of it all,
   I will walk in your way.

3. I had mastered it all,
       all my answers were true,
   but when I heard your call
       all your questions were new;
   all the ways that you came,
       the disguises you wore,
   you were just not the same,
       not the same anymore.
   Still in spite of the loss
       and in spite of the pain,
   still in spite of it all
       I will find you again,
   still in spite of it all
       I will find you again.

Kevin Nichols

s 3

1. Now the green blade riseth
       from the buried grain,
   wheat that in the dark earth
       many days has lain;
   love lives again,
       that with the dead has been:
   love is come again
       like wheat that springeth green.

2. In the grave they laid him,
       Love whom men had slain,
   thinking that never
       he would wake again,
   laid in the earth
       like grain that sleeps unseen:
   love is come again
       like wheat that springeth green.

3. Forth he came at Easter,
       like the risen grain,
   he that for three days
       in the grave had lain,
   quick from the dead
       my risen Lord is seen:
   love is come again
       like wheat that springeth green.

4. When our hearts are wintry,
     grieving or in pain,
   thy touch can call us
     back to life again,
   fields of our heart
     that dead and bare have been:
   love is come again
     like wheat that springeth green.

J. M. C. Crum

s 4

St. David

1. O Great Saint David,
     still we hear thee call us,
   unto a life that knows
     no fear of death;
   Yea, down the ages,
     will thy words enthral us,
   strong happy words:
     'Be joyful, keep the faith'.

Chorus:
On Cambria's sons stretch out
   thy hands in blessing;
For our dear land
   thy help we now implore.
Lead us to God,
   with humble hearts confessing
Jesus, Lord and King
   for evermore.

2. Christ was the centre rock
     of all thy teaching,
   God's holy will —
     the splendour of its theme.
   His grace informed,
     his love inflamed thy preaching
   Christ's sway on earth,
     the substance of thy dream.

Chorus: On Cambria's sons, etc.

3. In early childhood,
     choosing Jesus only,
   Thy fervour showed his yoke
     was light and sweet
   and thus for thee,
     life's journey was not lonely —
   the path made plain
     by prints of wounded feet.

Chorus: On Cambria's sons, etc.

4. O glorious saint,
     we wander in the dark;
   With thee we seek
     our trusted guide in Rome.
   Help him to steer
     on earth Saint Peter's barque,
   that we may safely reach
     our heavenly home.

Chorus: On Cambria's sons, etc.

Francis E. Mostyn (1860-1939)

s 5

1. Saint Andrew,
     called to follow Christ,
   to learn to fish for men;
   sought out his brother Peter first
   and brought him to the Lord.

2. Then with five thousand to be fed
   in desert wild and drear;
   'twas Andrew found a boy with bread
   and brought him to the Lord.

3. And when the Greeks
     through Philip sought
   that Jesus they might see;
   'twas Andrew first whom Philip brough
   to bring them to the Lord.

4. So may we, this St Andrew's-tide,
   share Andrew's burning zeal;
   and fish for men both far and wide,
   to bring them to the Lord.

Frank Gibson

s 6

1. Hail, holy Joseph, hail!
   husband of Mary, hail!
   Chaste as the lily flower
   in Eden's peaceful vale.

2. Hail, holy Joseph, hail!
   Father of Christ esteemed,
   Father be thou to those
   thy foster Son redeemed.

3. Hail, holy Joseph, hail!
   Prince of the house of God,
   may his blest graces be
   by thy pure hands bestowed.

4. Hail, holy Joseph, hail!
   comrade of angels, hail:
   cheer thou the hearts that faint,
   and guide the steps that fail.

5. Hail, holy Joseph, hail!
   God's choice wert thou alone;
   to thee the Word made flesh
   was subject as a Son.

6. Mother of Jesus, bless,
   and bless, ye saints on high,
   all meek and simple souls
   that to Saint Joseph cry.

Frederick William Faber (1814-1863)

s 7

Lord make me an instrument
    of thy peace.

1. Where there is hatred,
       let me sow love,
   Where there is injury, pardon.

2. Where there is doubt,
       let me bring faith.
   Where there's despair, hope.

3. Where there is darkness,
       let me bring light.
   Where there is sadness, joy.

4. Grant I may not seek
       to be consoled as to console;
   not seek to be understood
       as to understand;
   to be loved as to love.

5. For it is in giving
       that we receive,
   in pardoning
       that we are pardoned;
   and it is in giving
       that we are born to eternal life.

Words (Based on St Francis of Assisi)

s 8

1. Spirit of God
       in the clear running water,
   blowing to greatness
       the trees on the hill.
   Spirit of God
       in the finger of morning,
   fill the earth, bring it to birth
       and blow where you will.
   Blow, blow, blow till I be but breath
       of the Spirit blowing in me.

2. Down in the meadow
       the willows are moaning,
   sheep in the pasture-land
       cannot lie still.
   Spirit of God
       creation is groaning,
   fill the earth, bring it to birth
       and blow where you will.
   Blow, blow, blow till I be but breath
       of the Spirit blowing in me.

3. I saw the scar
       of a year that lay dying,
   heard the lament
       of a lone whip-poorwill.
   Spirit of God
       see that cloud crying,
   fill the earth, bring it to birth
       and blow where you will.
   Blow, blow, blow till I be but breath
       of the Spirit blowing in me.

4. Spirit of God,
       every man's heart is lonely,
   watching and waiting
       and hungry until,
   Spirit of God,
       man longs that you only,

   fulfill the earth, bring it to birth
       and blow where you will.
   Blow, blow, blow till I be but breath
       of the Spirit blowing in me.

Medical Mission Sisters

*(Index for Supplement:
                see inside back cover.)*

Celebration Hymnal

MAYHEW - McCRIMMON
Great Wakering

First Published in Great Britain in 1976 by
MAYHEW - McCRIMMON LTD
Great Wakering
Essex

Reprinted 1982, Reprinted 1983, Reprinted 1984

ISBN 0 85597 094 4

Cover: Jim Bowler

Printed and bound in Great Britain by
Bemrose Printing, Confidential & Information Products, Derby

1

1. Abide with me,
   fast falls the eventide;
   the darkness deepens,
   Lord, with me abide!
   When other helpers fail,
   and comforts flee,
   help of the helpless,
   O abide with me.

2. Swift to its close
   ebbs out life's little day;
   earth's joys grow dim,
   its glories pass away;
   change and decay
   in all around I see;
   O thou who changest not,
   abide with me.

3. I need thy presence
   every passing hour;
   what but thy grace
   can foil the tempter's power?
   Who like thyself
   my guide and stay can be?
   Through cloud and sunshine,
   O abide with me.

4. I fear no foe with thee
   at hand to bless;
   ills have no weight,
   and tears no bitterness.
   Where is death's sting?
   Where, grave, thy victory?
   I triumph still,
   if thou abide with me.

5. Hold thou thy Cross before
   my closing eyes;
   shine through the gloom,
   and point me to the skies;
   heaven's morning breaks,
   and earth's vain shadows flee:
   in life, in death, O Lord,
   abide with me!

   H. F. Lyte (1793-1847)

2

1. Accept, O Father, in thy love,
   these humble gifts of bread and
   wine,
   that with ourselves we offer thee,
   returning gifts already thine.

2. Behold this host and chalice, Lord,
   to thee in heaven the gifts we raise;
   through them may we our homage
   pay,
   our adoration and our praise.

3. No earthly claim to grace is ours,
   save what thy sacrifice has won;
   grant then thy grace, fulfil our
   needs,
   and may thy will in ours be done.

   J. Clifford Evers

3

1. All creation, bless the Lord.
   Earth and heaven, bless the Lord.
   Spirits, powers, bless the Lord.
   Praise him for ever.
   Sun and moon, bless the Lord.
   Stars and planets, bless the Lord.
   Dews and showers, bless the Lord.
   Praise him for ever.

2. Winds and breezes, bless the Lord.
   Spring and Autumn, bless the Lord.
   Winter, Summer, bless the Lord.
   Praise him for ever.
   Fire and heat, bless the Lord.
   Frost and cold, bless the Lord.
   Ice and snow, bless the Lord.
   Praise him for ever.

3. Night and daytime, bless the Lord.
   Light and darkness, bless the Lord.
   Clouds and lightning, bless the Lord.
   Praise him for ever.
   All the earth, bless the Lord.
   Hills and mountains, bless the Lord.
   Trees and flowers, bless the Lord.
   Praise him for ever.

4. Springs and rivers, bless the Lord.
Seas and oceans, bless the Lord.
Whales and fishes, bless the Lord.
Praise him for ever.
Birds and insects, bless the Lord.
Beasts and cattle, bless the Lord.
Let all creatures bless the Lord.
Praise him for ever.

5. Let God's people bless the Lord.
Men and women, bless the Lord.
All creation, bless the Lord.
Praise him for ever.
Let God's people bless the Lord.
Men and women, bless the Lord.
All creation, bless the Lord.
Praise him for ever.

Hayward Osborne

4

1. All creatures of our God and King,
lift up your voice and with us sing
alleluia, alleluia!
Thou burning sun with golden
beam,
thou silver moon with softer gleam:

O praise him, O praise him,
alleluia, alleluia, alleluia.

2. Thou rushing wind that art so
strong,
ye clouds that sail in heaven along,
O praise him, alleluia!
Thou rising morn, in praise rejoice,
ye lights of evening, find a voice:

3. Thou flowing water, pure and clear,
make music for thy Lord to hear,
alleluia, alleluia!
Thou fire so masterful and bright,
that givest man both warmth and
light:

4. Dear mother earth, who day by day
unfoldest blessings on our way,
O praise him, alleluia!
The flowers and fruits that in thee
grow
let them his glory also show.

5. And all ye men of tender heart,
forgiving others, take your part,
O sing ye, alleluia!
Ye who long pain and sorrow bear,
praise God and on him cast your
care:

6. And thou, most kind and gentle
death,
waiting to hush our latest breath,
O praise him, alleluia!
Thou leadest home the child of
God,
and Christ our Lord the way hath
trod:

7. Let all things their Creator bless,
and worship him in humbleness,
O praise him, alleluia!
Praise, praise the Father, praise the
Son,
and praise the Spirit, Three in One.

W. H. Draper (1855-1933)
Based on the Cantico di Frate Sole of
St. Francis of Assisi (1182-1226)

5

1. Alleluia, alleluia,
alleluia, alleluia,
alleluia, alleluia,
alleluia, alleluia.

2. Jesus is Lord, . . .

3. And I love him, . . .

4. Christ is risen, . . .

Traditional

6

Alleluia, alleluia!
I will praise the Father
for all of my life,
I will sing to my God
as long as I live,
alleluia, alleluia, alleluia!

1. Do not place all your trust
    in the power of man:
   he cannot save.
   His schemes will all perish
       when he yields up his breath
   at the end of his day.

2. But so happy the man
       who will trust in his God:
   he will find help.
   For he is the maker
       of the heavens and earth
   and of all that these hold.

3. All the searchers for justice,
       for freedom, for love,
   he will fulfil.
   The widow, the orphan,
       and the blind and the lame
   in his love are restored.

Based on Psalm 146
by Michael Cockett

7

1. Alleluia, sing to Jesus,
   his the sceptre, his the throne,
   alleluia, his the triumph,
   his the victory alone:
   hark the songs of peaceful Sion
   thunder like a mighty flood:
   Jesus, out of every nation,
   hath redeemed us by his blood.

2. Alleluia, not as orphans
   are we left in sorrow now;
   alleluia, he is near us,
   faith believes, nor questions how;
   though the cloud from sight received
                                    him
   when the forty days were o'er,
   shall our hearts forget his promise,
   'I am with you evermore'?

3. Alleluia, Bread of Angels,
   thou on earth our food, our stay;
   alleluia, here the sinful
   flee to thee from day to day;
   intercessor, friend of sinners,
   earth's Redeemer, plead for me,
   where the songs of all the sinless
   sweep across the crystal sea.

4. Alleluia, King eternal
   thee the Lord of lords we own;
   alleluia, born of Mary,
   earth thy footstool, heaven thy
                                    throne;
   thou within the veil hast entered,
   robed in flesh, our great High Priest;
   thou on earth both priest and
                                    victim
   in the Eucharistic Feast.

W. Chatterton Dix (1837-98)

8

All glory, laud and honour,
to thee, Redeemer King,
to whom the lips of children
made sweet hosannas ring.

1. Thou art the King of Israel,
   thou David's royal Son,
   who in the Lord's name comest,
   the King and blessed one.

2. The company of angels
   are praising thee on high,
   and mortal men and all things
   created make reply.

3. The people of the Hebrews
   with palms before thee went:
   our praise and prayer and anthems
   before thee we presen

4. To thee before thy passion
   they sang their hymns of praise;
   to thee now high exalted
   our melody we raise.

5. Thou didst accept their praises,
   accept the prayers we bring,
   who in all good delightest,
   thou good and gracious king.

St Theodulph of Orleans (821),
tr. J. M. Neale

9

1. All hail the power of Jesus' name;
   let angels prostrate fall;
   bring forth the royal diadem
   To crown him, crown him,
   crown him,
   crown him Lord of all.

2. Crown him, ye martyrs of your
   God,
   who from his altar call;
   praise him whose way of pain ye
   trod,
   and crown him Lord of all.

3. Ye prophets who our freedom won,
   ye searchers, great and small,
   by whom the work of truth is done,
   now crown him Lord of all.

4. Sinners, whose love can ne'er forget
   the wormwood and the gall,
   go spread your trophies at his feet,
   and crown him Lord of all.

5. Bless him, each poor oppresséd race
   that Christ did upward call;
   his hand in each achievement trace,
   and crown him Lord of all.

6. Let every tribe and every tongue
   to him their hearts enthral:
   lift high the universal song,
   and crown him Lord of all.

   E. Perronet (1762-92), and others

10

1. All people that on earth do dwell,
   sing to the Lord with cheerful voice;
   him serve with fear, his praise forth
   tell,
   come ye before him and rejoice.

2. The Lord, ye know, is God indeed,
   without our aid he did us make;
   we are his folk, he doth us feed
   and for his sheep he doth us take.

3. O enter then his gates with praise,
   approach with joy his courts unto;
   praise, laud, and bless his name
   always,
   for it is seemly so to do.

4. For why? the Lord our God is good:
   his mercy is for ever sure;
   his truth at all times firmly stood,
   and shall from age to age endure.

5. To Father, Son and Holy Ghost,
   the God whom heaven and earth
   adore,
   from men and from the angel-host
   be praise and glory evermore.

   William Kethe, Day's Psalter (1560)

11

1. All that I am, all that I do,
   all that I'll ever have,
   I offer now to you.
   Take and sanctify these gifts
   for your honour, Lord.
   Knowing that I love and serve you
   is enough reward.
   All that I am, all that I do,
   all that I'll ever have
   I offer now to you.

2. All that I dream, all that I pray,
   all that I'll ever make,
   I give to you today.
   Take and sanctify these gifts
   for your honour, Lord.
   Knowing that I love and serve you
   is enough reward.
   All that I am, all that I do,
   all that I'll ever have
   I offer now to you.

   Sebastian Temple

12

All the nations of the earth,
praise the Lord who brings to birth
the greatest star, the smallest flower.
Alleluia.

1. Let the heavens praise the Lord.
   Alleluia.
   Moon and stars, praise the Lord.
   Alleluia.

2. Snow capped mountains,
      praise the Lord.
   Alleluia.
   Rolling hills, praise the Lord.
   Alleluia.

3. Deep sea water, praise the Lord.
   Alleluia.
   Gentle rain, praise the Lord.
   Alleluia.

4. Roaring lion, praise the Lord.
   Alleluia.
   Singing birds, praise the Lord.
   Alleluia.

5. Kings and princes, praise the Lord.
   Alleluia.
   Young and old, praise the Lord.
   Alleluia.

Michael Cockett

13

1. All things bright and beautiful,
   all creatures great and small,
   all things wise and wonderful,
   the Lord God made them all.

2. Each little flower that opens,
   each little bird that sings,
   he made their glowing colours,
   he made their tiny wings.

3. The purple-headed mountain,
   the river running by,
   the sunset and the morning,
   that brightens up the sky.

4. The cold wind in the winter,
   the pleasant summer sun,
   the ripe fruits in the garden,
   he made them every one.

5. The tall trees in the greenwood,
   the meadows for our play,
   the rushes by the water,
   to gather every day.

6. He gave us eyes to see them,
   and lips that we may tell
   how great is God Almighty,
   who has made all things well.

C. F. Alexander (1818-95)

14

1. All this world belongs to Jesus,
   ev'rything is his by right;
   all on the land, all in the sea;
   ev'rything is his by right.

2. Shining stars in all their beauty
   are outnumbered by his gifts.
   Sand on the shore, stars in the sky,
   are outnumbered by his gifts.

3. Ev'ry foot that starts a-dancing
   taps a rhythm full of hope;
   full of his joy, full of his hope,
   taps a rhythm full of hope.

4. All that's good reflects his goodness;
   may it lead us back to him.
   All that is good, all that is true,
   may it lead us back to him.

5. So give thanks for what he's given;
   touch and taste, and feet to dance;
   eyes for the lights, ears for the sound,
   for the wonders of our Lord.

Willard F. Jabusch

15

1. All ye who seek a comfort sure
   in trouble and distress,
   whatever sorrow vex the mind,
   or guilt the soul oppress:

2. Jesus, who gave himself for you
   upon the cross to die,
   opens to you his sacred heart;
   oh, to that heart draw nigh.

3. Ye hear how kindly he invites;
   ye hear his words so blest:
   'All ye that labour come to me,
   and I will give you rest.'

4. Jesus, thou joy of saints on high,
   thou hope of sinners here,
   attracted by those loving words
   to thee I lift my prayer.

5. Wash thou my wounds in that dear
   blood,
   which forth from thee doth flow;
   new grace, new hope inspire, a new
   and better heart bestow.

   18th c., tr. Edward Caswall

16

*All you peoples, clap your hands
and shout for joy.
The Lord has made all mankind one,
so raise your voices high.*

1. All creation shows
   the glory of the Lord.
   The earth proclaims his handiwork,
   the sky cries out his word.
   Night and day sing out
   the glories all about,
   so praise the Lord with shouts of
   joy.

2. The king of all the earth
   has made his message known,
   that we should offer him ourselves
   and ev'rything we own.
   We do this by the way
   we live through ev'ry day.
   So live each day in peace and joy.

3. The kingdom of the Lord
   was made for all the good;
   those who want to live in peace
   and brotherhood.
   So with our fellow man
   let's all join hand to hand
   and praise the Lord with shouts of
   joy.

4. Let ev'ry man alive
   remember your command,
   that ev'ry day in ev'ry way
   we love our fellow man.
   If this command is done,
   the vict'ry will be won,
   and we'll live in peace and joy.

   Ray Repp

17

1. Almighty Father, Lord most high,
   who madest all, who fillest all,
   thy name we praise and magnify,
   for all our needs on thee we call.

2. We offer to thee of thine own,
   ourselves and all that we can bring,
   in bread and cup before thee shown,
   our universal offering.

3. All that we have we bring to thee,
   yet all is naught when all is done,
   save that in it thy love can see
   the sacrifice of thy dear Son.

4. By this command in bread and cup,
   his body and his blood we plead;
   what on the cross he offer'd up
   is here our sacrifice indeed.

5. For all thy gifts of life and grace,
   here we thy servants humbly pray
   that thou would'st look upon the
   face
   of thine anointed Son today.

   *Vincent Stuckley Stratton Coles
   (1845-1929)*

18

1. Almighty Father, take this bread
   thy people offer thee;
   where sins divide us, take instead
   one fold and family.

2. The wine we offer soon will be
   Christ's blood, redemption's price;
   receive it, Holy Trinity,
   this holy sacrifice.

3. O God, by angels' choirs adored,
   thy name be praised on earth;
   on all men be that peace outpoured
   once promised at his birth.

Anonymous

19

1. Amazing grace! How sweet the
                         sound
   that saved a wretch like me.
   I once was lost but now I'm found,
   was blind, but now I see.

2. 'Twas grace that taught my heart to
                              fear,
   and grace my fears relieved.
   How precious did that grace appear
   the hour I first believed.

3. Through many dangers, toils and
                            snares
   I have already come.
   'Tis grace hath brought me safe thus
                              far,
   and grace will lead me home.

4. The Lord has promised good to me;
   his word my hope secures.
   He will my shield and portion be
   as long as life endures.

John Newton

20

1. And did those feet in ancient time
   walk upon England's mountains
                         green?
   And was the holy Lamb of God
   on England's pleasant pastures
                          seen?
   And did the countenance divine
   shine forth upon our clouded hills?
   And was Jerusalem buildéd here
   among those dark Satanic mills?

2. Bring me my bow of burning gold!
   Bring me my arrows of desire!
   Bring me my spear! O clouds,
                       unfold!
   Bring me my chariot of fire!
   I will not cease from mental fight,
   nor shall my sword sleep in my
                             hand,
   till we have built Jerusalem
   in England's green and pleasant
                              land.

William Blake (1757-1827)

21

1. Angels we have heard in heaven
   sweetly singing o'er our plains,
   and the mountain-tops in answer
   echoing their joyous strains.

Gloria in excelsis Deo.

2. Shepherds, why this exultation?
   Why your rapturous strain prolong?
   Tell us of the gladsome tidings,
   which inspire your joyous song.

3. Come to Bethlehem, and see him
   o'er whose birth the angels sing,
   come, adore, devoutly kneeling,
   Christ the Lord, the new-born king.

4. See him in a manger lying
   whom the choir of angels praise!
   Mary, Joseph, come to aid us
   while our hearts in love we raise.

James Chadwick (1813-82)

22

1. Angels we have heard on high
   sweetly singing o'er our plains,
   and the mountains in reply
   echo still their joyous strains.

   Gloria in excelsis Deo.

2. Shepherds, why this jubilee?
   Why your rapturous strain prolong?
   Say, what may your tidings be,
   which inspire your heavenly song.

3. Come to Bethlehem and see
   him whose birth the angels sing:
   come, adore on bended knee
   the infant Christ, the new-born
   King.

4. See within a manger laid,
   Jesus, Lord of heaven and earth!
   Mary, Joseph, lend your aid
   to celebrate our Saviour's birth.

   James Chadwick (1813-82)

23

*Ask, and you will receive.
Seek, and you will find.
Knock, and the door will be opened
for the love of the Lord has no end.*

1. Is there any man here,
      when his son asks for bread,
   would turn him away
      with a stone instead?
   Is there any man here,
      when his son asks for meat,
   would then give him
      a poisonous snake to eat?

2. So then how could your Father
      in heaven above,
   who knows so much more
      of the ways of love,
   so then how could your Father
      refuse what is good,
   when you ask in the name
      of the Son he loves?

3. So whatever you ask
      you will always receive,
   whatever you seek
      you will always find.
   For my Father will give
      to all those who believe
   in the Spirit of love
      that will never end.

   Michael Cockett

24

1. As with gladness men of old,
   did the guiding star behold,
   as with joy they hailed its light,
   leading onward, beaming bright,
   so, most gracious God, may we
   evermore be led to thee.

2. As with joyful steps they sped,
   to that lowly manger-bed,
   there to bend the knee before
   him whom heaven and earth adore,
   so may we with willing feet
   ever seek thy mercy-seat.

3. As they offered gifts most rare,
   at that manger rude and bare,
   so may we with holy joy,
   pure, and free from sin's alloy,
   all our costliest treasures bring,
   Christ, to thee our heavenly King.

4. Holy Jesu, every day
   keep us in the narrow way;
   and, when earthly things are past,
   bring our ransomed souls at last
   where they need no star to guide,
   where no clouds thy glory hide.

5. In the heavenly country bright
   need they no created light,
   thou its Light, its Joy, its Crown,
   thou its Sun which goes not down;
   there for ever may we sing
   alleluias to our King.

   William Chatterton Dix (1837-98)

25

1. Attend and keep this happy fast
   I preach to you this day.
   Is this the fast that pleases me
   that takes your joy away?
   Do I delight in sorrow's dress,
   says God, who reigns above,
   the hanging head, the dismal look,
   will they attract my love?

2. But is this not the fast I choose,
   that shares the heavy load;
   that seeks to bring the poor man in
   who's weary of the road;
   that gives the hungry bread to eat,
   to strangers gives a home;
   that does not let you hide your face
   from your own flesh and bone?

3. Then like the dawn your light will
   break,
   to life you will be raised.
   And men will praise the Lord for
   you;
   be happy in your days.
   The glory of the Lord will shine,
   and in your steps his grace.
   And when you call he'll answer you;
   he will not hide his face.

   Roger Ruston, after Isaiah 58: 5-9

26

1. At the cross her station keeping,
   stood the mournful mother
   weeping,
   close to Jesus to the last;

2. Through her heart, his sorrow
   sharing,
   all his bitter anguish bearing,
   now at length the sword has pass'd.

3. Oh, how sad and sore distress'd
   was that mother highly blest,
   of the sole-begotten One.

4. Christ above in torment hangs;
   she beneath beholds the pangs
   of her dying glorious Son.

5. Is there one who would not weep,
   whelm'd in miseries so deep,
   Christ's dear mother to behold?

6. Can the human heart refrain
   from partaking in her pain,
   in that mother's pain untold?

7. Bruised, derided, cursed, defiled,
   she beheld her tender child,
   all with bloody scourges rent;

8. For the sins of his own nation,
   saw him hang in desolation,
   till his spirit forth he sent.

9. O thou mother! fount of love!
   Touch my spirit from above,
   make my heart with thine accord:

10. Make me feel as thou hast felt;
    make my soul to glow and melt
    with the love of Christ my Lord.

11. Holy Mother, pierce me through,
    in my heart each wound renew
    of my Saviour crucified.

12. Let me share with thee his pain
    who for all my sins was slain,
    who for me in torments died.

13. Let me mingle tears with thee,
    mourning him who mourn'd for me,
    all the days that I may live:

14. By the cross with thee to stay,
    there with thee to weep and pray,
    is all I ask of thee to give.

15. Virgin of all virgins best,
    listen to my fond request:
    let me share thy grief divine;

16. Let me, to my latest breath,
    in my body bear the death
    of that dying son of thine.

17. Wounded with his every wound,
    steep my soul till it hath swoon'd
    in his very blood away.

18. Be to me, O Virgin, nigh,
    lest in flames I burn and die,
    in his awful judgement day.

19. Christ, when thou shalt call me
hence,
be thy mother my defence,
be thy cross my victory.

20. While my body here decays,
may my soul thy goodness praise,
safe in paradise with thee.

Ascribed to Jacopone da Todi (d.1306),
tr. E. Caswall

27

1. At the Lamb's high feast we sing
praise to our victorious king,
who hath washed us in the tide
flowing from his piercéd side.
Praise we him whose love divine
gives the guests his blood for wine,
gives his body for the feast,
love the victim, love the priest.

2. Where the paschal blood is poured,
Death's dark angel sheathes his
sword;
Israel's hosts triumphant go
through the wave that drowns the
foe.
Christ the Lamb, whose blood was
shed.
Paschal victim, paschal bread;
with sincerity and love
eat we manna from above.

3. Mighty victim from the sky,
powers of hell beneath thee lie;
death is conquered in the fight;
thou hast brought us life and light,
now thy banner thou dost wave;
vanquished Satan and the grave;
angels join his praise to tell —
see o'erthrown the prince of hell.

4. Paschal triumph, paschal joy,
only sin can this destroy;
from the death of sin set free
souls re-born, dear Lord, in thee.
Hymns of glory, songs of praise,
Father, unto thee we raise.
Risen Lord, all praise to thee,
ever with the Spirit be.

7th c., tr. Robert Campbell

28

1. At the name of Jesus
every knee shall bow,
every tongue confess him
King of glory now;
'tis the Father's pleasure
we should call him Lord,
who from the beginning,
was the mighty Word.

2. At his voice creation
sprang at once to sight,
all the Angel faces,
all the hosts of light,
thrones and dominations,
stars upon their way,
all the heavenly orders,
in their great array.

3. Humbled for a season,
to receive a name
from the lips of sinners
unto whom he came,
faithfully he bore it
spotless to the last,
brought it back victorious
when from death he passed:

4. Bore it up triumphant
with its human light
through all ranks of creatures,
to the central height,
to the throne of Godhead,
to the Father's breast,
filled it with the glory
of that perfect rest.

5. Name him, brothers, name him,
with love as strong as death;
but with awe and wonder,
and with bated breath.
He is God the Saviour,
he is Christ the Lord,
ever to be worshipped,
trusted, and adored.

6. In your hearts enthrone him;
   there let him subdue
   all that is not holy,
   all that is not true;
   crown him as your captain,
   in temptation's hour
   let his will enfold you
   in its light and power.

7. Brothers, this Lord Jesus
   shall return again,
   with his Father's glory,
   with his angel train,
   for all wreaths of empire
   meet upon his brow,
   and our hearts confess him
   King of glory now.

   Caroline Maria Noel (1817-77)

29

1. Ave Maria, O Maiden, O Mother,
   fondly thy children are calling on
   thee;
   thine are the graces unclaimed by
   another,
   sinless and beautiful Star of the sea.

   Mater amabilis, ora pro nobis,
   pray for thy children who call upon
   thee;
   Ave sanctissima, Ave purissima
   sinless and beautiful Star of the sea.

2. Ave Maria, the night shades are
   falling,
   softly, our voices arise unto thee;
   earth's lonely exiles for succour are
   calling,
   sinless and beautiful Star of the sea.

3. Ave Maria, thy children are
   kneeling,
   words of endearment are murmured
   to thee;
   softly thy spirit upon us is stealing,
   sinless and beautiful Star of the sea.

   'Sister M.'

30

1. Away in a manger,
   no crib for a bed,
   the little Lord Jesus
   laid down his sweet head,
   the stars in the bright sky
   looked down where he lay,
   the little Lord Jesus
   asleep on the hay.

2. The cattle are lowing,
   the baby awakes,
   but little Lord Jesus
   no crying he makes.
   I love thee, Lord Jesus!
   Look down from the sky,
   and stay by my side
   until morning is nigh.

3. Be near me, Lord Jesus;
   I ask thee to stay
   close by me for ever,
   and love me, I pray.
   Bless all the dear children
   in thy tender care,
   and fit us for heaven,
   to live with thee there.

   J. Kirkpatrick

31

1. Battle is o'er,
   hell's armies flee:
   raise we the cry of victory
   with abounding joy resounding,
   alleluia.

2. Christ who endured
   the shameful tree,
   o'er death triumphant welcome we,
   our adoring praise outpouring,
   alleluia.

3. On the third morn
   from death rose he,
   clothed with what light in heaven
   shall be,
   our unswerving faith deserving,
   alleluia.

4. Hell's gloomy gates
   yield up their key,
   paradise door thrown wide we see;
   never-tiring be our choiring,
   alleluia.

5. Lord, by the stripes
   men laid on thee,
   grant us to live from death set free,
   this our greeting still repeating,
   alleluia.

Simphonia Sirenum (1695)
tr. Ronald Arbuthnott Knox

32

1. Be still, and know I am with you,
   be still, I am the Lord.
   I will not leave you orphans.
   I leave with you my world.
   Be one.

2. You fear the light may be fading,
   you fear to lose your way.
   Be still, and know I am near you.
   I'll lead you to the day
   and the sun.

3. Be glad the day you have sorrow,
   be glad, for then you live.
   The stars shine only in darkness,
   and in your need I give
   my peace.

Sister Jude

33

1. Be still and know that I am God,
   be still and know that I am God,
   be still and know that I am God.

2. I am the Lord that healeth thee,
   I am the Lord that healeth thee,
   I am the Lord that healeth thee.

3. In thee, O Lord, I put my trust,
   in thee, O Lord, I put my trust,
   in thee, O Lord, I put my trust.

Anonymous

34

1. Bethlehem! of noblest cities
   none can once with thee compare;
   thou alone the Lord from heaven
   didst for us incarnate bear.

2. Fairer than the sun at morning
   was the star that told his birth,
   to the lands their God announcing,
   hid beneath a form of earth.

3. By its lambent beauty guided,
   see the eastern kings appear;
   see them bend, their gifts to offer —
   gifts of incense, gold and myrrh.

4. Solemn things of mystic meaning!
   Incense doth the God disclose;
   gold a royal child proclaimeth;
   Myrrh a future tomb foreshows.

5. Holy Jesu, in they brightness
   to the gentile world display'd,
   with the Father and the Spirit,
   endless praise to thee be paid.

Aurelius Prudentius (348-413),
tr. E. Caswall

35

1. Be thou my vision,
      O Lord of my heart,
   naught be all else to me
      save that thou art;
   thou my best thought
      in the day and night,
   waking or sleeping,
      thy presence my light.

2. Be thou my wisdom,
      be thou my true word,
   I ever with thee and
      thou with me, Lord;
   thou my great Father,
      and I thy true son;
   thou in me dwelling,
      and I with thee one.

3. Be thou my breast-plate,
     my sword for the fight,
   be thou my armour,
     and be thou my might,
   thou my soul's shelter,
     and thou my high tower,
   raise thou me heavenward,
     O Power of my power.

4. Riches I heed not,
     nor man's empty praise,
   thou mine inheritance
     through all my days;
   thou, and thou only,
     the first in my heart,
   high King of heaven,
     my treasure thou art!

5. High King of heaven
     when battle is done,
   grant heaven's joy to me,
     O bright heaven's sun;
   Christ of my own heart,
     whatever befall,
   still be my vision,
     O Ruler of all.

> *Irish (8th C.), tr. Mary Byrne,*
> *versified by Eleanor Hull*

36

1. Blest are the pure in heart,
   for they shall see our God;
   the secret of the Lord is theirs,
   their soul is Christ's abode.

2. The Lord who left the heavens
   our life and peace to bring,
   to dwell in lowliness with men,
   their pattern and their king.

3. Still to the lowly soul
   he doth himself impart
   and for his dwelling and his throne
   chooseth the pure in heart.

4. Lord, we thy presence seek;
   may ours this blessing be:
   give us a pure and lowly heart,
   a temple meet for thee.

> *Verses 1 and 3 by John Keble*
> *(1792-1866) verses 2 and 4 from*
> *W. J. Hall's Psalms and Hymns (1836)*

37

1. Breathe on me, Breath of God,
   fill me with life anew,
   that I may love what thou dost love,
   and do what thou wouldst do.

2. Breathe on me, Breath of God,
   until my heart is pure:
   until with thee I have one will
   to do and to endure.

3. Breathe on me, Breath of God,
   till I am wholly thine,
   until this earthly part of me
   glows with thy fire divine.

4. Breathe on me, Breath of God,
   so shall I never die,
   but live with thee the perfect life
   of thine Eternity.

> *Edwin Hatch (1835-89)*

38

1. Bring, all ye dear-bought nations,
                              bring,
   your richest praises to your king,
                  alleluia, alleluia,
   that spotless Lamb, who more than
                              due,
   paid for his sheep, and those sheep
                              you,
   Alleluia.

2. That guiltless Son, who bought
                       your peace,
   and made his Father's anger cease,
   then, life and death together fought,
   each to a strange extreme were
                           brought.

3. Life died, but soon revived again,
   and even death by it was slain.
   Say, happy Magdalen, oh, say,
   what didst thou see there by the
                              way?

4. "I saw the tomb of my dear Lord,
   I saw himself, and him adored,
   I saw the napkin and the sheet,
   that bound his head and wrapt his
                                feet."

5. "I heard the angels witness bear,
   Jesus is ris'n; he is not here;
   go, tell his followers they shall see,
   thine and their hope in Galilee."

6. We, Lord, with faithful hearts and
                                voice,
   on this thy rising day rejoice.
   O thou, whose power o'ercame the
                                grave,
   by grace and love us sinners save.

   Wipo (11th C.),
   tr. Walter Kirkham Blount

39

1. Bring flowers of the rarest,
   bring blossoms the fairest,
   from garden and woodland
      and hillside and dale;
   our full hearts are swelling,
   our glad voices telling
   the praise of the loveliest
      flower of the vale.

   O Mary we crown thee
      with blossoms today.
   Queen of the Angels
      and Queen of the May.
   O Mary we crown thee
      with blossoms today,
   Queen of the Angels
      and Queen of the May.

2. Their lady they name thee,
   their mistress proclaim thee.
   Oh, grant that thy children
      on earth be as true,
   as long as the bowers
   are radiant with flowers
   as long as the azure shall
      keep its bright hue.

3. Sing gaily in chorus,
   the bright angels o'er us
   re-echo the strains we
   begin upon earth;
   their harps are repeating
   the notes of our greeting,
   for Mary herself is the
   cause of our mirth.

   Anonymous

40

1. By the blood that flow'd from thee
   in thy grievous agony;
   by the traitor's guileful kiss,
   filling up thy bitterness;

   Jesus, saviour, hear our cry;
   thou wert suff'ring once as we:
   now enthron'd in majesty
   countless angels sing to thee.

2. By the cords that, round thee cast,
   bound thee to the pillar fast,
   by the scourge so meekly borne,
   by the purple robe of scorn.

3. By the thorns that crown'd thy
                                head,
   by the sceptre of a reed;
   by thy foes on bending knee,
   mocking at thy royalty.

4. By the people's cruel jeers;
   by the holy women's tears;
   by thy footsteps, faint and slow,
   weigh'd beneath thy cross of woe;

5. By thy weeping mother's woe;
   by the sword that pierced her
                                through,
   when in anguish standing by,
   on the cross she saw thee die.

   Frederick William Faber (1814-63)

41

1. Christ be beside me,
   Christ be before me,
   Christ be behind me,
   King of my heart.
   Christ be within me,
   Christ be below me,
   Christ be above me,
   never to part.

2. Christ on my right hand,
   Christ on my left hand,
   Christ all around me,
   shield in the strife.
   Christ in my sleeping,
   Christ in my sitting,
   Christ in my rising,
   light of my life.

3. Christ be in all hearts
   thinking about me,
   Christ be in all tongues
   telling of me.
   Christ be the vision
   in eyes that see me,
   in ears that hear me,
   Christ ever be.

Adapted from 'St. Patrick's Breastplate'
by James Quinn

42

1. Christ is King of earth and heaven!
   Let his subjects all proclaim
   in the splendour of his temple
   honour to his holy name.

2. Christ is King! No soul created
   can refuse to bend the knee
   to the God made man who reigneth
   as 'twas promised, from the tree.

3. Christ is King! Let humble sorrow
   for our past neglect atone,
   for the lack of faithful service
   to the Master whom we own.

4. Christ is King! Let joy and gladness
   greet him; let his courts resound
   with the praise of faithful subjects
   to his love in honour bound.

5. Christ is King! In health and
   sickness,
   till we breathe our latest breath,
   till we greet in highest heaven,
   Christ the victor over death.

Ivor J. E. Daniel (1883-1967)

43

Christ is our king,
  let the whole world rejoice!
May all the nations
  sing out with one voice!
Light of the world,
  you have helped us to see
that all men are brothers
  and all men one day will be free.

1. He came to open
     the eyes of the blind,
   letting the sunlight pour
     into their minds.
   Vision is waiting for
     those who have hope.
   He is the light of the world.

2. He came to speak
     tender words to the poor,
   he is the gateway and
     he is the door.
   Riches are waiting for all
     those who hope.
   He is the light of the world.

3. He came to open
     the doors of the gaol,
   he came to help the
     downtrodden and frail.
   Freedom is waiting for
     all those who hope.
   He is the light of the world.

4. He came to open
     the lips of the mute,
   letting them speak out
     with courage and truth.
   His words are uttered by
     all those who hope.
   He is the light of the world.

5. He came to heal all
     the crippled and lame,
   sickness took flight at the
     sound of his name.
   Vigour is waiting for
     all those who hope.
   He is the light of the world.

6. He came to love
     every man on this earth
   and through his Spirit he
     promised rebirth.
   New life is waiting for
     all those who hope.
   He is the light of the world.

Estelle White

44

1. Christ the Lord is risen today!
   Christians, haste your vows to pay,
   offer ye your praises meet
   at the paschal victim's feet;
   for the sheep the Lamb hath bled,
   sinless in the sinner's stead.
   Christ the Lord is ris'n on high;
   now he lives, no more to die.

2. Christ, the victim undefiled,
   man to God hath reconciled
   when in strange and awful strife
   met together death and life;
   Christians, on this happy day
   haste with joy your vows to pay.
   Christ the Lord is ris'n on high;
   Now he lives, no more to die.

3. Say, O wond'ring Mary, say,
   what thou sawest on thy way.
   "I beheld, where Christ had lain,
   empty tomb and angels twain,
   I beheld the glory bright
   of the rising Lord of light;
   Christ my hope is ris'n again;
   now he lives, and lives to reign."

4. Christ, who once for sinners bled,
   now the first-born from the dead,
   throned in endless might and
                           power,
   lives and reigns for evermore.
   Hail, eternal hope on high!
   Hail, thou king of victory!
   Hail, thou Prince of life adored!
   Help and save us, gracious Lord.

Wipo 11th c., tr. Jane Elizabeth Leeson

45

1. Colours of day
     dawn into the mind,
   the sun has come up,
     the night is behind.
   Go down in the city,
     into the street,
   and let's give the message
     to the people we meet.

*So light up the fire
     and let the flame burn,
open the door, let Jesus return.
Take seeds of his Spirit,
     let the fruit grow,
tell the people of Jesus,
     let his love show.*

2. Go through the park,
     on into the town;
   the sun still shines on
     it never goes down.
   The light of the world
     is risen again;
   the people of darkness
     are needing our friend.

3. Open your eyes,
     look into the sky,
   the darkness has come,
     the sun came to die.
   The evening draws on,
     the sun disappears,
   but Jesus is living,
     and his Spirit is near.

*Sue McClellan, John Pac
and Keith Ryecroft*

46

1. Come, adore this wondrous presence,
   bow to Christ, the source of grace.
   Here is kept the ancient promise
   of God's earthly dwelling-place.
   Sight is blind before God's glory,
   faith alone may see his face.

2. Glory be to God the Father,
   praise to his co-equal Son,
   adoration to the Spirit,
   bond of love, in Godhead one.
   Blest be God by all creation
   joyously while ages run.

   St Thomas Aquinas (1227-74)
   translated by James Quinn

47

1. Come, Christian people,
   take heed what I say:
   Here, in this stable,
   your King was born today.

   Star of wisdom, child of gladness,
   tell him all your troubles.
   Mary's boy has banished sadness,
   why be sorrowful now?

2. Not much to look at
   – simply straw and hay –
   yet on that carpet
   your King was laid today.

3. Man, are you listening?
   Take heed what I say:
   Here on this planet
   your King still lives today.

   John Glynn

48

Come, come, come to the manger,
children, come
to the children's King;
sing, sing, chorus of Angels,
stars of morning o'er Bethlehem sing.

1. He lies 'mid the beasts of the stall,
   who is Maker and Lord of us all;
   the wintry wind blows cold and
                              dreary,
   see, he weeps, the world is weary;
   Lord, have pity and mercy on me!

2. He leaves all his glory behind,
   to be born and to die for mankind,
   with grateful beasts his cradle
                              chooses,
   thankless man his love refuses;
   Lord, have pity and mercy on me!

3. To the manger of Bethlehem come,
   to the Saviour Emmanuel's home;
   the heav'nly hosts above are singing,
   set the Christmas bells a-ringing;
   Lord, have pity and mercy on me.

   Anonymous

49

1. Come down, O love divine,
   seek thou this soul of mine,
   and visit it with thine own
      ardour glowing;
   O comforter, draw near,
   within my heart appear,
   and kindle it, thy holy
      flame bestowing.

2. O let it freely burn,
   till earthly passions turn
   to dust and ashes in its
      heat consuming;
   and let thy glorious light
   shine ever on my sight,
   and clothe me round, the while my
      path illuming.

3. Let holy charity
   mine outward vesture be,
   and lowliness become mine
      inner clothing;
   true lowliness of heart,
   which takes the humbler part,
   and o'er its own shortcomings
   weeps with loathing.

4. And so the yearning strong,
   with which the soul will long,
   shall far outpass the power of
        human telling;
   for none can guess its grace,
   till he become the place
   wherein the Holy Spirit
        makes his dwelling.

Bianco da Siena d.1434,
tr. Richard Frederick Littledale

50

1. Come, Holy Ghost, Creator, come
   from thy bright heavenly throne,
   come, take possession of our souls,
   and make them all thine own.

2. Thou who art called the Paraclete,
   best gift of God above,
   the living spring, the living fire,
   sweet unction and true love.

3. Thou who are sev'nfold in thy grace,
   finger of God's right hand;
   his promise, teaching little ones
   to speak and understand.

4. O guide our minds with thy blest
        light,
   with love our hearts inflame;
   and with thy strength, which ne'er
        decays,
   confirm our mortal frame.

5. Far from us drive our deadly foe;
   true peace unto us bring;
   and through all perils lead us safe
   beneath thy sacred wing.

6. Through thee may we the Father
        know,
   through thee th'eternal Son,
   and thee the Spirit of them both,
   thrice-blessed Three in One.

7. All glory to the Father be,
   with his co-equal Son:
   the same to thee, great Paraclete,
   while endless ages run.

Ascribed to Rabanus Maurus (776-856)
tr. Anonymous

51

1. Come, Lord Jesus, come.
   Come, take my hands,
   take them for your work.
   Take them for your service Lord.
   Take them for your glory, Lord,
   Come, Lord Jesus, come.
   Come, Lord Jesus, take my hands.

2. Come, Lord Jesus, come.
   Come, take my eyes,
   may they shine with joy.
   Take them for your service, Lord.
   Take them for your glory, Lord.
   Come, Lord Jesus, come.
   Come, Lord Jesus, take my eyes.

3. Come, Lord Jesus, come.
   Come, take my lips,
   may they speak your truth.
   Take them for your service, Lord.
   Take them for your glory, Lord.
   Come, Lord Jesus, come.
   Come, Lord Jesus, take my lips.

4. Come, Lord Jesus, come.
   Come take my feet,
   may they walk your path.
   Take them for your service, Lord.
   Take them for your glory, Lord.
   Come, Lord Jesus, come.
   Come, Lord Jesus, take my feet.

5. Come, Lord Jesus, come.
   Come, take my heart,
   fill it with your love.
   Take it for your service, Lord.
   Take it for your glory, Lord.
   Come, Lord Jesus, come.
   Come, Lord Jesus, take my heart.

6. Come, Lord Jesus, come.
   Come, take my life,
   take it for your own.
   Take it for your service, Lord.
   Take it for your glory, Lord.
   Come, Lord Jesus, come.
   Come, Lord Jesus, take my life.

Kevin Mayhew

52

1. Come, my brothers, praise the Lord,
     alleluia.
   He's our God and we are his,
     alleluia.

2. Come to him with songs of praise,
     alleluia.
   Songs of praise, rejoice in him,
     alleluia.

3. For the Lord is a mighty God,
     alleluia.
   He is king of all the world,
     alleluia.

4. In his hands are valleys deep,
     alleluia.
   In his hands are mountain peaks,
     alleluia.

5. In his hands are all the seas,
     alleluia.
   And the lands which he has made,
     alleluia.

6. Praise the Father, praise the Son,
     alleluia.
   Praise the Spirit, the Holy One,
     alleluia.

Traditional

53

1. Come, praise the Lord, the almighty,
     the King of all nations!
   Tell forth his fame, O ye peoples,
     with loud acclamations!
         His love is sure;
         faithful his word shall endure,
   steadfast through all generations!

2. Praise to the Father most gracious,
     the Lord of creation!
   Praise to his Son, the Redeemer
     who wrought our salvation!
         O heav'nly Dove,
         praise to thee, fruit of their
           love.
   Giver of all consolation!

Psalm 116, versified by James Quinn

54

1. Come to the Lord
     and gather round his table.
   Gather round his table
     and come to the Lord.

2. Speak to the Lord
     and gather round his table.
   Gather round his table
     and speak to the Lord.

3. Sing to the Lord
     and gather round his table.
   Gather round his table
     and sing to the Lord.

4. Clap to the Lord
     and gather round his table.
   Gather round his table
     and clap to the Lord.

5. Dance to the Lord
     and gather round his table.
   Gather round his table
     and dance to the Lord.

Estelle White

55

1. Come, ye thankful people, come,
   raise the song of harvest-home!
   All be safely gathered in,
   ere the winter storms begin;
   God, our maker, doth provide
   for our wants to be supplied;
   come to God's own temple come;
   raise the song of harvest-home!

2. We ourselves are God's own field,
   fruit unto his praise to yield;
   wheat and tares together sown,
   unto joy or sorrow grown;
   first the blade and then the ear,
   then the full corn shall appear:
   grant, O harvest Lord, that we
   wholesome grain and pure may be.

3. For the Lord our God shall come,
   and shall take his harvest home;
   from his field shall purge away
   all that doth offend, that day,
   give his angels charge at last
   in the fire the tares to cast,
   but the fruitful ears to store
   in his garner evermore.

4. Then, thou Church triumphant,
                                come,
   raise the song of harvest-home;
   all be safely gathered in,
   free from sorrow, free from sin,
   there for ever purified
   in God's garner to abide:
   come, ten thousand angels, come,
   raise the glorious harvest-home!

   Henry Alford (1810-71)

56

1. Crown him with many crowns,
   the Lamb upon his throne;
   hark, how the heavenly anthem
                                drowns
   all music but its own:
   awake, my soul, and sing
   of him who died for thee,
   and hail him as thy matchless King
   through all eternity.

2. Crown him the Virgin's Son,
   the God incarnate born,
   whose arm those crimson trophies
                                won
   which now his brow adorn;
   fruit of the mystic rose,
   as of that rose the stem,
   the root, whence mercy ever flows,
   the babe of Bethlehem.

3. Crown him the Lord of love;
   behold his hands and side,
   rich wounds, yet visible above,
   in beauty glorified:
   no angel in the sky
   can fully bear that sight,
   but downward bends his burning eye
   at mysteries so bright.

4. Crown him the Lord of peace,
   whose power a sceptre sways,
   from pole to pole, that wars may
                                cease,
   absorbed in prayer and praise:
   his reign shall know no end,
   and round his pierced feet
   fair flowers of Paradise extend
   their fragrance ever sweet.

5. Crown him the Lord of heaven,
   one with the Father known,
   and the blest Spirit through him
                                given
   from yonder triune throne:
   all hail, Redeemer, hail,
   for thou hast died for me;
   thy praise shall never, never fail
   throughout eternity.

   Matthew Bridges (1800-94)

57

1. Daily, daily, sing to Mary,
   sing my soul, her praises due;
   all her feasts, her actions worship,
   with the heart's devotion true.
   Lost in wond'ring contemplation
   be her majesty confessed:
   call her Mother, call her Virgin,
   happy Mother, Virgin blest.

2. She is mighty to deliver;
   call her, trust her lovingly.
   When the tempest rages round thee,
   she will calm the troubled sea.
   Gifts of heaven she has given,
   noble Lady! to our race:
   she, the Queen, who decks her
                                subjects,
   with the light of God's own grace.

3. Sing, my tongue, the Virgin's
                                trophies,
   who for us her Maker bore;
   for the curse of old inflicted,
   peace and blessings to restore.
   Sing in songs of praise unending,
   sing the world's majestic Queen;
   weary not nor faint in telling
   all the gifts she gives to men.

4. All my senses, heart, affections,
   strive to sound her glory forth;
   spread abroad the sweet memorials,
   of the Virgin's priceless worth,
   where the voice of music thrilling,
   where the tongues of eloquence,
   that can utter hymns beseeming
   all her matchless excellence?

5. All our joys do flow from Mary,
   all then join her praise to sing;
   trembling sing the Virgin Mother,
   Mother of our Lord and King,
   while we sing her awful glory,
   far above our fancy's reach,
   let our hearts be quick to offer
   love the heart alone can teach.

Ascribed to St. Bernard of Cluny
(12th c.), tr. Henry Bittleston

58

Day by day in the market place
I play my flute all day.
I have piped to them all,
   but nobody dances.
Day by day in the market place
I play my flute all day,
and whoever you be,
   won't you dance with me.

1. At Cana, when my mother pleaded
   that they were short of wine,
   I gave them all the wine they needed;
   their happiness was mine.

2. Once, when I found poor Peter
                           quaking,
   I let him walk the sea.
   I filled their fishing nets to breaking
   that day in Galilee.

3. While all the world despised the
                           sinner
   I showed him hope again,
   and gave the honours at that dinner
   to Mary Magdalene.

4. Lazarus from the tomb advancing
   once more drew life's sweet breath.
   You too will leave the churchyard
                           dancing,
   for I have conquered death.

Aimé Duval

59

1. Day is done, but Love unfailing
   dwells ever here;
   shadows fall, but hope, prevailing,
   calms every fear.
   Loving Father, none forsaking,
   take our hearts, of Love's own making,
   watch our sleeping, guard our waking,
   be always near!

2. Dark descends, but Light unending
   shines through our night;
   you are with us, ever lending
   new strength to sight;
   one in love, your truth confessing,
   one in hope of heaven's blessing,
   may we see, in love's possessing,
   love's endless light!

3. Eyes will close, but you, unsleeping,
   watch by our side;
   death may come: in love's safe keeping
   still we abide.
   God of love, all evil quelling,
   sin forgiving, fear dispelling,
   stay with us, our hearts indwelling,
   this eventide!

James Quinn

60

1. Dear Lord and Father of mankind,
   forgive our foolish ways!
   Re-clothe us in our rightful mind,
   in purer lives thy service find,
   in deeper reverence praise,
   in deeper reverence praise.

2. In simple trust like theirs who heard
   beside the Syrian sea,
   the gracious calling of the Lord,
   let us, like them, without a word,
   rise up and follow thee,
   rise up and follow thee.

3. O Sabbath rest by Galilee!
   O calm of hills above,
   where Jesus knelt to share with thee
   the silence of eternity,
   interpreted by love!
   interpreted by love!

4. Drop thy still dews of quietness,
   till all our strivings cease;
   take from our souls the strain and
   stress,
   and let our ordered lives confess.
   The beauty of thy peace.
   The beauty of thy peace.

5. Breathe through the heats of our
   desire
   thy coolness and thy balm;
   let sense be dumb, let flesh retire;
   speak through the earthquake, wind
   and fire,
   O still small voice of calm!
   O still small voice of calm!

   John Greenleaf Whittier (1807-92)

61

1. Dear maker of the starry skies,
   light of believers evermore,
   Jesu, redeemer of mankind,
   be near us who thine aid implore.

2. When man was sunk in sin and death,
   lost in the depth of Satan's snare,
   love brought thee down to cure our
   ills,
   by taking of those ills a share.

3. Thou for the sake of guilty men
   permitting thy pure blood to flow,
   didst issue from thy virgin shrine
   and to the cross a victim go.

4. So great the glory of thy might,
   if we but chance thy name to sound,
   at once all heaven and hell unite
   in bending low with awe profound.

5. Great judge of all, in that last day,
   when friends shall fail and foes
   combine,
   be present then with us, we pray,
   to guard us with thy arm divine.

6. To God the Father with the Son,
   and Holy Spirit, one and three,
   be honour, glory, blessing, praise,
   all through the long eternity.

   7th c., tr. Edward Caswall

62

1. Ding dong! merrily on high
   in heav'n the bells are ringing,
   ding dong! verily the sky
   is riv'n with angels singing.

   Gloria, hosanna in excelsis!

2. E'en so here below, below,
   let steeple bells be swungen,
   and io, io, io,
   by priest and people sungen.

3. Pray you, dutifully prime
   your matin chime, ye ringers;
   may you beautifully rime
   your evetime song, ye singers.

   George Ratcliffe Woodward
   (1848-1934)

63

Do not worry over what to eat,
what to wear or put upon your feet.
Trust and pray,
   go do your best today,
then leave it in the hands
   of the Lord.
Leave it in the hands of the Lord.

1. The lilies of the field,
      they do not spin or weave,
   yet Solomon was not
      arrayed like one of these.
   The birds of the air,
      they do not sow or reap,
   but God tends to them,
      like a shepherd tends his sheep.

2. The Lord will guide you
      in his hidden way,
   show you what to do
      and tell you what to say.
   When you pray for rain,
      go build a dam to store
   ev'ry drop of water
      you have asked him for.

3. The Lord knows all your
      needs before you ask.
   Only trust in him
      for he will do the task
   of bringing in your life
      whatever you must know.
   He'll lead you through the darkness
      wherever you must go.

                    Sebastian Temple

64

1. Do you know that the Lord
      walks on earth?
   Do you know he is living here now?
   He is waiting for all men
      to recognise him here.
   Do you know that the Lord
      walks on earth?

2. Do you know that he walks
      in disguise?
   Do you know he's in crowds
      ev'rywhere?
   Every place that you go,
      you may find that he is there.
   Do you know that the Lord's
      in disguise?

3. Do you know that the Lord
      thirsts so much?
   Do you know that he's sitting
      in jail?
   Ev'rywhere he is hungry
      and naked in the cold.
   Do you know he's rejected
      without care?

4. Do you know he is crucified
      each day?
   Do you know that he suffers
      and dies?
   Ev'rywhere he is lonely
      and waiting for a call.
   Do you know he is sick
      all alone?

5. Do you know that he wants
      to be free?
   Do you know he wants help
      from you and me?
   He has need of our hands
      and our feet and hearts to serve.
   Do you know he can work
      through men?

6. Do you know that the Lord
      dwells in men?
   Do you know he resides
      in their hearts?
   His face is shining
      in everyone we meet.
   Do you know he's disguised
      as ev'ry man?

7. Do you know that the Lord
      walks on earth?
   Do you know he is living here now?
   He is waiting for all men
      to recognise him here.
   Do you know he's disguised
      as ev'ry man?

                    Sebastian Temple

65

1. Draw nigh, and take
      the body of our Lord;
   and drink the holy blood
      for you outpoured;
   saved by that body,
      hallowed by that blood,
   whereby refreshed
      we render thanks to God.

2. Salvation's giver,
      Christ the only Son,
   by that his cross and blood
      the victory won,
   offered was he for
      greatest and for least;
   himself the victim,
      and himself the priest.

3. Victims were offered
      by the law of old,
   that, in a type,
      celestial mysteries told.
   He, ransomer from
      death and light from shade,
   giveth his holy grace
      his saints to aid.

4. Approach ye then with
      faithful hearts sincere,
   and take the safeguard
      of salvation here,
   he that in this world
      rules his saints and shields,
   to all believers
      life eternal yields.

5. With heav'nly bread
      makes them that hunger whole,
   gives living waters
      to the thirsty soul,
   Alpha and Omega,
      to whom shall bow
   all nations at the doom,
      is with us now.

*From the Antiphonary of Bennchar
(7th C.), tr. J. M. Neale*

66

1. Dust, dust, and ashes
      lie over on my grave.
   Dust, dust and ashes
      lie over on my grave.
   Dust, dust and ashes
      lie over on my grave,
   and the Lord shall bear
      my spirit home,
   and the Lord shall bear
      my spirit home.

2 They crucified my saviour
      and nailed him to the cross. . .

3. And Mary came a-running,
      her saviour for to see. . .

4. The angels said: "He's not here,
      he's gone to Galilee. . .

5. He rose, he rose, he rose up,
      he rose up from the dead. . .

Traditional

67

1. Eternal Father, strong to save,
   whose arm doth bind the restless
                                    wave,
   who bidd'st the mighty ocean deep,
   it's own appointed limits keep:
   O hear us us when we cry to thee
   For those in peril on the sea.

2. O Saviour, whose almighty word
   the winds and waves submissive
                                   heard,
   who walkedst on the foaming deep
   and calm amid its rage didst sleep:
   O hear us when we cry to thee
   for those in peril on the sea.

3. O sacred Spirit, who didst brood
   upon the waters dark and rude,
   and bid their angry tumult cease,
   and give, for wild confusion, peace:
   O hear us when we cry to thee
   for those in peril on the sea.

4. O Trinity of love and power,
   our brethren shield in danger's hour.
   From rock and tempest, fire and foe,
   protect them whereso'er they go,
   and ever let there rise to thee
   glad hymns of praise from land and
                                    sea.

W. Whiting (1825-78)

68

1. Faith of our fathers, living still
   in spite of dungeon, fire and sword;
   oh, how our hearts
   beat high with joy
   when e'er we hear that glorious
   word!

   Faith of our fathers! Holy Faith!
   We will be true to thee till death,
   we will be true to thee till death.

2. Our fathers, chained in prisons dark,
   were still in heart
   and conscience free;
   how sweet would be their children's
   fate,
   if they, like them, could die for thee!

3. Faith of our fathers, Mary's prayers,
   shall win our country back to thee;
   and through the truth
   that comes from God
   England shall then indeed be free.

4. Faith of our fathers, we will love
   both friend and foe in all our strife,
   and preach thee too,
   as love knows how,
   by kindly words and virtuous life.

   Frederick William Faber (1814-63)

69

1. Father and life-giver,
   grace of Christ impart;
   he, the word incarnate –
   food for mind and heart.
   Children of the promise,
   homage now we pay;
   sacrificial banquet
   cheers the desert way.

2. Wine and bread the symbols –
   love and life convey,
   offered by your people,
   work and joy portray.
   All we own consigning,
   nothing is retained;
   tokens of our service,
   gifts and song contain.

3. Transformation wondrous –
   water into wine;
   mingled in the Godhead
   we are made divine.
   Birth into his body
   brought us life anew,
   total consecration –
   fruit from grafting true.

4. Christ, the head and members
   living now as one,
   offered to the Father
   by this holy Son;
   and our adoration
   purified we find,
   through the Holy Spirit
   breathing in mankind.

   A. J. Newman

70

1. Father most holy,
      merciful and loving,
   Jesu, redeemer,
      ever to be worshipped,
   life-giving Spirit,
      Comforter most gracious,
   God everlasting.

2. Three in a wondrous
      unity unbroken,
   one perfect Godhead,
      love that never faileth,
   light of the angels,
      succour of the needy,
   hope of all living.

3. All thy creation
      serveth its creator,
   thee every creature
      praiseth without ceasing,
   we too would sing
      the psalms of true devotion:
   hear, we beseech thee.

4. Lord God almighty,
      unto thee be glory,
   one in three persons,
      over all exalted.
   Thine, as is meet,
      be honour, praise and blessing
   now and forever.

   10th c., tr. A. E. Alston

71

1. Father, within thy house today
we wait thy kindly love to see:
since thou hast said in truth that
they
who dwell in love are one with thee,
bless those who for thy blessing
wait;
their love accept and consecrate.

2. Blest Spirit, who with life and light
didst quicken chaos to thy praise,
whose energy, in sin's despite,
still lifts our nature up to grace,
bless those who here in troth
consent,
Creator, crown thy sacrament.

3. Great one in three, of whom are
named
all families in earth and heaven,
hear us, who have thy promise
claimed,
and let a wealth of grace be given,
grant them in life and death to be
each knit to each, and both to thee.

Robert Hugh Benson (1871-1914)

72

*Feed us now, O Son of God,
as you fed them long ago.*

1. The people came to hear you,
the poor, the lame, the blind.
They asked for food to save them,
you fed them body and mind.

2. The ones who didn't listen,
the rich, the safe, the sure,
they didn't think they needed
the offering of a cure.

3. It's hard for us to listen,
things haven't changed at all.
We've got the things we wanted;
we don't want to hear your call.

4. Yet millions still have hunger,
disease, no homes, and fear.
We offer them so little,
and it costs them very dear.

5. So help us see the writing,
written clear upon the wall:
he who doesn't feed his neighbour
will get no food at all.

Peter Allen

73

1. Fight the good fight with all thy
might,
Christ is thy strength, and Christ
thy right;
lay hold on life and it shall be
thy joy and crown eternally.

2. Run the straight race through God's
good grace,
lift up thine eyes and seek his face;
life with its way before us lies,
Christ is the path, and Christ the
prize.

3. Cast care aside, upon thy Guide
lean, and his mercy will provide
lean, and the trusting soul shall prove
Christ is its life, and Christ its love.

4. Faint not nor fear, his arms are near,
he changeth not, and thou art dear;
only believe, and thou shalt see
that Christ is all in all to thee.

J. S. B. Monsell (1811-75)

74

1. Fill my house unto the fullest.
Eat my bread and drink my wine.
The love I bear is held from no-one.

*All I own
and all I do
I give to you.*

2. Take my time unto the fullest.
Find in me the trust you seek,
and take my hands to you
outreaching.

3. Christ our Lord with love enormous
from the cross his lesson taught
– to love all men as I have loved you.

4. Join with me as one in Christ-love.
   May our hearts all beat as one,
   and may we give ourselves
                          completely.

   Peter Kearney

75

1. Firmly I believe and truly
   God is three, and God is one,
   and I next acknowledge duly
   manhood taken by the Son.

2. And I trust and hope most fully
   in that manhood crucified;
   and each thought and deed unruly
   do to death, as he has died.

3. Simply to his grace and wholly
   light and life and strength belong;
   and I love supremely, solely,
   him the holy, him the strong.

4. And I hold in veneration,
   for the love of him alone,
   Holy Church, as his creation,
   and her teachings, as his own.

5. Adoration aye be given,
   with and through the angelic host,
   to the God of earth and heaven,
   Father, Son and Holy Ghost.

   John Henry Newman (1801-90)

76

1. Follow Christ and love the world
      as he did,
   when he walked upon the earth.
   Love each friend and enemy
      as he did.
   In God's eyes we have equal worth.

2. Follow Christ and serve the world
      as he did
   when he ministered to ev'ryone.
   Serve each friend and enemy
      as he did
   so that the Father's will be done.

3. He said: "Love each other
      as I love you.
   By this all men will know you're mine.
   As I served you I ask that you do.
   This new commandment I assign."

4. Follow Christ and love the world
      as he did
   when he walked upon the earth.
   Love each friend and enemy
      as he did.
   In God's eyes we have equal worth.

   Sebastian Temple

77

1. For all the saints
      who from their labours rest,
   who thee by faith
      before the world confest,
   thy name, O Jesus
      be for ever blest.

   Alleluia, alleluia!

2. Thou wast their rock,
      their fortress, and their might;
   thou, Lord, their captain
      in the well-fought fight;
   thou in the darkness drear
      their one true light.

3. O may thy soldiers,
      faithful, true, and bold,
   fight as the saints who
      nobly fought of old,
   and win, with them,
      the victor's crown of gold.

4. O blest communion!
      fellowship divine!
   We feebly struggle,
      they in glory shine;
   yet all are one in thee,
      for all are thine.

5. And when the strife is fierce,
      the warfare long,
   steals on the ear the
      distant triumph-song,
   and hearts are brave again,
      and arms are strong.

6. The golden evening
      brightens in the west;
   soon, soon to faithful
      warriors cometh rest:
   sweet is the calm of
      paradise the blest.

7. But lo! there breaks a
      yet more glorious day;
   the saints triumphant
      rise in bright array:
   the king of glory
      passes on his way.

8. From earth's wide bounds,
      from ocean's farthest coast,
   through gates of pearl streams
      in the countless host,
   singing to Father,
      Son and Holy Ghost.

William Walsham How (1823-97)

78

1. Forth in the peace of Christ we go;
   Christ to the world with joy
      we bring;
   Christ in our minds, Christ on
      our lips,
   Christ in our hearts, the world's
      true King.

2. King of our hearts, Christ makes
      us kings;
   kingship with him his servants gain;
   with Christ, the Servant-Lord of all,
   Christ's world we serve to share
      Christ's reign.

3. Priests of the world, Christ sends
      us forth
   the world of time to consecrate,
   the world of sin by grace to heal,
   Christ's world in Christ to re-create.

4. Christ's are our lips, his word we
      speak;
   prophets are we whose deeds
      proclaim
   Christ's truth in love that we may be
   Christ in the world, to spread
      Christ's name.

5. We are the Church; Christ bids
      us show
   that in his Church all nations find
   their hearth and home where
      Christ restores
   true peace, true love, to all mankind.

James Quinn, S.J.

79

1. Forth in thy name, O Lord, I go,
   my daily labour to pursue;
   thee, only thee, resolved to know,
   in all I think or speak or do.

2. The task thy wisdom hath assigned
   O let me cheerfully fulfil;
   in all my works thy presence find,
   and prove thy good and perfect will.

3. Thee may I set at my right hand,
   whose eyes my inmost substance
      see,
   and labour on at thy command,
   and offer all my works to thee.

4. Give me to bear thy easy yoke,
   and every moment watch and pray,
   and still to things eternal look,
   and hasten to thy glorious day;

5. For thee delightfully employ
   whate'er thy bounteous grace hath
      given,
   and run my course with even joy,
   and closely walk with thee to
      heaven.

Charles Wesley (1707-88)

80

1. Forty days and forty nights
   thou wast fasting in the wild;
   forty days and forty nights
   tempted still, yet unbeguiled:

2. Sunbeams scorching all the day,
   chilly dew-drops nightly shed,
   prowling beasts about thy way,
   stones thy pillow, earth thy bed.

3. Let us thy endurance share
   and from earthly greed abstain
   with thee watching unto prayer,
   with thee strong to suffer pain.

4. Then if evil on us press,
   flesh or spirit to assail,
   victor in the wilderness,
   help us not to swerve or fail!

5. So shall peace divine be ours;
   holier gladness ours shall be,
   come to us angelic powers,
   such as ministered to thee.

6. Keep, O keep us, Saviour dear,
   ever constant by thy side,
   that with thee we may appear
   at the eternal Eastertide.

George Hunt Smyttan (1822-70)
and others

81

1. From the deep I lift my voice,
   hear my cry, O God;
   listen, Lord, to my appeal,
   none but you can help.

2. If you count our grievous sins,
   no man will be spared,
   but your mercy still forgives,
   in your love we trust.

3. Night and day my spirit waits,
   longs to see my God,
   like a watchman, weary, cold,
   waiting for the dawn.

4. Open-handed is the Lord,
   swift to pardon us:
   he will lead his people free,
   clean from all their sins.

5. Glory be to God our Lord,
   merciful and kind,
   Father, Son and Holy Ghost,
   now and evermore.

Paraphrased from Psalm 129
by Luke Connaughton

82

1. From the depths we cry to thee,
   God of sovereign majesty!
   Hear our chants and hymns of
                              praise;
   bless our Lent of forty days.

2. Though our consciences proclaim
   our transgressions and our shame,
   cleanse us, Lord, we humbly plead,
   from our sins of thought and deed.

3. Lord, accept our Lenten fast
   and forgive our sinful past,
   that we may partake with thee
   in the Easter mystery.

Based on Psalm 129
by Sister M. Teresine

83

1. Give me peace, O Lord, I pray,
   in my work and in my play,
   and inside my heart and mind,
   Lord, give me peace.

2. Give peace to the world, I pray,
   let all quarrels cease today.
   May we spread your light and love.
   Lord, give us peace.

Estelle White

84

1. Give me joy in my heart,
         keep me praising,
   give me joy in my heart I pray.
   Give me joy in my heart
         keep me praising.
   Keep me praising till the end of day.

   Sing hosanna! Sing hosanna!
   Sing hosanna to the King of Kings!
   Sing hosanna! Sing hosanna!
   Sing hosanna to the King!

2. Give me peace in my heart,
         keep me resting,
   give me peace in my heart I pray.
   Give me peace in my heart,
         keep me resting.
   Keep me resting till the end of day.

3. Give me love in my heart,
      keep me serving,
   give me love in my heart, I pray.
   Give me love in my heart,
      keep me serving,
   keep me serving 'till the end of day.

Traditional

85

1. Give me yourself
      O Jesus Christ my brother,
   give me yourself
      O Jesus Christ my Lord.

2. Give me your peace,
      O Jesus Christ my brother,
   give me your peace,
      O Jesus Christ my Lord.

3. Give me your love,
      O Jesus Christ my brother,
   give me your love,
      O Jesus Christ my Lord.

4. Give me your heart,
      O Jesus Christ my brother,
   give me your heart,
      O Jesus Christ my Lord.

Estelle White

86

1. Glorious God, King of creation,
   we praise you, we bless you,
      we worship you in song.
   Glorious God, in adoration,
   at your feet we belong.

   Lord of life, Father almighty,
   Lord of hearts, Christ the King.
   Lord of love, Holy Spirit,
   to whom we homage bring.

2. Glorious God, magnificent, holy,
   we love you, adore you,
      and come to you in pray'r.
   Glorious God, mighty, eternal,
   we sing your praise ev'rywhere.

Sebastian Temple

87

Glory be to God, the King of kings.
Hosanna, hosanna!
Raise your voices
let the whole world sing.
Hosanna, hosanna.

1. Praise him sun and moon and all that
   gives the world its light,
   planets and the galaxies and
   shooting stars at night.

2. Butterflies and silken moths and
   spiders in their webs,
   praise him streams and rounded
                              stones that
   line a river bed.

3. Praise him concrete, glass and steel
   that form a city's face,
   piston rods and generators,
   satellites in space.

4. Praise him all the oceans and the
   waves upon the shore,
   albatross and kittiwake and
   seagulls as they soar.

5. Praise him all you people from the
   near and distant lands,
   praise him for the fruitful earth,
   his loving gift to man.

   Glory be to God, the King of kings.
   Hosanna, hosanna!
   Raise your voices
   let the whole world sing.
   Hosanna, hosanna, hosanna,
   hosanna, hosanna.

Estelle White

88

1. Glory be to Jesus,
   who in bitter pains
   poured for me the life-blood,
   from his sacred veins.

2. Grace and life eternal
   in that blood I find:
   blest be his compassion,
   infinitely kind.

3. Blest through endless ages
   be the precious stream,
   which from endless torment
   doth the world redeem.

4. There the fainting spirit
   drinks of life her fill;
   there as in a fountain
   laves herself at will.

5. Abel's blood for vengeance
   pleaded to the skies,
   but the blood of Jesus
   for our pardon cries.

6. Oft as it is sprinkled
   on our guilty hearts,
   Satan in confusion
   terror-struck departs.

7. Oft as earth exulting
   wafts its praise on high,
   hell with horror trembles;
   heaven is filled with joy.

8. Lift ye, then, your voices;
   swell the mighty flood;
   louder still and louder,
   praise the precious blood.

18th c., tr. Edward Caswall

89

1. Glory to God, glory to God,
   glory to the Father.
   Glory to God, glory to God,
   glory to the Father.
   To him be glory for ever.
   To him be glory for ever.
   Alleluia, amen.
   Alleluia, amen,
   alleluia, amen,
   alleluia, amen.

2. Glory to God, glory to God,
   Son of the Father.
   Glory to God, glory to God,
   Son of the Father.
   To him be glory for ever.
   To him be glory for ever.
   Alleluia, amen.
   Alleluia, amen,
   alleluia, amen,
   alleluia, amen.

3. Glory to God, glory to God,
   glory to the Spirit.
   Glory to God, glory to God,
   glory to the Spirit.
   To him be glory for ever.
   To him be glory for ever.
   Alleluia, amen.
   Alleluia, amen,
   alleluia, amen,
   alleluia, amen.

Peruvian

90

1. Glory to thee, Lord God!
   in faith and hope we sing.
   Through this completed sacrifice
   our love and praise we bring.
   We give thee for our sins
   a price beyond all worth,
   which none could ever fitly pay
   but this thy Son on earth.

2. Here is the Lord of all,
   to thee in glory slain;
   of worthless givers, worthy gift
   a victim without stain.
   Through him we give thee thanks,
   with him we bend the knee,
   in him be all our life, who is
   our one true way to thee.

3. So may this sacrifice
   we offer here this day,
   be joined with our poor lives in all
   we think and do and say.
   By living true to grace,
   for thee and thee alone,
   our sorrows, labours, and our joys
   will be his very own.

   John Greally

91

1. Glory to thee, my God, this night
   for all the blessings of the light;
   keep me, O keep me, King of kings,
   beneath thy own almighty wings.

2. Forgive me, Lord, for thy dear Son,
   the ill that I this day have done,
   that with the world, myself and
                                   thee,
   I, ere I sleep, at peace may be.

3. Teach me to live, that I may dread
   the grave as little as my bed;
   teach me to die, that so I may
   rise glorious at the awful day.

4. O may my soul on thee repose,
   and with sweet sleep mine eyelids
                                  close,
   sleep that may me more vigorous
                                   make
   to serve my God when I awake.

5. Praise God, from whom all blessings
                                   flow;
   praise him, all creatures here below;
   praise him above, ye heavenly host;
   praise Father, Son, and Holy Ghost.

   T. Ken (1637-1711)

92

Go, tell it on the mountain,
over the hills and ev'rywhere.
Go, tell it on the mountain
that Jesus Christ is born.

1. While shepherds kept their watching
   o'er wand'ring flocks by night,
   behold from out of heaven
   there shone a holy light.

2. And lo, when they had seen it,
   they all bowed down and prayed,
   they travelled on together
   to where the Babe was laid.

3. When I was a seeker,
   I sought both night and day:
   I asked my Lord to help me
   and he showed me the way.

4. He made me a watchman
   upon the city wall,
   And if I am a Christian,
   I am the least of all.

   Traditional

93

1. God be in my head, and in my
                          understanding;
   God be in mine eyes, and in my
                          looking;
   God be in my mouth, and in my
                          speaking;
   God be in my heart, and in my
                          thinking;
   God be at mine end, and at my
                          departing.

   Book of Hours (1514)

94

1. God everlasting, wonderful,
    and holy,
Father most gracious,
    we who stand before thee
here at thine altar,
    as thy Son has taught us,
come to adore thee.

2. Countless the mercies thou hast
    lavished on us,
source of all blessing
    to all creatures living;
to thee we render,
    for thy love o'erflowing.
Humble thanksgiving.

3. Now in remembrance of our
    great redeemer,
dying on Calvary,
    rising and ascending,
through him we offer
    what he ever offers,
sinners befriending.

4. Strength to the living,
    rest to the departed,
grant, Holy Father,
    through this pure oblation:
may the life-giving
    bread for ever bring us
health and salvation.

Harold Riley

95

1. Godhead here in hiding,
    whom I do adore,
masked by these bare shadows,
    shape and nothing more,
see, Lord, at thy service
    low lies here a heart
lost, all lost in wonder
    at the God thou art.

2. Seeing, touching, tasting
    are in thee deceived;
how says trusty hearing?
    That shall be believed;
what God's Son hath told me,
    take for truth I do;
truth himself speaks truly,
    or there's nothing true.

3. On the cross thy Godhead
    made no sign to men;
here thy very manhood
    steals from human ken;
both are my confession,
    both are my belief;
and I pray the prayer
    of the dying thief.

4. I am not like Thomas,
    wounds I cannot see,
but can plainly call thee
    Lord and God as he;
this faith each day deeper
    be my holding of,
daily make me harder
    hope and dearer love.

5. O thou our reminder
    of Christ crucified,
living Bread, the life of
    us for whom he died,
lend this life to me then;
    feed and feast my mind,
there be thou the sweetness
    man was meant to find.

6. Jesu, whom I look at
    shrouded here below,
I beseech thee send me
    what I long for so,
some day to gaze on thee
    face to face in light
and be blest for ever
    with thy glory's sight.

Ascribed to St. Thomas Aquinas
(1227-74), tr. Gerard Manley Hopkins

96

1. God is love
and the one who lives in love
lives in God,
and God lives in him.
And we have come to know
and have believed
the love which God has for us.
God is love
and the one who lives in love
lives in God,
and God lives in him.

2. God is hope . . .

3. God is peace . . .

4. God is joy . . .

Anonymous

97

1. God is love: his the care,
tending each, everywhere.
God is love, all is there!
Jesus came to show him,
that mankind might know him!

Sing aloud, loud, loud!
Sing aloud, loud, loud!
God is good!
God is truth! God is beauty!
Praise him!

2. None can see God above;
all have here man to love;
thus may we Godward move,
finding him in others,
holding all men brothers:

3. Jesus lived here for men:
strove and died, rose again,
rules our hearts, now as then;
for he came to save us
by the truth he gave us:

4. To our Lord praise we sing,
light and life, friend and king,
coming down love to bring,
pattern for our duty,
showing God in beauty:

Percy Dearmer (1867-1936)

98

1. God of mercy and compassion,
look with pity upon me;
Father, let me call thee Father,
'tis thy child returns to thee.

Jesus Lord, I ask for mercy;
let me not implore in vain:
all my sins I now detest them,
never will I sin again.

2. By my sins I have deserved
death and endless misery,
hell with all its pain and torments,
and for all eternity.

3. By my sins I have abandon'd
right and claim to heaven above,
where the saints rejoice for ever,
in a boundless sea of love.

4. See our Saviour, bleeding, dying,
on the cross of Calvary;
to that cross my sins have nail'd
him,
yet he bleeds and dies for me.

E. Vaughan (1827-1908)

99

1. God's spirit is in my heart.
He has called me and set me apart.
This is what I have to do,
what I have to do.

He sent me to give
the Good News to the poor,
tell prisoners that they are
prisoners no more,
tell blind people that they can see,
and set the downtrodden free,
and go tell ev'ryone
the news that the Kingdom of God
has come,
and go tell ev'ryone
the news that God's kingdom
has come.

2. Just as the Father sent me,
   so I'm sending you out to be
   my witnesses throughout the world,
   the whole of the world.

3. Don't carry a load in your pack,
   you don't need two shirts on your
   back.
   A workman can earn his own keep,
   can earn his own keep.

4. Don't worry what you have to say,
   don't worry because on that day
   God's spirit will speak in your heart,
   will speak in your heart.

Alan Dale

100

1. Going home, going home,
   I'm a-going home.
   Quiet like, some still day,
   I'm just going home.
   It's not far, just close by,
   through an open door.
   Work all done, care laid by,
   going to fear no more.
   Mother's there expecting me,
   father's waiting too.
   Lots of folk gathered there,
   all the friends I knew,
   all the friends I knew.

2. Morning star lights the way,
   restless dreams all done.
   Shadows gone, break of day,
   real life just begun.
   There's no break, there's no end,
   just a living on,
   wide awake, with a smile,
   going on and on.
   Going home, going home,
   I'm just going home.
   It's not far, just close by,
   through an open door.
   I'm just going home.

William Arms Fisher

101

1. Gonna lay down
      my sword and shield
   down by the riverside,
   down by the riverside,
   down by the riverside,
   Gonna lay down
      my sword and shield
   down by the riverside.
   I ain't gonna study war no more.

   I ain't gonna study war no more.

2. Gonna walk with
      the Prince of Peace
   down by the riverside,
   down by the riverside,
   down by the riverside.
   Gonna walk with
      the Prince of Peace
   down by the riverside.
   I ain't gonna study war no more.

3. Gonna shake hands
      around the world
   down by the riverside,
   down by the riverside,
   down by the riverside.
   Gonna shake hands
      around the world
   down by the riverside.
   I ain't gonna study war no more.

Traditional Spiritual

102

1. Go, the Mass is ended,
   children of the Lord.
   Take his Word to others
   as you've heard it spoken to you.
   Go, the Mass is ended,
   go and tell the world
   the Lord is good, the Lord is kind,
   and he loves ev'ryone.

2. Go, the Mass is ended,
   take his love to all.
   Gladden all who meet you,
   fill their hearts with hope and
                             courage.
   Go, the Mass is ended,
   fill the world with love,
   and give to all what you've received
   — the peace and joy of Christ.

3. Go, the Mass is ended,
   strengthened in the Lord,
   lighten ev'ry burden,
   spread the joy of Christ around you.
   Go, the Mass is ended,
   take his peace to all.
   This day is yours to change the
                             world
   — to make God known and loved.

   Sister Marie Lydia Pereira

103

1. Great Saint Andrew, friend of Jesus,
   lover of his glorious cross,
   early by his voice effective
   called from ease to pain and loss,
   strong Saint Andrew, Simon's
                             brother,
   who with haste fraternal flew,
   fain with him to share the treasure
   which, at Jesus' lips, he drew.

2. Blest Saint Andrew, Jesus' herald,
   true apostle, martyr bold,
   who, by deeds his words confirming,
   sealed with blood the truth he told.
   Ne'er to king was crown so
                             beauteous,
   ne'er was prize to heart so dear,
   as to him the cross of Jesus
   when its promised joys drew near.

3. Loved Saint Andrew, Scotland's
                             patron,
   watch thy land with heedful eye,
   rally round the cross of Jesus
   all her storied chivalry!
   To the Father, Son, and Spirit,
   fount of sanctity and love,
   give we glory, now and ever,
   with the saints who reign above.

   Frederick Oakeley (1802-80)

104

1. Guide me, O thou great redeemer,
   pilgrim through this barren land;
   I am weak, but thou art mighty,
   hold me with thy powerful hand:
   Bread of heaven,
   feed me till I want no more.

2. Open now the crystal fountain,
   whence the healing stream doth
                             flow;
   let the fire and cloudy pillar
   lead me all my journey through;
   strong Deliverer,
   be thou still my strength and shield.

3. When I tread the verge of Jordan,
   bid my anxious fears subside;
   death of death, and hell's
                             destruction,
   land me safe on Canaan's side;
   songs of praises,
   I will ever give to thee.

   W. Williams (1717-91),
   tr. P. and W. Williams

105

1. Hail, glorious Saint Patrick,
      dear saint of our isle,
   on us thy poor children
      bestow a sweet smile;
   and now thou art high
      in the mansions above,
   on Erin's green valleys
   look down in thy love.
   On Erin's green valleys,
      on Erin's green valleys,
   on Erin's green valleys
      look down in thy love.

2. Hail, glorious Saint Patrick!
      thy words were once strong
   against Satan's wiles and
      an infidel throng;
   not less is thy might
      where in heaven thou art;
   O, come to our aid,
      in our battle take part.

3. In the war against sin,
      in the fight for the faith,
   dear saint, may thy children
      resist unto death;
   may their strength be in meekness,
      in penance, in prayer,
   Their banner the Cross
      which they glory to bear.

4. Thy people, now exiles
      on many a shore,
   shall love and revere thee
      till time be no more;
   and the fire thou hast kindled
      shall ever burn bright,
   Its warmth undiminished,
      undying its light.

5. Ever bless and defend the sweet
      land of our birth,
   where the shamrock still blooms
      as when thou wert on earth,
   and our hearts shall yet burn,
      wheresoever we roam,
   For God and Saint Patrick,
      and our native home.

   Sister Agnes

106

1. Hail, Queen of heav'n, the ocean
                              star,
      guide of the wand'rer here below;
      thrown on life's surge, we claim thy
                              care;
   save us from peril and from woe.
   Mother of Christ, star of the sea,
   pray for the wanderer, pray for me.

2. O gentle, chaste and spotless maid,
   we sinners make our prayers
                        through thee;
   remind thy son that he has paid
   the price of our iniquity.
   Virgin most pure, star of the sea,
   pray for the sinner, pray for me.

3. Sojourners in this vale of tears,
   to thee, blest advocate, we cry;
   pity our sorrows, calm our fears,
   and soothe with hope our misery.
   Refuge in grief, star of the sea,
   pray for the mourner, pray for me.

4. And while to him who reigns above,
   in Godhead One, in Persons Three,
   the source of life, of grace, of love,
   homage we pay on bended knee,
   do thou, bright Queen, star of the
                              sea,
   pray for thy children, pray for me.

   John Lingard (1771-1851)

107

1. Hail, Redeemer, King divine!
   Priest and Lamb, the throne is thine,
   King, whose reign shall never cease,
   Prince of everlasting peace.

   Angels, saints and nations sing:
   'Praised be Jesus Christ, our King;
   Lord of life, earth, sky and sea,
   King of love on Calvary.'

2. King whose name creation thrills,
   rule our minds, our hearts, our wills,
   till in peace each nation rings
   with thy praises, King of kings.

3. King most holy, King of truth,
   guide the lowly, guide the youth;
   Christ thou King of glory bright,
   be to us eternal light.

4. Shepherd-King, o'er mountains steep,
   homeward bring the wandering
                              sheep,

   shelter in one royal fold
   states and kingdoms, new and old.

   Patrick Brennan

8. Ever upward let us move,
   wafted on the wings of love;
   looking when our Lord shall come,
   longing, sighing after home.

   *Charles Wesley (1707-88), Thomas
   Cotterill (1779-1823) and others*

108

1. Hail the day that sees him rise,
                              alleluia!

   To his throne above the skies;
                              alleluia!
   Christ, the Lamb for sinners given,
                              alleluia!
   Enters now the highest heaven,
                              alleluia!

2. There for him high triumph waits;
   lift your heads, eternal gates!
   He hath conquered death and sin;
   take the king of glory in!

3. Circled round with angel-powers,
   their triumphant Lord and ours;
   wide unfold the radiant scene,
   take the king of glory in!

4. Lo, the heaven its Lord receives,
   yet he loves the earth he leaves;
   though returning to his throne,
   still he calls mankind his own.

5. See! he lifts his hands above,
   see! he shows the prints of love;
   hark! his gracious lips bestow,
   blessings on his Church below.

6. Still for us he intercedes,
   his prevailing death he pleads;
   near himself prepares our place,
   he the first-fruits of our race.

7. Lord, though parted from our sight,
   far above the starry height,
   grant our hearts may thither rise,
   seeking thee above the skies.

109

1. Hail, thou star of ocean,
   portal of the sky;
   ever virgin Mother
   of the Lord most high.
   Oh! by Gabriel's Ave,
   utter'd long ago,
   Eva's name reversing,
   'stablish peace below.

2. Break the captive's fetters,
   light on blindness pour,
   all our ills expelling,
   every bliss implore.
   Show thyself a mother;
   offer him our sighs,
   who for us incarnate
   did not thee despise.

3. Virgin of all virgins,
   to thy shelter take us;
   gentlest of the gentle,
   chaste and gentle make us.
   Still, as on we journey,
   help our weak endeavour;
   till with thee and Jesus
   we rejoice for ever.

4. Through the highest heaven,
   to the almighty Three,
   Father, Son and Spirit,
   One same glory be.

   9th c., tr. Edward Caswall

110

1. Hail to the Lord's anointed!
   Great David's greater son;
   hail, in the time appointed,
   his reign on earth begun!
   he comes to break oppression,
   to set the captive free;
   to take away transgression,
   and rule in equity.

2. He shall come down like showers
   upon the fruitful earth,
   and love, joy, hope, like flowers,
   spring in his path to birth:
   before him on the mountains
   shall peace the herald go;
   and righteousness in fountains
   from hill to valley flow.

3. Kings shall fall down before him,
   and gold and incense bring;
   all nations shall adore him,
   his praise all people sing;
   to him shall prayer unceasing
   and daily vows ascend;
   his kingdom still increasing
   a kingdom without end.

4. O'er every foe victorious,
   he on his throne shall rest,
   from age to age more glorious,
   all-blessing and all-blest;
   the tide of time shall never
   his covenant remove;
   his name shall stand for ever;
   that name to us is love.

   James Montgomery (1771-1854)

111

Happy the man
   who wanders with the Lord.
Happy the man
   who knows how to live.
Happy the man
   who never seeks reward,
giving because he loves to give.
He seeks no gold, he wants no gain.

He knows those things
   are all in vain.
He needs no praise nor honour, too.
His only motto:
   'To your own self be true.'
Happy the man
   who learned how to pray.
Happy the man
   who has a burning goal.
Happy the man
   whose service needs no pay.
This man has found his own soul.
Happy the man,
   happy the man of the Lord.

   Sebastian Temple

112

1. Hark! a herald voice is calling:
   'Christ is nigh' it seems to say;
   'Cast away the dreams of darkness,
   O ye children of the day!'

2. Startled at the solemn warning,
   let the earth-bound soul arise;
   Christ, her sun, all sloth dispelling,
   shines upon the morning skies.

3. Lo! the Lamb, so long expected,
   comes with pardon down from
   heaven;
   let us haste, with tears of sorrow,
   one and all to be forgiven;

4. So when next he comes with glory,
   wrapping all the earth in fear,
   may he then as our defender
   on the clouds of heaven appear.

5. Honour, glory, virtue, merit,
   to the Father and the Son,
   with the co-eternal Spirit,
   while unending ages run.

   6th c., tr. Edward Caswall

113

1. Hark, the herald angels sing,
   glory to the new-born King;
   peace on earth and mercy mild,
   God and sinners reconciled:
   joyful all ye nations rise,
   join the triumph of the skies,
   with the angelic host proclaim,
   Christ is born in Bethlehem.

   Hark, the herald Angels sing,
   glory to the new-born King.

2. Christ, by highest heaven adored,
   Christ, the everlasting Lord,
   late in time behold him come,
   offspring of a Virgin's womb!
   Veiled in flesh the Godhead see,
   hail the incarnate Deity!
   Pleased as man with man to dwell,
   Jesus, our Emmanuel.

3. Hail the heaven-born Prince of
                            peace!
   Hail the Son of Righteousness!
   Light and life to all he brings
   risen with healing in his wings;
   mild he lays his glory by,
   born that man no more may die,
   born to raise the sons of earth,
   born to give them second birth.

   Charles Wesley (1743),
   George Whitefield (1753),
   Martin Madan (1760), and others

114

Haul, haul away.
Haul, haul away.
Cast the nets wide
   and sink the nets deep
and it's haul, haul away.

1. Oh, he sat in the boat
      and he spoke to the crowd.
   Haul, haul away.
   And his voice wasn't soft
      and his voice wasn't loud.
   Haul, haul away.
   And he spoke of the just
      and the pure and the free,
   and his voice caught the air
      like a net in the sea.
   And it's . . .

2. He said: "Cast your nets wide
      where the water is deep."
   Haul, haul away.
   "Oh, cast the nets wide
      and sink the nets deep."
   Haul, haul away.
   "Though we've worked through the
   night and we've nothing to show,
   we will try once again
      just because you say so."
   And it's . . .

3. Oh the catch it was huge
      and the boat it was small.
   Haul, haul away.
   His friends came to help
      when they heard Peter call.
   Haul, haul away.
   "You must leave us," said Peter,
      "for we're men of sin."
   But he said: "Come with me
      and be fishers of men."
   And it's . . .

   Michael Cockett

115

1. Help, Lord, the souls that thou hast
                                  made,
   the souls to thee so dear,
   in prison for the debt unpaid
   of sin committed here.

2. These holy souls, they suffer on,
   resigned in heart and will,
   until thy high behest is done,
   and justice has its fill.

3. For daily falls, for pardoned crime
   they joy to undergo
   the shadow of thy cross sublime,
   the remnant of thy woe.

4. Oh, by their patience of delay,
   their hope amid their pain,
   their sacred zeal to burn away
   disfigurement and stain;

5. Oh, by their fire of love, not less
   in keenness than the flame;
   oh, by their very helplessness,
   oh, by thy own great name;

6. Good Jesus, help! sweet Jesus aid
   the souls to thee most dear,
   in prison for the debt unpaid
   of sins committed here.

   John Henry Newman (1801-90)

116

1. Here's a child for you, O Lord,
   we shall cherish, we shall care.
   We'll be faithful to your Word
   for we want this child to share
   your lovelight.

2. May he hold his head up high,
   graceful, joyful, strong of limb.
   May his eyes be clear and bright,
   seeing beauty in all things
   that you've made.

3. We were young ourselves, O Lord,
   we were eager, we were fresh
   like the opening buds of spring,
   and we wanted happiness
   in your way.

4. Then, at times, we went astray,
   we were foolish, we were weak,
   and the innocence we had
   vanished like the trace of feet
   when snow melts.

5. But we come, O Lord and king,
   at your bidding, and we pray
   that the precious gift we bring
   will grow stronger every day
   in your love.

6. By the water poured out here
   and our promise, we believe,
   he will master every fear,
   and at last will come to see
   your Godhead.

   Estelle White

117

1. He's got the whole world
   in his hand.
   He's got the whole world
   in his hand.
   He's got the whole wide world
   in his hand.
   He's got the whole world
   in his hand.

2. He's got you and me, brother . . .

3. He's got you and me, sister . . .

4. He's got everybody here . . .

5. He's got the whole world . . .

118 *Traditional*

1. He was born like you and I
   in a body which must die,
   yet his death was not for ever,
   he lives on.
   Who is this, like you and I
   who was born to live and die,
   yet his death was not for ever,
   he lives on?

   Deep, deep, deep,
   is the mystery I sing.
   Dark, dark, dark is the riddle.
   He was born like you and I
   in a body which must die,
   yet his death was not for ever:
   he lives on.

2. Not a soul, so it is said,
   saw him raised up from the dead,
   yet by now the story's known
   throughout the world.
   Who is this whom it is said
   no one saw raised from the dead,
   yet by now the story's known
   throughout the world?

3. His believers, when they've met,
   know he's there with them, and yet
   he's with God (what makes us
       think that's somewhere else?)
   Who is this who, when they've met,
   is right there with them, and yet
   he's with God (what makes us
       think that's somewhere else?)

Hubert Richards

119

1. He who would valiant be
   'gainst all disaster,
   let him in constancy
   follow the master
   there's no discouragement
   shall make him once relent
   his first avowed intent
   to be a pilgrim.

2. Who so beset him round
   with dismal stories,
   do'but themselves confound:
   his strength the more is.
   No foes shall stay his might
   though he with giants fight:
   he will make good his right
   to be a pilgrim.

3. Since, Lord, thou dost defend
   us with thy Spirit,
   we know we at the end
   shall life inherit.
   Then fancies flee away!
   I'll fear not what men say,
   I'll labour night and day
   to be a pilgrim.

Percy Dearmer (1867-1936),
after John Bunyan (1628-88)

120

1. Holy Father, God of might,
   throned amid the hosts of light,
   take our life, our strength, our love,
   King of earth and heaven above.

2. Hear the songs your people raise,
   songs of joyful thanks and praise,
   calling all created things
   to adore you, King of kings.

3. Christ, be with us as we go,
   let this blind world see and know,
   burning in our lives, the sight
   of its only saving light.

4. So, all men will bless your name,
   and your kingship all proclaim,
   praising with the heavenly host
   Father, Son and Holy Ghost.

Anonymous

121

1. Holy God, we praise thy name;
   Lord of all, we bow before thee!
   All on earth thy sceptre own,
   all in heaven above adore thee.
   Infinite thy vast domain,
   everlasting is thy reign.

2. Hark! the loud celestial hymn,
   angel choirs above are raising;
   cherubim and seraphim,
   in unceasing chorus praising,
   fill the heavens with sweet accord,
   holy, holy, holy Lord.

3. Holy Father, holy Son,
   Holy Spirit, three we name thee.
   While in essence only one.
   Undivided God we claim thee;
   and adoring bend the knee,
   while we own the mystery.

4. Spare thy people, Lord, we pray,
   by a thousand snares surrounded;
   keep us without sin to-day;
   never let us be confounded.
   Lo, I put my trust in thee,
   never, Lord, abandon me.

C. A. Walworth (1820-1900)

122

1. Holy, holy, holy, holy.
   Holy, holy, holy Lord
      God almighty.
   And we lift our hearts before you
      as a token of our love.
   Holy, holy, holy, holy.

2. Gracious Father, gracious Father,
   we are glad to be your children,
      gracious Father.
   And we lift our heads before you
      as a token of our love,
   gracious Father, gracious Father.

3. Precious Jesus, precious Jesus,
   we are glad you have redeemed us,
      precious Jesus.
   And we lift our hands before you
               as a token of our love,
   precious Jesus, precious Jesus.

4. Holy Spirit, Holy Spirit,
   come and fill our hearts anew,
      Holy Spirit.
   And we lift our voice before you
      as a token of our love,
   Holy Spirit, Holy Spirit.

5. Hallelujah, hallelujah,
   hallelujah, hallelujah,
      hallelujah.
   And we lift our hearts before you
      as a token of our love,
   hallelujah, hallelujah.

Jimmy Owens

123

1. Holy, holy, holy!
      Lord God almighty!
   Early in the morning
      our song shall rise to thee;
   holy, holy, holy!
      Merciful and mighty!
   God in three persons,
      blessed Trinity!

2. Holy, holy, holy!
      All the saints adore thee.
   Casting down their golden crowns
      around the glassy sea;
   Cherubim and seraphim
      falling down before thee,
   which wert, and art,
      and evermore shalt be.

3. Holy, holy, holy!
      Though the darkness hide thee,
   though the eye of sinful man
      thy glory may not see,
   only thou art holy,
      there is none beside thee,
   perfect in power,
      in love, and purity.

4. Holy, holy, holy!
      Lord God almighty!
   All thy works shall praise thy name,
      in earth, and sky, and sea;
   holy, holy, holy!
      Merciful and mighty!
   God in three persons,
      blessed Trinity!

Reginald Heber (1783-1875)

124

1. Holy Spirit, Lord of light,
   from the clear celestial height,
   thy pure beaming radiance give;
   come, thou Father of the poor,
   come with treasures which endure;
   come, thou light of all that live!

2. Thou, of all consolers best,
   thou, the soul's delightsome guest,
   dost refreshing peace bestow:
   thou in toil art comfort sweet;
   pleasant coolness in the heat;
   solace in the midst of woe.

3. Light immortal, light divine,
   visit thou these hearts of thine,
   and our inmost being fill:
   if thou take thy grace away,
   nothing pure in man will stay;
   all his good is turned to ill.

4. Heal our wounds, our strength
                                renew;
   on our dryness pour thy dew;
   wash the stains of guilt away:
   Bend the stubborn heart and will;
   melt the frozen, warm the chill;
   guide the steps that go astray.

5. Thou, on those who evermore
   thee confess and thee adore,
   in thy sevenfold gifts descend:
   Give them comfort when they die;
   give them life with thee on high;
   give them joys that never end.

Ascribed to Stephen Langton (d.1228)
tr. Edward Caswall

125

1. Holy Spirit of fire,
   flame everlasting,
        so bright and clear,
   speak this day in our hearts.
   Lighten our darkness
        and purge us of fear,
   Holy Spirit of fire.

   The wind can blow or be still,
   or water be parched by the sun.
   A fire can die into dust:
   but here the eternal Spirit of God
   tells us a new world's begun.

2. Holy Spirit of love,
   strong are the faithful
        who trust your pow'r.
   Love who conquer our will,
   teach us the words of
        the gospel of peace,
   Holy Spirit of love.

3. Holy Spirit of God,
   flame everlasting,
        so bright and clear,
   speak this day in our hearts.
   Lighten our darkness
        and purge us of fear,
   Holy Spirit of God.

                        John Glynn

126

1. Holy Virgin, by God's decree,
   you were called eternally;
   that he could give
        his Son to our race.
   Mary, we praise you,
        hail full of grace.

   Ave, ave, ave, Maria.

2. By your faith and loving accord,
   as the handmaid of the Lord,
   you undertook
        God's plan to embrace.
   Mary, we thank you,
        hail full of grace.

3. Refuge for your children so weak,
   sure protection all can seek.
   Problems of life
        you help us to face.
   Mary, we trust you,
        hail full of grace.

4. To our needy world of today
   love and beauty you portray,
   showing the path
        to Christ we must trace.
   Mary, our mother,
        hail, full of grace.

                        J-P. Lécot
          tr. W. Raymond Lawrence

127

1. How dark was the stable
        where Jesus was born?
   How dark was the stable
        that was his first home?
   It was dark as the sky
        on a black winter's night,
   when the stars will not shine
        and the moon gives no light.

2. How cold was the stable
        where Jesus was born?
   How cold was the stable
        that was his first home?
   It was cold as the frost
        on a white window pane;
   it was cold as a heart
        that has known no love.

3. How light was the stable
   when Jesus was born?
   How light was the stable
   he made his first home?
   It was light as the star
   that was shining that night;
   it was light as an angel
   in splendour and might.

4. How warm was the stable
   when Jesus was born?
   How warm was the stable
   he made his first home?
   It was warm as the love
   of that first Christmas morn;
   it was warm as our hearts
   in which Jesus is born.

Michael Cockett

128

1. I am the bread of life.
   He who comes to me
   will never be hungry.
   I will raise him up.
   I will raise him up.
   I will raise him up to eternal life.
   I am the bread of life.

2. I am the spring of life.
   He who hopes in me
   will never be thirsty.
   I will raise him up.
   I will raise him up.
   I will raise him up to eternal life.
   I am the spring of life.

3. I am the way of life.
   He who follows me
   will never be lonely.
   I will raise him up.
   I will raise him up.
   I will raise him up to eternal life.
   I am the way of life.

4. I am the truth of life.
   He who looks for me
   will never seek blindly.
   I will raise him up.
   I will raise him up.
   I will raise him up to eternal life.
   I am the truth of life.

5. I am the life of life.
   He who dies with me
   will never die vainly.
   I will raise him up.
   I will raise him up.
   I will raise him up to eternal life.
   I am the life of life.

David Konstant

129

1. I believe in God almighty,
   who made heav'n and earth.
   I believe in one Lord,
   Jesus Christ, his only Son.
   God from God and Light from Light,
   the one true God above,
   with the Father he is one,
   creator of all things.

   Oh I believe in God almighty
   who made heav'n and earth.
   Yes, I believe in God almighty
   who made heav'n and earth.

2. Through the Spirit, born of Mary,
   God became a man.
   For our sake he suffered death.
   They nailed him to a cross.
   But no earthly grave could hold
   the Lord of heav'n and earth;
   bursting forth he rose again,
   just as the prophets said.

3. Forty days he walked the earth,
   a dead man come alive.
   Then he bid his friends farewell,
   returning to his heav'n
   He will come again to judge
   the living and the dead.
   He is Lord of all the worlds;
   his kingdom has no end.

4. I believe in God the Father,
   Spirit and the Son.
   I believe the Church is holy,
   universal, one.
   And through water all our guilt
   is cleansed—we are made new.
   Dying we will rise again
   to live for ever more.

Kevin Mayhew

130

1. I believe in God, the Father;
   I believe in God, his Son;
   I believe in God, their Spirit;
   each is God, yet God is one.

2. I believe what God has spoken
   through his Church, whose word is
           true;
   boldly she proclaims his Gospel,
   ever old, yet ever new.

3. All my hope is in God's goodness,
   shown for us by him who died,
   Jesus Christ, the world's Redeemer,
   spotless Victim crucified.

4. All my love is Love eternal;
   in that Love I love mankind.
   Take my heart, O Heart once broken,
   take my soul, my strength, my mind.

5. Father, I have sinned against you;
   look on me with eyes of love;
   seek your wand'ring sheep,
           Good Shepherd;
   grant heav'n's peace, O heav'nly Dove.

6. Bless'd be God, the loving Father;
   bless'd be God, his only Son;
   bless'd be God, all-holy Spirit;
   bless'd be God, for ever one.

                              James Quinn

131

1. I danced in the morning
   when the world was begun,
   and I danced in the moon
   and the stars and the sun,
   and I came down from heaven and
   I danced on the earth,
   at Bethlehem
   I had my birth.

   Dance, then, wherever you may be,
   I am the Lord of the Dance, said he.
   And I'll lead you all
        wherever you may be,
   and I'll lead you all
        in the dance, said he.

2. I danced for the scribe
   and the pharisee,
   but they would not dance
   and they wouldn't follow me.
   I danced for the fishermen,
   for James and John;
   they came with me
   and the dance went on.

3. I danced on the Sabbath
   and I cured the lame.
   The holy people they
   said it was a shame.
   They whipped and they stripped
   and they hung me on high,
   and they left me there
   on the cross to die.

4. I danced on a Friday
   when the sky turned black.
   It's hard to dance
   with the devil on your back.
   They buried my body
   and they thought I'd gone
   but I am the dance
   and I still go on.

5. They cut me down
   and I leapt up high.
   I am the life
   that'll never, never die
   I'll live in you
   if you'll live in me.
   I am the Lord
   of the Dance, said he.

                              Sydney Carter

132

1. I'll sing a hymn to Mary,
   the Mother of my God,
   the Virgin of all virgins,
   of David's royal blood.
   O teach me, holy Mary,
   a loving song to frame,
   when wicked men blaspheme thee,
   to love and bless thy name.

2. O noble Tower of David,
   of gold and ivory,
   the Ark of God's own promise,
   the gate of heav'n to me,
   to live and not to love thee,
   would fill my soul with shame;
   when wicked men blaspheme thee,
   I'll love and bless thy name.

3. The Saints are high in glory,
   with golden crowns so bright;
   but brighter far is Mary,
   upon her throne of light.
   O that which God did give thee,
   let mortal ne'er disclaim;
   when wicked men blaspheme thee,
   I'll love and bless thy name.

4. But in the crown of Mary,
   there lies a wondrous gem,
   as Queen of all the Angels,
   which Mary shares with them:
   no sin hath e'er defiled thee,
   so doth our faith proclaim;
   when wicked men blaspheme thee,
   I'll love and bless thy name.

   John Wyse (1825-98)

133

1. Immaculate Mary!
   Our hearts are on fire,
   that title so wondrous
   fills all our desire.

   Ave, ave, ave Maria!
   Ave, ave, ave Maria!

2. We pray for God's glory,
   may his kingdom come!
   We pray for his vicar,
   our father, and Rome.

3. We pray for our mother
   the church upon earth,
   and bless, sweetest Lady,
   the land of our birth.

4. O Mary! O mother!
   Reign o'er us once more,
   be England thy 'dowry'
   as in days of yore.

5. We pray for all sinners,
   and souls that now stray
   from Jesus and Mary,
   in heresy's way.

6. For poor, sick, afflicted
   thy mercy we crave;
   and comfort the dying
   thou light of the grave.

7. There is no need, Mary,
   nor ever has been,
   which thou canst not succour,
   Immaculate Queen.

8. In grief and temptation,
   in joy or in pain,
   we'll ask thee, our mother,
   nor seek thee in vain.

9. O bless us, dear Lady,
   with blessings from heaven.
   And to our petitions
   let answer be given.

10. In death's solemn moment,
    our mother, be nigh;
    as children of Mary
    O teach us to die.

11. And crown thy sweet mercy
    with this special grace,
    to behold soon in heaven
    God's ravishing face.

12. Now to God be all glory
    and worship for aye,
    and to God's virgin mother
    an endless Ave.

    Anonymous

134

1. Immortal, invisible,
    God only wise,
   in light inaccessible
      hid from our eyes,
   most blessed, most glorious,
      the Ancient of Days,
   almighty, victorious,
      thy great name we praise.

2. Unresting, unhasting,
      and silent as light;
   nor wanting, nor wasting,
      thou rulest in might —
   thy justice like mountains
      high-soaring above
   thy clouds which are fountains
      of goodness and love.

3. To all life thou givest,
      to both great and small;
   in all life thou livest,
      the true life of all;
   we blossom and flourish
      as leaves on the tree,
   and wither and perish;
      but naught changeth thee.

4. Great Father of glory,
      pure Father of light,
   thine angels adore thee,
      all veiling their sight;
   all laud we would render:
      O help us to see
   'tis only the splendour
      of light hideth thee.

W. Chalmers Smith (1825-1908)
Based on 1 Tim. 1: 17

135

1. In bread we bring you, Lord,
      our bodies' labour.
   In wine we offer you
      our spirits' grief.
   We do not ask you, Lord,
      who is my neighbour?
   But stand united now,
      one in belief.

Oh we have gladly heard
   your Word, your holy Word,
and now in answer, Lord,
   our gifts we bring.
Our selfish hearts make true,
   our failing faith renew,
our lives belong to you,
   our Lord and King.

2. The bread we offer you
      is blessed and broken,
   and it becomes for us
      our spirits' food.
   Over the cup we bring
      your Word is spoken;
   make it your gift to us,
      your healing blood.
   Take all that daily toil
      plants in our heart's poor soil
   take all we start and spoil,
      each hopeful dream,
   the chances we have missed,
      the graces we resist,
   Lord, in thy Eucharist,
      take and redeem.

Kevin Nichols

136

1. In Christ there is no east or west,
   in him no south or north,
   but one great fellowship of love
   throughout the whole wide earth.

2. In him shall true hearts ev'rywhere
   their high communion find.
   His service is the golden cord
   close-binding all mankind.

3. Join hands, then, brothers of the
                              faith
   whate'er your race may be.
   Who serves my Father as a son
   is surely kin to me.

4. In Christ now meet both east and
                              west,
   in him meet south and north.
   All Christly souls are one in him
   throughout the whole wide earth.

John Oxenham (1852-1941)

137

1. In the bleak midwinter,
   frosty wind made moan,
   earth stood hard as iron,
   water like a stone;
   snow had fallen, snow on snow,
   snow on snow,
   in the bleak midwinter
   long ago.

2. Our God, heaven cannot hold him
   nor earth sustain;
   Heaven and earth shall flee away,
   when he comes to reign.
   In the bleak midwinter
   a stable-place sufficed
   the Lord God Almighty,
   Jesus Christ.

3. Enough for him, whom Cherubim
   worship night and day,
   a breastful of milk,
   and a mangerful of hay:
   enough for him, whom angels
   fall down before,
   the ox and ass and camel
   which adore.

4. Angels and archangels
   may have gathered there,
   Cherubim and Seraphim
   thronged the air.
   But only his mother
   in her maiden bliss
   worshipped the beloved
   with a kiss.

5. What can I give him,
   poor as I am?
   If I were a shepherd
   I would bring a lamb;
   if I were a wise man
   I would do my part;
   yet what I can I give him —
   give my heart.

   Christina G. Rossetti (1830-94)

138

1. In the earth the small seed
      is hidden and
   lies unseen until
      it is bidden by
   springtime stirrings up
      to the sunlight and
   summer ripening.
   Golden is the harvest
      and precious the
   bread that you are,
   and give to us, Lord.

2. In the vineyard branches
      are cut away
   so that fresh young shoots
      may, with ev'ry day,
   bend beneath the fruit
      as it ripens and
   fills with promise.
   Golden is the harvest
      and precious the
   wine that you are
   and give to us, Lord.

3. In me, Oh my Lord, plant
      the seed of love
   nourished by your body
      and by your blood.
   May my soul take wings
      and rise upwards to
   new awakenings!
   Golden is the light of
      your Godhead that
   by love you have,
   and give to us, Lord.

   Estelle White

139

1. Into one we all are gathered
      through the love of Christ.
   Let us then rejoice with gladness.
      In him we find love.
   Let us fear and love the living God,
   and love and cherish all mankind.

   Where charity and love are,
      there is God.

2. Therefore, when we are together
      in the love of Christ,
   let our minds know no division,
      strife or bitterness;
   may the Christ our God be in our
                              midst.
   Through Christ our Lord all love is
                              found.

3. May we see your face in glory,
      Christ our loving God.
   With the blessed saints of heaven
      give us lasting joy.
   We will then possess true happiness,
   and love for all eternity.

   Adapted from "Ubi Caritas et Amor"
                by Michael Cockett

140

1. I saw the grass, I saw the trees
   and the boats along the shore.
   I saw the shapes of many things
   I had only sensed before.
   And I saw the faces of men
      more clearly
   than if I had never been blind,
   the lines of envy around their lips
   and the greed
      and the hate in their eyes.
   And I turned away,
      yes, I turned away,
   for I had seen the perfect face
      of a real and proper man,
   the man who brought me
      from the dark
   into light, where life began.

2. I hurried then away from town
   to a quiet, lonely place.
   I found a clear, unruffled pool
   and I gazed upon my face.
   And I saw the image of me
      more clearly
   than if I had never been blind.
   The lines of envy around the lips
   and the greed
      and the hate in the eyes.
   And I turned away,
      yes, I turned away,
   for I had seen the perfect face
      of a real and proper man,
   the man who'd brought me
      from the dark
   into light, where life began.

3. I made my way into the town,
   to the busy, crowded streets,
   the shops and stalls and alley-ways,
   to the squalor and the heat.
   And I saw the faces of men
      more clearly
   than if I had never been blind,
   the lines of sorrow around their lips
   and the child
      looking out from their eyes,
   and I turned to them,
      yes, I turned to them,
   remembering the perfect face
      of a real and proper man,
   the man who'd brought me
      from the dark
   into light, where life began.

   Estelle White

141

I sing a song to you, Lord,
a song of love and praise.
All glory be to you, Lord,
through everlasting days.

1. Holy, holy, holy,
   mighty Lord and God.
   He who was and is now,
   and who is to come.

2. Worthy is the slain Lamb,
   honour him and praise.
   We rejoice with gladness,
   sing our love today.

3. He has used his power,
   has begun his reign.
   So rejoice, you heavens,
   and proclaim his name.

4. Shine your light on us, Lord,
   let us know your way.
   Be our guide for ever,
   make us yours today.

Richard Beaumont

142

1. I sing the Lord God's praises,
   I answer to his call.
   His servant-girl he raises,
   she will be blessed by all.
   The Lord God gives his power
   to her who loves his name;
   o'er her his strength will tower,
   his mercies will remain.

2. Proud-hearted men he scatters,
   the strong will pass away;
   and for the kind and gentle
   there dawns the Lord's own day.
   Woe to the rich and mighty!
   He feeds and satisfies
   those who for justice hunger,
   and to him turn their eyes.

3. A Saviour he had promised
   to Abram long ago;
   and now to his own people
   his mercy he will show.
   Come let us praise our Father,
   for he fulfils his word,
   and sends his Holy Spirit
   through Jesus Christ our Lord.

W. F. Harwood

143

1. It came upon the midnight clear,
   that glorious song of old,
   from angels bending near the earth
   to touch their harps of gold;
   'Peace on the earth, good will to men,
   from heaven's all-gracious King!

The world in solemn stillness lay
to hear the angels sing.

2. Yet with the woes of sin and strife
   the world has suffered long;
   beneath the angel-strain have rolled
   two thousand years of wrong;
   and man, at war with man, hears not
   the love-song which they bring:
   O hush the noise, ye men of strife,
   and hear the angels sing!

3. For lo, the days are hastening on,
   by prophets seen of old,
   when with the ever-circling years
   shall come the time foretold,
   when the new heaven and earth
                        shall own
   the prince of peace their king,
   and all the world send back the song
   which now the angels sing.

E. H. Sears (1810-76)

144

It's me, it's me, it's me, O Lord,
standin' in the need of pray'r.
It's me, it's me it's me, O Lord,
standin' in the need of pray'r.

1. Not my brother or my sister,
      but it's me, O Lord,
   standin' in the need of prayer.
   Not my brother or my sister,
      but it's me, O Lord,
   standin' in the need of pray'r.

2. Not my mother or my father,
      but it's me, O Lord,
   standin' in the need of prayer.
   Not my mother or my father,
      but it's me, O Lord,
   standin' in the need of pray'r.

3. Not the stranger or my neighbour,
      but it's me, O Lord,
   standin' in the need of prayer.
   Not the stranger or my neighbour,
      but it's me, O Lord,
   standin' in the need of pray'r.

Negro Spiritual

145

1. I watch the sunrise
   lighting the sky,
   casting its shadows near.
   And on this morning
   bright though it be,
   I feel those shadows near me.

   But you are always
   close to me
   following all my ways.
   May I be always
   close to you
   following all your ways, Lord.

2. I watch the sunlight
   shine through the clouds,
   warming the earth below.
   And at the mid-day
   life seems to say:
   "I feel your brightness near me."
   For you are always . . .

3. I watch the sunset
   fading away,
   lighting the clouds with sleep.
   And as the evening
   closes its eyes
   I feel your presence near me.
   For you are always . . .

4. I watch the moonlight
   guarding the night,
   waiting till morning comes.
   The air is silent,
   earth is at rest —
   only your peace is near me.
   Yes, you are always . . .

   John Glynn

146

1. I will give you glory,
   O God, my King.
   I will bless your name for ever.
   I will bless you day, after day.

   Day after day, after day, after day,
   after day, after day, after day.

2. I will sing your praises,
   O God, my King.
   I will bless your name for ever.
   I will bless you day, after day.

3. I will give you honour,
   O God, my King.
   I will bless your name for ever.
   I will bless you day, after day.

   Malcolm Campbell-Carr

147

1. I wonder as I wander
      out under the sky,
   how Jesus the Saviour
      did come for to die
   for poor ord'n'ry people
      like you and like I.
   I wonder as I wander
      out under the sky.

2. When Mary birthed Jesus,
   'twas in a cow's stall
   with wise men and farmers
      and shepherds and all.
   But high from God's heaven
      a star's light did fall,
   and the promise of ages
      it did then recall.

3. If Jesus had wanted
      for any wee thing,
   a star in the sky, or
      a bird on the wing,
   or all of God's angels
      in heav'n for to sing,
   he surely could have it,
      'cause he was the king.

   Traditional

148

1. January brings the snow,
   and the white frost glistens;
   I'm a child full of love,
   speak, Lord, and I'll listen.

2. March means sun and wind and rain,
   springtime flowers dancing.
   I am young, growing fast,
   wanting all the answers.

3. Maytime blossoms fill the air,
   here's a time for pleasure!
   Keep me safe, O my Lord,
   in my work and leisure.

4. In July the trees are tall,
   butterflies are roving.
   In my prime, may I be
   faithful in my loving.

5. In September's golden fields
   harvesters are reaping,
   and my mind gathers in
   mem'ries worth the keeping.

6. In November there are mists
   jewelling the grasses.
   Now my steps lose their spring;
   how each moment passes!

7. Come December days grow short
   and they say my life's through;
   but, my Lord, it's been good,
   and I want to thank you.

Estelle White

149

1. Jerusalem the golden,
   with milk and honey blest,
   beneath thy contemplation
   sink heart and voice oppressed.
   I know not, ah, I know not
   what joys await us there,
   what radiancy of glory,
   what bliss beyond compare.

2. They stand, those halls of Sion,
   all jubilant with song,
   and bright with many an angel,
   and all the martyr throng;
   the prince is ever in them,
   the daylight is serene;
   the pastures of the blessed
   are decked in glorious sheen.

3. There is the throne of David;
   and there, from care released,
   the shout of them that triumph,
   the song of them that feast;
   and they, who with their leader
   have conquered in the fight,
   for ever and for ever
   are clad in robes of white.

4. O sweet and blessed country,
   the home of God's elect!
   O sweet and blessed country
   that eager hearts expect!
   Jesus, in mercy bring us
   to that dear land of rest;
   who art, with God the Father
   and Spirit, ever blest.

From 'De Contemptu Mundi'
St. Bernard of Cluny, tr. J. M. Neale

150

1. Jesu, lover of my soul!
   Let me to thy bosom fly,
   while the nearer waters roll,
   while the tempest still is high;
   hide me, O my Saviour, hide,
   till the storm of life is past;
   safe into the haven guide,
   O receive my soul at last.

2. Other refuge have I none;
   hangs my helpless soul on thee;
   leave, ah! leave me not alone,
   still support and comfort me.
   All my trust on thee is stayed,
   all my help from thee I bring;
   cover my defenceless head
   with the shadow of thy wing.

3. Thou, O Christ, art all I want;
more than all in thee I find;
raise the fallen, cheer the faint,
heal the sick and lead the blind,
just and holy is thy name;
I am all unrighteousness;
false and full of sin I am,
thou art full of truth and grace.

4. Plenteous grace with thee is found,
grace to cover all my sin
let the healing streams abound;
make and keep me pure within.
Thou of life the fountain art,
freely let me take of thee;
spring thou up within my heart,
rise to all eternity.

Charles Wesley (1707-88)

151

1. Jesu, meek and lowly,
Saviour, pure and holy,
on thy love relying,
come I to thee flying.

2. Prince of life and power,
my salvation's tower,
on the cross I view thee,
calling sinners to thee.

3. There behold me gazing
at the sight amazing;
bending low before thee,
helpless I adore thee.

4. See the red wounds streaming,
with Christ's life-blood gleaming,
blood for sinners flowing,
pardon free bestowing,

5. Fountains rich in blessing,
Christ's fond love expressing,
thou my aching sadness
turnest into gladness.

6. Lord in mercy guide me,
be thou e'er beside me,
In thy ways direct me,
'neath thy wings protect me.

A. H. Collins (1827-1919)

152

1. Jesu, the very thought of thee
with sweetness fills my breast;
but sweeter far thy face to see,
and in thy presence rest.

2. Nor voice can sing, nor heart can
frame,
nor can the memory find,
a sweeter sound than thy blest name,
O Saviour of mankind.

3. O hope of every contrite heart,
O joy of all the meek,
to those who fall, how kind thou art,
how good to those who seek!

4. But what to those who find? Ah, this
nor tongue nor pen can show;
the love of Jesus, what it is
none but his lovers know.

5. Jesu, our only joy be thou,
as thou our prize wilt be;
Jesu, be thou our glory now,
and through eternity.

11th c.,tr. Edward Caswall

153

1. Jesus Christ is risen today,
alleluia!
Our triumphant holy day,
alleluia!
Who did once, upon the cross,
alleluia!
Suffer to redeem our loss,
alleluia!

2. Hymns of praise then let us sing,
alleluia!
Unto Christ, our heavenly king,
alleluia!
Who endured the cross and grave,
alleluia!
Sinners to redeem and save,
alleluia!

3. But the pains that he endured,
alleluia!
Our salvation have procured;
alleluia!

Now above the sky he's king,
    alleluia!
Where the angels ever sing,
    alleluia!

Lyra Davidica (1708) and the
Supplement (1816).
Based partly on 'Surrexit Christus
hodie. (14th c.)

154

1. Jesus, gentlest Saviour,
    God of might and power,
    thou thyself art dwelling
    in us at this hour.
    Nature cannot hold thee,
    heav'n is all too strait
    for thine endless glory,
    and thy royal state.

2. Yet the hearts of children,
    hold what worlds cannot,
    and the God of wonders
    loves the lowly spot.
    Jesus, gentlest Saviour,
    thou art in us now,
    fill us full of goodness,
    till our hearts o'erflow.

3. Pray the prayer within us
    that to heaven shall rise;
    sing the song that angels
    sing above the skies;
    multiply our graces,
    chiefly love and fear;
    and, dear Lord, the chiefest,
    grace to persevere.

Frederick William Faber (1814-63)

155

1. Jesus, Lord, I'll sing a song
    that's soft and low for you,
    so you can join with me
    and sing it too.
    You have said that when we pray,
    then you are praying too,
    and when your Father hears us,
    he hears you.

Our Father who art in heaven,
hallowed be thy name,
hallowed be thy name.

2. I believe that you are here
    with me and praying too.
    Your Father loves me
    because I love you.
    Jesus, Lord, I'll sing a song that's
    soft and low for you,
    so you can join with me
    and sing it too.

Briege O'Hare

156

1. Jesus is God! The solid earth,
    the ocean broad and bright,
    the countless stars, the golden dust,
    that strew the skies at night,
    the wheeling storm, the dreadful
                                    fire,
    the pleasant wholesome air,
    the summer's sun, the winter's frost,
    his own creations were.

2. Jesus is God! the glorious bands
    of golden angels sing
    songs of adoring praise to him,
    their maker and their king.
    He was true God in Bethlehem's
                                    crib,
    on Calvary's cross true God,
    he who in heaven eternal reigned,
    in time on earth abode.

3. Jesus is God! Let sorrow come,
    and pain and every ill;
    all are worth while, for all are means
    his glory to fulfil;
    worth while a thousand years of life
    to speak one little word,
    if by our Credo we might own
    the Godhead of our Lord.

Frederick William Faber (1814-63)

157

1. Jesus, my Lord, my God, my all,
   how can I love thee as I ought?
   And how revere this wondrous gift
   so far surpassing hope or thought?

   Sweet Sacrament, we thee adore;
   Oh, make us love thee more and
   more.

2. Had I but Mary's sinless heart
   to love thee with, my dearest King,
   Oh, with what bursts of fervent
                                    praise
   thy goodness, Jesus, would I sing!

3. Ah, see! within a creature's hand
   the vast Creator deigns to be,
   reposing, infant-like, as though
   on Joseph's arm, or Mary's knee.

4. Thy body, soul, and Godhead, all;
   O mystery of love divine!
   I cannot compass all I have,
   for all thou hast and art are mine;

5. Sound, sound, his praises higher
                                   still,
   and come, ye angels, to our aid;
   'tis God, 'tis God, the very God
   whose power both man and angels
                                    made.

   Frederick William Faber (1814-63)

158

1. Jesus! thou art coming,
   holy as thou art,
   thou, the God who made me,
   to my sinful heart.
   Jesus! I believe it,
   on thy only word;
   kneeling, I adore thee,
   as my king and Lord.

2. Who am I, my Jesus,
   that thou com'st to me?
   I have sinned against thee,
   often grievously;
   I am very sorry
   I have caused thee pain.
   I will never, never,
   wound thy heart again.

3. Put thy kind arms round me,
   feeble as I am;
   thou art my Good Shepherd,
   I, thy little lamb;
   since thou comest, Jesus,
   now to be my guest,
   I can trust thee always,
   Lord, for all the rest.

4. Dearest Lord, I love thee,
   with my whole heart,
   not for what thou givest,
   but for what thou art.
   Come, oh, come, sweet Saviour!
   Come to me, and stay,
   for I want thee, Jesus,
   more than I can say.

5. Ah! what gift or present,
   Jesus, can I bring?
   I have nothing worthy
   of my God and King;
   but thou art my shepherd:
   I, thy little lamb,
   take myself, dear Jesus,
   all I have and am.

6. Take my body, Jesus,
   eyes, and ears and tongue;
   never let them, Jesus,
   help to do thee wrong.
   Take my heart, and fill it
   full of love for thee;
   all I have I give thee,
   give thyself to me.

   'S.N.D.'

159

1. Just a closer walk with thee,
   grant it, Jesus if you please;
   daily walking close to thee,
   let it be, dear Lord, let it be.

2. Through the day of toil that's near,
   if I fall, dear Lord, who cares.
   Who with me my burden share?
   None but thee, dear Lord, none but
           thee.

3. When my feeble life is o'er,
   time for me will be no more.
   Guide me gently, safely on
   to the shore, dear Lord, to the
           shore.

   Traditional

160

1. Keep we the fast that men of old
   learned from on high in mystic
           ways,
   till yonder sun hath duly told
   his hallowed tale of forty days.

2. This covenant, long since revealed
   to patriarchs and ardent seers,
   Christ by his own example sealed,
   author of time, and Lord of years.

3. More wisely therefore let us walk,
   sparing of food and wine and sleep;
   over our trifles and our talk
   more jealous be the watch we keep.

4. Still by our sins, O Lord, we grieve
   thy love, so full of pardon free:
   author of mercy, still reprieve
   the souls that turn again to thee.

5. Remember whence our fashion
           came,
   frail creatures, yet thy creatures still,
   crush, for the glory of thy name,
   the murm'rings of our stubborn will.

6. The guilt that dooms us put away,
   with larger grace our prayers
           requite,
   at last, and ever from this day,
   teach us to live as in thy sight.

7. Hear us, O Trinity sublime,
   and undivided unity;
   so let this consecrated time
   bring forth thy fruits abundantly.

   St. Gregory the Great (540-604)
   tr. R. A. Knox

161

1. King of glory, king of peace,
   I will love thee;
   and that love may never cease,
   I will move thee.
   Thou hast granted my request,
   thou hast heard me;
   thou didst note my working breast,
   thou hast spared me.

2. Wherefore with my utmost art,
   I will sing thee.
   And the cream of all my heart
   I will bring thee,
   though my sins against me cried,
   thou didst clear me;
   and alone, when they replied,
   thou didst hear me.

3. Seven whole days, not one in seven,
   I will praise thee;
   in my heart, though not in heaven,
   I can raise thee.
   Small it is, in this poor sort
   to enrol thee:
   e'en eternity's too short
   to extol thee.

   George Herbert (1593-1633)

162

1. Kum ba yah, my Lord,
      kum ba yah,
   kum ba yah, my Lord,
      kum ba yah!
   Kum ba yah, my Lord,
      kum ba yah!
   O Lord, kum ba yah.

2. Someone's crying, Lord,
      kum ba yah,
   someone's crying, Lord,
      kum ba yah!
   Someone's crying, Lord,
      kum ba yah!
   O Lord, kum ba yah.

3. Someone's singing, Lord,
      kum ba yah,
   someone's singing, Lord,
      kum ba yah!
   Someone's singing, Lord,
      kum ba yah!
   O Lord, kum ba yah.

4. Someone's praying, Lord,
      kum ba yah,
   someone's praying, Lord,
      kum ba yah!
   Someone's praying, Lord,
      kum ba yah!
   O Lord, kum ba yah.

Spiritual

163

1. Leader now on earth no longer,
   soldier of th'eternal king,
   victor in the fight for heaven,
   we thy loving praises sing.

   Great Saint George,
   our patron, help us,
   in the conflict be thou nigh;
   help us in that daily battle,
   where each one must win or die.

2. Praise him who in deadly battle
   never shrank from foeman's sword,
   proof against all earthly weapon,
   gave his life for Christ the Lord.

3. Who, when earthly war was over,
   fought, but not for earth's renown;
   fought, and won a nobler glory,
   won the martyr's purple crown.

4. Help us when temptation presses,
   we have still our crown to win,
   help us when our soul is weary
   fighting with the powers of sin.

5. Clothe us in thy shining armour,
   place thy good sword in our hand;
   teach us how to wield it, fighting
   onward towards the heavenly land.

6. Onward, till, our striving over,
   on life's battlefield we fall,
   resting then, but ever ready,
   waiting for the angel's call.

Joseph W. Reeks (1849-1900)

164

1. Lead, kindly light
      amid th'encircling gloom,
   lead thou me on;
   the night is dark,
      and I am far from home,
   lead thou me on.
   Keep thou my feet;
      I do not ask to see
   the distant scene;
      one step enough for me.

2. I was not ever thus,
      nor prayed that thou
   shouldst lead me on;
   I loved to choose
      and see my path; but now
   lead thou me on.
   I loved the garish day,
      and, spite of fears,
   pride ruled my will;
      remember not past years.

3. So long thy power
      hath blest me, sure it still
   will lead me on
   o'er moor and fen,
      o'er crag and torrent, till
   the night is gone,
   and with the morn
      those angel faces smile
   which I have loved
      long since, and lost awhile.

   John Henry Newman (1801-90)

165

1. Lead us, heav'nly Father, lead us
   o'er the world's tempestuous sea:
   guard us, guide us, keep us, feed us,
   for we have no help but thee;
   yet possessing ev'ry blessing
   if our God our Father be.

2. Saviour, breathe forgiveness o'er us,
   all our weakness thou dost know,
   thou didst tread this earth before us,
   thou didst feel its keenest woe;
   lone and dreary, faint and weary,
   through the desert thou didst go.

3. Spirit of our God, descending,
   fill our hearts with heavenly joy,
   love with every passion blending,
   pleasure that can never cloy;
   thus provided, pardoned, guided,
   nothing can our peace destroy.

   J. Edmeston (1791-1867)

166

1. Let all mortal flesh keep silence
   and with fear and trembling stand,
   ponder nothing earthly-minded:
   for with blessing in his hand,
   Christ our God on earth descendeth,
   our full homage to demand.

2. King of kings, yet born of Mary,
   as of old on earth he stood
   Lord of lords, in human vesture —
   in the Body and the Blood.
   He will give to all the faithful
   his own Self for heavenly Food.

3. Rank on rank the host of heaven
   spreads its vanguard on the way,
   as the Light of Light descendeth
   from the realms of endless day,
   that the powers of hell may vanish
   as the darkness clears away.

4. At his feet the six-winged Seraph;
   Cherubim with sleepless eye,
   veil their faces to the Presence,
   as with ceaseless voice they cry,
   alleluia, alleluia,
   alleluia, Lord most high.

   Liturgy of St. James, tr. G. Moultrie

167

1. Let all that is within me cry holy.
   Let all that is within me cry holy.
   Holy, holy, holy
      is the Lamb that was slain.

2. Let all that is within me cry mighty.
   Let all that is within me cry mighty.
   Mighty, mighty, mighty
      is the Lamb that was slain.

3. Let all that is within me cry worthy.
   Let all that is within me cry worthy.
   Worthy, worthy, worthy
      is the Lamb that was slain.

4. Let all that is within me cry blessed.
   Let all that is within me cry blessed.
   Blessed, blessed, blessed
      is the Lamb that was slain.

5. Let all that is within me cry Jesus.
   Let all that is within me cry Jesus.
   Jesus, Jesus, Jesus
      is the Lamb that was slain.

   Traditional

168

1. Let all the world
   in every corner sing,
   my God and King!
   The heav'ns are not too high,
   his praise may thither fly;
   the earth is not too low,
   his praises there may grow.
   Let all the world
   in every corner sing,
   my God and King!

2. Let all the world
   in every corner sing,
   my God and King!
   The church with psalms must shout,
   no door can keep them out;
   but, above all, the heart
   must bear the longest part.
   Let all the world
   in every corner sing,
   my God and King!

   George Herbert (1593-1633)

169

1. Let us break bread together
      on our knees.
   Let us break bread together
      on our knees.
   When I fall on my knees
      with my face to the rising sun,
   Oh Lord, have mercy on me.

2. Let us drink wine together . . .

3. Let us praise God together . . .

   Traditional

170

1. Let's make peace in our hearts.
   Let's make peace in our hearts.
   Let's make true peace in our hearts.
   Let's make true peace in our hearts.

2. Let's take peace into the world.
   Let's take peace into the world.
   Let's take true peace into the world.
   Let's take true peace into the world.

3. Let's share peace with ev'ryone.
   Let's share peace with ev'ryone.
   Let's share true peace with ev'ryone.
   Let's share true peace with ev'ryone.

4. My peace I leave with you.
   My peace I give to you.
   Not as the world gives do I give,
   but true peace I give unto you.

   Sebastian Temple

171

1. Let us, with a gladsome mind,
   praise the Lord, for he is kind;

   For his mercies aye endure,
   ever faithful, ever sure.

2. Let us blaze his name abroad,
   for of gods he is the God;

3. He, with all-commanding might,
   filled the new-made world with
                                    light;

4. He the golden-tressed sun
   caused all day his course to run:

5. And the horned moon at night,
   'mid her spangled sisters bright:

6. All things living he doth feed,
   his full hand supplies their need:

7. Let us, with a gladsome mind,
   praise the Lord, for he is kind.

   John Milton (1608-75),
   based on Ps. 136

172

1. Light of our darkness, Word of God,
   sent to illumine our earthly night,
   you we salute with singing hearts,
   bathed in the splendour of your
   light.

2. Sword that can pierce the inmost
   soul,
   stripping whatever thoughts are
   there,
   cut to the marrow of our minds,
   enter our hearts and lay them bare.

3. Vessel of God's abundant life,
   bearer of truth that sets us free,
   breaking the deadly grasp of sin,
   work in our hearts your mystery.

4. Word that has overcome the world,
   seed of immortal destiny,
   grow in our hearts, that we may live
   sharing your deathless victory.

   Richard Connolly

173

1. Little flower in the ground,
   petals falling all around.
   Summer's past and Autumn's here
   and now we know your end is near.

2. Seeds that fall on to the ground
   by the winds are scattered round.
   Some will feed the Winter birds,
   and some will nestle in the earth.

3. Some will last the Winter through
   'till the Spring makes all things new.
   See the flower newly grown
   from seeds the Winter wind has
   sown.

4. Praise the Lord in heav'n above,
   who shows us all the way of love.
   Praise him for the dying year.
   If Winter comes then Spring is near.

   Michael Cockett

174

1. Little Jesus, sweetly sleep,
   do not stir;
   we will lend a coat of fur,
   we will rock you,
   rock you, rock you,
   we will rock you,
   rock you, rock you,
   see the fur to keep you warm
   snugly round your tiny form.

2. Mary's little baby sleep,
   sweetly sleep,
   sleep in comfort, slumber deep;
   we will rock you,
   rock you, rock you,
   we will rock you,
   rock you, rock you,
   we will serve you all we can,
   darling , darling little man.

   Czech., tr. O.B.C.

175

1. Long ago in Bethlehem,
   you were lying in a manger
   in the midst of human danger,
   at your mother's knee.
   Hosanna, alleluia,
   hosanna, alleluia,
   hosanna, alleluia,
   at your mother's knee.

2. Now as King we hail the baby,
   living faith proclaims the story
   of that humble manger glory,
   stabled in the hay.
   Hosanna, alleluia,
   hosanna, alleluia,
   hosanna, alleluia,
   Christ is King today.

   Ian Sharp

176

1. Look down, O Mother Mary,
   from thy bright throne above;
   cast down upon thy children
   one only glance of love;
   and if a heart so tender
   with pity flows not o'er,
   then turn away, O Mother,
   and look on us no more.

   Look down O Mother Mary,
   from thy bright throne above,
   cast down upon thy children,
   one only glance of love.

2. See how, ungrateful sinners,
   we stand before thy Son;
   his loving heart upbraids us
   the evil we have done,
   but if thou wilt appease him,
   speak for us but one word;
   for thus thou canst obtain us,
   the pardon of Our Lord.

3. O Mary, dearest Mother,
   if thou wouldst have us live,
   say that we are thy children,
   and Jesus will forgive.
   Our sins make us unworthy
   that title still to bear,
   but thou art still our mother;
   then show a mother's care.

4. Unfold to us thy mantle,
   there stay we without fear;
   what evil can befall us
   if, mother, thou art near?
   O kindest, dearest mother
   thy sinful children save;
   look down on us with pity,
   who thy protection crave.

   St. Alphonsus (1696-1787),
   tr. Edmund Vaughan

177

1. Lord accept the gifts we offer
   at this Eucharistic feast,
   bread and wine to be transformed
   now
   through the action of thy priest
   take us too, Lord, and transform us,
   be thy grace in us increased.

2. May our souls be pure and spotless
   as the host of wheat so fine;
   may all stain of sin be crushed out,
   like the grape that forms the wine,
   as we, too, become partakers,
   in this sacrifice divine.

3. Take our gifts, almighty Father,
   living God, eternal, true,
   which we give through Christ, our
   Saviour,
   pleading here for us anew
   grant salvation to all present,
   and our faith and love renew.

   Sister M. Teresine

178

1. Lord, for tomorrow and its needs
   I do not pray;
   keep me, my God, from stain of sin,
   just for today.

2. Let me both diligently work
   and duly pray;
   let me be kind in word and deed,
   just for today.

3. Let me be slow to do my will,
   prompt to obey;
   help me to mortify my flesh,
   just for today.

4. Let me no wrong or idle word
   unthinking say;
   set thou a seal upon my lips,
   just for today.

5. Let me in season, Lord, be grave,
   in season, gay;
   let me be faithful to thy grace,
   just for today.

6. And if today my tide of life
   should ebb away,
   give me thy sacraments divine,
   sweet Lord, today.

7. So, for tomorrow and its needs
   I do not pray;
   but keep me, guide me, love me,
   Lord,
   just for today.

   Sister M. Xavier

179

1. Lord, Jesus Christ,
   you have come to us
   you are one with us, Mary's son.
   Cleansing our souls from all their sin,
   pouring your love and goodness in,
   Jesus our love for you we sing,
   living Lord.

2. Lord Jesus Christ,
   now and ev'ry day
   teach us how to pray, Son of God.
   You have commanded us to do
   this in remembrance, Lord, of you
   Into our lives your pow'r breaks
                              through,
   living Lord.

3. Lord Jesus Christ,
   you have come to us,
   born as one of us, Mary's Son.
   Led out to die on Calvary,
   risen from death to set us free,
   living Lord Jesus, help us see
   you are Lord.

4. Lord Jesus Christ,
   I would come to you,
   live my life for you, Son of God.
   All your commands I know are true,
   your many gifts will make me new,
   into my life your pow'r breaks
                              through,
   living Lord.

Patrick Appleford

180

1. Lord Jesus, think on me,
   and purge away my sin;
   from earthborn passions set me free,
   and make me pure within.

2. Lord Jesus, think on me,
   with care and woe oppressed;
   let me thy loving servant be,
   and taste thy promised rest.

3. Lord Jesus, think on me
   amid the battle's strife;
   in all my pain and misery
   be thou my health and life.

4. Lord Jesus, think on me,
   nor let me go astray;
   through darkness and perplexity
   point thou the heavenly way.

5. Lord Jesus, think on me,
   when flows the tempest high:
   when on doth rush the enemy,
   O Saviour, be thou nigh.

6. Lord Jesus, think on me,
   that, when the flood is past,
   I may the eternal brightness see,
   and share thy joy at last.

Bishop Synesius (375-430)
tr. A. W. Chatfield

181

1. Lord of all hopefulness,
   Lord of all joy,
   whose trust, ever child-like,
   no cares could destroy,
   be there at our waking,
   and give us, we pray,
   your bliss in our hearts, Lord,
   at the break of the day.

2. Lord of all eagerness,
   Lord of all faith,
   whose strong hands were skilled
   at the plane and the lathe,
   be there at our labours,
   and give us, we pray,
   your strength in our hearts, Lord,
   at the noon of the day.

3. Lord, of all kindliness,
   Lord of all grace,
   your hands swift to welcome,
   your arms to embrace,
   be there at our homing,
   and give us, we pray,
   your love in our hearts, Lord,
   at the eve of the day.

4. Lord of all gentleness,
   Lord of all calm,
   whose voice is contentment,
   whose presence is balm,
   be there at our sleeping,
   and give us, we pray,
   your peace in our hearts, Lord,
   at the end of the day.

   Jan Struther (1901-53)

182

1. Lord, we pray for golden peace,
   peace all over the land,
   may all men dwell in liberty,
   all walking hand in hand.

   Banish fear and ignorance,
   hunger, thirst and pain.
   Banish hate and poverty,
   let no man live in vain,
   let no man live in vain.

2. Keep all men for ever one,
   one in love and in grace.
   And wipe away all war and strife,
   give freedom to each race.

3. Let your justice reign supreme.
   Righteousness always done.
   Let goodness rule the hearts of men
   and evil overcome.

   Sebastian Temple

183

1. Lord, who throughout these forty
                              days
   for us didst fast and pray,
   teach us with thee to mourn our sins,
   and at thy side to stay.

2. As thou with Satan didst contend,
   and didst the victory win,
   O give us strength in thee to fight,
   in thee to conquer sin.

3. As thirst and hunger thou didst bear,
   so teach us, gracious Lord,
   to die to self, and daily live
   by thy most holy word.

4. And through these days of
                              penitence,
   and through thy Passiontide,
   yea, evermore, in life and death,
   Lord Christ, with us abide.

   Claudia Frances Hernaman (1838-98)

184

1. Love divine, all loves excelling,
   joy of heaven, to earth come down,
   fix in us thy humble dwelling,
   all thy faithful mercies crown.

2. Jesus, thou art all compassion,
   pure unbounded love thou art;
   visit us with thy salvation,
   enter every trembling heart.

3. Come, almighty to deliver,
   let us all thy life receive;
   suddenly return, and never,
   never more thy temples leave.

4. Thee we would be always blessing,
   serve thee as thy hosts above;
   pray, and praise thee without
                              ceasing,
   glory in thy perfect love.

5. Finish then thy new creation,
   pure and sinless let us be;
   let us see thy great salvation
   perfectly restored in thee.

6. Changed from glory into glory,
   till in heaven we take our place,
   till we cast our crowns before thee,
   lost in wonder, love, and praise.

   Charles Wesley (1707-88)

185

1. Love is his word, love is his way,
   feasting with men, fasting alone,
   living and dying, rising again,
   love, only love, is his way.

   Richer than gold
     is the love of my Lord:
   better than splendour and wealth.

2. Love is his way, love is his mark,
   sharing his last Passover feast,
   Christ at his table, host to the
                           Twelve,
   love, only love, is his mark.

3. Love is his mark, love is his sign,
   bread for our strength, wine for our
                           joy,
   "This is my body, this is my blood,"
   love, only love, is his sign.

4. Love is his sign, love is his news,
   "Do this," he said, "lest you forget
   all my deep sorrow, all my dear
                           blood,"
   love, only love, is his news.

5. Love is his news, love is his name,
   we are his own, chosen and called,
   family, brethren, cousins and kin.
   Love, only love, is his name.

6. Love is his name, love is his law.
   Hear his command, all who are his:
   "Love one another, I have loved
                           you."
   Love, only love, is his law.

7. Love is his law, love is his word:
   love of the Lord, Father and Word,
   love of the Spirit, God ever one,
   love, only love, is his word.

   Luke Connaughton

186

1. Loving Father, from thy bounty
   choicest gifts unnumbered flow:
   all the blessings of salvation,
   which to Christ thy Son we owe,
   all the gifts that by thy bidding
   nature's hands on us bestow!

2. Here thy grateful children gather,
   offering gifts of bread and wine;
   these we give to thee in homage,
   of our love the loving sign,
   and restore to thee creation,
   given to man, yet ever thine!

3. Soon will come Christ's loving
                           presence,
   on our love to set his seal!
   Body broken, Blood shed for us,
   bread and wine will then reveal!
   bread and wine, though these no
                           longer,
   flesh and blood will yet conceal!

   James Quinn, S.J.

187

1. Loving shepherd of thy sheep,
   keep me, Lord, in safety keep;
   nothing can thy pow'r withstand,
   none can pluck me from thy hand.

2. Loving shepherd, thou didst give
   thine own life that I might live;
   may I love thee day by day,
   gladly thy sweet will obey.

3. Loving shepherd, ever near,
   teach me still thy voice to hear;
   suffer not my steps to stray
   from the strait and narrow way.

4. Where thou leadest may I go,
   walking in thy steps below;
   then before thy Father's throne,
   Jesu, claim me for thine own.

   Jane E. Leeson (1807-82)

188

1. Maiden, yet a mother,
   daughter of thy Son,
   high beyond all other,
   lowlier is none;
   thou the consummation
   planned by God's decree,
   when our lost creation
   nobler rose in thee!

2. Thus his place prepared,
   he who all things made
   'mid his creatures tarried,
   in thy bosom laid;
   there his love he nourished,
   warmth that gave increase
   to the root whence flourished
   our eternal peace.

3. Noon on Sion's mountain
   is thy charity;
   hope its living fountain
   finds, on earth, in thee:
   lady, such thy power,
   he, who grace would buy
   not as of thy dower,
   without wings would fly.

   Dante Alighieri (1265-1321)
   tr. R. A. Knox

189

1. Make me a channel of your peace.
   Where there is hatred,
      let me bring your love.
   Where there is injury,
      your pardon, Lord.
   And where there's doubt,
      true faith in you.

2. Make me a channel of your peace.
   Where there's despair in life,
      let me bring hope.
   Where there is darkness
      only light,
   and where there's sadness
      ever joy.

3. Oh, Master,
      grant that I may never seek
   so much to be consoled
      as to console,
   to be understood as to understand,
   to be loved, as to love,
      with all my soul.

4. Make a channel of your peace.
   It is in pardoning
      that we are pardoned,
   in giving to all men
      that we receive,
   and in dying that we're
      born to eternal life.

   Sebastian Temple

190

1. Man of Galilee
   will you come and stand by me
   through the length of each working
                               day?
   Bless, O Lord, my efforts, I pray.

2. Man who healed the blind
   open up the eyes of my mind
   to the needs of my fellow man.
   Help me give with open hands.

3. Man of bread and of wine
   show me by the means of this sign
   that I share your life and your light
   with the neighbour here at my side.

4. Man of Calvary
   give me strength and will to be free
   of the weight of self-pity's chains,
   then my trials will be but gains.

5. Man at God's right hand,
   will you help me understand
   that in you, when my breath is
                               stilled,
   all my longings will be fulfilled?

   Estelle White

191

1. Many times I have turned
      from the way of the Lord,
   many times
      I have chosen the darkness.
   In the light of the day,
      when the shadows are gone,
   all I see is my sin
      in its starkness.

   Jesus came to bring us mercy.
   Jesus came to bring us life again.
   He loves us, he loves us, he loves us!

2. I confess I have sinned
      in the sight of the Lord,
   through my pride,
      through my malice and weakness.
   I've rejected the promise
      that comes from the cross
   where the Lord hung above
      us in meakness.

3. With a word, with a deed,
      with a failure to act,
   with a thought
      that was evil and hateful,
   I confess to you,
      brothers and sisters of mine,
   I have sinned and
      been proven ungrateful.

4. Through my fault, through my fault,
      through my serious fault,
   I confess to you,
      Lord, all my sinning.
   But look down on me, Lord,
      grant your pardon and peace;
   with your help, I've a
      new life beginning.

   Willard F. Jabusch

192

1. Mary immaculate,
      star of the morning,
   chosen before
      the creation began,
   chosen to bring,
      for thy bridal adorning,
   woe to the serpent
      and rescue to man.

2. Here, in an orbit
      of shadow and sadness
   veiling thy splendour,
      thy course thou hast run;
   now thou art throned in all glory
      and gladness,
   crowned by the hand
      of thy saviour and Son.

3. Sinners, we worship
      thy sinless perfection,
   fallen and weak,
      for thy pity we plead;
   grant us the shield
      of thy sovereign protection,
   measure thine aid
      by the depth of our need.

4. Frail is our nature,
      and strict our probation,
   watchful the foe
      that would lure us to wrong,
   succour our souls
      in the hour of temptation,
   Mary immaculate
      tender and strong.

5. See how the wiles
      of the serpent assail us,
   see how we waver
      and flinch in the fight;
   let thine immaculate
      merit avail us,
   make of our weakness
      a proof of thy might.

6. Bend from thy throne
      at the voice of our crying;
   bend to this earth
      which thy footsteps have trod;
   stretch out thine arms
      to us living and dying,
   Mary immaculate,
      mother of God.

   F. W. Weatherell

193

May the peace of Christ
    be with you today,
may the peace of Christ
    be with you today,
may the love of Christ,
the joy of Christ,
may the peace of Christ be yours.

Kevin Mayhew

194

1. Merrily on, merrily on
    flow the bright waters
        that carry a song,
    a song that is sung
        of the love of the Lord,
    a love that is endless
        and ever outpoured.

2. Father above, Father above,
    source of our life and
        our strength and our love,
    as fresh as the spring
        that is limpid and clear,
    your presence is young
        and will always be near.

3. Son from on high, Son from on high,
    you who united
        the earth and the sky,
    Oh, cleanse us with water
        and fill us with peace,
    our river of mercy
        who never will cease.

4. Spirit of God, Spirit of God,
    breathe on the waters
        and flow in the flood,
    and open the flood-gates
        that lead to the sea
    — the ocean is open
        and boundless and free!

5. Merrily on, merrily on
    flow the bright waters
        that carry a song,
    a song that is sung
        of the love of the Lord,
    a love that is endless
        and ever outpoured.

John Glynn

195

1. Mine eyes have seen the glory
        of the coming of the Lord.
    He is trampling out the vintage
    where the grapes of wrath are stored.
    He has loosed the fateful lightning
        of his terrible swift sword.
    His truth is marching on.

    Glory, glory halleluja!
    Glory, glory halleluja!
    Glory, glory halleluja!
    His truth is marching on.

2. I have seen him in the watchfires
        of a hundred circling camps.
    They have gilded him an altar
        in the evening dews and damps.
    I can read his righteous sentence
        by the dim and flaring lamps.
    His day is marching on.

3. He has sounded forth the trumpet
        that shall never sound retreat.
    He is sifting out the hearts of men
        before his judgement seat.
    O, be swift my soul to answer him,
        be jubilant my feet!
    Our God is marching on.

4. In the beauty of the lilies
        Christ was born across the sea
    with a glory in his bosom
        that transfigures you and me.
    As he died to make men holy,
        let us die to make men free.
    Whilst God is marching on.

Julia Ward Howe (1819-1910)

196

1. Morning has broken
   like the first morning,
   blackbird has spoken
   like the first bird.
   Praise for the singing!
   Praise for the morning!
   Praise for them, springing
   fresh from the Word!

2. Sweet the rain's new fall
   sunlit from heaven,
   like the first dew-fall
   on the first grass.
   Praise for the sweetness
   of the wet garden,
   sprung in completeness
   where his feet pass.

3. Mine is the sunlight!
   Mine is the morning
   born of the one light
   Eden saw play!
   Praise with elation,
   praise ev'ry morning,
   God's re-creation
   of the new day!

   Eleanor Farjeon (1881-1965)

197

1. "Moses I know you're the man,"
   the Lord said.
   "You're going to work out my
      plan,"
   the Lord said.
   "Lead all the Israelites
      out of slavery."
   And I shall make them a
      wandering race
   called the people of God."

   So ev'ry day we're on our way,
   for we're a travelling,
   *   wandering race*
   called the people of God.

2. "Don't get too set in your ways,"
   the Lord said.
   "Each step is only a phase,"
   the Lord said.
   "I'll go before you and
      I shall be a sign
   to guide my travelling,
      wandering race.
   You're the people of God."

3. "No matter what you may do,"
   the Lord said,
   "I shall be faithful and true,"
   the Lord said.
   "My love will strengthen you
      as you go along,
   for you're my travelling,
      wandering race.
   You're the people of God."

4. "Look at the birds in the air,"
   the Lord said,
   "They fly unhampered by care,"
   the Lord said.
   "You will move easier
      if you're travelling light,
   for you're a wandering,
      vagabond race.
   You're the people of God."

5. "Foxes have places to go,"
   the Lord said.
   "But I've no home here below,"
   the Lord said.
   "So if you want to be
      with me all your days,
   keep up the moving and
      travelling on.
   You're the people of God."

   Estelle White

198

1. Most ancient of all mysteries,
   before thy throne we lie;
   have mercy now, most merciful,
   most Holy Trinity.

2. When heaven and earth were yet
   unmade,
   when time was yet unknown,
   thou, in thy bliss and majesty,
   didst live and love alone.

3. Thou wert not born; there was no
   fount,
   from which thy being flowed;
   there is no end which thou canst
   reach:
   but thou art simply God.

4. How wonderful creation is,
   the work that thou didst bless;
   and oh, what then must thou be like,
   Eternal Loveliness!

5. Most ancient of all mysteries,
   still at thy throne we lie;
   have mercy now, most merciful,
   most Holy Trinity.

   Frederick William Faber (1814-63)

2. Though poverty and work and woe
   the masters of my life may be,
   when times are worst, who does not
   know
   darkness is light with love of thee?
   darkness is light with love of thee?

3. But scornful men have coldly said
   thy love was leading me from God;
   and yet in this I did but tread
   the very path my Saviour trod,
   the very path my Saviour trod.

4. They know but little of thy worth
   who speak these heartless words to
   me;
   for what did Jesus love on earth
   one half so tenderly as thee?
   one half so tenderly as thee?

5. Get me the grace to love thee more;
   Jesus will give if thou wilt plead;
   and, Mother! when life's cares are
   o'er,
   oh, I shall love thee then indeed!
   oh, I shall love thee then indeed!

6. Jesus, when his three hours were run,
   bequeath'd thee from the cross to me,
   and oh! how I love thy Son,
   sweet Mother! if I love not thee?
   sweet Mother! if I love not thee?

   Frederick William Faber (1814-63)

200

1. *My glory and the lifter of my head,*
   my glory and the lifter of my head,
   for thou, O Lord, art a shield to me,
   my glory and the lifter of my head.
   I cried unto the Lord with my voice,
   I cried unto the Lord with my voice,
   I cried unto the Lord with my voice,
   and he heard me out of his holy hill.

   From Scripture

199

1. Mother of Mercy, day by day
   my love of thee grows more and
   more;
   thy gifts are strewn upon my way,
   like sands upon the great seashore,
   like sands upon the great seashore.

201

1. My God accept my heart this day,
   and make it wholly thine,
   that I from thee no more may stray,
   no more from thee decline.

2. Before the cross of him who died,
   behold, I prostrate fall;
   let every sin be crucified,
   and Christ be all in all.

3. Anoint me with thy heavenly grace,
   and seal me for thine own,
   that I may see thy glorious face,
   and worship at thy throne.

4. Let every thought, and work and
   word
   to thee be ever given,
   then life shall be thy service, Lord,
   and Death the gate of heaven.

5. All glory to the Father be,
   all glory to the Son,
   all glory, Holy Ghost, to thee,
   while endless ages run.

Matthew Bridges (1800-94)

202

1. My God, and is thy table spread,
   and does thy cup with love o'er-
   flow?
   Thither be all thy children led,
   and let them all thy sweetness know.

2. Hail, sacred feast, which Jesus
   makes!
   Rich banquet of his flesh and blood!
   Thrice happy he, who here partakes
   that sacred stream, that heavenly
   food.

3. O let thy table honoured be,
   and furnished well with joyful
   guests;
   and may each soul salvation see,
   that here its sacred pledges tastes.

Philip Doddridge (1702-51)

203

1. My God, how wonderful thou art,
   thy majesty how bright
   how beautiful thy mercy-seat
   in depths of burning light.

2. How dread are thine eternal years
   O everlasting Lord!
   By prostrate spirits day and night
   incessantly adored.

3. How beautiful, how beautiful
   the sight of thee must be,
   thine endless wisdom, boundless
   power
   and awful purity!

4. Oh, how I fear thee, living God!
   with deepest, tenderest fears,
   and worship thee with trembling hope
   and penitential tears.

5. Yet I may love thee too, O Lord,
   almighty as thou art,
   for thou hast stooped to ask of me
   the love of my poor heart.

6. No earthly father loves like thee,
   no mother e'er so mild
   bears and forbears as thou hast done
   with me thy sinful child.

7. Father of Jesus, love's reward,
   what rapture will it be,
   prostrate before thy throne to lie,
   and gaze and gaze on thee!

Frederick William Faber (1814-63)

204

1. My God I love thee, not because
   I hope for heav'n thereby;
   nor yet that those who love thee not
   are lost eternally.

2. Thou, O my Jesus, thou didst me
   upon the cross embrace;
   for me didst bear the nails and spear
   and manifold disgrace.

3. And griefs and torments numberless
   and sweat of agony;
   e'en death itself — and all for one
   who was thine enemy.

4. Then why, O Blessed Jesu Christ
   should I not love thee well;
   not for the sake of winning heaven,
   or of escaping hell;

5. Not with the hope of gaining aught;
   not seeking a reward,
   but, as thyself hast loved me
   O ever-loving Lord?

6. E'en so I love thee, and will love,
   and in thy praise will sing;
   solely because thou art my God
   and my eternal king.

   17th c., tr. Edward Caswall

205

1. My God loves me.
   His love will never end.
   He rests within my heart
   for my God loves me.

2. His gentle hand
   he stretches over me.
   Though storm-clouds
        threaten the day
   he will set me free.

3. He comes to me
   in sharing bread and wine.
   He brings me life that will reach
   past the end of time.

4. My God loves me,
   his faithful love endures.
   And I will live like a child
   held in love secure.

5. The joys of love
   as offerings now we bring.
   The pains of love will be lost
   in the praise we sing.

   Verse 1 *Anonymous*
   Verses 2-5 *Sandra Joan Billington*

206

1. My song is love unknown,
   my Saviour's love to me,
   love to the loveless shown,
   that they might lovely be.
   O who am I,
   that for my sake,
   my Lord should take
   frail flesh and die?

2. He came from his blest throne,
   salvation to bestow;
   but men made strange, and none
   the longed-for Christ would know,
   but O, my friend,
   my friend indeed,
   who at my need
   his life did spend!

3. Sometimes they strew his way,
   and his sweet praises sing;
   resounding all the day
   hosannas to their King;
   then 'Crucify!'
   is all their breath,
   and for his death
   they thirst and cry.

4. Why, what hath my Lord done?
   What makes this rage and spite?
   He made the lame to run,
   he gave the blind their sight.
   Sweet injuries!
   Yet they at these
   themselves displease,
   and 'gainst him rise.

5. They rise, and needs will have
   my dear Lord made away;
   a murderer they save,
   the Prince of Life they slay.
   Yet cheerful he
   to suffering goes,
   that he his foes
   from thence might free.

6. In life, no house, no home
   my Lord on earth might have:
   in death no friendly tomb
   but what a stranger gave.
   What may I say?
   Heaven was his home;
   but mine the tomb
   wherein he lay.

7. Here might I stay and sing,
   no story so divine,
   never was love, dear King,
   never was grief like thine.
   This is my Friend,
   in whose sweet praise
   I all my days
   could gladly spend.

   Samuel Crossman (c. 1624-84)

207

1. New praises be given
      to Christ newly crowned,
   who back to his heaven
      a new way hath found;
   God's blessedness sharing
      before us he goes,
   what mansions preparing,
      what endless repose!

2. His glory still praising
      on thrice holy ground
   the apostles stood gazing,
      his mother around;
   with hearts that beat faster,
      with eyes full of love,
   they watched while their master
      ascended above.

3. "No star can disclose him",
      the bright angels said;
   "Eternity knows him,
      your conquering head;
   those high habitations,
      he leaves not again,
   till, judging all nations,
      on earth he shall reign".

4. Thus spoke they and straightway,
      where legions defend
   heaven's glittering gateway,
      their Lord they attend,
   and cry, looking thither,
      "Your portals let down
   for him who rides hither
      in peace and renown".

5. They asked, who keep sentry
      in that blessed town,
   "Who thus claimeth entry,
      a king of renown?"
   "The Lord of all valiance",
      that herald replied,
   "Who Satan's battalions
      laid low in their pride".

6. Grant, Lord, that our longing
      may follow thee there,
   on earth who are thronging
      thy temples with prayer;
   and unto thee gather,
      Redeemer, thine own
   where thou with thy Father
      dost sit on the throne.

   St. Bede the Venerable (673-735)
   tr. R. A. Knox

208

1. Now come to me all you who seek
   and place your trust in me.
   For I have comfort for the weak,
   the strength to set you free.
   And, just as gentle blades of grass
   can crack the hardened earth,
   creation will be yours at last
   when love is brought to birth.

2. Now come to me all you who seek
   and place your trust in me.
   For I will comfort those who mourn
   and make the blind to see.
   However dark the stormy night
   the sun will raise the dawn,
   and you will live beneath the light
   of love in darkness born.

3. Now come to me all you who seek
and place your trust in me.
For I bring peace to those at war
and set the captives free.
Just as in cutting sun-ripe wheat
we count the summer's worth,
so shall all those who justice seek
be there at love's new birth.

Michael Cockett

209

1. Now Jesus said:
"We'll bake some bread,
so bring me flour and water.
Then bring me salt
and bring me yeast;
I'll bake for you a splendid feast,
and we will join and drink a toast
to friendship ever after."

2. They found the flour,
they found the salt,
they found a jug of water.
But, though they searched
around the town,
an ounce of yeast
could not be found.
They came to him
with eyes cast down
and told him of their failure.

3. Then Jesus said:
"Do not be sad,
we'll mix the flour and water.
And though we bake
unleavened bread,
if you will be the yeast instead,
the bread will rise up from the dead
and feed you ever after."

Michael Cockett

210

1. Now Jesus said:
"You must love one another,
pass it on, pass it on,"
And Jesus said:
"Call all men your brother,
come to me, learn to love,
pass it on, pass it on."

2. So Peter said:
"You must love one another,
pass it on, pass it on."
So Peter said:
"Call all men your brother,
come to me, learn to love,
pass it on, pass it on."

3. The people said . . .

4. My Father said . . .

5. Now I can say . . .

Michael Cockett

211

1. Now thank we all our God,
with heart and hands and voices,
who wondrous things hath done,
in whom this world rejoices;
who from our mother's arms
hath blessed us on our way
with countless gifts of love,
and still is ours today.

2. O may this bounteous God
through all our life be near us
with ever joyful hearts
and blessed peace to cheer us;
and keep us in his grace,
and guide us when perplexed,
and free us from all ills
in this world and the next.

3. All praise and thanks to God
the Father now be given
the Son and him who reigns
with them in highest heaven,
the one Eternal God,
whom earth and heaven adore;
for thus it was, is now,
and shall be evermore.

Martin Rinkart (1586-1649),
tr. Catherine Winkworth

212

1. Now with the fast-departing light,
   maker of all! We ask of thee,
   of thy great mercy, through the
                                    night
   our guardian and defence to be.

2. Far off let idle visions fly;
   no phantom of the night molest:
   curb thou our raging enemy,
   that we in chaste repose may rest.

3. Father of mercies! hear our cry:
   hear us, O sole-begotten Son!
   Who, with the Holy Ghost most
                                    high,
   reignest while endless ages run.

   7th c., tr. Edward Caswall

213

1. O bread of heaven, beneath this veil
   thou dost my very God conceal;
   my Jesus, dearest treasure, hail;
   I love thee and adoring kneel;
   each loving soul by thee is fed
   with thine own self in form of bread.

2. O food of life, thou who dost give
   the pledge of immortality;
   I live; no, 'tis not I that live;
   God gives me life, God lives in me:
   he feeds my soul, he guides my ways,
   and every grief with joy repays.

3. O bond of love, that dost unite
   the servant to his living Lord;
   could I dare live, and not requite
   such love   then death were meet
                                    reward:
   I cannot live unless to prove
   some love for such unmeasured love.

4. Beloved Lord in heaven above,
   there, Jesus, thou awaitest me;
   to gaze on thee with changeless love,
   yes, thus I hope, thus shall it be:
   for how can he deny me heaven
   who here on earth himself hath
                                    given?

   St. Alphonsus (1696-1787)
   tr. Edward Vaughan

214

1. O come, all ye faithful,
   joyful and triumphant,
   O come ye, O come ye to Bethlehem;
   come and behold him,
   born the king of angels:

   O come, let us adore him,
   O come, let us adore him,
   O come, let us adore him,
   Christ the Lord.

2. God of God,
   light of light,
   lo! he abhors not the virgin's womb;
   very God,
   begotten not created:

3. Sing, choirs of angels,
   sing in exultation,
   sing all ye citizens of heaven above:
   glory to God
   in the highest:

4. Yea, Lord, we greet thee,
   born this happy morning,
   Jesu, to thee be glory given;
   word of the Father,
   now in flesh appearing:

   18th c., tr. Frederick Oakeley

215

1. O come and mourn with me awhile;
   see, Mary calls us to her side;
   O come and let us mourn with her;

   Jesus our love, Jesus our love,
   is crucified.

2. Have we no tears to shed for him,
   while soldiers scoff and men deride?
   Ah! look how patiently he hangs;

3. How fast his feet and hands are
   nailed,
   his blessed tongue with thirst is tied;
   his failing eyes are blind with blood;

4. Seven times he spoke, seven words
   of love,
   and all three hours his silence cried.
   For mercy on the souls of men;

5. O break, O break, hard heart of
   mine:
   thy weak self-love and guilty pride
   his Pilate and his Judas were:

6. A broken heart, a fount of tears,
   ask, and they will not be denied;
   a broken heart, love's cradle is;

7. O love of God! O sin of man!
   In this dread act your strength is
   tried;
   and victory remains with love;

   Frederick William Faber (1814-63)

216

1. O come, O come, Emmanuel,
   and ransom captive Israel,
   that mourns in lonely exile here
   until the Son of God appear:

   Rejoice, rejoice! Emmanuel
   shall come to thee, O Israel.

2. O come, thou Rod of Jesse, free
   thine own from Satan's tyranny;
   from depths of hell thy people save,
   and give them vict'ry o'er the grave:

3. O come, thou dayspring, come and
   cheer
   our spirits by thine advent here;
   disperse the gloomy clouds of night,
   and death's dark shadows put to
   flight:

4. O come, thou key of David, come
   and open wide our heavenly home;
   make safe the way that leads on high,
   and close the path to misery.

5. O come, O come, thou Lord of
   might,
   who to thy tribes on Sinai's height
   in ancient times didst give the law
   in cloud and majesty and awe:

   From the 'Great O Antiphons'
   (12th-13th c.), tr. John Mason Neale

217

1. O Father, now the hour has come,
   so glorify your Son,
   that he may give eternal life
   to those who hope in him.

2. Through Jesus Christ, your only Son,
   the Word has now been sown,
   so honour him with glory now,
   the saviour of the world.

3. O Father of the Word of Truth,
   the world has known you not,
   but through the Son that you have
   sent
   your love is in our hearts.

4. He is no longer in this world,
   he has returned to you.
   So, holy Father, make us one
   as he is one with you.

5. May all good men be joined as one,
   as Father with the Son,
   that through the unity of love,
   the whole world may believe.

6. Through glory given to the Son,
   the Father will reveal
   the joy complete, the bond of love,
   mysterious Three in One.

   Michael Cockett

218

1. O Father, take in sign of love
   these gifts of bread and wine!
   With them we give our very selves,
   to be for ever thine!

2. These gifts another gift will be,
   thy Son in very deed,
   for us a willing victim made,
   the Lamb on whom we feed!

3. These are the gifts thy Son did bless
   the night before he died.
   By which he showed himself a priest
   and victim crucified!

4. He now has given us as our own
   his offering made to thee:
   his body broken, Blood outpoured,
   for us on Calvary!

5. This bread his Body will become,
   this wine his Blood will be!
   Our humble gifts will be the gift
   that is most dear to thee!

6. This perfect gift thou wilt restore
   to greatest and to least,
   to make all one in love and joy
   in thy communion-feast!

   James Quinn, S.J.

219

1. Of the glorious body telling,
   O my tongue, its myst'ries sing,
   and the blood, all price excelling,
   which the world's eternal king,
   in a noble womb once dwelling,
   shed for this world's ransoming.

2. Giv'n for us, for us descending,
   of a virgin to proceed,
   man with man in converse blending,
   scattered he the gospel seed,
   'till his sojourn drew to ending,
   which he closed in wondrous deed.

3. At the last great supper lying,
   circled by his brethren's band,
   meekly with the law complying,
   first, he finished its command.

Then, immortal food supplying,
gave himself with his own hand.

4. Word made flesh, by word he
   maketh
   very bread his flesh to be;
   man in wine Christ's blood
   partaketh,
   and if senses fail to see,
   faith alone the true heart waketh,
   to behold the mystery.

5. Therefore, we before him bending,
   this great sacrament revere;
   types and shadows have their ending,
   for the newer rite is here;
   faith, our outward sense befriending,
   makes the inward vision clear.

6. Glory let us give, and blessing,
   to the Father and the Son;
   honour, might and praise addressing,
   while eternal ages run;
   ever too his love confessing,
   who from both, with both is one.

   St. Thomas Aquinas (1127-74),
   tr. J. M. Neale, E. Caswall and others

220

1. O Godhead hid, devoutly I adore
   thee,
   who truly art within the forms
   before me;
   to thee my heart I bow with
   bended knee,
   as failing quite in contemplating
   thee.

2. Sight, touch, and taste in thee are
   each deceived,
   the ear alone most safely is
   believed:
   I believe all the Son of God has
   spoken;
   than truth's own word there is no
   truer token.

3. God only on the cross lay hid from
   view;
   but here lies hid at once the
   manhood too:

and I, in both professing my belief,
make the same prayer as the
  repentant thief.

4. Thy wounds, as Thomas saw, I do
    not see;
  yet thee confess my Lord and God
    to be;
  make me believe thee ever more and
    more,
  In thee my hope, in thee my love to
    store.

5. O thou memorial of our Lord's own
    dying!
  O bread that living art and vivifying!
  Make ever thou my soul on thee to
    live;
  ever a taste of heavenly sweetness
    give.

6. O loving Pelican! O Jesus, Lord!
  Unclean I am, but cleanse me in thy
    blood;
  of which a single drop, for sinners
    spilt,
  is ransom for a world's entire guilt.

7. Jesus, whom for the present veiled
    I see,
  what I so thirst for, oh, vouchsafe
    to me:
  that I may see thy countenance
    unfolding,
  and may be blest thy glory in
    beholding.

> *St. Thomas Aquinas (1227-74),*
> *tr. Edward Caswall*

221

1. O God of earth and altar,
  bow down and hear our cry,
  our earthly rulers falter,
  our people drift and die;
  the walls of gold entomb us,
  the swords of scorn divide,
  take not thy thunder from us,
  but take away our pride.

2. From all that terror teaches,
  from lies of tongue and pen,
  from all the easy speeches
  that comfort cruel men,
  from sale and profanation
  of honour and the sword,
  from sleep and from damnation,
  deliver us, good Lord!

3. Tie in a living tether
  the prince and priest and thrall,
  bind all our lives together,
  smite us and save us all;
  in ire and exultation
  aflame with faith, and free,
  lift up a living nation,
  a single sword to thee.

> *G. K. Chesterton (1874-1936)*

222

1. O God, our help in ages past,
  our hope for years to come,
  our shelter from the stormy blast,
  and our eternal home;

2. Beneath the shadow of thy throne,
  thy saints have dwelt secure;
  sufficient is thine arm alone,
  and our defence is sure.

3. Before the hills in order stood,
  or earth received her frame,
  from everlasting thou art God,
  to endless years the same.

4. A thousand ages in thy sight,
  are like an evening gone;
  short as the watch that ends the
                                night
  before the rising sun.

5. Time, like an ever-rolling stream,
  bears all its sons away;
  they fly forgotten, as a dream
  dies at the opening day.

6. O God, our help in ages past,
  our hope for years to come,
  be thou our guard while troubles
                                last,
  and our eternal home.

> *Isaac Watts (1674-1748)*

223

1. O God, thy people gather,
   obedient to thy word,
   around thy holy altar,
   to praise thy name, O Lord;
   for all thy loving kindness
   our grateful hearts we raise;
   but pardon first the blindness
   of all our sinful ways.

2. Thou art our loving Father,
   thou art our holiest Lord,
   but we have sinned against thee,
   by thought and deed and word.
   Before the court of heaven
   we stand and humbly pray
   our sins may be forgiven,
   our faults be washed away.

3. Though sinful, we implore thee
   to turn and make us live,
   that so we may adore thee,
   and our due offering give,
   and may the prayers and voices
   of thy glad people rise,
   as thy whole Church rejoices
   in this great sacrifice.

   Anthony Nye

224

1. O God, we give ourselves today
   with this pure host to thee,
   the selfsame gift which thy dear Son
   gave once on Calvary.

2. Entire and whole, our life and love
   with heart and soul and mind,
   for all our sins and faults and needs,
   thy Church and all mankind.

3. With humble and with contrite heart
   this bread and wine we give
   because thy Son once gave himself
   and died that we might live.

4. Though lowly now, soon by thy
   word
   these offered gifts will be
   the very body of our Lord,
   his soul and deity.

5. His very body, offered up
   a gift beyond all price,
   he gives to us, that we may give
   in loving sacrifice.

6. O Lord, who took our human life,
   as water mixed with wine,
   grant through this sacrifice that we
   may share thy life divine.

   Anthony Nye

225

Oh living water, refresh my soul.
Oh living water, refresh my soul
Spirit of joy, Lord of creation.
Spirit of hope, Spirit of peace.

1. Spirit of God,
   Spirit of God.

2. Oh set us free,
   Oh set us free.

3. Come, pray in us,
   come, pray in us.

   Rosalie Vissing

226

1. Oh Lord,
   all the world belongs to you,
   and you are always making
   all things new.
   What is wrong you forgive,
   and the new life you give
   is what's turning the world
   upside down.

2. The world's
   only loving to its friends,
   but you have brought us love that
   never ends;
   loving enemies too,
   and this loving with you
   is what's turning the world
   upside down.

3. This world
   lives divided and apart.
   You draw all men together
   and we start
   in your body to see
   that in fellowship we

can be turning the world
   upside down.

4. The world
      wants the wealth to live in state,
   but you show us a new way
      to be great:
   like a servant you came,
   and if we do the same,
   we'll be turning the world
      upside down.

5. Oh Lord
      all the world belongs to you,
   and you are always making
      all things new.
   Send your Spirit on all
   in your Church whom you call
   to be turning the world
      upside down.

Patrick Appleford

227

1. O Lord, my God,
      when I in awesome wonder,
   consider all the worlds
      thy hand has made,
   I see the stars,
      I hear the rolling thunder,
   thy pow'r throughout
      the universe displayed.

   Then sings my soul,
      my Saviour God to thee:
   How great thou art,
      how great thou art.
   Then sings my soul,
      my Saviour God to thee:
   How great thou art,
      how great thou art.

2. And when I think
      that God, his Son not sparing,
   sent him to die, I
      scarce can take it in
   that on the cross,
      my burden gladly bearing,
   he bled and died
      to take away my sin.

3. When Christ shall come
      with shout of acclamation
   and take me home,
      what joy shall fill my heart;
   when I shall bow
      in humble adoration,
   and there proclaim;
      my God, how great thou art.

Unknown

228

1. O holy Lord, by all adored,
   our trespasses confessing,
   to thee this day thy children pray,
   our holy faith professing!
   Accept, O king, the gifts we bring,
   our songs of praise, the prayers we
                                    raise,
   and grant us, Lord, thy blessing.

2. To God on high be thanks and
                              praise,
   who deigns our bond to sever;
   his care shall guide us all our days,
   and harm shall reach us never,
   on him we rest with faith assured;
   of all that live he is the Lord,
   for ever and for ever.

M. F. Bell (1862-1947)

229

1. Oh sinner man,
      where you going to run to?
   Oh, sinner man,
      where you going to run to?
   Oh, sinner man,
      where you going to run to?
   all on that day?

2. Run to the moon,
      moon won't you hide me?
   Run to the sea,
      sea won't you hide me?
   Run to the sun,
      sun won't you hide me?
   all on that day?

3. Lord said: "Sinner Man,
      the moon'll be a-bleeding."
   Lord said: "Sinner Man,
      the sea'll be a-sinking."
   Lord said: "Sinner Man,
      the sun'll be a-freezing."
   all on that day.

4. Run to the Lord:
      "Lord, won't you hide me?"
   Run to the Lord:
      "Lord, won't you hide me?"
   Run to the Lord:
      "Lord, won't you hide me?"
   all on that day.

5. Lord said: "Sinner Man,
      you should have been a-praying!"
   Lord said: "Sinner Man,
      you should have been a-praying!"
   Lord said: "Sinner Man,
      you should have been a-praying!"
   all on that day.

Traditional

230

1. Oh, the Lord looked down
      from his window in the sky,
   said: "I created man
      but I can't remember why!
   Nothing but fighting
      since creation day.
   I'll send a little water
      and wash them all away."
   Oh, the Lord came down
      and looked around a spell.
   There was Mister Noah
      behaving mighty well.
   And that is the reason
      the Scriptures record
   Noah found grace
      in the eyes of the Lord.

   *Noah found grace
      in the eyes of the Lord.
   Noah found grace
      in the eyes of the Lord.
   Noah found grace
      in the eyes of the Lord
   and he left him high and dry.*

2. The Lord said: "Noah,
      there's going to be a flood,
   there's going to be some water,
      there's going to be some mud,
   so take off your hat, Noah,
      take off your coat,
   get Sham, Ham and Japhat
      and build yourself a boat."
   Noah said: "Lord,
      I don't believe I could."
   The Lord said: "Noah,
      get yourself some wood.
   You never know what
      you can do till you try.
   Build it fifty cubits wide
      and thirty cubits high."

3. Noah said: "There she is,
      there she is Lord!"
   The Lord said: "Noah,
      it's time to get aboard.
   Take of each creature
      a he and a she
   and of course take Mrs Noah
      and the whole family."
   Noah said: "Lord,
      it's getting mighty dark."
   The Lord said: "Noah,
      get those creatures in the ark."
   Noah said: "Lord,
      it's beginning to pour."
   The Lord said: "Noah,
      hurry up and close the door."

4. The ark rose up
      on the bosom of the deep.
   After forty days
      Mr Noah took a peep.
   He said: "We're not moving, Lord,
      where are we at?"
   The Lord said: "You're sitting
      right on Mount Ararat."
   Noah said: "Lord,
      it's getting nice and dry."
   The Lord said: "Noah,
      see my rainbow in the sky.
   Take all your creatures
      and people the earth
   and be sure that you're not
      more trouble than you're worth."

231

1. Oh, the love of my Lord
   is the essence
   of all that I love here on earth.
   All the beauty I see
   he has given to me
   and his giving is gentle as silence.

2. Every day, every hour,
   every moment
   have been blessed by
   the strength of his love.
   At the turn of each tide
   he is there at my side,
   and his touch is as gentle as silence.

3. There've been times when I've turned
   from his presence,
   and I've walked other paths,
   other ways.
   But I've called on his name
   in the dark of my shame,
   and his mercy was gentle as silence.

Estelle White

232

1. Oh when the saints go marching in,
   oh when the saints go marching in,
   I want to be in that number,
   when the saints go marching in.

2. Oh when the drums begin to bang,
   oh when the drums begin to bang,
   I want to be in that number,
   when the drums begin to bang.

3. Oh when the stars fall from the sky,
   oh when the stars fall from the sky,
   I want to be in that number,
   when the stars fall from the sky.

4. Oh when the moon turns into blood,
   oh when the moon turns into blood,
   I want to be in that number,
   when the moon turns into blood.

5. Oh when the sun turns into fire,
   oh when the sun turns into fire,
   I want to be in that number,
   when the sun turns into fire.

6. Oh when the fires begin to blaze,
   oh when the fires begin to blaze,
   I want to be in that number,
   when the fires begin to blaze.

7. Oh when the Lord calls out the
                            names,
   oh when the Lord calls out the
                            names,
   I want to be in that number,
   when the Lord calls out the names.

Traditional

233

1. O Jesus Christ, remember,
   when thou shalt come again,
   upon the clouds of heaven,
   with all thy shining train;
   when every eye shall see thee
   in deity revealed,
   who now upon this altar
   in silence art concealed.

2. Remember then, O Saviour,
   I supplicate of thee,
   that here I bowed before thee
   upon my bended knee;
   that here I owned thy presence,
   and did not thee deny,
   and glorified thy greatness
   though hid from human eye.

3. Accept, divine Redeemer,
   the homage of my praise;
   be thou the light and honour
   and glory of my days.
   Be thou my consolation
   when death is drawing nigh;
   be thou my only treasure
   through all eternity.

Edward Caswall (1814-78)

234

1. O king of might and splendour
   creator most adored,
   this sacrifice we render
   to thee as sov'reign Lord.
   May these our gifts be pleasing
   unto thy majesty,

mankind from sin releasing
who have offended thee.

2. Thy body thou hast given,
   thy blood thou hast outpoured,
   that sin might be forgiven,
   O Jesus, loving Lord.
   As now with love most tender,
   thy death we celebrate,
   our lives in self-surrender
   to thee we consecrate.

Dom Gregory Murray, O.S.B.

235

1. O little town of Bethlehem,
   how still we see thee lie!
   Above thy deep and dreamless sleep
   the silent stars go by.
   Yet, in thy dark streets shineth
   the everlasting light;
   the hopes and fears of all the years
   are met in thee tonight.

2. O morning stars, together
   proclaim the holy birth,
   and praises sing to God the King,
   and peace to men on earth;
   for Christ is born of Mary;
   and, gathered all above,
   while mortals sleep, the angels keep
   their watch of wondering love.

3. How silently, how silently,
   the wondrous gift is given!
   So God imparts to human hearts
   the blessings of his heaven.
   No ear may hear his coming;
   but in this world of sin,
   where meek souls will receive him, still
   the dear Christ enters in.

4. Where children pure and happy
   pray to the blessed Child,
   where misery cries out to thee,
   Son of the mother mild;
   where charity stands watching
   and faith holds wide the door,
   the dark night wakes, the glory
                             breaks,
   and Christmas comes once more.

Phillips Brooks (1835-93)

236

1. O Mother blest, whom God bestows
   on sinners and on just,
   what joy, what hope thou givest
                             those
   who in thy mercy trust.

Thou art clement, thou art chaste,
Mary, thou art fair;
of all mothers sweetest, best;
none with thee compare.

2. O heavenly mother, mistress sweet!
   It never yet was told
   that suppliant sinner left thy feet
   unpitied, unconsoled.

3. O mother pitiful and mild,
   cease not to pray for me;
   for I do love thee as a child,
   and sigh for love of thee.

4. Most powerful mother, all men
                             know
   thy Son denies thee nought;
   thou askest, wishest it, and lo!
   his power thy will hath wrought.

5. O mother blest, for me obtain
   ungrateful though I be,
   to love that God who first could
                             deign
   to show such love for me.

St. Alphonsus Liquori (1699-1787),
tr. Edmund Vaughan

237

1. O my Lord, within my heart
   pride will have no home,
   every talent that I have
   comes from you alone.

And like a child at rest
close to its mother's breast,
safe in your arms
my soul is calmed.

2. Lord, my eyes do not look high
   nor my thoughts take wings,
   for I can find treasures in
   ordinary things.

3. Great affairs are not for me,
   deeds beyond my scope,
   in the simple things I do
   I find joy and hope.

   Estelle White

238

1. Once in royal David's city
   stood a lowly cattle shed,
   where a Mother laid her baby
   in a manger for his bed:
   Mary was that Mother mild,
   Jesus Christ her little child.

2. He came down to earth from
   heaven,
   who is God and Lord of all,
   and his shelter was a stable
   and his cradle was a stall;
   with the poor, and mean, and lowly,
   lived on earth our Saviour holy.

3. And through all his wondrous
   childhood
   he would honour and obey,
   love, and watch the lowly maiden
   in whose gentle arms he lay;
   Christian children all must be
   mild, obedient, good as he.

4. For he is our childhood's pattern,
   day by day like us he grew;
   he was little, weak and helpless,
   tears and smiles like us he knew;
   and he feeleth for our sadness,
   and he shareth in our gladness.

5. And our eyes at last shall see him
   through his own redeeming love,
   for that child so dear and gentle
   is our Lord in heaven above;
   and he leads his children on
   to the place where he is gone.

6. Not in that poor lowly stable,
   with the oxen standing by,
   we shall see him; but in heaven,
   set at God's right hand on high;
   when like stars his children crowned
   all in white shall wait around.

   Cecil Francis Alexander (1818-95)

239

1. On Jordan's bank the Baptist's cry
   announces that the Lord is nigh,
   come then and hearken, for he
   brings
   glad tidings from the King of kings.

2. Then cleansed be every Christian
   breast,
   and furnished for so great a guest!
   Yea, let us each our hearts prepare,
   for Christ to come and enter there.

3. For thou art our salvation, Lord,
   our refuge and our great reward;
   without thy grace our souls must
   fade,
   and wither like a flower decayed.

4. Stretch forth thy hand, to heal our
   sore,
   and make us rise, to fall no more;
   once more upon thy people shine,
   and fill the world with love divine.

5. All praise, eternal Son, to thee
   whose advent sets thy people free,
   whom, with the Father, we adore,
   and Holy Ghost, for evermore.

   C. Coffin (1676-1749), tr. J. Chandler

240

1. On this house your blessing, Lord.
   On this house your grace bestow.
   On this house your blessing, Lord.
   May it come and never go.
   Bringing peace and joy
   and happiness,
   bringing love that knows no end.
   On this house your blessing Lord.
   On this house your blessing send.

2. On this house your loving, Lord.
   May it overflow each day.
   On this house your loving, Lord.
   May it come and with us stay.
   Drawing us in love
   and unity
   by the love received from you.
   On this house your loving, Lord.
   May it come each day anew.

3. On this house your giving, Lord.
   May it turn and ever flow.
   On this house your giving, Lord.
   On this house your wealth bestow.
   Filling all our hopes
   and wishes, Lord,
   in the way you know is best.
   On this house your giving, Lord.
   May it come and with us rest.

4. On this house your calling, Lord.
   May it come to us each day.
   On this house your calling, Lord.
   May it come to lead the way.
   Filling us with nobler
   yearnings, Lord,
   calling us to live in you.
   On this house your calling, Lord.
   May it come each day anew.

Sister M. Pereira

241

1. Onward, Christian soldiers,
   marching as to war,
   with the Cross of Jesus
   going on before.
   Christ the royal Master
   leads against the foe;
   forward into battle,
   see, his banners go!

   Onward, Christian soldiers,
   marching as to war,
   with the Cross of Jesus
   going on before.

2. At the sign of triumph
   Satan's legions flee;
   on then, Christian soldiers,
   on to victory.
   Hell's foundations quiver
   at the shout of praise;
   brothers, lift your voices,
   loud your anthem raise.

3. Like a mighty army
   moves the Church of God.
   Brothers, we are treading
   where the Saints have trod;
   we are not divided,
   all one body we,
   one in hope and doctrine,
   one in charity.

4. Crowns and thrones may perish,
   kingdoms rise and wane,
   but the Church of Jesus
   constant will remain;
   gates of hell can never
   'gainst that Church prevail;
   we have Christ's own promise,
   and that cannot fail.

5. Onward, then, ye people,
   join our happy throng,
   blend with ours your voices
   in the triumph song;
   glory, laud, and honour
   unto Christ the King;
   this through countless ages
   men and angels sing.

S. Baring-Gould (1834-1924)

242

1. Open your ears, O Christian people,
   open your ears and hear Good News.
   Open your hearts
       O royal priesthood
    God has come to you.
   God has spoken to his people,
   alleluia.
   And his words are words of wisdom,
   alleluia.

2. Israel comes to greet the Saviour,
   Judah is glad to see his day.
   From East and West the
       the peoples travel,
   he will show the way.

3. He who has ears to hear his message;
   he who has ears, then let him hear.
   He who would learn
       the way of wisdom,
   let him hear God's words.

                            W. F. Jabusch

243

1. O perfect love,
       all human thought transcending,
   lowly we kneel
       in prayer before thy throne.
   That theirs may be
       the love which knows no ending
   whom thou for evermore
       dost join in one.

2. O perfect life,
       be thou their full assurance
   of tender charity
       and steadfast faith,
   of patient hope,
       and quiet, brave endurance,
   with childlike trust
       that fears nor pain nor death.

3. Grant them the joy
       which brightens earthly sorrow,
   grant them the peace
       which calms all earthly strife;
   and to life's day
       the glorious unknown morrow
   that dawns upon
       eternal love and life.

Dorothy Francis Gurney (1858-1932)

244

1. O praise ye the Lord!
       praise him in the height;
   rejoice in his word,
       ye angels of light;
   ye heavens, adore him,
       by whom ye were made,
   and worship before him,
       in brightness arrayed.

2. O praise ye the Lord!
       praise him upon earth,
   in tuneful accord,
       ye sons of new birth.
   Praise him who hath brought you
       his grace from above,
   praise him who hath taught you
       to sing of his love.

3. O praise ye the Lord,
       all things that give sound;
   each jubilant chord
       re-echo around;
   loud organs, his glory
       forth tell in deep tone,
   and, sweet harp, the story
       of what he hath done.

4. O praise ye the Lord!
       thanksgiving and song
   to him be outpoured
       all ages along;
   for love in creation,
       for heaven restored,
   for grace of salvation,
       O praise ye the Lord!

Henry Williams Baker (1821-77),
based on Psalms 148 and 150

245

1. O Priest and Victim, Lord of life,
   throw wide the gates of paradise!
   We face our foes in mortal strife;
   thou art our strength:
   O heed our cries!

2. To Father, Son and Spirit blest,
   one only God, be ceaseless praise!
   May he in goodness grant us rest
   in heav'n, our home,
   for endless days!

   St Thomas Aquinas (1227-74)
   tr. James Quinn, S.J.

246

1. O purest of creatures!
   Sweet mother, sweet maid;
   the one spotless womb
   wherein Jesus was laid.
   Dark night hath come down
   on us, mother, and we
   look out for thy shining,
   sweet star of the sea.

2. Deep night hath come down on
   this rough-spoken world.
   And the banners of darkness
   are boldly unfurled;
   and the tempest-tossed Church,
   all her eyes are on thee.
   They look to thy shining,
   sweet star of the sea.

3. He gazed on thy soul,
   it was spotless and fair;
   for the empire of sin,
   it had never been there;
   none ever had owned thee,
   dear mother, but he,
   and he blessed thy clear shining,
   sweet star of the sea.

4. Earth gave him one lodging;
   'twas deep in thy breast,
   and God found a home where
   the sinner finds rest;
   his home and his hiding-place,
   both were in thee;
   he was won by thy shining,
   sweet star of the sea.

5. Oh, blissful and calm
   was the wonderful rest
   that thou gavest thy God
   in thy virginal breast;
   for the heaven he left
   he found heaven in thee,
   and he shone in thy shining,
   sweet star of the sea.

   Frederick William Faber (1814-63)

247

1. O sacred head sore wounded,
   defiled and put to scorn,
   O kingly head surrounded
   with mocking crown of thorn,
   what sorrow mars thy grandeur?
   Can death thy bloom deflower?
   O countenance whose splendour
   the hosts of heaven adore.

2. Thy beauty, long-desirèd,
   hath vanished from our sight;
   thy power is all expired,
   and quenched the light of light.
   Ah me! for whom thou diest,
   hide not so far thy grace:
   show me, O love most highest,
   the brightness of thy face.

3. I pray thee, Jesu, own me,
   me, shepherd good, for thine;
   who to thy fold hast won me,
   and fed with truth divine.
   Me guilty, me refuse not;
   incline thy face to me,
   this comfort that I lose not
   on earth to comfort thee.

4. In thy most bitter passion
   my heart to share doth cry,
   with thee for my salvation
   upon the cross to die.
   Ah, keep my heart thus movèd
   to stand thy cross beneath,
   to mourn thee, well-beloved,
   yet thank thee for thy death.

5. My days are few, O fail not,
   with thine immortal power,
   to hold me that I quail not
   in death's most fearful hour:
   that I may fight befriended,
   and see in my last strife
   to me thine arms extended
   upon the cross of life.

   Paulus Gerhardt (1607-76),
   tr. Robert Bridges

248

1. O Sacred Heart,
   our home lies deep in thee;
   on earth thou art an exile's rest,
   in heav'n the glory of the blest,
   O Sacred Heart.

2. O Sacred Heart,
   thou fount of contrite tears;
   where'er those living waters flow,
   new life to sinners they bestow,
   O Sacred Heart.

3. O Sacred Heart,
   bless our dear native land;
   may England's sons in truth e'er
                              stand,
   with faith's bright banner still in
                              hand,
   O Sacred Heart.

4. O Sacred Heart,
   our trust is all in thee,
   for though earth's night be dark
                          and drear,
   thou breathest rest where thou art
                              near,
   O Sacred Heart.

5. O Sacred Heart,
   when shades of death shall fall,
   receive us 'neath thy gentle care,
   and save us from the tempter's snare,
   O Sacred Heart.

6. O Sacred Heart,
   lead exiled children home,
   where we may ever rest near thee,
   in peace and joy eternally,
   O Sacred Heart.

   Francis Stanfield (1835-1914)

249

1. O thou, who at
      thy Eucharist didst pray
   that all thy Church
      might be for ever one.
   grant us at every
      Eucharist to say
   with longing heart and soul,
      "Thy will be done".
   O may we all one bread,
      one body be,
   one through this sacrament of unity.

2. For all thy Church,
      O Lord, we intercede;
   make thou our sad
      divisions soon to cease;
   draw us the nearer
      each to each, we plead,
   by drawing all to thee,
      O Prince of peace;
   thus may we all one
      bread, one body be,
   one through this sacrament of unity.

3. We pray thee too
      for wanderers from thy fold,
   O bring them back,
      good shepherd of the sheep,
   back to the faith which
      saints believed of old,
   back to the Church which still
      that faith doth keep;
   soon may we all one bread,
      one body be,
   one through this sacrament of unity.

4. So, Lord, at length
    When sacraments shall cease,
may we be one
    with all thy Church above,
one with thy saints in
    one unbroken peace,
one with thy saints in one
    unbounded love:
more blessed still, in peace
    and love to be
one with the Trinity in unity.

William Harry Turton (1856-1938)

250

1. O Trinity, most blessed light,
   O unity of sovereign might,
   as now the fiery sun departs,
   shed thou thy beams within our
                                    hearts.

2. To thee our morning song of praise,
   to thee our evening prayer we raise;
   thee may our souls for evermore,
   in lowly reverence adore.

3. All praise to God the Father be,
   all praise, eternal Son, to thee,
   whom with the Spirit we adore,
   for ever and for evermore.

St. Ambrose (340-397), tr. J. M. Neale

251

1. Our Father, who art in heaven,
   hallowed be thy name.
   Thy kingdom come thy will be
                                    done,
   hallowed be thy name,
   hallowed be thy name.

2. On earth as it is in heaven,
   hallowed be thy name.
   Give us this day our daily bread,
   hallowed be thy name,
   hallowed be thy name.

3. Forgive us our trespasses,
   hallowed be thy name,
   as we forgive those who trespass
                                    against us,
   hallowed be thy name,
   hallowed be thy name.

4. And lead us not into temptation,
   hallowed be thy name,
   but deliver us from all that is evil,
   hallowed be thy name,
   hallowed be thy name.

5. For thine is the kingdom, the power
                                    and the glory,
   hallowed be thy name,
   for ever, and for ever and ever,
   hallowed be thy name,
   hallowed be thy name.

6. Amen, amen, it shall be so,
   hallowed be thy name.
   Amen, amen, it shall be so,
   hallowed be thy name,
   hallowed be thy name.

Traditional Caribbean

252

1. Out and away
       the mountains are calling!
   Voices are clear
       and wide as the sky!
   Where is the music
       I hear in my heart:
   soars over valleys
       as swift as a lark;
   echoes the joy that has
       scattered the dark: I am free.

2. Hear the wind sigh
       through leaves that are falling;
   see the wind sway
       the trees that are dry.
   Silent the darkness
       where thunder-clouds form;
   still is the world as
       it waits for the storm:
   now comes the lightning that
       heralds the dawn of the rain.

3. Water is clear,
    as clear as the moonlight;
dew on the ground,
    a tear in the eye.
Rivers and torrents
    have vanished before;
oceans have coastlines
    and continents shores:
Boundless the flow that's
    unlocking the doors of my heart.

4. Free as the day
    my spirit is flying:
eagles have wings,
    but none strong as these!
Where have I found it,
    this life newly-grown?
Gently, my heart says
    it's not of my own:
deeper beyond me the Spirit
    has blown — he is love.

John Glynn

253

1. O worship the King
    all glorious above;
O gratefully sing
    his power and his love:
our shield and defender,
    the ancient of days,
pavilioned in splendour,
    and girded with praise.

2. O tell of his might,
    O sing of his grace,
whose robe is the light,
    whose canopy space.
His chariots of wrath,
    the deep thunder-clouds form,
and dark is his path
    on the wings of the storm.

3. This earth, with its store
    of wonders untold,
almighty, thy power
    hath founded of old;
hath stablished it fast
    by a changeless decree,
and round it hath cast,
    like a mantle, the sea.

4. Thy bountiful care
    what tongue can recite?
It breathes in the air,
    it shines in the light;
it streams from the hills,
    it descends to the plain,
and sweetly distils
    in the dew and the rain.

5. Frail children of dust,
    and feeble as frail,
in thee do we trust,
    nor find thee to fail;
thy mercies how tender!
How firm to the end!
Our maker, defender,
    redeemer, and friend.

6. O measureless might,
    ineffable love,
while angels delight
    to hymn thee above,
thy humbler creation,
    though feeble their lays,
with true adoration
    shall sing to thy praise.

Robert Grant (1779-1838)

254

1. Peace is flowing like a river,
    flowing out through you and me,
    spreading out into the desert,
    setting all the captives free.

2. Love is flowing like a river . . .

3. Joy is flowing like a river . . .

4. Hope is flowing like a river . . .

Anonymous

255

1. Peace is the gift of heaven to earth,
   softly enfolding our fears.
   Peace is the gift of
       Christ to the world,
   given for us.
   He is the Lamb who bore
       the pain of peace.

2. Peace is the gift of Christ
       to his Church,
   wound of the lance of his love.
   Love is the pain he
       suffered for man,
   offered to us:
   Oh, to accept the wound
       that brings us peace!

3. Joy is the gift the Spirit imparts,
   born of the heavens and earth.
   We are his children,
       children of joy,
   people of God:
   He is our Lord, our peace,
       our love, our joy!

John Glynn

256

*Peacemakers to be called
    the sons of God.
Peacemakers to be called
    the sons of God.*

1. Seeing the crowd,
   Jesus went up to the hill.
   There he sat down
   and was joined by his friends.
   Then he began to speak to them,
   and this is what he said:
   You must be . . .

2. Happy the gentle,
   for I give to them the earth.
   Happy the mourners,
   I will comfort their distress.
   Happy are those who thirst and
   hunger after what is right.
   They shall be . . .

Malcolm Campbell-Carr

257

1. Peace, perfect peace,
       is the gift of Christ our Lord.
   Peace, perfect peace,
       is the gift of Christ our Lord.
   Thus, says the Lord
       will the world know my friends.
   Peace, perfect peace,
       is the gift of Christ our Lord.

2. Love, perfect love . . .

3. Faith, perfect faith . . .

4. Hope, perfect hope . . . .

5. Joy, perfect joy . . .

Kevin Mayhew

258

1. People of God,
       give praise to his name,
   praise everlasting is his,
   brought to his feast
       as guests in his house,
   praise everlasting is his,
   enter with joy, the Spirit is here,
   praise everlasting is his,
   gladly receive the word that is life,
   praise everlasting is his.

2. Sing with one voice,
       one love in your heart,
   praise everlasting is his,
   love that the Saviour
       bears to us all;
   praise everlasting is his,
   friend for the friendless, neighbour
       for foe,
   praise everlasting is his,
   Christ for all peoples, we are his sign,
   praise everlasting is his.

3. All that we have
   and all that we are,
   praise everlasting is his,
   all is his gift,
   his token of love,
   praise everlasting is his,
   all to be loved, made profit for love,
   praise everlasting is his,
   all to be taken home to the Lord,
   praise everlasting is his.

4. Praise for his glory,
   thanks for his gifts,
   praise everlasting is his,
   God everlasting, one that is three,
   praise everlasting is his,
   offer him praise,
   the Lord of all might,
   praise everlasting is his,
   majesty, glory, age upon age,
   praise everlasting is his.

Luke Connaughton

259

1. Praise him, praise him,
   praise him in the morning,
   praise him in the noontime.
   Praise him, praise him,
   praise him when the sun goes down.

2. Love him, . . .

3. Trust him, . . .

4. Serve him, . . .

5. Jesus, . . .

Anonymous

260

1. Praise, my soul, the king of heaven!
   To his feet thy tribute bring.
   Ransomed, healed, restored, forgiven,
   who like me his praise should sing?
   Praise him! Praise him!
   Praise him! Praise him!
   Praise the everlasting king!

2. Praise him for his grace and favour
   to our fathers in distress;

praise him still the same for ever,
slow to chide and swift to bless.
Praise him! Praise him!
Praise him! Praise him!
Glorious in his faithfulness!

3. Father-like he tends and spares us;
   well our feeble frame he knows;
   in his hands he gently bears us,
   rescues us from all our foes.
   Praise him! Praise him!
   Praise him! Praise him!
   Widely as his mercy flows!

4. Angels, help us to adore him;
   ye behold him face to face;
   sun and moon bow down before
                                    him,
   dwellers all in time and space.
   Praise him! Praise him!
   Praise him! Praise him!
   Praise with us the God of grace!

Henry Francis Lyte (1793-1847)

261

Praise the Lord, and sing hallelujah,
hallelujah, hallelujah.
Praise the Lord, and sing hallelujah,
hallelujah, hallelujah.

1. Praise him for the sun and
   for the stars above,
   hallelujah, hallelujah.
   Praise him with your brothers
   for he is the God of love,
   hallelujah, hallelujah.

2. Praise him when you're happy,
   praise him when you're sad,
   hallelujah, hallelujah.
   He's the God who saves us
   and his message makes us glad,
   hallelujah, hallelujah.

3. Praise him in the morning,
   praise him in the night,
   hallelujah, hallelujah.
   Praise him in the thunder
   for he is the God of might,
   hallelujah, hallelujah.

Gerald O'Mahony

262

1. Praise to the Holiest in the height,
   and in the depth be praise,
   in all his words most wonderful,
   most sure in all his ways.

2. O loving wisdom of our God!
   When all was sin and shame,
   a second Adam to the fight,
   and to the rescue came.

3. O wisest love! that flesh and blood
   which did in Adam fail,
   should strive afresh against the foe,
   should strive and should prevail;

4. And that a higher gift than grace
   should flesh and blood refine,
   God's presence and his very self,
   and Essence all divine.

5. O generous love! that he who smote
   in man for man the foe,
   the double agony in man
   for man should undergo.

6. And in the garden secretly
   and on the Cross on high,
   should teach his brethren, and
   inspire
   to suffer and to die.

7. Praise to the Holiest in the height,
   and in the depth be praise,
   in all his words most wonderful,
   most sure in all his ways.

   John Henry Newman (1801-90)

263

Praise to the Lord our God,
let us sing together,
lifting our hearts and our voices
to sing with joy and gladness.
Come along, along, along,
and sing with . . .

   Estelle White

264

1. Praise to the Lord, the Almighty,
   the King of creation!
   O my soul, praise him,
   for he is your health and
   salvation.
   All you who hear,
   now to his altar draw near,
   join in profound adoration.

2. Praise to the Lord, let us offer
   our gifts at his altar;
   let not our sins and transgressions
   now cause us to falter.
   Christ, the High Priest,
   bids us all join in his feast.
   Victims with him on the altar.

3. Praise to the Lord, oh, let all that
   is in us adore him!
   All that has life and breath,
   come now in praises before him.
   Let the Amen sound from
   his people again,
   now as we worship before him.

   Joachim Neander (1650-80),
   tr. C. Winkworth

265

1. Praise we now the Lord our God,
   all mankind in chorus;
   ceaselessly let seraphim,
   angels, pow'rs and cherubim
   sing with joy their praise of him,
   holy, Lord of Sabaoth.

2. All the earth and sea and sky,
   glorify their maker,
   blessed martyrs, prophets grand,
   Christ's beloved apostle-band,
   holy Church in every land.
   Sing his praise for ever.

3. Hail thou king of glory, Christ,
   born before all ages!
   Born of Mary, Virgin pure,
   thou didst us from death secure,
   opening wide to mankind poor,
   stores of heavenly treasure.

4. Seated now at God's right hand,
   bless thy chosen people;
   rule o'er us, dear Lord, we pray,
   keep us free from sin this day,
   save us, Lord, without delay,
   lest we be confounded.

5. In the solemn day of doom,
   we shall hear thy judgment;
   but remember, Lord, we cry,
   in that day when we shall die,
   how thy blood on us did lie,
   signing us thy people.

6. Praise we yet the Lord our God,
   throned in triune splendour:
   praise the Father, Lord of might,
   praise the Son, redeemer bright,
   praise the Spirit, source of light,
   through eternal ages.

D. McRoberts

266

1. Praise we our God with joy
   and gladness never ending;
   angels and saints with us
   their grateful voices blending.
   He is our Father dear,
   o'er filled with parent's love;
   mercies unsought, unknown,
   he showers from above.

2. He is our shepherd true;
   with watchful care unsleeping,
   on us, his erring sheep
   an eye of pity keeping;
   he with a mighty arm
   the bonds of sin doth break,
   and to our burden'd hearts
   in words of peace doth speak.

3. Graces in copious stream
   from that pure fount are welling,
   where, in our heart of hearts,
   our God hath set his dwelling.
   His word our lantern is;
   his peace our comfort still;
   his sweetness all our rest;
   our law, our life, his will.

Frederick Oakeley (1802-80) and others

267

1. Promised Lord, and Christ is he,
   may we soon his kingdom see.

   *Come, O Lord, quickly come,
   come in glory, come in glory,
   come in glory, quickly come.*

2. Teaching, healing once was he,
   may we soon his kingdom see.

3. Dead and buried once was he,
   may we soon his kingdom see.

4. Risen from the dead is he,
   may we soon his kingdom see.

5. Soon to come again is he,
   may we soon his kingdom see.
   *Come, O Lord, quickly come,
   in our lifetime, in our lifetime,
   in our lifetime may it be.*

*Roger Ruston,
based on a Jewish Passover Song*

268

1. Reap me the earth
   as a harvest to God,
   gather and bring it again,
   all that is his,
   to the Maker of all.
   Lift it and offer it high.

   *Bring bread, bring wine,
   give glory to the Lord;
   whose is the earth but God's,
   whose is the praise but his?*

2. Go with your song
   and your music with joy,
   go to the altar of God.
   Carry your offerings,
   fruits of the earth,
   work of your labouring hands.

3. Gladness and pity
   and passion and pain,
   all that is mortal in man,
   lay all before him,
   return him his gift,
   God, to whom all shall go home.

Peter Icarus

269

Rejoice in the Lord always,
and again I say rejoice.
Rejoice in the Lord always,
and again I say rejoice.
Rejoice, rejoice,
and again I say rejoice.
Rejoice, rejoice,
and again I say rejoice.

from Scripture

270

1. Rejoice! the Lord is King!
Your Lord and King adore;
mortals, give thanks and sing,
and triumph evermore:

   *Lift up your heart,
   lift up your voice;
   rejoice, again I say, rejoice.*

2. Jesus the Saviour reigns,
the God of truth and love;
when he had purged our stains,
he took his seat above:

3. His kingdom cannot fail;
he rules o'er earth and heaven;
the keys of death and hell
are to our Jesus given:

4. He sits at God's right hand
till all his foes submit,
and bow to his command,
and fall beneath his feet:

Charles Wesley (1707-88)

271

1. Ride on! ride on in majesty!
Hark, all the tribes hosanna cry;
thy humble beast pursued his road
with palms and scattered garments
strowed.

2. Ride on! ride on in majesty!
In lowly pomp ride on to die;
O Christ, thy triumphs now begin
o'er captive death and conquered
sin.

3. Ride on! ride on in majesty!
The wingèd squadrons of the sky,
look down with sad and wondering
eyes
to see the approaching sacrifice.

4. Ride on! ride on in majesty!
Thy last and fiercest strife is nigh;
the Father, on his sapphire throne
expects his own anointed Son.

5. Ride on! ride on in majesty!
In lowly pomp ride on to die;
bow thy meek head to mortal pain,
then take, O God, thy power, and
reign.

H. H. Milman (1791-1868)

272

1. Round me falls the night,
Saviour be my light;
through the hours in darkness
shrouded
let me see thy face unclouded.
Let thy glory shine
in this heart of mine.

2. Earthly work is done,
earthly sounds are none;
rest in sleep and silence seeking,
let me hear thee softly speaking;
in my spirit's ear
whisper: "I am near".

3. Blessed heav'nly light
shining through earth's night;
voice that oft' of love has told me,
arms, so strong, to clasp and hold
me;
thou thy watch will keep,
Saviour o'er my sleep.

W. Romanis

273

1. Seasons come, seasons go,
   moon-struck tides will ebb and flow;
   when I forget my constant one
   he draws me back, he brings me
   home.

   O love, my love,
   I hear you far away.
   a distant storm
   that will refresh the day.

2. Seasons come, seasons go,
   petals fall though flowers grow;
   and when I doubt love lifts a hand
   and scatters stars like grains of sand.
   Oh love, my love,
   I see you passing by
   like birds that fearlessly
   possess the sky.

3. Seasons come, seasons go,
   times to reap and times to sow;
   but you are love, a fruitful vine,
   in ev'ry season yielding wine.
   I hear my love
   in laughter and in song,
   no day too short,
   no winter night too long.

   Michael Cockett

274

1. See, amid the winter's snow,
   born for us on earth below,
   see, the tender lamb appears,
   promised from eternal years.

   Hail, thou ever-blessed morn,
   hail, redemption's happy dawn!
   Sing through all Jerusalem,
   Christ is born in Bethlehem.

2. Lo, within a manger lies
   he who built the starry skies;
   he who, throned in heights sublime,
   sits amid the cherubim.

3. Say, ye holy shepherds, say,
   what your joyful news today?
   Wherefore have ye left your sheep
   on the lonely mountain steep?

4. 'As we watched at dead of night,
   lo, we saw a wondrous light;
   angels, singing peace on earth,
   told us of the Saviour's birth.'

5. Sacred infant, all divine,
   what a tender love was thine,
   thus to come from highest bliss,
   down to such a world as this!

6. Virgin mother, Mary blest,
   by the joys that fill thy breast,
   pray for us, that we may prove
   worthy of the Saviour's love.

   Edward Caswall (1814-78)

275

1. See us, Lord, about thine altar;
   though so many, we are one;
   many souls by love united
   in the heart of Christ thy Son.

2. Hear our prayers, O loving Father,
   hear in them thy Son, our Lord;
   hear him speak our love and worship,
   as we sing with one accord.

3. Once were seen the blood and water;
   now he seems but bread and wine;
   then in human form he suffered,
   now his form is but a sign.

4. Wheat and grape contain the
   meaning;
   food and drink he is to all;
   one in him, we kneel adoring,
   gathered by his loving call.

5. Hear us yet; so much is needful
   in our frail, disordered life;
   stay with us and tend our weakness
   till that day of no more strife.

6. Members of his mystic body
   now we know our prayer is heard,
   heard by thee, because thy children
   have received th' eternal word.

   John Greally

276

Shalom, my friend,
  shalom my friend, shalom, shalom,
the peace of Christ
  I give you today, shalom, shalom.

Sandra Joan Billington

277

1. Silent night, holy night,
   all is calm, all is bright,
   round yon virgin mother and child;
   holy infant so tender and mild:
   sleep in heavenly peace,
   sleep in heavenly peace.

2. Silent night, holy night.
   Shepherds quake at the sight,
   glories stream from heaven afar,
   heavenly hosts sing alleluia:
   Christ, the Saviour is born,
   Christ, the Saviour is born.

3. Silent night, holy night.
   Son of God, love's pure light
   radiant beams from thy holy face,
   with the dawn of redeeming grace:
   Jesus, Lord, at thy birth,
   Jesus, Lord, at thy birth.

Joseph Mohr (1792-1848),
tr. J. Young

278

Sing, my soul. Sing, my soul.
Sing, my soul, of his mercy.
Sing, my soul. Sing, my soul.
Sing, my soul, of his mercy.

1. The Lord is good to me.
   His light will shine on me.
   When city lights would blind my
                                    eyes.
   He hears my silent call.
   His hands help when I fall.
   His gentle voice stills my sighs.

2. The Lord is good to me.
   His word will set me free
   when men would tie me to the
                                  ground.

He mocks my foolish ways
with love that never fails.
When I'm most lost then I'm found.

3. The Lord is good to me.
   I hear him speak to me.
   His voice is in the rain that falls.
   He whispers in the air
   of his unending care.
   If I will hear, then he calls.

Michael Cockett

279

1. Sing, my tongue, the glorious battle,
   sing the last, the dread affray;
   o'er the cross, the victor's trophy,
   sound the high triumphal lay;
   how, the pains of death enduring,
   earth's redeemer won the day.

2. Faithful cross! above all other,
   one and only noble tree!
   None in foliage, none in blossom,
   none in fruit thy peer may be;
   sweetest wood and sweetest iron!
   Sweetest weight is hung on thee.

3. Bend, O lofty tree, thy branches,
   thy too rigid sinews bend;
   and awhile the stubborn hardness,
   which thy birth bestowed, suspend;
   and the limbs of heaven's high
                                    monarch,
   gently on thine arms extend.

4. Thou alone wast counted worthy
   this world's ransom to sustain,
   that by thee a wrecked creation
   might its ark and haven gain,
   with the sacred blood anointed
   of the Lamb that hath been slain.

5. Praise and honour to the Father,
   praise and honour to the Son,
   praise and honour to the Spirit,
   ever three and ever one,
   one in might and one in glory,
   while eternal ages run.

Venantius Fortunatus (530-609),
tr. J. M. Neale

280

1. Sing of the bride
   and sing of the groom,
   and the wine that was flowing free,
   when the Lord was a guest
   at the wedding feast
   in a town in Galilee.

   Fill the pots with water
   and raise the glasses high,
   for the Lord has come to Cana
   and changed water into wine.

2. Sing of the bride
   and sing of the groom,
   and the feasting all night and day,
   with the wine running short
   at the wedding feast
   to the stewards' sad dismay.

3. "Please will you help,
   they have no more wine,"
   said a mother to her only son.
   He said: "Woman, don't you know
   you can't turn to me,
   for my time has not yet come."

4. "Wait till the day
   and wait till the time
   for the cross and for Calvary,
   but until that time
   here's a fine new wine
   with a taste that's fine and free."

5. Drink to the bride
   and drink to the groom
   at the wedding in Galilee,
   and drink to the life
   that is like new wine
   to all men who wish to be free.

   Michael Cockett

281

1. Sing of Mary, pure and lowly,
   virgin mother undefiled.
   Sing of God's own Son most holy,
   who became her little child.
   Fairest child of fairest mother,
   God, the Lord, who came to earth,
   Word made flesh, our very brother,
   takes our nature by his birth.

2. Sing of Jesus, son of Mary,
   in the home at Nazareth.
   Toil and labour cannot weary
   love enduring unto death.
   Constant was the love he gave her,
   though he went forth from her side,
   forth to preach and heal and suffer,
   till on Calvary he died.

3. Glory be to God the Father,
   glory be to God the Son;
   glory be to God the Spirit,
   glory to the three in one.
   From the heart of blessed Mary,
   from all saints the song ascends
   and the Church the strain re-echoes
   unto earth's remotest ends.

   Anonymous (c. 1914)

282

Sing, sing, sing, sing, sing, sing!
Sing! people of God, sing!
Sing with one accord.
Sing! people of God,
sing your praises to the Lord.

1. O Lord, how glorious over all
   the good earth is your name.
   You have exalted your majesty
   over ev'ry hill and plain.
   From the mouths of the little ones
   you fashion endless praise
   to silence all the vengeful ones
   and glorify your ways.

2. When we behold the heavens
   where your creation shines,
   the moon and stars you set in place
   to stand the test of time,
   what is man that you should mind,
   his sons that you should care?
   A little less than angels
   you have crowned him ev'rywhere.

3. You've given us dominion
over all that you have made.
We're masters of your handiwork
and rule them unafraid.
We're lords of the fish and birds,
of beasts both wild and tame.
O Lord, how glorious over all
the good earth is your name.

Sebastian Temple

283

1. Sing praises to God, sing praises,
sing praises to God, sing praises,
for he is the king of all the earth,
sing praises to his name.

2. Give glory to God, give glory,
give glory to God, give glory,
for he is the king of all the earth,
give glory to his name.

3. Give honour to God, give honour,
give honour to God, give honour,
for he is the king of all the earth,
give honour to his name.

Anonymous

284

1. Sing praises to the living God,
glory, hallelujah.
Come, adore the living God,
glory, hallelujah.
Though sun and moon may pass away
his words will ever stay.
His power is for evermore,
glory, hallelujah.

*Glory to the Trinity.
The undivided Unity,
the Father, Son and Spirit one,
from whom all life
and greatness come.*

2. And to the living God we sing,
glory hallelujah.
Let our love and praises ring,
glory hallelujah.
To all his sons he always gives
his mercy and his love.
So praise him now for evermore,
glory hallelujah.

3. And to the God who cannot die,
glory hallelujah.
To the living God we cry,
glory hallelujah.
He promised to be with us and
he lives in ev'ry one.
We love him now for evermore,
glory hallelujah.

Sebastian Temple

285

1. Sleep, holy babe,
upon thy mother's breast;
great Lord of earth and sea and sky,
how sweet it is to see thee lie
in such a place of rest.

2. Sleep, holy babe;
thine angels watch around,
all bending low, with folded wings,
before th'incarnate King of kings,
in reverent awe profound.

3. Sleep, holy babe,
while I with Mary gaze
in joy upon that face awhile,
upon the loving infant smile,
which there divinely plays.

4. Sleep, holy babe,
ah, take thy brief repose,
too quickly will thy slumbers break,
and thou to lengthen'd pains awake,
that death alone shall close.

5. O lady blest,
sweet Virgin, hear my cry;
forgive the wrong that I have done
to thee, in causing thy dear Son
upon the cross to die.

Edward Caswall (1814-78)

286

1. Songs of thankfulness and praise,
   Jesus, Lord to thee we raise,
   manifested by the star
   to the sages from afar;
   branch of royal David's stem,
   in thy birth at Bethlehem;
   anthems be to thee addressed;
   God in man made manifest.

2. Manifest at Jordan's stream,
   prophet, Priest and King supreme,
   and at Cana wedding-guest,
   in thy Godhead manifest,
   manifest in power divine,
   changing water into wine;
   anthems be to thee addressed;
   God in man made manifest.

3. Manifest in making whole,
   palsied limbs and fainting soul,
   manifest in valiant fight,
   quelling all the devil's might,
   manifest in gracious will,
   ever bringing good from ill;
   anthems be to thee addressed;
   God in man made manifest.

4. Sun and moon shall darkened be,
   stars shall fall, the heavens shall flee.
   Christ will then like lightning shine.
   All will see his glorious sign.
   All will see the judge appear;
   all will then the trumpet hear;
   thou by all wilt be confessed;
   God in man made manifest.

5. Grant us grace to see thee, Lord,
   mirrored in thy holy word;
   may we imitate thee now
   and be pure, as pure art thou;
   that we like to thee may be
   at thy great Epiphany,
   and may praise thee, ever blest,
   God in man made manifest.

   Christopher Wordsworth (1807-85)

287

Sons of God, hear his holy Word!
Gather round the table of the Lord!
Eat his Body, drink his Blood,
and we'll sing a song of love.
Allelu, allelu, allelu, alleluia.

1. Brothers, sisters, we are one,
   and our life has just begun.
   In the Spirit we are young.
   We can live for ever.

2. Shout together to the Lord
   who has promised our reward:
   happiness a hundredfold,
   and we'll live forever.

3. Jesus gave a new command
   that we love our fellow man
   till we reach the promised land,
   where we'll live forever.

4. If we want to live with him;
   we must also die with him;
   die to selfishness and sin,
   and we'll rise forever.

5. Make the world a unity,
   make all men one family
   till we meet the Trinity
   and live with them forever.

6. With the Church we celebrate;
   Jesus' coming we await,
   so we make a holiday,
   so we'll live forever.

   James Theim

288

1. Soul of my Saviour,
   sanctify my breast;
   Body of Christ,
   be thou my saving guest;
   Blood of my Saviour,
   bathe me in thy tide,
   wash me with water
   flowing from thy side.

2. Strength and protection
   may thy Passion be;
   O Blessed Jesus
   hear and answer me;
   deep in thy wounds, Lord,
   hide and shelter me;
   so shall I never,
   never part from thee.

3. Guard and defend me
   from the foe malign;
   in death's dread moments
   make me only thine;
   call me, and bid me
   come to thee on high,
   when I may praise thee
   with thy saints for aye.

Ascribed to John XXII (1249-1334),
tr. Anonymous

289

Spirit of the living God,
   fall afresh on me.
Spirit of the living God,
   fall afresh on me.
Break me, melt me,
   mould me, fill me.
Spirit of the living God,
   fall afresh on me.

Michael Iverson

290

1. Star of ocean, lead us;
   God for mother claims thee,
   ever Virgin names thee;
   gate of heaven, speed us.

2. Ave to thee crying
   Gabriel went before us;
   peace do thou restore us,
   Eva's knot untying.

3. Loose the bonds that chain us,
   darkened eyes enlighten,
   clouded prospects brighten,
   heavenly mercies gain us.

4. For thy sons thou carest;
   offer Christ our praying —
   still thy word obeying —
   whom on earth thou barest.

5. Purer, kinder maiden
   God did never fashion;
   pureness and compassion
   grant to hearts sin-laden.

6. From that sin release us,
   shield us, heavenward faring,
   heaven, that is but sharing
   in thy joy with Jesus.

7. Honour, praise and merit
   to our God address we;
   Three in One confess we,
   Father, Son and Spirit.

9th c., tr. R. A. Knox

291

Steal away, steal away,
steal away to Jesus.
Steal away, steal away home.
I ain't got long to stay here.

1. My Lord, he calls me.
   He calls me by the thunder.
   The trumpet sounds within my soul;
   I ain't got long to stay here.

2. Green trees are bending,
   the sinner stands a-trembling.
   The trumpet sounds within my soul;
   I ain't got long to stay here.

3. My Lord, he calls me,
   he calls me by the lightning.
   The trumpet sounds within my soul;
   I ain't got long to stay here.

Negro Spiritual

292

Suffer little children
to come unto me,
for theirs is the kingdom of heaven.
Suffer little children
to come unto me.
for theirs is the kingdom
of the Lord.

1. There came unto him
   children, little children,
   that he might lay his hands
      upon them,
   pray for and bless them,
   children, little children,
   gathered round our Lord.

2. The disciples said:
   "Children, little children,
   leave the Master to his prayer.
   Begone and stay not,
   children, little children,
   gathered round our Lord."

3. But Jesus said:
   "Children, little children,
   stay my blessing to receive.
   Forbid you not that
   children, little children,
   shall gather round the Lord."

4. "For you must be like
   children, little children,
   humble, simple, pure in heart.
   For it is to these
   children, little children,
   the kingdom of heav'n belongs."

Philip Green

293

1. Sweet heart of Jesus,
      fount of love and mercy,
   today we come,
      thy blessing to implore;
   O touch our hearts,
      so cold and so ungrateful,
   and make them, Lord,
      thine own for evermore.

Sweet heart of Jesus, we implore,
O make us love thee more and more.

2. Sweet heart of Jesus,
      make us know and love thee,
   unfold to us
      the treasures of thy grace;
   that so our hearts,
      from things of earth uplifted,
   may long alone
      to gaze upon thy face.

3. Sweet heart of Jesus,
      make us pure and gentle,
   and teach us how
      to do thy blessed will;
   to follow close
      the print of thy dear footsteps,
   and when we fall
      — sweet heart, oh, love us still.

4. Sweet heart of Jesus,
      bless all hearts that love thee,
   and may thine own
      heart ever blessed be,
   bless us, dear Lord,
      and bless the friends we cherish,
   and keep us true
      to Mary and to thee.

Traditional

294

1. Sweet sacrament divine,
   hid in thy earthly home,
   lo! round thy lowly shrine,
   with suppliant hearts we come;
   Jesus, to thee our voice we raise,
   in songs of love and heartfelt praise,
   sweet sacrament divine.

2. Sweet sacrament of peace,
   dear home of every heart,
   where restless yearnings cease,
   and sorrows all depart,
   there in thine ear all trustfully
   we tell our tale of misery,
   sweet sacrament of peace.

3. Sweet sacrament of rest,
   Ark from the ocean's roar,
   within thy shelter blest
   soon may we reach the shore,
   save us, for still the tempest raves;
   save, lest we sink beneath the waves
   sweet sacrament of rest.

4. Sweet sacrament divine,
   earth's light and jubilee,
   in thy far depths doth shine
   thy Godhead's majesty;
   sweet light, so shine on us, we pray,
   that earthly joys may fade away,
   sweet sacrament divine.

   Francis Stanfield (1835-1914)

295

1. Sweet Saviour, bless us ere we go,
   thy word into our minds instil;
   and make our lukewarm hearts to
   glow
   with lowly love and fervent will.

   *Through life's long day
   and death's dark night,
   O gentle Jesus, be our light.*

2. The day is done; its hours have run,
   and thou hast taken count of all,
   the scanty triumphs grace has won,
   the broken vow, the frequent fall.

3. Grant us, dear Lord, from evil ways,
   true absolution and release;
   and bless us more than in past days
   with purity and inward peace.

4. Do more than pardon; give us joy,
   sweet fear and sober liberty,
   and loving hearts without alloy,
   that only long to be like thee.

5. Labour is sweet, for thou hast toiled,
   and care is light, for thou hast cared;
   let not our works with self be soiled.
   Nor in unsimple ways ensnared.

6. For all we love – the poor, the sad,
   the sinful – unto thee we call;
   oh let thy mercy make us glad,
   thou art our Jesus and our all.

   Frederick William Faber (1814-63)

296

1. Take my hands
   and make them as your own,
   and use them for your
   Kingdom here on earth.
   Consecrate them to your care,
   anoint them for
   your service where
   you may need your gospel to be sown.

2. Take my hands.
   They speak now for my heart,
   and by their actions
   they will show their love.
   Guard them on their daily course,
   be their strength
   and guiding force
   to ever serve the Trinity above.

3. Take my hands.
   I give them to you, Lord.
   Prepare them for the
   service of your name.
   Open them to human need
   and by their love
   they'll sow your seed
   so all may know
   the love and hope you give.

   Sebastian Temple

297

Take our bread, we ask you,
take our hearts, we love you,
take our lives, oh Father,
we are yours, we are yours.

1. Yours as we stand
      at the table you set,
   yours as we eat the bread
      our hearts can't forget.
   We are the signs
      of your life with us yet;
   we are yours, we are yours.

2. Your holy people
      stand washed in your blood,
   Spirit filled, yet hungry,
      we await your food.
   Poor though we are,
      we have brought ourselves to you:
   we are yours, we are yours,

Joseph Wise

298

1. Thank you
      for giving me the morning.
   Thank you for ev'ry day that's new.
   Thank you
      that I can know my worries
   can be cast on you.

2. Thank you
      for all my friends and brothers.
   Thank you for all the men that live.
   Thank you
      for even greatest enemies
   I can forgive.

3. Thank you,
      I have my occupation.
   Thank you
      for ev'ry pleasure small.
   Thank you
      for music, light and gladness.
   Thank you for them all.

4. Thank you
      for many little sorrows.
   Thank you for ev'ry kindly word.
   Thank you
      for ev'rywhere your guidance
   reaches ev'ry land.

5. Thank you,
      I see your Word has meaning.
   Thank you, I know your Spirit here.
   Thank you
      because you love all people,
   those both far and near.

6. Thank you,
      O Lord, you spoke unto us.
   Thank you that for our words you care
   Thank you,
      O Lord, you came among us,
   bread and wine to share.

7. Thank you,
      O Lord, your love is boundless.
   Thank you that I am full of you.
   Thank you,
      you made me feel so glad and
   thankful as I do.

Walter van der Haas
and Peter-Paul van Lelyveld

299

1. The bakerwoman
      in her humble lodge
   received a grain of wheat from God.
   For nine whole months
      the grain she stored.
   Behold the handmaid of the Lord.
   Make us the bread, Mary, Mary.
   Make us the bread,
      we need to be fed.

2. The bakerwoman took
      the road which led
   to Bethlehem, the house of bread.
   To knead the bread she laboured
      through the night,
   and brought it forth about midnight.
   Bake us the bread, Mary, Mary.
   Bake us the bread,
      we need to be fed.

3. She baked the bread for thirty years
   by the fire of her love
       and the salt of her tears,
   by the warmth of a heart
       so tender and bright,
   and the bread was golden
       brown and white.
   Bring us the bread, Mary, Mary.
   Bring us the bread,
       we need to be fed.

4. After thirty years
       the bread was done.
   It was taken to town
       by her only son;
   the soft white bread to be given free
   to the hungry people of Galilee.
   Give us the bread, Mary, Mary.
   Give us the bread,
       we need to be fed.

5. For thirty coins the bread was sold,
   and a thousand teeth so cold,
       so cold
   tore it to pieces on a Friday noon
   when the sun turned black
       and red the moon.
   Break us the bread, Mary, Mary.
   Break us the bread,
       we need to be fed.

6. And when she saw
       the bread so white,
   the living bread she had made
       at night,
   devoured as wolves might
       devour a sheep,
   the bakerwoman began to weep.
   Weep for the bread, Mary, Mary.
   Weep for the bread,
       we need to be fed.

7. But the bakerwoman's only son
   appeared to his friends
       when three days had run
   on the road which to Emmaus led,
   and they knew him in
       the breaking of bread.
   Lift up your head, Mary, Mary.
   Lift up your head,
       for now we've been fed.

Hubert Richards

300

1. The Church's one foundation,
   is Jesus Christ, her Lord;
   she is his new creation,
   by water and the Word;
   from heav'n he came and sought her
   to be his holy bride,
   with his own blood he bought her,
   and for her life he died.

2. Elect from every nation,
   yet one o'er all the earth,
   her charter of salvation
   one Lord, one faith, one birth;
   one holy name she blesses,
   partakes one holy food,
   and to one hope she presses,
   with every grace endued.

3. 'Mid toil, and tribulation,
   and tumult of her war,
   she waits the consummation
   of peace for evermore;
   till with the vision glorious
   her longing eyes are blest,
   and the great Church victorious
   shall be the Church at rest.

4. Yet she on earth hath union
   with God the Three in One,
   and mystic sweet communion
   with those whose rest is won:
   O happy ones and holy!
   Lord, give us grace that we
   like them, the meek and lowly
   on high may dwell with thee.

S. J. Stone (1830-1900)

301

1. The coming of our God
   our thoughts must now employ;
   then let us meet him on the road
   with songs of holy joy.

2. The co-eternal Son,
   a maiden's offspring see;
   a servant's form Christ putteth on,
   to set his people free.

3. Daughter of Sion, rise
   to greet thine infant king,
   nor let thy stubborn heart despise
   the pardon he doth bring.

4. In glory from his throne
   again will Christ descend,
   and summon all that are his own
   to joys that never end.

5. Let deeds of darkness fly
   before the approaching morn,
   for unto sin 'tis ours to die,
   and serve the virgin-born.

6. Our joyful praises sing
   to Christ, that set us free;
   like tribute to the Father bring,
   and, Holy Ghost, to thee.

Charles Coffin (1676-1749),
tr. R. Campbell

302

1. The day of resurrection!
   Earth, tell it out abroad;
   the Passover of gladness
   the Passover of God!
   From death to life eternal,
   from earth unto the sky,
   our Christ hath brought us over
   with hymns of victory.

2. Our hearts be pure from evil,
   that we may see aright
   the Lord in rays eternal
   of ressurection-light;
   And listening to his accents,
   may hear so calm and plain
   his own 'All hail' and, hearing,
   may raise the victor strain.

3. Now let the heavens be joyful,
   and earth her song begin,
   the round world keep high triumph,
   and all that is therein;
   Let all things seen and unseen
   their notes of gladness blend,
   for Christ the Lord hath risen,
   our joy that hath no end.

St. John Damascene (c. 750),
tr. J. M. Neale

303

1. The day thou gavest Lord, is ended:
   the darkness falls at thy behest;
   to thee our morning
      hymns ascended;
   thy praise shall sanctify our rest.

2. We thank thee that thy Church
      unsleeping,
   while earth rolls onward into light,
   through all the world her
      watch is keeping,
   and rests not now by day or night.

3. As o'er each continent and island
   the dawn leads on another day,
   the voice of prayer is
      never silent,
   nor dies the strain of praise away.

4. The sun that bids us rest is waking
   our brethren 'neath the western sky
   and hour by hour fresh
      lips are making
   thy wondrous doings heard on high.

5. So be it, Lord; thy throne shall
      never,
   like earth's proud empire, pass away;
   thy kingdom stands, and
      grows for ever,
   till all thy creatures own thy sway.

John Ellerton (1826-93)

304

1. The farmer in the fertile field is
   sowing, sowing.
   The seed is good,
      the shoots of corn are
   growing, growing, growing, growing.

2. An enemy with darnel seed is
   sowing, sowing.
   The weed that fights
      the growing corn is
   choking, choking, choking, choking.

3. Together till the harvest they'll be
   growing, growing.
   But then what has
      been sown we will be
   reaping, reaping, reaping, reaping.

4. The corn is taken to the barn for
   storing, storing.
   The weed is cast
      into the fire for
   burning, burning, burning, burning.

Michael Cockett

305

1. The first Nowell the angel did say
   was to certain poor shepherds in
      fields as they lay:
   in fields where they lay keeping
      their sheep,
   on a cold winter's night that was
      so deep.

   Nowell, Nowell, Nowell, Nowell,
   born is the King of Israel!

2. They looked up and saw a star,
   shining in the east, beyond them
      far,
   and to the earth it gave great light,
   and so it continued both day and
      night.

3. And by the light of that same star,
   three wise men came from country
      far.
   To seek for a king was their intent,
   and to follow the star wherever it
      went.

4. This star drew nigh to the north-
      west,
   o'er Bethlehem it took its rest,
   and there it did both stop and stay
   right over the place where Jesus lay

5. Then entered in those wise men
      three,
   full reverently upon their knee,
   and offered there in his presence,
   their gold and myrrh and
      frankincense.

6. Then let us all with one accord
   sing praises to our heavenly Lord,
   that hath made heaven and earth of
      nought,
   and with his blood mankind hath
      bought.

Traditional Old English

306

1. The God whom earth,
      and sea, and sky,
   adore and laud and magnify,
   who o'er their threefold fabric
                              reigns,
   the Virgin's spotless womb contains.

2. The God whose will
      by moon and sun,
   and all things in due course is done,
   is borne upon a maiden's breast
   by fullest heavenly grace possessed.

3. How blest that mother,
      in whose shrine
   the great Artificer divine,
   whose hand contains the earth and
                                 sky,
   vouchsafed, as in his ark, to lie!

4. Blest, in the message Gabriel brought;
   blest, by the work the Spirit wrought;
   from whom the great desire of earth,
   took human flesh and human birth.

5. All honour, laud and glory be,
   O Jesus, virgin-born, to thee!
   All glory, as is ever meet
   to Father and to Paraclete.

*Ascribed to Venantius Fortunatus
(530-609), tr. J. M. Neale*

307

1. The green life rises from the earth,
   the life of sun and rain and soil,
   in seed and shoot, in grain and grape,
   in food and drink for men.

   *Praise be to God for all his gifts,
   praise for the bread and wine.*

2. The Lord of Spring, the Lord of Life,
   made bread his body, wine his blood.
   The life of earth, the life of God,
   becomes the life of man.

3. We take in hand the bread and wine,
   reminder of the dying Lord.
   This food, this drink, this feast of joy
   gives Christ's own life to us.

4. "The Son of Man must die," said he,
   "my death will raise you all to life.
   No blade is born, no harvest reaped,
   until the seed has died.

5. "These are the signs of death and life,
   the bread you break, the cup you share:
   my dying gift in which I live,
   my death is life to you."

6. Give praise to God who gave this gift,
   his very Son, to bring us life.
   The Father's life in him is ours,
   his Spirit breathes in us.

Luke Connaughton

308

1. The head that once was crowned
                              with thorns
   is crowned with glory now:
   a royal diadem adorns
   the mighty victor's brow.

2. The highest place that heaven
                              affords
   is his, is his by right.
   The King of kings and Lord of lords,
   and heaven's eternal light;

3. The joy of all who dwell above,
   the joy of all below,
   to whom he manifests his love,
   and grants his name to know.

4. To them the cross, with all its shame
   with all its grace is given;
   their name an everlasting name,
   their joy the joy of heaven.

5. They suffer with their Lord below,
   they reign with him above,
   their profit and their joy to know
   the mystery of his love.

6. The cross he bore is life and health,
   though shame and death to him;
   his people's hope, his people's
                              wealth,
   their everlasting theme.

Thomas Kelly (1769-1854)

309

1. The heav'nly Word, proceeding forth
   yet leaving not the Father's side,
   accomplishing his work on earth
   had reached at length life's eventide.

2. By false disciple to be giv'n
   to foemen for his life athirst,
   himself, the very bread of heav'n,
   he gave to his disciples first.

3. He gave himself in either kind,
   he gave his flesh, he gave his blood;
   in love's own fullness thus designed,
   of the whole man to be the food.

4. O saving victim, opening wide
   the gate of heav'n to man below,
   our foes press on from every side;
   thine aid supply, thy strength
                       bestow.

5. To thy great name be endless praise,
   Immortal Godhead, one in three;
   O grant us endless length of days
   in our true native land with thee.

St. Thomas Aquinas (1227-74),
tr. J. M. Neale

310

The King of glory comes
the nation rejoices
open the gates before him,
lift up your voices.

1. Who is the King of glory
   how shall we call him?
   He is Emmanuel,
   the promised of ages.

2. In all of Galilee,
   in city and village,
   he goes among his people,
   curing their illness.

3. Sing then of David's Son,
   our Saviour and brother;
   in all of Galilee
   was never another.

4. He gave his life for us,
   the pledge of salvation.
   He took upon himself
   the sins of the nation.

5. He conquered sin and death;
   he truly has risen.
   And he will share with us
   his heavenly vision.

W. F. Jabusch

311

1. The King of love my Shepherd is,
   whose goodness faileth never;
   I nothing lack if I am his
   and he is mine for ever.

2. Where streams of living water flow
   my ransomed soul he leadeth,
   and where the verdant pastures grow
   with food celestial feedeth.

3. Perverse and foolish oft I strayed
   but yet in love he sought me,
   and on his shoulder gently laid,
   and home, rejoicing, brought me.

4. In death's dark vale I fear no ill
   with thee, dear Lord, beside me;
   thy rod and staff my comfort still,
   thy cross before to guide me.

5. Thou spread'st a table in my sight,
   thy unction grace bestoweth:
   and O what transport of delight
   from thy pure chalice floweth!

6. And so through all the length of
                       days
   thy goodness faileth never;
   good Shepherd, may I sing thy praise
   within thy house for ever.

Henry Williams Baker (1821-77)

312

1. The Lord's my shepherd, I'll not
                       want,
   he makes me down to lie
   in pastures green. He leadeth me
   the quiet waters by.

2. My soul he doth restore again,
   and me to walk doth make
   within the paths of righteousness,
   e'en for his own name's sake.

3. Yea, though I walk in death's dark
vale,
yet will I fear none ill.
For thou art with me, and thy rod
and staff me comfort still.

4. My table thou hast furnishèd
in presence of my foes,
my head thou dost with oil anoint,
and my cup overflows.

5. Goodness and mercy all my life
shall surely follow me.
And in God's house for evermore
my dwelling-place shall be.

Paraphrased from Ps. 22(23)
in the "Scottish Psalter" 1650

313

1. The Mass is ended, all go in peace.
We must diminish,
and Christ increase.
We take him with us
where'er we go
that through our actions
his life may show.

2. We witness his love to ev'ryone
by our communion
with Christ the Son.
We take the Mass to
where men may be,
so Christ may shine forth
for all to see.

3. Thanks to the Father
who shows the way.
His life within us
throughout each day.
Let all our living
and loving be
to praise and honour
the Trinity.

4. The Mass is ended, all go in peace.
We must diminish
and Christ increase.
We take him with us
where'er we go
that through our actions
his life may show.

Sebastian Temple

314

1. The prophet in his hunger
asked for bread.
He asked the poor
and famine was their guest.
They saw starvation
walking in the street,
the doomed who thought
to eat their last and die.

2. It is the Lord
who lights the blinded eye,
who lends the poor his wealth,
the weak his strength,
who feeds us with
his everlasting love,
and pours for men
his justice like strong wine.

3. Because the widow
offered of her last,
and opened to his need
her empty hand,
Elijah promised her:
"You shall not want.
Your larder never shall
be clean of food."

4. The widow and the orphan
are his care;
whom none will else defend,
he will defend:
he puts the strutting pride
of tyrants down,
and raises up the lowly
from the dust.

5. See, in the temple,
how with gestures wide,
the rich men cast
their casual gold to God,
the widow offers
all her dwindling purse,
the pence of poverty —
a richer gift.

Luke Connaughton

315

1. The race that long in darkness pined
   has seen a glorious light:
   the people dwell in day, who dwelt
   in death's surrounding night.

2. To hail thy rise, thou better sun,
   the gathering nations come,
   joyous as when the reapers bear
   the harvest treasures home.

3. To us a child of hope is born,
   to us a Son is given;
   him shall the tribes of earth obey,
   him all the hosts of heaven.

4. His name shall be the Prince of Peace
   for evermore adored,
   the Wonderful, the Counsellor,
   the great and mighty Lord.

5. His power increasing still shall
                              spread,
   his reign no end shall know;
   justice shall guard his throne above,
   and peace abound below.

   John Morison (1749-98)

316

1. There is a green hill far away,
   without a city wall,
   where the dear Lord was crucified
   who died to save us all.

2. We may not know, we cannot tell,
   what pains he had to bear,
   but we believe it was for us
   he hung and suffered there.

3. He died that we might be forgiven,
   he died to make us good;
   that we might go at last to heaven,
   saved by his precious blood.

4. There was no other good enough
   to pay the price of sin;
   he only could unlock the gate
   of heaven, and let us in.

5. O, dearly, dearly has he loved,
   and we must love him too,
   and trust in his redeeming blood,
   and try his works to do.

   Cecil Frances Alexander (1818-95)

317

1. There is a world
       where people come and go
   about their ways and
       never care to know
   that ev'ry step
       they take is placed on roads
   made out of men
       who had to carry loads too hard
       to bear.

   "That world's not ours,"
       that's what we always say.
   "We'll build a new one
       but some other day."
   When will we wake
       from comfort and from ease,
   and strive together
       to create a world of love and peace?

2. There is a world
       where people walk alone,
   and have around them
       men with hearts of stone,
   who would not spare
       one second of their day,
   or spend their breath
       in order just to say: "Your pain
   is mine."

3. There is a world
       where brothers cannot meet
   with one another
       where the tramp of feet
   brings men of ice,
       men who would force apart
   friends of all races
       having but one heart, a heart of
   love.

   Estelle White

318

1. The royal banners forward go,
   the cross shines forth in mystic glow,
   where he in flesh, our flesh who
   made,
   our sentence bore, our ransom paid.

2. There whilst he hung, his sacred side
   by soldier's spear was open'd wide,
   to cleanse us in the precious flood
   of water mingled with his blood.

3. Fulfill'd is now what David told
   in true prophetic song of old,
   how God the heathen's king should
   be;
   for God is reigning from the tree.

4. O tree of glory, tree most fair,
   ordain'd those holy limbs to bear,
   how bright in purple robe it stood,
   the purple of a saviour's blood!

5. Upon its arms, like balance true,
   he weigh'd the price for sinners due,
   the price which none but he could
   pay:
   and spoil'd the spoiler of his prey.

6. To thee, eternal Three in One,
   let homage meet by all be done,
   as by the cross thou dost restore,
   so rule and guide us evermore.

   Venantius Fortunatus (530-609),
   tr. J. M. Neale and others

319

1. The Spirit of the Lord
     is now upon me
   to heal the broken heart
     and set the captives free,
   to open prison doors
     and make the blind to see.
   The Spirit of the Lord
     is now on me.

   Anonymous

320

1. The tree of life grows in Paradise,
   and its roots reach out ev'rywhere:
   to the North, to the South,
     to the East and West
   and all its branches
     praise the living God!

2. The fire of life burns in Paradise,
   and its flames reach out ev'rywhere:
   to the North, to the South,
     to the East and West,
   its warmth and light shall
     praise the living God!

3. The book of life is read in Paradise,
   and its name's called out ev'rywhere:
   to the North, to the South,
     to the East and West,
   and all its pages
     praise the living God!

4. The Lord of life lives in Paradise,
   and his arms reach out ev'rywhere:
   to the North, to the South,
     to the East and West,
   and all his friends shall
     praise the living God!

   James Thiem

321

1. The Virgin Mary had a baby boy,
   the Virgin Mary had a baby boy,
   the Virgin Mary had a baby boy,
   and they said that his name was
                                    Jesus

   He came from the glory,
   he came from the glorious kingdom.
   He came from the glory,
   he came from the glorious kingdom.
   Oh yes, believer,
   Oh yes, believer.
   He came from the glory,
   he came from the glorious kingdom.

2. The angels sang
       when the baby was born . . .
   and proclaimed him
       the Saviour Jesus.

3. The wise men saw
       where the baby was born . . .
   and they saw
       that his name was Jesus.

Traditional West Indian

322

1. The wandering flock of Israel
   is scattered and far
       from home and hope;
   the Shepherd alone,
       with crook and staff,
   can find them and lead
       and keep them safe.

   He made and upheld us,
       granted grace;
   his smile is our peace,
       his word our hope.

2. I walk on the heights,
       I climb and cling,
   the terror beneath,
       the ice aloft.
   I look for his tracks,
       await his hand
   to help and to hold,
       to guide and save.

3. I thirst for his word
       as grass in drought,
   dry, brittle and barren,
       parched and brown;
   no shower can fall,
       no sap rise green
   no hope, if the Lord
       should send no rain.

4. Creator of all,
       your craftman's care
   with fashioning hand
       caressed our clay:
   this vine is the work
       your hands have wrought,
   your love is the sun,
       our soil of growth.

J. Smith

323

1. They hung him on a cross,
       they hung him on a cross,
   they hung him on a cross for me.
   One day when I was lost,
       they hung him on a cross,
   they hung him on a cross for me.

2. They whipped him up the hill, . . .

3. They speared him in the side, . . .

4. The blood came streaming down . . .

5. He hung his head and died, . . .

6. He's coming back again, . . .

Spiritual

324

1. They say I am wise
    and they say I am King.
   I'm a carpenter's son
    and I don't own a thing.
   They say I am rich
    and they say I am poor,
   and when I came knocking
    they bolted the door.

2. They asked me for bread
    and they asked for a sign.
   I gave them some bread
    and I gave them some wine.
   The bread was my body,
    the wine was my blood.
   They still turned away from me
    looking for food.

3. They shouted with joy.
    They laid palms on the road,
   but into the town
    on a donkey I rode.
   They said: "Do not go
    for we can't stand the loss."
   The very next morning
    they gave me a cross.

4. They brought me down low
    though they hung me up high.
   They brought me to life
    though they left me to die.
   They buried me deep
    with a stone at my head,
   but I am the living
    and they are the dead.

Michael Cockett

325

1. This day God gives me
   strength of high heaven,
   sun and moon shining,
    flame in my hearth,
   flashing of lightning,
   wind in its swiftness,
   deeps of the ocean,
    firmness of earth.

2. This day God sends me
   strength as my steersman,
   might to uphold me,
    wisdom as guide.
   Your eyes are watchful,
   your ears are listening,
   your lips are speaking,
    friend at my side.

3. God's way is my way,
   God's shield is round me,
   God's host defends me,
    saving from ill.
   Angels of heaven,
   drive from me always
   all that would harm me,
    stand by me still.

4. Rising, I thank you,
   mighty and strong One,
   King of creation,
    giver of rest,
   firmly confessing
   Threeness of Persons,
   Oneness of Godhead,
    Trinity blest.

Adapted from St. Patrick's Breastplate

James Quinn, S.J.

326

1. This is the image of the queen
   who reigns in bliss above;
   of her who is the hope of men,
   whom men and angels love.
   Most holy Mary, at thy feet
   I bend a suppliant knee;
   in this thy own sweet month of May,
   do thou remember me.

2. The homage offered at the feet
   of Mary's image here
   to Mary's self at once ascends
   above the starry sphere.
   Most holy Mary, at thy feet
   I bend a suppliant knee;
   in all my joy, in all my pain,
   do thou remember me.

3. How fair soever be the form
   which here your eyes behold,
   its beauty is by Mary's self
   excell'd a thousandfold.
   Most holy Mary, at thy feet,
   I bend a suppliant knee;
   in my temptations each and all,
   do thou remember me.

4. Sweet are the flow'rets we have
                             culled,
   this image to adorn;
   but sweeter far is Mary's self,
   that rose without a thorn.
   Most holy Mary, at thy feet
   I bend a suppliant knee;
   when on the bed of death I lie,
   do thou remember me.

5. O lady, by the stars that make
   a glory round thy head;
   and by the pure uplifted hands,
   that for thy children plead;
   when at the judgment-seat I stand,
   and my dread saviour see;
   when waves of night around me roll
   O then remember me.

Edward Caswall (1814-78)

327

1. This is my will,
   my one command,
   that love should dwell
   among you all.
   This my will
   that you should love
   as I have shown
   that I love you.

2. No greater love
   a man can have
   than that he die
   to save his friends.
   You are my friends
   if you obey
   all I command
   that you should do.

3. I call you now
   no longer slaves;
   no slave knows all
   his master does.
   I call you friends,
   for all I hear
   my Father say
   you hear from me.

4. You chose not me,
   but I chose you,
   that you should go
   and bear much fruit.
   I called you out
   that you in me
   should bear much fruit
   that will abide.

5. All that you ask
   my Father dear
   for my name's sake
   you shall receive.
   This is my will,
   my one command,
   that love should dwell
   in each, in all.

James Quinn S.J.

328

1. This joyful Eastertide,
   away with sin and sorrow,
   my love, the Crucified,
   hath sprung to life this morrow:

   Had Christ, that once was slain,
   ne'er burst his three-day prison,
   our faith had been in vain:
   but now hath Christ arisen.

2. My flesh in hope shall rest,
   and for a season slumber:
   till trump from east to west
   shall wake the dead in number:

3. Death's flood hath lost his chill,
   since Jesus crossed the river:
   lover of souls, from ill
   my passing soul deliver:

   George Ratclife Woodward
   (1849-1934)

2. On Monday he
      gave me the gift of love,
   Tuesday peace came from above.
   On Wednesday he
      told me to have more faith,
   on Thursday he
      gave me a little more grace.
   Friday he told me just to
      watch and pray,
   Saturday he told me just
      what to say.
   On Sunday he gave me
      the power divine
   to let my little light shine.

   Traditional

329

This little light of mine,
I'm gonna let it shine.
This little light of mine,
I'm gonna let it shine.
This little light of mine,
I'm gonna let it shine,
let it shine, let it shine, let it shine.

1. The light that shines
      is the light of love,
   lights the darkness from above.
   It shines on me
      and it shines on you,
   and shows what the
      power of love can do.
   I'm gonna shine my light
      both far and near,
   I'm gonna shine my light
      both bright and clear.
   Where there's a dark corner
      in this land
   I'm gonna let my little light shine.

330

1. Thou wilt keep him in perfect peace,
   thou wilt keep him in perfect peace,
   thou wilt keep him in perfect peace
   whose mind is stayed on thee.

2. Marvel not, I say unto you,
   marvel not, I say unto you,
   marvel not, I say unto you,
   you must be born again.

3. Though your sins as scarlet be,
   though your sins as scarlet be,
   though your sins as scarlet be,
   they shall be white as snow.

4. If the Son shall set you free,
   if the Son shall set you free,
   • if the Son shall set you free,
   you shall be free indeed.

   Anonymous

331

1. Thy hand, O God, has guided
   thy flock from age to age;
   the wondrous tale is written,
   full clear, on ev'ry page;
   our fathers owned thy goodness,
   and we their deeds record;
   and both of this bear witness:
   one Church, one Faith, one Lord.

2. Thy heralds brought glad tidings
   to greatest, as to least;
   they bade men rise, and hasten
   to share the great king's feast;
   and this was all their teaching,
   in every deed and word,
   to all alike proclaiming
   one Church, one Faith, one Lord.

3. When shadows thick were falling,
   and all seemed sunk in night,
   thou, Lord, didst send thy servants,
   thy chosen sons of light.
   On them and on thy people
   thy plenteous grace was poured,
   and this was still their message:
   one Church, one Faith, one Lord.

4. Through many a day of darkness,
   through many a scene of strife,
   the faithful few fought bravely,
   to guard the nation's life.
   Their gospel of redemption,
   sin pardoned, man restored,
   was all in this enfolded:
   one Church, one Faith, one Lord.

5. And we, shall we be faithless?
   Shall hearts fail, hands hang down?
   Shall we evade the conflict,
   and cast away our crown?
   Not so: in God's deep counsels
   some better thing is stored;
   we will maintain, unflinching,
   one Church, one Faith, one Lord.

6. Thy mercy will not fail us,
   nor leave thy work undone;
   with thy right hand to help us
   the vict'ry shall be won;
   and then, by men and angels
   thy name shall be adored.
   And this shall be their anthem:
   one Church, one Faith, one Lord.

E. H. Plumptre (1821-91)

332

1. To Christ the Lord of worlds we
   sing,
   the nations' universal king.
   Hail, conqu'ring Christ, whose reign
   alone
   over our hearts and souls we own.

2. Christ, who art known the prince of
   peace,
   bid all rebellious tumults cease;
   call home thy straying sheep, and
   hold
   for ever in one faithful fold.

3. For this, thine arms, on Calvary,
   were stretched across th' empurpled
   tree,
   and the sharp spear that through
   thee ran
   laid bare the heart that burned for
   man.

4. For this, in forms of bread and wine
   lies hid the plenitude divine,
   and from thy wounded body runs
   the stream of life to all thy sons.

5. May those who rule o'er men below
   thee for their greater sovereign
   know,
   and human wisdom, arts, and laws,
   in thee repose as in their cause.

6. Let kingly signs of pomp and state
   unto thy name be dedicate,
   city and hearth and household be
   under thy gentle sceptre free.

7. Praise be to Christ, whose name and
                              throne
   o'er every throne and name we own;
   and equal praises still repeat
   the Father and the Paraclete.

   Roman Breviary, tr. W. H. Shewring

333

1. To Christ, the Prince of peace,
   and Son of God most high,
   the father of the world to come,
   sing we with holy joy.

2. Deep in his heart for us
   the wound of love he bore;
   that love wherewith he still inflames
   the hearts that him adore.

3. O Jesu, victim blest,
   what else but love divine
   could thee constrain to open thus
   that sacred heart of thine?

4. O fount of endless life,
   O spring of water clear,
   O flame celestial, cleansing all
   who unto thee draw near!

5. Hide us in thy dear heart,
   for thither we do fly;
   there seek thy grace through life, in
                                   death
   thine immortality.

6. Praise to the Father be,
   and sole-begotten Son;
   praise, holy Paraclete, to thee
   while endless ages run.

   Catholicum Hymnologium
   Germanicum (1587) tr. E. Caswall

334

1. To Jesus' Heart, all burning
   with fervent love for men,
   my heart with fondest yearning
   shall raise its joyful strain.

   While ages course along,
   blest be with loudest song
   the sacred heart of Jesus
   by ev'ry heart and tongue.
   The sacred heart of Jesus
   by ev'ry heart and tongue.

2. O Heart, for me on fire
   with love no man can speak,
   my yet untold desire
   God gives me for thy sake.

3. Too true, I have forsaken
   thy love for wilful sin;
   yet now let me be taken
   back by thy grace again.

4. As thou are meek and lowly,
   and ever pure of heart,
   so may my heart be wholly
   of thine the counterpart.

5. When life away is flying,
   and earth's false glare is done;
   still, sacred Heart, in dying
   I'll say I'm all thine own.

   Aloys Schlor (1805-52),
   tr. A. J. Christie

335

1. To the name that brings salvation
   honour, worship, laud we pay:
   that for many a generation
   hid in God's foreknowledge lay;
   but to ev'ry tongue and nation
   Holy Church proclaims today.

2. Name of gladness, name of pleasure,
   by the tongue ineffable,
   name of sweetness passing measure,
   to the ear delectable;
   'tis our safeguard and our treasure,
   'tis our help 'gainst sin and hell.

3. 'Tis the name of adoration,
   'tis the name of victory;
   'tis the name for meditation
   in the vale of misery;
   'tis the name for veneration
   by the citizens on high.

4. 'Tis the name by right exalted
   over every other name:
   that when we are sore assaulted
   puts our enemies to shame:
   strength to them that else had
   halted,
   eyes to blind, and feet to lame.

5. Jesu, we thy name adoring,
   long to see thee as thou art:
   of thy clemency imploring
   so to write it in our heart,
   that hereafter, upward soaring,
   we with angels may have part.

   15th c., tr. J. M. Neale

336

1. Trust is in the eyes
   of a tiny babe
   leaning on his mother's breast.
   In the eager beat
   of a young bird's wings
   on the day it leaves the nest.

   It is the living Spirit
   filling the earth, bringing to birth
   a world of love and laughter,
   joy in the light of the Lord.

2. Hope is in the rain
   that makes crystal streams
   tumble down a mountain side,
   and in every man
   who repairs his nets,
   waiting for the rising tide.

3. Love is in the hearts
   of all those who seek
   freedom for the human race.
   Love is in the touch
   of the hand that heals,
   and the smile that lights a face.

4. Strength is in the wind
   as it bends the trees,
   warmth is in the bright red flame,
   light is in the sun
   and the candle-glow,
   cleansing are the ocean's waves.

337 *Estelle White*

1. Unto us is born a Son,
   King of quires supernal;
   see on earth his life begun,
   of lords the Lord eternal,
   of lords the Lord eternal.

2. Christ, from heav'n descending low,
   comes on earth a stranger:
   ox and ass their owner know
   becradled in a manger,
   becradled in a manger.

3. This did Herod sore affray,
   and grievously bewilder:
   so he gave the word to slay,
   and slew the little childer,
   and slew the little childer.

4. Of his love and mercy mild
   this the Christmas story,
   and O that Mary's gentle Child
   might lead us up to glory!
   Might lead us up to glory!

5. O and A and A and O
   cum cantibus in choro,
   let the merry organ go,
   Benedicamus Domino,
   Benedicamus Domino.

   15th c., tr. G. R. Woodward

338

1. Vaster far than any ocean,
   deeper than the deepest sea
   is the love of Christ my Saviour,
   reaching through eternity.

2. But my sins are truly many,
   is God's grace so vast, so deep?
   Yes, there's grace o'er sin
                     abounding,
   grace to pardon, grace to keep.

3. Can he quench my thirst for ever?
   Will his Spirit strength impart?
   Yes, he gives me living water
   springing up within my heart.

Author unknown

339

1. Virgin, wholly marvellous,
   who didst bear God's Son for us,
   worthless is my tongue and weak
   of thy purity to speak.

2. Who can praise thee as he ought?
   Gifts, with every blessing fraught,
   gifts that bring the gifted life,
   thou didst grant us, Maiden-Wife.

3. God became thy lowly Son,
   made himself thy little one,
   raising men to tell thy worth
   high in heav'n as here on earth.

4. Heav'n and earth, and all that is
   thrill today with ecstasies,
   chanting glory unto thee,
   singing praise with festal glee.

5. Cherubim with fourfold face,
   are no peers of thine in grace;
   and the six-wing'd seraphim
   shine, amid thy splendour, dim.

6. Purer art thou than are all
   heav'nly hosts angelical,
   who delight with pomp and state
   on thy beauteous Child to wait.

St. Ephrem Syrus (c. 307-373),
tr. J. W. Atkinson

340

Walk with me, oh my Lord,
through the darkest night
     and brightest day.
Be at my side, oh Lord,
hold my hand
     and guide me on my way.

1. Sometimes the road seems long,
   my energy is spent.
   Then, Lord, I think of you
   and I am given strength.

2. Stones often bar my path
   and there are times I fall,
   but you are always there
   to help me when I call.

3. Just as you calmed the wind
   and walked upon the sea,
   conquer, my living Lord,
   the storms that threaten me.

4. Help me to pierce the mists
   that cloud my heart and mind
   so that I shall not fear
   the steepest mountain-side.

5. As once you healed the lame
   and gave sight to the blind,
   help me when I'm downcast
   to hold my head up high.

Estelle White

341

1. We are gathering together unto him.
   We are gathering together unto him.
   Unto him shall the gath'ring
      of the people be.
   We are gathering together unto him.

2. We are offering together unto him.
   We are offering together unto him.
   Unto him shall the offering
      of the people be.
   We are offering together unto him.

3. We are singing together unto him.
   We are singing together unto him.
   Unto him shall the singing
      of the people be.
   We are singing together unto him.

4. We are praying together unto him.
   We are praying together unto him.
   Unto him shall the praying
      of the people be.
   We are praying together unto him.

Anonymous

342

1. We are one in the Spirit,
   we are one in the Lord,
   we are one in the Spirit
   we are one in the Lord,
   and we pray that all unity
   may one day be restored.

   *And they'll know we are Christians
   by our love, by our love,
   yes, they'll know we are Christians
   by our love.*

2. We will walk with each other,
   we will walk hand in hand.
   We will walk with each other,
   we will walk hand in hand.
   And together we'll spread the news
   that God is in our land.

3. We will work with each other,
   we will work side by side.
   We will work with each other,
   we will work side by side.
   And we'll guard each man's dignity
   and save each man's pride.

4. All praise to the Father
   from whom all things come,
   and all praise to Christ Jesus,
   his only Son,
   and all praise to the Spirit
   who makes us one.

Peter Scholtes

343

1. We bring our gifts to the Lord,
      our God.
   We bring our gifts to the Lord,
      our God.

2. We bring our love to the Lord,
      our God.
   We bring our love to the Lord,
      our God.

3. We bring ourselves to the Lord,
      our God.
   We bring ourselves to the Lord,
      our God.

Estelle White

344

1. We celebrate this festive day
   with pray'r and joyful song.
   Our Father's house is home to us,
   we know that we belong.

   *The bread is broken, wine is poured,
   a feast to lift us up!
   Then thank the Lord who gives
                           himself
   as food and saving cup!*

2. The door is open, enter in
   and take your place by right.
   For you've been chosen as his guest
   to share his love and light.

3. We come together as the twelve
came to the Upper Room.
Our host is Jesus Christ the Lord,
now risen from the tomb.

4. Who travels needs both food and
drink
to help him on his way.
Refreshed and strong we'll journey
on
and face another day.

5. Who shares this meal receives the
Lord
who lives, though he was dead.
So death can hold no terrors now
for those who eat this bread.

Willard F. Jabusch

345

1. We gather together
as brothers and sisters
for Jesus our Lord truly lives.
He's risen in glory;
the full gospel story,
what freedom and courage it gives.

*He binds up the wounded
and the broken.
He gives the poor his chalice
and his bread.
The Father has raised him,
together we'll praise him,
and march with the Lord
at our head.*

2. For mother and father,
for sister and brother,
for children and husband and wife,
his Word spreads like flame,
for all people came,
bringing peace and the seeds of new
life.

3. God takes what is foolish,
he chooses the weakest
to put wise and strong both to
shame.
Give thanks to the Father,
we live in Christ Jesus,
bow low and sing sweetly his name.

Willard F. Jabusch

346

1. We plough the fields and scatter
the good seed on the land,
but it is fed and watered
by God's almighty hand;
he sends the snow in winter,
the warmth to swell the grain,
the breezes and the sunshine,
and soft refreshing rain.

*All good gifts around us
are sent from heav'n above,
then thank the Lord,
O thank the Lord for all his love.*

2. He only is the maker
of all things near and far;
he paints the wayside flower,
he lights the ev'ning star.
The winds and waves obey him,
by him the birds are fed:
much more to us his children,
he gives our daily bread.

3. We thank thee then, O Father,
for all things bright and good:
the seed-time and the harvest,
our life, our health, our food.
No gifts have we to offer
for all thy love imparts,
but that which thou desirest,
our humble, thankful hearts.

*M. Claudius (1740-1815),
tr. J. M. Campbell*

347

1. Were you there
    when they crucified my Lord?
 Were you there
    when they crucified my Lord?
 Oh sometimes it causes me
    to tremble, tremble, tremble.
 Were you there
    when they crucified my Lord?

2. Were you there
    when they nailed him to a tree? . . .

3. Were you there
    when they pierced him in the side?

4. Were you there
    when the sun refused to shine? . . .

5. Were you there
    when they laid him in the tomb? . .

6. Were you there
    when he rose from out the tomb? .

Negro Spiritual

348

1. We shall overcome,
    we shall overcome,
    we shall overcome some day.
 Oh, deep in my heart I do believe
    that we shall overcome some day.

2. We'll walk hand in hand . . .

3. We shall live in peace . . .

4. We shall live with him . . .

Traditional

349

1. We three Kings of Orient are;
    bearing gifts we traverse afar,
    field and fountain, moor and
                                mountain,
    following yonder star.

 O Star of wonder, star of night,
 star with royal beauty bright,
 westward leading, still proceeding,
 guide us to thy perfect light.

2. Born a King on Bethlehem plain,
    gold I bring, to crown him again,
    King for ever, ceasing never,
    over us all to reign.

3. Frankincense to offer have I,
    Incense owns a Deity nigh.
    Prayer and praising, all men raising,
    worship him, God most high.

4. Myrrh is mine, its bitter perfume
    breathes a life of gathering gloom;
    sorrowing, sighing, bleeding, dying,
    sealed in the stone-cold tomb.

5. Glorious now behold him arise,
    King and God and sacrifice;
    alleluia, alleluia,
    earth to heaven replies.

 John Henry Hopkins (1822-1900)

350

1. We will walk through the valley
    in the shadow of death.
 We will walk through the darkness
    without fear.
 Though the night may be long,
    the dark enclosing,
 we know Jesus,
    our morning light is near.

2. He has walked through the valley
    of the shadow of death,
 he has walked through the night of
    fear alone.
 Though the darkness had gathered
    to destroy him
 he was there at
    the rising of the sun.

3. We will walk in the glory
    of the bright morning sun,
 we will walk in the light that
    guides our way.
 For with Jesus the lord of
    light beside us
 we will walk in
    the glory of the day.

 Michael Cockett

351

1. What can we offer you,
   Lord our God?
   How can we worship you
   as you deserve?
   We can only offer
   what our lips do proclaim.
   We can only offer you
   humble acts of praise.
   But we offer this with Jesus
   our brother, Jesus your Son.
   We join with him,
   glory to you, O God!
   We join with him,
   glory to you, O God!

2. What can we offer you,
   Lord our God?
   How can we thank you
   for all that you've done?
   We can only say it,
   Lord God, we thank you so.
   We can only try to live
   grateful lives, O Lord.
   But we offer this with Jesus,
   our brother, Jesus your Son.
   We join with him,
   our thanks to you, O God.
   We join with him,
   our thanks to you, O God.

3. What can we offer you,
   Lord our God?
   How do we prove we are
   truly sorry, Lord?
   We can say it often,
   God, sorry that we are.
   We can try to prove it,
   Lord, by the way we live.
   And we offer this with Jesus,
   our brother, Jesus, your Son.
   We join with him,
   forgive our sins, O God.
   We join with him,
   forgive our sins, O God.

4. What can we offer you,
   Lord our God?
   Dare we present you with
   another call for help?
   We just have to say it,
   Lord God, we need you so.
   We just have to beg you,
   Lord, take us by the hand.
   And we offer this with Jesus,
   our brother, Jesus, your Son.
   We join with him,
   Lord, we need you so.
   We join with him,
   Lord, we need you so.

Tom Shelley

352

*Whatsoever you do
to the least of my brothers,
that you do unto me.*

1. When I was hungry
   you gave me to eat.
   When I was thirsty
   you gave me to drink.
   Now enter into the
   home of my Father.

2. When I was homeless
   you opened your door.
   When I was naked
   you gave me your coat.
   Now enter into the
   home of my Father.

3. When I was weary
   you helped me find rest.
   When I was anxious
   you calmed all my fears.
   Now enter into the
   home of my Father.

4. When in a prison
   you came to my cell.
   When on a sick bed
   you cared for my needs.
   Now enter into the
   home of my Father.

5. Hurt in a battle
   you bound up my wounds.
   Searching for kindness
   you held out your hands.
   Now enter into the
   home of my Father.

6. When I was Negro
   or Chinese or White,
   mocked and insulted,
   you carried my cross.
   Now enter into the
   home of my Father.

7. When I was aged
   you bothered to smile.
   When I was restless
   you listened and cared.
   Now enter into the
   home of my Father.

8. When I was laughed at
   you stood by my side.
   When I was happy
   you shared in my joy.
   Now enter into the
   home of my Father.

W. F. Jabusch

353

1. When I needed a neighbour
      were you there were you there?
   When I needed a neighbour
      were you there?
   And the creed and the colour
      and the name won't matter
      were you there?

2. I was hungry and thirsty, . . .

3. I was cold, I was naked, . . .

4. When I needed a shelter, . . .

5. When I needed a healer, . . .

6. Wherever you travel,
      I'll be there I'll be there.
   Wherever you travel, I'll be there.
   And the creed and the colour
      and the name won't matter,
      I'll be there.

Sydney Carter

354

1. When Israel was in Egypt's land,
   let my people go,
   oppressed so hard they could not
                                    stand,
   let my people go.

   Go down, Moses,
   way down in Egypt's land.
   Tell old Pharoah
   to let my people go.

2. The Lord told Moses what to do,
   let my people go,
   to lead the children of Israel
                                 through,
   let my people go.

3. Your foes shall not before you stand,
   let my people go,
   and you'll possess fair Canaan's land,
   let my people go.

4. O let us all from bondage flee,
   let my people go,
   and let us all in Christ be free,
   let my people go.

5. I do believe without a doubt,
   let my people go,
   a Christian has a right to shout,
   let my people go.

Negro Spiritual

355

1. When I survey the wondrous cross
   on which the Prince of Glory died,
   my richest gain I count but loss,
   and pour contempt on all my pride.

2. Forbid it, Lord, that I should boast,
   save in the death of Christ, my God:
   all the vain things that charm me
                                      most,
   I sacrifice them to his blood.

3. See from his head, his hands, his
                                    feet,
   sorrow and love flow mingled down:
   did e'er such love and sorrow meet,
   or thorns compose so rich a crown?

4. Were the whole realm of nature
                                    mine,
   that were an offering far too small;
   love so amazing, so divine,
   demands my soul, my life, my all.

                    Isaac Watts (1674-1748)

356

Where are you bound, Mary, Mary?
Where are you bound,
   Mother of God?

1. Beauty is a dove
      sitting on a sunlit bough,
   beauty is a pray'r
      without the need of words.
   Words are more than sounds
      falling off an empty tongue:
   Let it be according to his word.

2. Mary heard the word
      spoken in her inmost heart;
   Mary bore the Word
      and held him in her arms.
   Sorrow she has known,
      seeing him upon the cross
   – greater joy to see him rise again.

3. Where are we all bound,
      carrying the Word of God?
   Time and place are ours
      to make his glory known.
   Mary bore him first,
      we will tell the whole wide world:
   Let it be according to his word.

                              John Glynn

357

1. Where does the wind come from?
      Where is it going?
   You see the swaying tree,
   and all the grasses blowing.

You know the wind is there,
   but where?
There is no knowing.

2. Whence does the Spirit come?
   Where is his dwelling?
   You see the weary world
      so wilful, so rebelling.
   But still the Spirit breathes,
      and where,
   there is no telling.

                    Sister Mary Oswin

358

1. Where is love and loving-kindness,
      God is fain to dwell.
   Flock of Christ, who loved us,
      in one fold containèd,
   joy and mirth be ours, for mirth
      and joy he giveth,
   fear we still and love the God who
      ever liveth,
   each to other joined by charity
      unfeignèd.

2. Where is love and loving-kindness,
      God is fain to dwell.
   Therefore, when we meet, the
      flock of Christ, so loving,
   take we heed lest bitterness be
      there engendered;
   all our spiteful thoughts and
      quarrels be surrendered,
   seeing Christ is there, divine
      among us moving.

3. Where is love and loving-kindness,
      God is fain to dwell.
   So may we be gathered once
      again, beholding
   glorified the glory, Christ, of
      thy unveiling,
   there, where never ending joy,
      and never failing
   age succeeds to age eternally
      unfolding.

From the Office of the Mandatum,
                    tr. R. A. Knox

359

1. Where would we be
      without Christ our Lord?
   We would be lost
      and walking in darkness
   He is the lantern
      that lights up that darkness
   and he is the shepherd
      who finds the right path.

   So let the trumpet sound to the
      glory of God.
   He is our Lord, loving and wise.

2. Where would we be
      without Christ our Lord?
   We would be left
      to wander the desert.
   He is the beacon
      that leads us to safety,
   and he is the water
      that brings us new life.

3. Where would we be
      without Christ our Lord?
   We would be cold
      and starving and thirsty.
   He is the bread
      that is food for the spirit,
   and he is the wine of
      the new covenant.

4. Where would we be
      without Christ our Lord?
   He is the Son
      who saves all the nations.
   Through Christ the Son
      we are given the Spirit,
   and this is the Spirit
      who brings us new life.

   Michael Cockett

360

1. While shepherds watched
      their flocks by night,
   all seated on the ground,
   the Angel of the Lord came down,
   and glory shone around.

2. "Fear not," said he,
   (for mighty dread
   had seized their troubled mind)
   "Glad tidings of great joy I bring
   to you and all mankind.

3. "To you in David's
      town this day
   is born of David's line
   a Saviour, who is Christ the Lord;
   and this shall be the sign:

4. "The heavenly Babe
   you there shall find
   to human view displayed,
   all meanly wrapped in swathing
                              bands,
   and in a manger laid."

5. Thus spake the Seraph;
   and forthwith
   appeared a shining throng
   of Angels praising God, who thus
   addressed their joyful song:

6. "All glory be
   to God on high,
   and on the earth be peace,
   goodwill henceforth from heaven
                              to men
   begin and never cease".

   Nahum Tate (1652-1715)

361

With a song in our hearts
we shall go on our way,
to bring God's love to ev'ryone
we meet today.

Love, love, love is his name.
Love, love, love is his name.
Great, great, great is his name.
Great, great, great is his name.

With a . . .

Estelle White

362

Yahweh,
you are my strength and salvation.
Yahweh,
you are my rock and my shield.

1. When foes inside my soul
   assailed me,
   he heard my cry for help
   and came to my aid.

2. He bent the heav'ns and came
   in thunder.
   He flew to me and soared
   on wings of the wind.

3. The depths within my mind
   he showed me,
   the hidden thoughts that I
   did not know were there.

4. His arm stretched from on high
   and held me.
   He drew me from the deep,
   wild waters of self.

5. He is the lamp who lights
   the darkness.
   He guides me as I leap
   the ramparts of life.

6. I raise my voice and sing
   his glory.
   With all my heart I praise
   the God of my joy.

Estelle White

363

1. Ye choirs of new Jerusalem,
   your sweetest notes employ,
   the Paschal victory to hymn
   in strains of holy joy.

2. How Judah's Lion burst his chains,
   and crushed the serpent's head;
   and brought with him, from death's
                              domain,
   the long-imprisoned dead.

3. From hell's devouring jaws the prey
   alone our leader bore;
   his ransomed hosts pursue their way
   where he hath gone before.

4. Triumphant in his glory now
   his sceptre ruleth all:
   earth, heaven, and hell before him
                              bow
   and at his footstool fall.

5. While joyful thus his praise we sing,
   his mercy we implore,
   into his palace bright to bring,
   and keep us evermore.

6. All glory to the Father be,
   all glory to the Son,
   all glory, Holy Ghost, to thee,
   while endless ages run.

St. Fulbert of Chartres (c.1000),
tr. R. Campbell

364

1. Ye sons and daughters of the Lord!
   the king of glory, king adored,
   this day himself from death restored.

Alleluia!

2. All in the early
       morning grey
   went holy women
       on their way
   to see the tomb where Jesus lay.

3. Of spices pure
       a precious store
   in their pure hands
       those women bore,
   to anoint the sacred body o'er.

4. Then straightaway one
      in white they see,
   who saith, "Ye seek
      the Lord; but he
   is risen, and gone to Galilee".

5. This told they Peter,
      told they John;
   who forthwith to
      to the tomb are gone,
   but Peter is by John outrun.

6. That self-same night,
      while out of fear
   the doors were shut,
      their Lord most dear
   to his apostles did appear.

7. But Thomas, when
      of this he heard,
   was doubtful of
      his brethren's word;
   wherefore again
      there comes the Lord.

8. "Thomas, behold my side,"
      saith he;
   "My hands, my feet,
      my body see,
   and doubt not, but believe in me".

9. When Thomas saw
      that wounded side,
   the truth no longer
      he denied;
   "Thou art my Lord
      and God!" he cried.

10. Now let us praise
      the Lord most high,
   and strive his name
      to magnify
   on this great day,
      through earth and sky.

11. Whose mercy ever
      runneth o'er,
   whom men and angel
      hosts adore;
   to him be glory evermore.

17th c., tr. E. Caswall

365

1. Ye who own the faith of Jesus
   sing the wonders that were done,
   when the love of God the Father
   o'er our sin the victory won,
   when he made the Virgin Mary
   Mother of his only Son.

Hail, Mary, full of grace.

2. Blessed were the chosen people
   out of whom the Lord did come,
   blessèd was the land of promise
   fashioned for his earthly home;
   but more blessèd far the mother
   she who bore him in her womb.

3. Wherefore let all faithful people
   tell the honour of her name,
   let the Church in her foreshadowed
   part in her thanksgiving claim;
   what Christ's mother sang in
                              gladness
   let Christ's people sing the same

4. May the Mother's intercessions
   on our homes a blessing win,
   that the children all be prospered
   strong and fair and pure within,
   following our Lord's own footsteps,
   firm in faith and free from sin.

5. For the sick and for the aged,
   for our dear ones far away,
   for the hearts that mourn in secret,
   all who need our prayers today,
   for the faithful gone before us,
   may the holy Virgin pray.

6. Praise, O Mary, praise the Father,
   praise thy Saviour and thy Son,
   praise the everlasting Spirit,
   who hath made thee ark and throne.
   O'er all creatures high exalted,
   lowly praise the three in one.

V. S. S. Coles (1845-1929)

366 AMERICAN EUCHARIST

Lord, have mercy

Lord, have mercy.
   Lord, have mercy,
on your servants, Lord, have mercy.
God Almighty, just and faithful,
Lord have mercy.
   Lord, have mercy.

Christ, have mercy.
   Christ, have mercy,
gift from heaven, Christ have mercy.
Light of truth, and light of justice,
Christ, have mercy.
   Christ have mercy.

Lord, have mercy.
   Lord, have mercy,
on your servants, Lord, have mercy.
God almighty, just and faithful,
Lord, have mercy.
   Lord, have mercy.

Holy, holy, holy

Holy, holy, holy, holy,
Lord of hosts. You fill with glory
all the earth and all the heavens.
Sing hosanna, sing hosanna.

Blest and holy, blest and holy
he who comes now in the Lord's
                   name.
In the highest sing hosanna,
in the highest sing hosanna.

Lamb of God

Jesus, Lamb of God, have mercy,
bearer of our sins, have mercy.
Jesus, Lamb of God, have mercy,
bearer of our sins, have mercy.

Saviour of the world, Lord Jesus,
may your peace be with us always.
Saviour of the world, Lord Jesus,
may your peace be with us always.

Sandra Joan Billington

367 ISRAELI MASS

Lord, have mercy

Lord, have mercy.
   Lord, have mercy.
Lord, have mercy on us all.
Lord, have mercy.
   Lord, have mercy
Lord, have mercy on us all.

Christ, have mercy.
   Christ, have mercy.
Christ, have mercy on us all.
Christ, have mercy.
   Christ, have mercy.
Christ, have mercy on us all.

Lord, have mercy.
   Lord, have mercy.
Lord, have mercy on us all.
Lord, have mercy.
   Lord, have mercy.
Lord, have mercy on us all.

Holy, holy, holy

Holy, holy, holy, holy
Lord of power, Lord of might.
Heav'n and earth are filled with
                   glory.
 Sing hosanna evermore.

Blest and holy, blest and holy
he who comes from God on high.
Raise your voices, sing his glory,
praise his name for evermore.

Lamb of God

Lamb of God,
   you take away the sin,
the sin of all the world.
Give us mercy,
   give us mercy,
give us mercy, Lamb of God.
                (Repeat)
Lamb of God,
   you take away the sin,
the sin of all the world.
Grant us peace, Lord,
   grant us peace, Lord,
grant us peace, O Lamb of God.

Anthony Hamson

368 GEORDIE MASS

Lord have mercy
Lord, have mercy on us all.
Lord, have mercy on us.
Lord, have mercy on us all.
Lord, have mercy on us.

Christ, have mercy on us all.
Christ, have mercy on us.
Christ, have mercy on us all.
Christ, have mercy on us.

Lord, have mercy on us all.
Lord, have mercy on us.
Lord, have mercy on us all.
Lord, have mercy on us.

Holy, holy, holy
Holy, holy, holy Lord
God of might and God of pow'r.
Glory fills all heav'n and earth.
Sing to him hosanna!

Blessed is the one who comes
in the name of Christ our Lord.
Holy, holy, holy Lord.
Sing to him hosanna!

Lamb of God
Lamb of God, you take our sins,
take away our sins, Lord.
So have mercy on us all,
so have mercy on us.   *(Repeat)*

Lamb of God, you take our sins,
take away our sins, Lord.
Grant us peace, O grant us peace,
grant us peace for ever.

Anthony Hamson

369 MONMOUTHSHIRE MASS

Lord, have mercy
Lord, have mercy on us all.
Lord, have mercy on us.
Lord, have mercy on us all.
Lord, have mercy on us.

Christ, have mercy on us all.
Christ have mercy on us.
Christ, have mercy on us all
Christ have mercy on us.

Lord, have mercy on us all.
Lord, have mercy on us.
Lord, have mercy on us all.
Lord, have mercy on us.

Holy, holy, holy
Holy, holy, holy Lord,
God of might and power.
Glory fills all heav'n and earth.
Sing to him hosanna!

Blessed is the one who comes
bringing this great glory.
Praise and honour be to God.
Sing to him hosanna!

Lamb of God
Lamb of God, you take away
the sin of all the world.
Lamb of God, you take away
the sin of all the world.

Lamb of God, you take away
the sin of all the world.
Grant us peace, O Lamb of God,
grant us peace for ever.

Anthony Hamson

370 SWEDISH MASS

Lord, have mercy
Lord, have mercy on us all.
Lord, have mercy on us.
Lord, have mercy on us all.
Lord, have mercy on us.

Christ, have mercy on us all.
Christ, have mercy on us.
Christ, have mercy on us all.
Christ, have mercy on us.

Lord, have mercy on us all.
Lord, have mercy on us.
Lord, have mercy on us all.
Lord, have mercy on us.

Holy, holy, holy

Holy, holy, holy Lord,
earth is full of your glory.
Glory fills the heavens too.
Sing to him hosanna!

Blessed is the one who comes
bringing this great glory.
Holy, holy, holy Lord.
Sing to him hosanna!

Lamb of God

Lamb of God, O Jesus Christ,
take away our sins,
and have mercy on us all,
and have mercy on us.   *(Repeat)*

Lamb of God, O Jesus Christ,
take away our sins.
Grant us peace, O grant us peace,
grant us peace for ever.

Anthony Hamson

371 PILGRIM'S MASS

Lord have mercy

1. Lord, have mercy on my soul.
   Lord, have mercy on my soul.
   Lord, have mercy, Lord have mercy.
   Lord, have mercy on my soul.

2. Christ, have mercy on my soul,
   Christ have mercy on my soul.
   Christ, have mercy, Christ have
                                    mercy,
   Christ, have mercy on my soul.

3. Pray for me, pray for me,
   brothers and sisters, pray for me.
   Lord, have mercy on my soul.
   Lord, have mercy on my soul.

4. I confess that I have sinned,
   sinned in thought and word and
                                    deed,
   done the things I should not do,
   left undone what I should do.

Repeat Verse 1

Gloria

1. Glory be to God in heaven,
   glory be to God on high,
   glory be, we give you thanks
   for the glory of the universe.

2. Peace on earth to all creation,
   peace on earth to all God's friends,

peace on earth to everyone
through the mercy of our Lord
                              Jesus Christ.

3. Jesus Christ, the Son of the Father,
   Jesus Christ, the Son of Man,
   Jesus Christ, the Lamb of God
   who takes away the sins of the
                                    world.

4. Lamb of God, right hand of the
                                    Father,
   Lamb of God the sacrifice.
   Lamb of God who bore our sins,
   have mercy on us, receive our pray'r.

5. You alone are the Lord of creation,
   you alone are the Holy One,
   you alone are the three in one,
   the Father, the Son and the Spirit.

6. Glory be, glory be,
   glory be, glory be.   Amen.

Creed

1. I believe.
   I believe that God almighty
   made the world for us to use.
   I believe in good and evil
   and that we've the power to choose.

2. I believe.
   I believe in God the Father.
   I believe in God the Son.
   I believe that he was born
   on earth to save us every one.

3. I believe.
   I believe he loved and suffered,
   taught us how to live and die,
   showed us all the way to heaven
   in our hearts, not in the sky.

4. I believe.
   I believe that God the Spirit
   ever was since time began.
   I believe that he will judge our
   actions when we've lived our span.

5. I believe.
   I believe the church is holy,
   I believe the church is true.
   I believe the church was made for
   all men, not just me and you.

6. I believe.
Doubts and fears will fall upon us;
we must trust that God will guide.
Faith and hope and love will help us,
and in joy we will abide.

Sanctus

Holy, holy, holy Lord God of hosts.
Your glory fills all heaven and earth.
Hosanna in the highest.
Holy, holy, holy Lord God of hosts.
Blessed is he who comes in your name.
Hosanna in the highest.

Lord's Prayer

*Our Father, king of heav'n and earth
we praise thy sacred name.*

1. Thy kingdom come, thy will be done
   in thought and deed not in words
   alone.

2. Give us this day our daily bread,
   our spirits and our bodies fed.

3. And forgive us all our trespasses,
   while we in turn will do no less.

4. And keep us from temptation's way,
   and help us when we go astray.

Lamb of God
Lamb of God,
you take away the sins of the world,
have mercy on us.
Lamb of God,
you take away the sins of the world,
have mercy on us.
Lamb of God,
you take away the sins of the world,
have mercy on us, and grant us peace.

Gordon Rock

372

1. O salutaris hostia,
   Quae caeli pandis ostium,
   Bella premunt hostilia,
   Da robur, fer auxilium.

2. Uni trinoque Domino
   Sit sempiterna gloria,
   Qui vitam sine termino
   Nobis donet in patria. Amen.

373

English version

1. O saving victim, opening wide
   The gate of heav'n to man below;
   Our foes press on from ev'ry side;
   Thine aid supply, thy strength bestow.

2. To thy great name be endless praise,
   Immortal Godhead, one in three;
   O grant us endless length of days
   In our true native land with thee.
   Amen.

*St. Thomas Aquinas (1227-74),
tr. J.M. Neale, E. Caswall and others*

374

1. Tantum ergo Sacramentum
   Veneremur cernui:
   Et antiquum documentum
   Novo cedat ritui:
   Praestet fides supplementum
   Sensuum defectui.

2. Genitori, genitoque
   Laus et jubilatio,
   Salus, honor, virtus quoque
   Sit et benedictio;
   Procedenti ab utroque
   Compar sit laudatio. Amen.

375

English version

1. Therefore we, before him bending,
   This great sacrament revere;
   Types and shadows have their ending,
   For the newer rite is here;
   Faith, our outward sense befriending,
   Makes the inward vision clear.

2. Glory let us give, and blessing
   To the Father and the Son,
   Honour, might, and praise addressing,
   While eternal ages run;
   Ever too his love confessing
   Who from both, with both is one.
   Amen.

*St. Thomas Aquinas (1227-74),
tr. J.M. Neale, E. Caswall and others*

Index of First Lines

Abide with me 1
Accept, O Father, in thy love 2
All creation, bless the Lord 3
All creatures of our God and King 4
Alleluia 5
Alleluia, I will praise the Father 6
Alleluia, sing to Jesus 7
All glory, laud and honour 8
All hail the power of Jesus' name 9
All people that on earth do dwell 10
All that I am 11
All the nations of the earth 12
All things bright and beautiful 13
All this world belongs to Jesus 14
All ye who seek a comfort sure 15
All you peoples, clap your hands 16
Almighty Father, Lord most high 17
Almighty Father, take this bread 18
Amazing Grace 19
And did those feet in ancient time 20
Angels we have heard in heaven 21
Angels we have heard on high 22
Ask and you will receive 23
As with gladness men of old 24
Attend and keep this happy fast 25
At the cross her station keeping 26
At the Lamb's high feast we sing 27
At the name of Jesus 28
Ave Maria, O maiden, O mother 29
Away in a manger 30
Battle is o'er, hell's armies flee 31
Be still and know I am with you 32
Be still and know that I am God 33
Bethlehem of noblest cities 34
Be thou my vision, O Lord of my
  heart 35
Blest are the pure in heart 36
Breathe on me breath of God 37
Bring, all ye dear-bought nations
  bring 38
Bring flowers of the rarest 39
By the blood that flowed 40
Christ be beside me 41
Christ is king of earth and heaven 42
Christ is our King 43
Christ the Lord is risen today 44

Colours of day 45
Come, adore this wondrous
  presence 46
Come, Christian people 47
Come, come, come to the manger 48
Come down, O love divine 49
Come, Holy Ghost, Creator, come 50
Come, Lord Jesus, come 51
Come, my brothers 52
Come, praise the Lord 53
Come to the Lord 54
Come, ye thankful people, come 55
Crown him with many crowns 56
Daily, daily sing to Mary 57
Day by day in the market place 58
Day is done, but love unfailing 59
Dear Lord and Father of mankind 60
Dear maker of the starry skies 61
Ding! dong! merrily on high 62
Do not worry 63
Do you know that the Lord 64
Draw nigh, and take the body 65
Dust, dust and ashes 66
Eternal Father, strong to save 67
Faith of our fathers 68
Father and life-giver 69
Father most holy 70
Father, within thy house today 71
Feed us now 72
Fight the good fight 73
Fill my house unto the fullest 74
Firmly I believe and truly 75
Follow Christ 76
For all the saints 77
Forth in the peace of Christ we go 78
Forth in thy name O Lord, I go 79
Forty days and forty nights 80
From the deep I lift my voice 81
From the depths we cry to thee 82
Give me peace, O Lord, I pray 83
Give me joy in my heart 84
Give me yourself 85
Glorious God, King of Creation 86
Glory be to God the King 87
Glory be to Jesus 88
Glory to God (Peruvian Gloria) 89

Glory to thee, Lord God	90	Into one we all are gathered	139
Glory to thee, my God, this night	91	I saw the grass	140
Go tell it on the mountain	92	I sing a song to you, Lord	141
God be in my head	93	I sing the Lord God's praises	142
God everlasting	94	It came upon a midnight clear	143
Godhead here in hiding	95	It's me, O Lord	144
God is love	96	I will give you glory	146
God is love: his the care	97	I wonder as I wander	147
God of mercy and compassion	98	January brings the snow	148
God's spirit is in my heart	99	Jerusalem the golden	149
Going home	100	Jesu, lover of my soul	150
Gonna lay down my sword	101	Jesu, meek and lowly	151
Go, the Mass is ended	102	Jesu, the very thought of thee	152
Great St. Andrew, friend of Jesus	103	Jesus Christ is risen today	153
Guide me, O thou great Redeemer	104	Jesus, gentlest Saviour	154
Hail, glorious St. Patrick	105	Jesus, Lord, I'll sing a song	155
Hail, Queen of heaven	106	Jesus is God! the solid earth	156
Hail Redeemer, King divine	107	Jesus, my Lord, my God, my all	157
Hail, the day that sees him rise	108	Jesus, thou art coming	158
Hail, thou star of ocean	109	Just a closer walk with thee	159
Hail to the Lord's anointed	110	Keep we the fast that men of old	160
Happy the man	111	King of glory, king of peace	161
Hark! a herald voice is calling	112	Kum ba yah	162
Hark! the herald angels sing	113	Leader now on earth no longer	163
Haul away	114	Lead, kindly light	164
Help, Lord, the souls	115	Lead us, heavenly Father, lead us	165
Here's a child for you, O Lord	116	Let all mortal flesh keep silence	166
He's got the whole world	117	Let all that is within me	167
He was born like you and I	118	Let all the world	168
He who would valiant be	119	Let us break bread together	169
Holy Father, God of might	120	Let's make peace in our hearts	170
Holy God we praise thy name	121	Let us with a gladsome mind	171
Holy, holy, holy Lord	122	Light of our darkness	172
Holy, holy, holy Lord God	123	Little flower in the ground	173
Holy Spirit, Lord of light	124	Little Jesus sweetly sleep	174
Holy Spirit of fire	125	Long ago in Bethlehem	175
Holy Virgin, by God's decree	126	Look down, O Mother Mary	176
How dark was the stable	127	Lord, accept the gifts we offer	177
I am the bread of life	128	Lord for tomorrow and its needs	178
I believe in God almighty	129	Lord, Jesus Christ	179
I believe in God, the Father	130	Lord Jesus, think on me	180
I danced in the morning	131	Lord of all hopefulness	181
I'll sing a hymn to Mary	132	Lord, we pray for golden peace	182
Immaculate Mary	133	Lord, who throughout these forty	
Immortal, invisible, God only wise	134	days	183
In bread we bring you, Lord	135	Love divine, all loves excelling	184
In Christ there is no east or west	136	Love is his word, love is his way	185
In the bleak mid-winter	137	Loving Father, from thy bounty	186
In the earth the small seed	138	Loving shepherd of thy sheep	187

Maiden, yet a mother	188	O my Lord, within my heart	237
Make me a channel of your peace	189	Once in royal David's city	238
Man of Galilee	190	On Jordan's bank the Baptist's cry	239
Many times I have turned	191	On this house your blessing, Lord	240
Mary immaculate	192	Onward Christian soldiers	241
May the peace of Christ	193	Open your ears	242
Merrily on	194	O perfect love	243
Mine eyes have seen the glory	195	O praise ye the Lord	244
Morning has broken	196	O Priest and Victim, Lord of life	245
Moses I know you're the man	197	O purest of creatures	246
Most ancient of all mysteries	198	O sacred head sore wounded	247
Mother of mercy, day by day	199	O sacred heart	248
My glory and the lifter	200	O thou, who at thy Eucharist	249
My God, accept my heart this day	201	O Trinity, most blessed light	250
My God, and is thy table spread	202	Our Father (Caribbean)	251
My God, how wonderful thou art	203	Out and away	252
My God, I love thee, not because	204	O worship the king	253
My God loves me	205	Peace is flowing like a river	254
My song is love unknown	206	Peace is the gift of heaven	255
New praises be given	207	Peacemakers	256
Now come to me all you who seek	208	Peace, perfect peace	257
Now Jesus said.	209	People of God, give praise	258
Now Jesus said: You must love	210	Praise him, praise him	259
Now thank we all our God	211	Praise my soul, the king of heaven	260
Now with the fast-departing light	212	Praise the Lord	261
O bread of heaven	213	Praise to the holiest	262
O come, all ye faithful	214	Praise to the Lord our God	263
O come and mourn with me	215	Praise to the Lord, the almighty	264
O come, O come Emmanuel	216	Praise we now the Lord our God	265
O Father, now the hour has come	217	Praise we our God with joy	266
O Father, take in sign of love	218	Promised Lord and Christ is he	267
Of the Glorious Body telling	219	Reap me the earth	268
O Godhead hid,	220	Rejoice in the Lord	269
O God of earth and altar	221	Rejoice! the Lord is King	270
O God, our help in ages past	222	Ride on, ride on in majesty	271
O God, thy people gather	223	Round me falls the night	272
O God, we give ourselves today	224	Seasons come, seasons go	273
Oh living water	225	See amid the winter's snow	274
Oh Lord, all the world	226	See us, Lord, about thine altar	275
Oh Lord, my God	227	Shalom	276
O Holy Lord, by all adored	228	Silent night	277
Oh, sinner man	229	Sing, my soul	278
Oh, the Lord looked down	230	Sing, my tongue	279
Oh the love of my Lord	231	Sing of the bride	280
Oh, when the Saints	232	Sing of Mary, pure and lowly	281
O Jesus Christ, remember	233	Sing, people of God	282
O King of might and splendour	234	Sing praises to God	283
O little town of Bethlehem	235	Sing praises to the living God	284
O mother blest	236	Sleep, holy babe	285

Songs of thankfulness and praise	286	To the name that brings salvation	335
Sons of God	287	Trust in the eyes of a tiny babe	336
Soul of my Saviour	288	Unto us is born a Son	337
Spirit of the living God	289	Vaster far than any ocean	338
Star of ocean, lead us	290	Virgin wholly marvellous	339
Steal away to Jesus	291	Walk with me, oh my Lord	340
Suffer little children	292	We are gathering together	341
Sweet heart of Jesus	293	We are one in the Spirit	342
Sweet Sacrament divine	294	We bring our gifts to the Lord	343
Sweet Saviour bless us 'ere we go	295	We celebrate this festive day	344
Take my hands	296	We gather together	345
Take our bread, we ask you	297	We plough the fields and scatter	346
Thank you	298	Were you there?	347
The bakerwoman	299	We shall overcome	348
The Church's one foundation	300	We three kings of Orient are	349
The coming of our God	301	We will walk through the valley	350
The day of resurrection	302	What can we offer you?	351
The day thou gavest, Lord	303	Whatsoever you do	352
The farmer in the fertile field	304	When I needed a neighbour	353
The first Nowell	305	When Israel was in Egypt's land	354
The God whom earth and sea	306	When I survey the wondrous cross	355
The green life rises from the earth	307	Where are you bound, Mary	356
The head that once was crowned	308	Where does the wind	357
The heavenly word,	309	Where is love and loving kindness	358
The King of Glory comes	310	Where would we be without Christ	359
The King of Love my shepherd is	311	While shepherds watched	360
The Lord's my shepherd	312	With a song in our hearts	361
The Mass is ended	313	Yahweh, you are my strength	362
The prophet in his hunger	314	Ye choirs of new Jerusalem	363
The race that long in darkness	315	Ye sons and daughters of the Lord	364
There is a green hill	316	Ye who own the faith of Jesus	365
There is a world	317		
The royal banners forward go	318		
The Spirit of the Lord	319	*Mass Settings*	
The tree of life	320	Geordie Mass	368
The Virgin Mary had a baby boy	321	American Eucharist	366
The wandering flock of Israel	322	Swedish Mass	370
They hung him on a cross	323	Monmouthshire Mass	369
They say I am wise	324	Israeli Mass	367
This day God give me	325	Pilgrim's Mass	371
This is the image of the Queen	326		
This is my will	327		
This joyful Eastertide	328	*Benediction*	
This little light of mine	329	O Salutaris	372
Thou wilt keep him	330	O saving victim	373
Thy hand, O God, has guided	331	Therefore, we before him bending	375
To Christ the Lord of worlds	332	Tantum Ergo	374
To Christ the Prince of peace	333		
To Jesus' heart all burning	334		

Acknowledgements

The publishers wish to express their gratitude to the following for permission to include copyright material in this book:

Alba House Communications, Canfield, Ohio 44406, for *What can we offer you* ©1977.

Christopher Alston for the words of *Father most holy*.

Belwin Mills Music Limited for the words and music of *Suffer little children*. Reproduced by kind permission of the copyright owners, Belwin Mills Music Limited, 250 Purley Way, Croydon, CR9 4QD.

Bosworth & Co Ltd, of 14/18 Heddon Street, London W1R 8DP, for the words and music of *Thank You*.

Geoffrey Chapman for the words of *Christ be beside me; This is my will; Come, adore this wondrous presence; Come, praise the Lord, the almighty; Day is done, but love unfailing; Forth in the peace of Christ we go; I believe in God the Father; Loving Father, from thy bounty; O Father take in sign of love; O Priest and victim* and *This day God gives me*.

Anne Conway for the words and music of *Be still and know I am with you*.

The Trustees of the Late Sir Walter Davies for the words and music of *God be in my head*.

B. Feldman & Co for the words and music of *Fill my house*.

F.E.L. Publications of Los Angeles for the words and music of *The tree of life; We are one in the spirit; Sons of God* and *All you peoples*.

Franciscan Communications Centre of Los Angeles for the words and music of *All that I am; Glorious God; Do not worry; Let's make peace in our hearts; Follow Christ; Lord we pray for golden peace; Sing, sing, sing; Happy the man; Make me a channel of your peace; The Mass is ended; Take my hands* and *Sing praises to the living God*.

John Glynn for the words of *I watch the sunrise*.

Gospel Light Publications, Shirley House, 27 Camden Road, London NW1 9LN, on behalf of Manna Music for *How great thou art*.

The Executors of the Late Dr B. Harwood for the music of *Let all the world* and *Thy hand, O God*.

David Higham Associates Limited, 5-8 Lower John Street, Golden Square, London W1R 4HA, for the words of *Morning has broken* by Eleanor Farjeon from 'The Children's Bells' published by Oxford University Press.

Rev Clifford Howell, SJ, for the words of *Glory to thee, O Lord; O God thy people gather; O God we give ourselves today* and *See us Lord about thine altar*.

The Literary Estate of Eleanor Hull and Chatto & Windus Limited for the words of *A Prayer* (*Be thou my vision*) from the Poem Book of Gael.

The Executrix of the Estate of the Late John Ireland for the music of *My song is love unknown*.

Michael Iverson for the words and music of *Spirit of the Living God*.

Rev Willard F. Jabusch for the words of *All this world belongs to Jesus; Many times I have turned; The King of glory comes; We celebrate this festive day; We gather together; Whatsoever you do* and *Open your ears*.

Lexicon Music for the words and music of *Holy, holy* from Come Together by Jimmy and Carol Owens ©1972 Lexicon Music (UK). All rights reserved. Used by permission.

Kevin Mayhew Limited, 55 Leigh Road, Leigh On Sea, Essex for the words and music of *Come Lord Jesus, come; I am the bread of life; He was born like you and I; May the peace of Christ be with you today; Peace, perfect peace* and *Seasons come, seasons go; Holy Virgin by God's decree;* and for the words of *My God loves me* (Vs 2-5) and the music of *Round me falls the night*.

SUPPLEMENT: INDEX OF FIRST LINES

God gives his people strength	S1
Hail holy Joseph, hail	S6
I have counted the cost	S2
Lord make me an instrument	S7
Now the green blade riseth	S3
O great St David	S4
Saint Andrew called to follow Christ	S5
Spirit of God	S8

──Celebration Hymnal──

The CELEBRATION HYMNAL has undergone extensive revision and up-dating. The new revised Volume 2, is combined with a wealth of psalmody and music for the Divine Office and will provide a valuable addition to the ever-popular CELEBRATION HYMNAL (Volume 1).

Available in the following editions:

The COMPLETE CELEBRATION HYMNAL

Words Only (Hymns 1-723 under one cover)   £1.75
ISBN 0 85597 371 4
Full Music (Vol.1 + 2 separately)   £19.95
ISBN 0 85597 250 5/368 4
Melody/Guitar (Vol.1 + 2 separately)
ISBN 0 85597 263 7/369 2   · in preparation

CELEBRATION HYMNAL Volume 2 (Revised)

Words Only   (Red)   £1.25
ISBN 0 85597 367 6
Full Music   (Red)   £10.50
ISBN 0 85597 368 4
Melody/Guitar   in preparation
ISBN 0 85597 369 2

CELEBRATION HYMNAL Volume 1
Words Only (Standard)   (Yellow) £1.30
ISBN 0 85597 094 4
Words Only (With Supplement) (Blue)   £1.35
ISBN 0 85597 230 0
Full Music   (Blue)   £10.50
ISBN 0 85597 250 5
Melody/Guitar   £3.95
ISBN 0 85597 263 7

DEMONSTRATION CASSETTES

Volume 2 (Revised) A. Nos.376-695   £19.50 + VAT
                   B. Nos.696-723   £3.50 + VAT
Volume 1   Nos.1-375   £22.50 + VAT

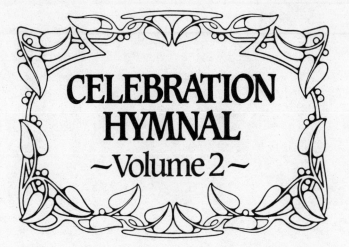

CELEBRATION HYMNAL
~Volume 2~

Completely Revised

Edited by Stephen Dean

MAYHEW McCRIMMON
Great Wakering Essex England

First published in 1984 by
MAYHEW McCRIMMON LTD

Compilation and all editorial
content © 1984 Mayhew McCrimmon Ltd

ISBN 0 85597 367 6

Editorial supervision: Joan McCrimmon,
Rosalind Pitcher and Michael Eldridge-Doyle
Cover: Jim Bowler
Lithographic artwork: Nick Snode

Typesetting: Phoenix Typesetting Ltd, Southend-on-Sea
Printed by Bemrose Printing, Derby, England

376

1. A certain traveller on his way
   was robbed and left to die;
   helpless by the road he lay
   and no one heard his cry.
   A certain priest came down that
     way,
   a man most dignified;
   'I will not get involved' said he,
   and passed on the other side.

   **Don't pass your neighbour by, my
     friend,**
   don't pass your neighbour by.
   Love your neighbour as yourself,
   don't pass your neighbour by.

2. A certain Levite came that way
   a man of wealth and pride,
   'I'm much too busy to stop'
     said he,
   and passed on the other side.
   But a certain man from Samaria,
   a stranger in the land,
   took pity on the injured man
   and lent a helping hand.

   Based on Luke 10: 25-37 by Mary Lu Walker
   © 1975 Missionary Society of St Paul the
   Apostle in the State of New York

377

   A child is born for us today,
   alleluia.
   He is our saviour and our God,
   alleluia.

1. Let our hearts resound with joy
   and sing a song of gladness
   for the Lord, our brother,
   is come and we are redeemed.

2. Tell the world of our good news:
   Jesus the Christ is among us,
   and his presence we celebrate
   offering peace and our joy to all.

3. Christ is born, the Christ has
     come!
   Sing everyone 'Alleluia!'
   Caught in wonder at this birth
   we worship God become man for
   us.

4. Glory to God, born today
   of the Virgin Mary,
   in a cave at Bethlehem:
   is there room in our lives for him?

5. His name shall be 'Emmanuel':
   'God-who-lives-among-us',
   Angels sing and shepherds cry:
   'Born is the saviour, our Lord!'

6. The magi went and worshipped
     him
   with gifts so precious and costly.
   In the fervour of their faith
   they sought the child who is Lord
     and King.

7. The Lord will make integrity
   and peace to grow in our times.
   A covenant he offers us:
   lasting joy will be ours to share.

8. Arise! Shine out, Jerusalem!
   The glory of Yahweh* has come
      to you.
   Lift up your eyes and look around!
   Radiant is your salvation!

   Instead of 'Yahweh' *you may
   prefer to substitute* 'God'

   Final Refrain
   **A child is born for us today,
   alleluia.
   He is our saviour and our God,
   alleluia.
   Alleluia, Alleluia.**

*Gregory Norbert © 1971 the Benedictine
Foundation of the State of Vermont, Inc*

378

1. A child is born in Bethlehem,
   alleluia;
   so leap with joy Jerusalem,
   alleluia, alleluia.

   **A new song let us sing
   for Christ is born
   let us adore
   and let our gladness ring.**

2. Through Gabriel the word has
      come,
   alleluia:
   The Virgin will conceive a son,
   alleluia, alleluia.

3. Within a manger now he lies,
   alleluia:
   Who reigns on high beyond the
      skies,
   alleluia, alleluia.

4. The shepherds hear the angel's
      word,
   alleluia:
   This child is truly Christ the Lord,
   alleluia, alleluia.

5. From Saba, from the rising sun,
   alleluia:
   With incense, gold, and myrrh
      they come,
   alleluia, alleluia.

6. Till with their gifts they enter in,
   alleluia:
   and kings adore the new-born
      King,
   alleluia, alleluia.

7. From virgin's womb this child is
      born,
   alleluia:
   the Light from Light who brings
      the dawn,
   alleluia, alleluia.

8. He comes to free us from our
      strife,
   alleluia;
   and share with us the Father's life,
   alleluia, alleluia.

9. At this the coming of the Word,
   alleluia;
   o come, let us adore the Lord,
   alleluia, alleluia.

10. To Father, Son, and Spirit praise,
    alleluia:
    from all his creatures all their
       days,
    alleluia, alleluia.

Latin, 14th Century, tr Ralph Wright, OSB, © 1980 ICEL

379

1. A mighty stronghold is our God,
   a sure defence and weapon.
   He'll help us out of every need
   whatever now may happen.
   The ancient evil fiend
   has deadly ill in mind;
   great power and craft are his,
   his armour gruesome is
   on earth is not his equal.

2. With our own strength is nothing
        done
   soon we are lost, dejected;
   but for us fights the rightful Man
   whom God himself elected.
   You ask: Who may this be?
   Christ Jesus it is he,
   the Lord Sabaoth's Son,
   our God, and he alone
   shall hold the field victorious.

3. And though the world were full
        of fiends
   all lurking to devour us,
   we tremble not nor fear their
        bands,
   they shall not overpower us.
   The prince of this world's ill
   may scowl upon us still,
   he cannot do us harm,
   to judgement he has come;
   one word can swiftly fell him.

4. The Word they must allow
        to stand –
   for this they win no merit;
   upon the field, so near at hand,
   he gives to us his Spirit.
   And though they take our life,
   goods, honour, child, and wife,
   though we must let all go,
   they will not profit so:
   to us remains the Kingdom.

   Martin Luther (1483-1546) tr by © Honor Mary Thwaites

380

A new Commandment I give unto you,
that you love one another as I have
   loved you,
that you love one another as I have
   loved you.

By this shall all men know that you
   are my disciples,
if you have love one for another.
By this shall all men know that you
   are my disciples,
if you have love for one another.

   Source unknown, based on John 13:34-35

381

1. A noble flow'r of Juda
   from tender roots has sprung,
   a rose from stem of Jesse,
   as prophets long had sung;
   a blossom fair and bright,
   that in the midst of winter
   will change to dawn our night.

2. The rose of grace and beauty
   of which Isaiah sings
   is Mary, virgin mother,
   and Christ the flow'r she brings.
   By God's divine decree
   she bore our loving Saviour
   who died to set us free.

3. To Mary, dearest mother,
   with fervent hearts we pray:
   grant that your tender infant
   will cast our sins away,
   and guide us with his love
   that we shall ever serve him
   and live with him above.

   German, 15th Century, paraphrased by
   Anthony G. Petti © Faber Music Ltd

382

1. A sign is seen in heaven,
   a maiden-mother fair;
   her mantle is the sunlight,
   and stars adorn her hair.
   The maiden's name is Mary;
   in love she brings to birth
   the Lord of all the ages,
   the King of all the earth.

2. Like moonlight on the hilltops
   she shines on all below,
   like sunlight on the mountains
   her Child outshines the snow.
   O Mary, Queen of mothers,
   still smile on young and old;
   bless hearth and home and
     harvest,
   bless farm and field and fold.

3. Pray, Mother, Queen in glory,
   before the Father's throne;
   praise God's eternal Wisdom,
   the Child who is your own;
   rejoice in God the Spirit,
   whose power let you conceive
   the Child of Eden's promise,
   O new and sinless Eve.

James Quinn, SJ. © Geoffrey Chapman Ltd

383

**Abba, Abba, Father,
you are the potter,
we are the clay,
the work of your hands.**

1. Mould us,
   mould us and fashion us
   into the image
   of Jesus, your Son.
   of Jesus, your Son.

2. Father,
   may we be one in you
   as he is in you
   and you are in him,
   and you are in him.

3. Glory,
   glory and praise to you,
   glory and praise to you
   for ever. Amen.
   For ever. Amen.

384

1. Abba, Father, send your Spirit . . .

   **Glory hallelujah, glory, Jesus
     Christ.
   Glory hallelujah, glory, Jesus
     Christ.**

2. I will give you living water . . .

3. If you seek me you will find me . . .

4. If you listen you will hear me . . .

5. Come, my children, I will teach
   you . . .

6. I'm your shepherd, I will lead
   you . . .

7. Peace I leave you, peace I give
   you . . .

8. I'm your life and resurrection . . .

9. Glory Father, glory Spirit . . .

*Other words from Scripture may be
substituted according to the occasion
or the season. For example, in Advent:*

1. Come, Lord Jesus, Light of
   nations . . .

2. Come, Lord Jesus, born of
   Mary . . .

3. Come, and show the Father's
   glory . . .

Ginny Vissing. © *1974 Shalom Community*

385

1. Across the years there echoes still
   the Baptist's bold assertion:
   the call of God to change of heart,
   repentance and conversion.

2. The word that John more boldly
      spoke
   in dying than in living
   now Christ takes up as he
      proclaims
   a Father all-forgiving.

3. The erring son he welcomes home
   when all is spent and squandered.
   He lovingly pursues the sheep
   that from the flock has wandered.

4. Forgive us, Lord, all we have done
   to you and one another.
   So often we have gone our way,
   forgetful of each other.

5. Forgetful of the cross they bear
   of hunger, want, oppression –
   grant, Lord, that we may make
      amends
   who humbly make confession.

Denis E. Hurley © *Archdiocese of Durban*

386

1. Again the Lord's own day is here,
   the day to Christian people dear,
   as week by week it bids them tell
   how Jesus rose from death and
   hell.

2. For by his flock the Lord declared
   his resurrection should be shared;
   and we who trust in him to save
   with him are risen from the grave.

3. We, one and all, of him possessed,
   are with exceeding treasures blest;
   for all he did and all he bore
   is shared by us for evermore.

4. Eternal glory, rest on high,
   a blesséd immortality,
   true peace and gladness, and a
      throne,
   are all his gifts and all our own.

5. And therefore unto thee we sing,
   O Lord of peace, eternal King;
   thy love we praise, thy name
      adore,
   both on this day and evermore.

Attributed to St Thomas a Kempis (1380-1471)
tr by J. M. Neale (1818-66) and others

387

**Alabaré, alabaré, alabaré a mi
Señor. (2)**

1. John saw the number of all those
      redeemed,
   and all were singing praises to the
      Lord.
   Thousands were praying, ten
      thousands rejoicing,
   and all were singing praises to the
      Lord.

2. There is no god as great as you,
   O Lord,
   there is none, there is none. (2)
   There is no god who does the
   mighty wonders
   that the Lord our God has
   done. (2)
   Neither with an army, nor with
   their weapons,
   but by the Holy Spirit's power. (2)
   And even mountains shall be
   moved, (3)
   by the Holy Spirit's power.

3. And even England * shall be
   saved (3)
   by the Holy Spirit's power.

   *or Scotland, Ireland, Wales, or
   wherever your live, or even a
   friend's name!*

   *('Alabaré a mi Señor is Spanish
   for 'I will praise my Lord')*

   Author unknown

388

1. All for Jesus, all for Jesus,
   this our song shall ever be;
   for we have no hope, nor Saviour,
   if we have not hope in Thee.

2. All for Jesus, thou wilt give us
   strength to serve thee, hour by
   hour;
   none can move us from thy
   presence,
   while we trust thy love and power.

3. All for Jesus, at thine altar
   thou wilt give us sweet content;
   there, dear Lord, we shall receive
   thee
   in the solemn sacrament.

4. All for Jesus, thou hast loved us;
   all for Jesus, thou hast died;
   all for Jesus, thou art with us;
   all for Jesus crucified.

5. All for Jesus, all for Jesus,
   this the Church's song must be;
   till, at last, her sons are gathered
   one in love and one in thee.

   J. Sparrow-Simpson © Novello & Co Ltd

389

1. All my hope on God is founded;
   he doth still my trust renew.
   Me through change and chance he
   guideth,
   only good and only true.
   God unknown, he alone
   call my heart to be his own.

2. Pride of man and earthly glory,
   sword and crown betray God's
   trust;
   what with lavish care man
   buildeth,
   tower and temple, fall to dust.
   But God's power, hour by hour,
   is my temple and my tower.

3. God's great goodness ay endureth,
   deep his wisdom, passing thought:
   splendour, light and life attend
   him,
   beauty springeth out of nought.
   Evermore, from his store
   new-born worlds rise and adore.

4. Still from man to God eternal
   sacrifice of praise be done,
   high above all praises praising
   for the gift of Christ his Son.
   Christ doth call one and all;
   Ye who follow shall not fall.

   *J. Neander (1650-80), paraphrased by R. S. Bridges
   (1844-1930)*

390

**All the earth proclaim the Lord,
sing your praise to God.**

1. Serve you the Lord, hearts filled
   with gladness.
   Come into his presence, singing
   for joy!

2. Know that the Lord is our creator.
   Yes, he is our Father; we are his
   sons.

3. We are the sheep of his green
   pasture,
   for we are his people; he is our
   God.

4. Enter his gates bringing
   thanksgiving,
   O enter his courts while singing
   his praise.

5. Our Lord is good, his love
   enduring,
   his word is abiding now with all
   men.

6. Honour and praise be to the
   Father,
   the Son, and the Spirit, world
   without end.

Based on Psalm 99 (100) by Lucien Deiss
© 1965 World Library Publications, Inc
All rights reserved. Printed with permission

391

**All you nations,
sing out your joy in the Lord:
Alleluia, alleluia!**

1. Joyfully shout, all you on earth,
   give praise to the glory of God;
   and with a hymn,
   sing out his glorious praise:
   Alleluia!

2. Lift up your hearts, sing to your
   God:
   tremendous his deeds among men!
   Vanquished your foes,
   struck down by power and might:
   Alleluia!

3. Let all the earth kneel in his sight,
   extolling his marvellous fame;
   honour his name,
   in highest heaven give praise:
   Alleluia!

4. Come forth and see all the great
   works
   that God has brought forth by his
   might;
   fall on your knees
   before his glorious throne:
   Alleluia!

5. Parting the seas with might and
   pow'r,
   he rescued his people from shame;
   let us give thanks
   for all his merciful deeds:
   Alleluia!

6. His eyes keep watch on all the
   earth,
   his strength is forever renewed;
   and let no man
   rebel against his commands;
   Alleluia!

7. Tested are we by God the Lord,
   as silver is tested by fire;
   burdened with pain,
   we fall ensnared in our sins:
   Alleluia!

8. Over our heads wicked men rode,
   we passed through the fire and the
   flood;
   then, Lord, you brought
   your people into your peace:
   Alleluia!

9. Glory and thanks be to the Father;
   honour and praise to the Son;
   and to the Spirit,
   source of life and of love:
   Alleluia!

*Based on Psalm 65 (66) by Lucien Deiss
© 1965 World Library Publications, Inc
All rights reserved. Printed with permission*

392

**Alleluia, alleluia, alleluia, Jesus
is alive!**

1. Praise the Lord
   for he is good eternally,
   and his loving kindness for us
   never fails.

2. His strong right hand
   overcomes and lifts us up;
   I'll never die, but live
   to praise his power to save.

3. For the stone rejected
   by the builder's sin
   has become the cornerstone
   of God's new House.

4. And he gives us the light
   wherewith to see;
   his intention is
   that we should live with him.

Based on Psalm 117 (118) © Bonaventure Hinwood

393

**Alleluia, alleluia, alleluia, may
God's Spirit come!**

1. Bless the Lord, my soul,
   for he is great and good:
   earth he has enriched
   with all his mighty works.

2. You send forth your Spirit,
   then creation starts,
   and you still renew
   all things upon the earth.

3. May the Lord find joy
   in all that he creates;
   and my thoughts about him
   fill my heart with joy.

Based on Psalm 103 (104) © 1974 Bonaventure Hinwood

394

**Alleluia! Alleluia! Alleluia,
Sons of God arise and follow
Alleluia! Alleluia!
sons of God arise and follow
the Lord.**

1. Come and be clothed in his
   righteousness;
   come join the band who are
   called by his name.

2. Look at the world which is bound
   by sin;
   walk into the midst of it
   proclaiming my life.

*Mimi Farra © 1971, 1975 Celebration Services
(International) Ltd*

395

**Alleluia, alleluia,
give thanks to the risen Lord.
Alleluia, alleluia,
give praise to his name.**

1. Jesus is Lord of all the earth.
   He is the King of creation.

2. Spread the good news o'er all the
   earth.
   Jesus has died and has risen.

3. We have been crucified with
   Christ.
   Now we shall live for ever.

4. God has proclaimed the just
   reward.
   Life for all men, alleluia.

5. Come, let us praise the living God,
   joyfully sing to our Saviour.

Don Fishel © 1973 The Word of God

396

Alleluia, alleluia!
1. Salvation and glory and pow'r
   belong to our God,
   allelluia!
   His judgements are true and just.

2. Praise our God, all you his
   servants,
   alleluia!
   You, who fear him, great and
   small.

3. The Lord, our God, the almighty,
   reigns,
   alleluia!
   Let us rejoice and exult and give
   him the glory.

4. The marriage of the Lamb has
   come,
   alleluia!
   And his Bride has made herself
   ready.

Based on Revelation 19:1-2, 5-7, from The Divine Office

397

1. Almighty Father, who for us thy
   Son didst give,
   that men and nations through his
   precious death might live,
   in mercy guard us, lest by sloth
   and selfish pride
   we cause to stumble those for
   whom the Saviour died.

2. We are thy stewards; thine our
   talents, wisdom, skill;
   our only glory that we may thy
   trust fulfill;
   that we thy pleasure in our
   neighbours' good pursue,
   if thou but workest in us both to
   will and do.

3. On just and unjust thou thy
   care dost freely shower;
   make us, thy children, free from
   greed and lust for power,
   lest human justice, yoked with
   man's unequal laws,
   oppress the needy and neglect
   the humble cause.

4. Let not thy worship blind us to
   the claims of love;
   but let thy manna lead us to the
   feast above,
   to seek the country which by faith
   we now possess,
   where Christ, our treasure, reigns
   in peace and righteousness.

George B. Caird © United Reformed Church

398

1. Angel-voices ever singing
   round thy throne of light,
   angel-harps for ever ringing,
   rest not day nor night;
   thousands only live to bless thee
   and confess thee Lord of might.

2. Thou who art beyond the farthest
   mortal eye can scan,
   can it be that thou regardest
   songs of sinful man?
   Can we know that thou art near
   us,
   and wilt hear us? Yes, we can.

3. Yes, we know that thou rejoicest
   o'er each work of thine;
   thou didst ears and hands and
   voices
   for thy praise design;
   craftsman's art and music's
   measure
   for thy pleasure all combine.

4. In thy house, great God, we offer
   of thine own to thee;
   and for thine acceptance proffer
   all unworthily;
   hearts and minds and hands and
   voices
   in our choicest psalmody.

5. Honour, glory, might and merit
   thine shall ever be,
   Father, Son, and Holy Spirit,
   Blessed Trinity!
   Of the best that thou hast given
   earth and heaven render thee.

F. Pott

399

1. An upper room did our Lord
   prepare
   for those he loved until the end:
   and his disciples still gather there,
   to celebrate their Risen Friend.

2. A lasting gift Jesus gave his own:
   to share his bread, his loving cup.
   Whatever burdens may bow us
   down,
   he by his cross shall lift us up.

3. And after Supper he washed their
   feet,
   for service, too, is sacrament.
   In him our joy shall be made
   complete –
   sent out to serve, as he was sent.

4. No end there is! We depart in
   peace.
   He loves beyond our uttermost:
   in every room in our Father's
   house
   he will be there, as Lord and Host.

F. Pratt Green © Stainer & Bell

400

1. As earth that is dry and parched
   in the sun
   lies waiting for rain,
   my soul is a desert, arid and waste;
   it longs for your Word, O Lord.

   **Come to the waters, all you
   who thirst;
   come now, and eat my bread.**

2. Though you have no money,
   come, buy my corn
   and drink my red wine.
   Why spend precious gold on
   what will not last?
   Hear me, and your soul will live.

3. As one on a journey strays
   from the road
   and falls in the dark,
   my mind is a wanderer,
   choosing wrong paths
   and longing to find a star.

4. The Lord is your light,
   the Lord is your strength;
   turn back to him now.
   For his ways are not the ways
   you would choose,
   and his thoughts are always new.

5. As rain from the mountains
   falls on the land
   and brings forth the seed,
   the word of the Lord sinks deep
   in our hearts,
   creating the flower of truth.

Isaiah 55: 1, 2, 6, 9 & 12, paraphrased by Anne Conway
© 1973 Anne Conway

401

1. As I kneel before you,
   as I bow my head in pray'r,
   take this day, make it yours
   and fill me with your love.

   Ave Maria, gratia plena,
   Dominus tecum, benedicta tu.

2. All I have I give you,
   ev'ry dream and wish are yours.
   Mother of Christ, Mother of mine,
   present them to my Lord.

3. As I kneel before you,
   and I see your smiling face,
   ev'ry thought, ev'ry word
   is lost in your embrace.

Maria Parkinson © 1978 Kevin Mayhew Ltd

402

1. As long as men on earth are
   living,
   and trees are yielding fruits on
   earth,
   you are our Father. Thanks we
   give you,
   for all that owes to you its birth.

2. You are our light and life and
   Saviour,
   you rescue us when we are dead.
   You gave your Son to be our
   neighbour.
   He feeds us with his living bread.

3. As long as human words are
   spoken
   and for each other we exist,
   your steadfastness remains
   unbroken;
   for Jesus' sake, your name be
   blessed.

4. You are the one who clothes the
   flowers,
   you feed the birds in all the land.
   You are our shelter: all my hours
   and all my days are in your hand.

5. Therefore, let all the world adore
   you.
   It is your love that brought it
   forth.
   You live among us, we before you.
   Your offspring are we, Praise the
   Lord!

Huub Oosterhuis and C. M. De Vries
© Sheed and Ward Ltd

403

As one body we are wed
by partaking of the self-same Bread;
and Jesus Christ of that body is the
head:
the holy Church of God.

1. I am the living bread which has
come down from heaven.
Anyone who eats this bread will
live for ever,
and the bread that I shall give
is my flesh for that life of the
world. *(John 6:51)*

2. On the same night that he was
betrayed, the Lord Jesus took
some bread
thanked God for it, and broke
it, and said:
'This is my body, which is given
up for you. *(1 Cor.11:23b-24)*

3. In the same way, after supper,
he took the cup and said:
'This cup is the new covenant in
my blood.
Do this in memory of me.'
So doing, we proclaim his
death, until he comes again.
(1 Cor.11:25-26)

4. Just as a human body, though it
is made up of many parts
these parts, though many, make
one body.
In the one Spirit we were all
baptised,
one Spirit given to us all to
drink. *(1 Cor.11:12-13)*

5. There is one body, there is one
Spirit

just as we were called into one
and the same hope.
There is one Lord, one faith,
one baptism
and one God, who is Father
over all. *(Ephesians 4:4-6)*

Words from Scripture:
Jean-Paul Lecot, W.R.
Lawrence, R.B.Kelly
© 1984 Kevin Mayhew Ltd

404

1. As the bridegroom to his chosen,
as the king unto his realm,
as the keep unto the castle,
as the pilot to the helm,
so, Lord, art thou to me.

2. As the fountain in the garden,
as the candle in the dark,
as the treasure in the coffer,
as the manna in the ark,
so, Lord, art thou to me.

3. As the music at the banquet,
as the stamp unto the seal,
as the medicine to the fainting,
as the wine-cup at the meal,
so, Lord, art thou to me.

4. As the ruby in the setting,
as the honey in the comb,
as the light within the lantern,
as the father in the home,
so, Lord, art thou to me.

5. As the sunshine in the heavens,
as the image in the glass,
as the fruit unto the fig-tree,
as the dew unto the grass,
so, Lord, art thou to me.

*Para from John Tauler (1330-61) by Emma Frances
Bevan (1827-1909)*

405

1. Awake, awake: fling off the night!
   For God has sent his glorious
       light;
   and we who live in Christ's new
       day
   must works of darkness put away.

2. Awake and rise, like men renewed,
   men with the Spirit's power
       endued.
   The light of life in us must glow,
   and fruits of truth and goodness
       show.

3. Let in the light; all sin expose
   to Christ, whose life no darkness
       knows.
   Before his cross for guidance
       kneel;
   his light will judge and, judging,
       heal.

4. Awake, and rise up from the dead,
   and Christ his light on you will
       shed.
   Its power will wrong desires
       destroy,
   and your whole nature fill with
       joy.

5. Then sing for joy, and use each
       day;
   give thanks for everything alway.
   Lift up your hearts; with one
       accord
   praise God through Jesus Christ
       our Lord.

J. R. Peacey (1896-1971) based on Ephesians 5:6-20
© Mildred Peacey

406

1. 'Bartimaeus, Bartimaeus,
   do you hear them, do you know?
   They have seen the prophet Jesus
   in the streets of Jericho.
   Bartimaeus, it is he!
   What a shame you cannot see.'

2. 'Son of David, Son of David
   walking in the blessed light,
   I a beggar ask no money.
   Lord, may I receive my sight?
   Son of David, pity me.
   You have power to make me see.'

3. 'Bartimaeus, Bartimaeus,
   you have eyes to know your need;
   you have eyes to know the Giver;
   surely this is sight indeed!
   Bartimaeus, come to me.
   Bartimaeus, you shall see.'

4. Son of David, Son of David
   kindle in the human soul.
   One blind faith like Bartimaeus;
   call us out, and make us whole.
   Son of David, source of light,
   Lord, may we receive our sight?

© 1982, 1984 Michael Hewlett

407

1. Be still, my soul: the Lord
       is on your side;
   bear patiently the cross
       of grief and pain;
   leave to your God
       to order and provide;
   in every change he faithful will
       remain.

Be still, my soul: your best,
  your heavenly friend
through thorny ways lead to a
  joyful end.

2 Be still, my soul: your God
  will undertake
to guide the future as he has
  the past.
Your hope, your confidence let
  nothing shake,
all now mysterious shall be clear
  at last.
Be still, my soul: the tempests
  still obey
his voice, who ruled them once
  on Galilee.

3. Be still, my soul: the hour is
  hastening on
when we shall be for ever with
  the Lord,
when disappointment, grief and
  fear are gone,
sorrow forgotten, love's pure
  joy restored.
Be still, my soul: when change
  and tears are past,
all safe and blessed we shall meet
  at last.

Katharina von Schlegel, tr by Jane L. Borthwick
(1813-1897)

408

1. Before Christ died
  he took some bread,
and then he took some wine.
'My body and my blood,' he said,
'a sacrificial sign.'

2. 'Now eat and drink, I am your
  food.
I promise you will see
your lives transformed, your
  hearts renewed;
you'll die and live with me.'

3. We drink this wine,
  we eat this bread,
as Jesus bade us do.
The covenant for which he bled
today we must renew.

4. By faith, in broken bread we see
the body of our Lord.
By faith, we know the wine to be
his holy blood outpoured.

5. Each time the church,
  for memory's sake,
repeats Christ's holy act,
each time we of that meal partake,
Christ's death we re-enact.

6. From sunrise to the setting sun
this death we will proclaim.
Each day Christ promises to come
until he comes again.

Peter de Rosa © 1970/1980 Mayhew McCrimmon Ltd

409

Bind us together, Lord,
bind us together
with cords that cannot be broken.
Bind us together, Lord,
bind us together,
bind us together with love.

1. There is only one God,
there is only one King,
there is only one Body,
that is why we sing:

2. Made for the glory of God,
   purchased by His precious Son,
   born with the right to be clean,
   for Jesus the victory has won.

3. You are the family of God,
   you are the promise divine,
   you are God's chosen desire,
   you are the glorious new wine.

Bob Gillman copyright © 1977 Thankyou Music,
PO Box 75, Eastbourne, BN23 6NW. Printed by permission

410

1. Blest are you, Lord, God of all
   creation,
   thanks to your goodness this
   bread we offer:
   fruit of the earth, work of our
   hands,
   it will become the bread of life.

   Blessed be God! Blessed be God!
   Blessed be God forever! Amen!
   Blessed be God! Blessed be God!
   Blessed be God forever! Amen!

2. Blest are you, Lord, God of all
   creation,
   thanks to your goodness this
   wine we offer:
   fruit of the earth, work of our
   hands,
   it will become the cup of life.

Aniceto Nazareth © 1980 Aniceto Nazareth,
St Pius College, Bombay 63

411

Blest be the Lord; blest be the Lord,
the God of mercy, the God who
saves.
I shall not fear the dark of night,
nor the arrow that flies by day.

1. He will release me from the nets
   of all my foes;
   He will protect me from their
   wicked hands.
   Beneath the shadow of His wings
   I will rejoice
   To find a dwelling place secure.

2. I need not shrink before the terrors
   of the night,
   Nor stand alone before the light
   of day.
   No harm shall come to me, no
   arrow strike me down,
   No evil settle in my soul.

3. Although a thousand strong have
   fallen at my side,
   I'll not be shaken with the Lord
   at hand.
   His faithful love is all the armour
   that I need
   To wage my battle with the foe.

Blest be the Lord, based on Psalm 90 (91)
by Daniel L. Schutte, SJ, copyright © 1976
by Daniel L. Schutte, SJ, and North America Liturgy
Resources, 10802 N 23rd Ave, Phoenix, AZ 85029, USA.
All rights reserved. Used with permission

412

1. Bread of the world, in mercy
   broken,
   wine of the soul, in mercy shed,
   by whom the words of life were
   spoken,
   and in whose death our sins are
   dead.

2. Look on the heart by sorrow
    broken,
   look on the tears by sinners shed;
   and be your feast to us the token
   that by your grace our souls are
   fed.

Reginald Heber (1783-1826)

4. Join then the movement of
    the love that frees,
   till people of whatever race
    or nation,
   will truly be themselves,
    stand on their feet,
   see eye to eye with laughter
    and elation.

Fred Kaan © 1975 Agapé

413

1. Break not the circle of enabling
    love,
   where people grow, forgiven
    and forgiving;
   break not that circle, make it
    wider still,
   till it includes, embraces all the
    living.

2. Come, wonder at this love
    that comes to life,
   where words of freedom are
    with humour spoken
   and people keep no score of
    wrong and guilt,
   but will that human bonds
    remain unbroken.

3. Come, wonder at the Lord
    who came and comes
   to teach the world the craft
    of hopeful craving
   for peace and wholeness that
    will fill the earth:
   he calls his people to creative
    living.

414

MAGNIFICAT

**Breathing the words of humble
    obedience true,
let it be so, and let it be done
    for you,
I am the handmaid of the Lord.**

1. My soul magnifies the Lord
    and my spirit rejoices in God my
     king.
   Henceforth all men will call me
    blessed
   because God has done great
    things for me.

2. His mercy spans each generation
    on those who fear him, holy is his
     name,
   he has shown the might of his
    arm,
   the proud he scattered with all
    their plans.

3. Mighty kings have been tumbled
    from their thrones,
   and exalted have been the lowly.
   He has filled the hungry with
    good things,
   the rich sent empty-handed away.

4. He has helped his servant Israel,
   to keep the promise made in time
      long past:
   his mercy shown to Abraham,
   and to all his descendants for ever.

Based on Luke 1:46-56 by Liz Powell and Jean Henriot © *Mayhew McCrimmon Ltd*

415

1. Bright star of morning, dawn on
      our darkness,
   Jesus our Master, our Lord and
      King,
   our hearts we give you now and
      forever,
   all that we care for to you we
      bring.

2. All of life's troubles, each daily
      burden
   are eased and lightened when you
      are near.
   Help us to stay close, trusting
      and child-like,
   calmed by your presence and free
      from fear.

3. Immortal Saviour, forgive our
      weakness,
   for you have known, Lord, our
      frailty.
   May we walk with you, safe in
      your love-light,
   each day and until eternity.

Estelle White © *Mayhew McCrimmon Ltd*

416

1. Brother Sun and Sister Moon,
   I seldom hear you,
   seldom hear your tune.
   Preoccupied with selfish misery.

2. Brother Wind and Sister Air,
   open my eyes to visions pure and
      fair
   that I may see the glory around
      me.

   I am God's creature,
   of him I am part.
   I feel his love
   awakening my heart.

3. Brother Sun and Sister Moon,
   I now do see you,
   I can hear your tune,
   so much in love with all I survey.

St Francis of Assisi, adapted by Donovan © *1973 Famous Music Corporation*

417

1. But I say unto you,
   love your enemies
   and pray for those who hurt you.
   Give to those who ask, don't turn
      away.

   And be like your Father in heaven
   above
   who causes his sun to shine on evil
   and good,
   and sends down his rain to quench
   all our thirst.
   In him we live and move and have
   our being.

2. If you forgive each other,
   so will God forgive you.
   Do not judge lest
   you be judg'd yourselves.

3. When you see the hungry,
   feed them from your table.
   For the poor and weary,
   be their wat'ring place.

Based on Luke 6:27ff. Beverlee Paine
© 1979 Celebration Services International Ltd

418

By his wounds we have been healed.

1. Christ suffered for you,
   leaving you an example
   that you should follow
   in his steps.

2. He committed no sin;
   no guile was found on his lips.
   When he was reviled,
   he did not revile in return.

3. When he suffered,
   he did not threaten;
   but he trusted in him
   who judges justly.

4. He himself bore our sins
   in his body on the tree,
   that we might die to sin
   and live to righteousness.

5. For you were straying like sheep,
   but now have returned
   to the shepherd
   and guardian of your souls.

1 Peter 2:21, 24 © Joseph Walshe, OSCO

419

1. By the Cross which did to death
   our only Saviour,
   this blessed vine from which
   grapes are gathered in:
   **Jesus Christ, we thank and bless
   you.**
   By the Cross which casts down fire
   upon our planet,
   this burning bush in which
   love is plainly shown:
   Jesus Christ, we glorify you.
   By the Cross on Calv'ry's hill
   securely planted,
   this living branch
   which can heal our ev'ry sin:
   **conquering God,
   we your Church proclaim you!**

2. By the Blood with which we
   marked
   the wooden lintels
   for our protection the night
   when God passed by:
   **Jesus Christ, we thank and bless
   you.**
   By the Blood which in our Exodus
   once saved us,
   when hell was sealed up
   by God's engulfing sea:
   Jesus Christ, we glorify you.
   By the Blood which kills the
   poison
   in bad fruitage,
   and gives new life
   to the dead sap in the tree:
   **conquering God,
   we your Church proclaim you!**

3. By the Death on Calv'ry's hill
   of him the First-born,

who bears the wood and the
flame for his own pyre:
**Jesus Christ, we thank and bless
you.**
By the Death, amid the thorns,
of God's own Shepherd,
the Paschal Lamb who was
  pierced
by our despair:
Jesus Christ, we glorify you.
By the Death of God's belov'd
outside his vineyard,
that he might change us
from murd'rer into heir:
**conquering God,
we your Church proclaim you!**

4. By the Wood which sings a song
of nuptial gladness,
of God who takes for bride
our human race:
**Jesus Christ, we thank and bless
you.**
By the Wood which raises up
in his full vigour
the Son of Man who draws
all men by his grace:
Jesus Christ, we glorify you.
By the Wood where he perfects
his royal Priesthood
in one High Priest
who for sin is sacrifice:
**conquering God,
we your Church proclaim you!**

5. Holy Tree which reaches up
from earth to heaven
that all the world may
exult in Jacob's God:
**Jesus Christ, we thank and bless
you.**

Mighty Ship which snatches us
from God's deep anger,
saves us, with Noah,
from drowning in the Flood:
Jesus Christ, we glorify you.
Tender Wood which gives to
brackish water sweetness,
and from the Rock shall strike
fountains for our food:
**conquering God,
we your Church proclaim you!**

Didier Rimaud, tr by F. Pratt Green
© Stainer & Bell Ltd

420

**Called to be servants,
called to be sons,
called to be daughters,
we're called to be one.
Called into service,
called to be free;
you are called to be you,
and I'm called to be me.**

1. Children, come, with wide open
eyes.
Look at the water; you have been
baptised.
You're free from the slav'ry that
bound you to sin,
so live now as children in the
kingdom of heav'n.

2. We are saints! Forgiveness is sure
not of ourselves, but the cross
Christ endured.
We're free from the Law that said
'You must provide!'
We're free to be servants; we're
called; we're baptised.

3. Jesus closed the dark pit of death.
   He has breathed on us with his
     holy breath.
   He gives us the faith to respond to
     his News.
   We're free to show mercy, to love,
     to be bruised.

© 1979 James G. Johnson

421

1. Child in the manger, infant of
     Mary;
   outcast and stranger, Lord of all;
   child who inherits all our
     transgressions,
   all our demerits on him fall.

2. Once the most holy child of
     salvation
   gently and lowly lived below;
   now as our glorious mighty
     Redeemer,
   see him victorious o'er each foe.

3. Prophets foretold him, infant of
     wonder;
   angels behold him on his throne:
   worthy our Saviour of all their
     praises;
   happy for ever are his own.

Mary Macdonald, tr by Lachlan Macbean

422

1. Christ be my way, my path to find
     the Father,
   my guide when there's no trusting
     sound or sight;
   Christ fill my mind to cleanse
     the understanding,

to be my truth, a beacon blazing
  bright;
Christ all I hope for,
  strengthening, upholding,
my breath of life, my pride and
  my delight.

**Truth on my tongue, his way
  to guide my walking
and I shall live, not I but
  Christ in me!**

2. No way but Christ, his cross
     the only signpost
   and he our road through death
     to blessedness;
   no safety else, no footing
     for the pilgrim,
   without his leading there's no
     guide nor guess:
   our way to where the Father
     waits in welcome
   to greet us home from night and
     wilderness.

3. We name him Lord, Truth rising
     like a tower
   above the world his coming shook
     and stirred:
   truth born in time, a child, and
     shown to shepherds
   when God's great glory on the
     hills was heard;
   truth born beyond all time, when
     first the Father
   pronounced his mighty
     all-creating Word.

4. Christ, Life of man, creation's
     mind and maker,
   hid deep in God before the
     world began,
   God born of God, the
     everlasting mercy,
   the Father's love, who stopped

and put on man:
man's life that ebbed beneath
   the nails, the crowning,
then burst in one white dawn
   death's narrow span.

Luke Connaughton © Mayhew McCrimmon Ltd

4. Go spread the news, he's not in
   the grave.
He has arisen, mankind to save.
Jesus' redeeming labours are
   done.
Even the battle with sin is won.

Tr from Swahili by Howard S. Olsen
© 1977 Augsburg Publishing House

423

1. Christ has arisen, Alleluia!
Rejoice and praise him; Alleluia!
For our Redeemer burst from
   the tomb,
even from death, dispelling its
   gloom.

Let us sing praise to him with
   endless joy.
Death's fearful sting he has come
   to destroy.
Our sins forgiving, Alleluia!
Jesus is living, Alleluia!

2. For three long days the grave did
   its worst,
until its strength by God was
   dispersed
He who gives life did death
   undergo,
and in its conquest his might
   did show.

3. The angel said to them, 'Do not
   fear,
you look for Jesus who is not here.
See for yourselves, the tomb is
   all bare:
only the grave-clothes are lying
   there.'

424

1. Christ is alive, with joy we sing;
we celebrate our risen Lord,
praising the glory of his name.
Alleluia, alleluia, alleluia.

2. He is the grain of wheat that died;
sown in distress and reaped in joy,
yielding a harvest of new life.
Alleluia, alleluia, alleluia.

3. He is the sun which brings the
   dawn:
he is the light of all the world,
setting us free from death and sin.
Alleluia, alleluia, alleluia.

4. He is the vine set in the earth,
sharing our life, becoming man,
that man might share in God's
   own life.
Alleluia, alleluia, alleluia.

5. Christ is alive, with joy we sing;
we celebrate our risen Lord,
praising the glory of his name.
Alleluia, alleluia, alleluia.

Pamela Stotter © 1978 Pamela Stotter

425

1. Christ is arisen from the grave's
   dark prison.
   We now rejoice with gladness;
   Christ will end all sadness.
   Lord, have mercy.

2. All our hopes were ended had
   Jesus not ascended
   from the grave triumphantly.
   For this, Lord Christ, we worship
   Thee.
   Lord, have mercy.

3. Alleluia! Alleluia! Alleluia!
   We now rejoice with gladness;
   Christ will end all sadness.
   Lord, have mercy.

Anon (11th Century) tr by Gustave Polack

426

1. Christ is coming
   to set the captives free,
   He is coming
   to rescue you and me.

   **Christ is coming from above
   bringing joy and bringing love.
   He is coming for you and me.**

2. Christ has come
   to a stable cold and bare;
   He is coming
   to a world where no one cares.

3. Christ is coming,
   bringing light where darkness
   reigned;
   He is coming
   where we gather in his name.

4. Christ is coming
   to this altar in our Mass;
   He is coming
   to a new home in our hearts.

5. Christ is coming,
   the Father's only Son;
   He is coming
   – his spirit makes us one.

© *1978 N. & K. Donnelly*

427

1. Christ is made the sure
   foundation,
   Christ the head and corner stone,
   chosen of the Lord, and precious,
   binding all the Church in one,
   holy Sion's help for ever,
   and her confidence alone.

2. All that dedicated city,
   dearly loved of God on high,
   in exultant jubilation
   pours perpetual melody,
   God the One in Three adoring
   in glad hymns eternally.

3. To this temple where we call you
   come, O Lord of Hosts, today;
   with your wonted loving kindness
   hear your people as they pray,
   and your fullest benediction
   shed within its walls alway.

4. Here vouchsafe to all your
   servants
   what they ask of you to gain,
   what they gain of you forever
   with the blessed to retain,
   and hereafter in your glory
   evermore with you to reign.

5. Praise and honour to the Father,
   praise and honour to the Son,
   praise and honour to the Spirit,
   ever Three and ever One,
   consubstantial, co-eternal,
   while unending ages run.

   Latin 7th or 8th Century, tr J. M. Neale
   (1818-66 alt)

428

1. Christ is the world's light,
   he and no other;
   born in our darkness,
   he became our brother.
   If we have seen him,
   we have seen the Father:
   glory to God on high.

2. Christ is the world's peace,
   he and no other;
   no man can serve him
   and despise his brother.
   Who else unites us,
   one in God the Father?
   Glory to God on high.

3. Christ is the world's life,
   he and no other,
   sold once for silver,
   murdered here, our brother
   he who redeems us,
   reigns with God the Father:
   glory to God on high.

4. Give God the glory,
   God and no other;
   give God the glory,
   Spirit, Son and Father;
   give God the glory,
   God in man, my brother:
   glory to God on high.

   F. Pratt Green © Stainer & Bell

429

1. Christ is the world's redeemer,
   the lover of the pure,
   the fount of heavenly wisdom,
   our trust and hope secure,
   the armour of his soldiers,
   the lord of earth and sky,
   our health while we are living,
   our life when we shall die.

2. Christ has our host surrounded
   with clouds of martyrs bright
   who wave their palms in triumph
   and fire us for the fight.
   For Christ the cross ascended
   to save a world undone
   and suffering for the sinful
   and full redemption won.

3. Down in the realm of darkness
   he lay a captive bound,
   but at the hour appointed
   he rose, a victor crowned,
   and now, to heaven ascended,
   he sits upon the throne
   in glorious dominion,
   his Father's and his own.

   St Columba (521-97) tr by Duncan McGregor

430

**Christ our Lord has come to save his
people!
Alleluia! Alleluia! Alleluia!**

1. Baptized in Christ our Lord,
   reborn to new life in our Saviour
   and Lord, alleluia!
   For we are the people whom God
   made his own
   through the blood of his own Son,
   our Lord Jesus Christ.

2. O come then, bless the Lord,
   the Father of all, who is love
       without end, alleluia!
   Before he created the world with
       great pow'r,
   we were chosen then in Christ,
   God made us his own.

3. Since time itself began
   God loved us and planned to
       adopt us in Christ, alleluia!
   He chose us to live in his glorious
       name,
   as his children and his friends, a
       people redeemed.

4. Be joyful in the Lord,
   rejoice and give thanks to the
       Father of all, alleluia!
   For Christ is alive and we live now
       in him;
   we are filled now with his life.
       Rejoice, praise his name!

5. With Christ we are made heirs
   and called to belong to the fam'ly
       of God, alleluia!
   Christ freed us from sin by his
       death on the cross,
   and has raised us up to life, a life
       without end.

6. Give glory to our God, the Father
       of all;
   to his Son, Jesus Christ, alleluia!
   And praise to the Spirit, the gift of
       his love.
   Let us sing out to the Lord for
       ever. Amen.

Paul Decha, tr by Sr Mary Lucia and Robert B. Kelly
© 1984 assigned to Kevin Mayhew Ltd

431

Christ our Pasch has been slain,
   alleluia!
Sing with joy, alleluia, alleluia,
   alleluia!

1. Pasch of the New Law,
   the Spirit's holy feast;
   O Pasch of Christ the Lord,
   who for us has come to earth!

2. Pasch of the New Law,
   O joy of all mankind;
   the doors of life are wide,
   giving life to us once more.

3. Pasch of the New Law,
   the banquet hall is full
   of guests the Lord has called,
   that all men may share his feast.

4. Pasch of the New Law,
   behold your baptized saints
   in robes of purest white
   for the marriage of the Lamb.

5. Pasch of the New Law,
   our souls' immortal flame
   shines forth in splendor bright,
   nevermore to cease its light.

6. Pasch of the New Law,
   O Christ who lives again:
   the pow'r of death you crushed,
   you have given us your life.

7. Pasch of the New Law,
   we pray to you, O Lord:
   stretch forth your blessed hands
   on the people you have saved.

8. Pasch of the New Law,
   O Christ, receive our songs;
   to you be glory, Lord,
   with all joy and praise. Amen!

*Lucien Deiss © 1965, 1966, 1973 World Library
Publications Inc. Reprinted with permission*

432

1. City of God, how broad and far
   outspread thy walls sublime!
   The true thy chartered freeman
      are,
   of every age and clime.

2. One holy Church, one army
      strong,
   one steadfast, high intent;
   one working band, one harvest
      song
   one King omnipotent.

3. How purely hath thy speech come
      down
   from man's primeval youth!
   How grandly hath thine empire
      grown,
   of freedom, love and truth!

4. How gleam thy watch-fires
      through the night
   with never-fainting ray!
   How rise thy towers, serene and
      bright,
   to meet the dawning day!

5. In vain the surge's angry shock,
   in vain the drifting sands:
   unharmed upon the eternal Rock
   the eternal City stands.

Samuel Johnson (1822-82)

433

1. Come, God's people, sing for joy,
   shout your songs of gladness;
   for the hope of Easter day
   overcomes our sadness.
   Come with all his people here,
   who with true affection,
   join again to celebrate
   Jesus' resurrection.

2. Years before, as Moses led
   Israel's sons and daughters
   from their bonds to Exodus
   through the Red Sea waters:
   so the living Lord of life
   speaks through our baptism
   of the new life that we share
   with him who is risen.

3. That first Easter he arose,
   his disciples greeting;
   Christians now throughout the
      world,
   still their Lord are meeting.
   Christ, who dies for all mankind,
   in his death brings healing;
   and his rising from the grave,
   God's power is revealing.

*St John Damascene (d 754), freely paraphrased
by Keith D. Pearson © 1976 Joint Board of Christian
Education of Australia and New Zealand*

434

1. Come, holy Lord, our faith renew,
   our little praise enough for you.

   **We ask your mercy, Lord,
   who bear your sacred name;
   your healing touch
   the glorious blessing we can claim.**

2. O Jesus, come, our hope on earth,
   from heaven you came to share
       our birth.

3. Come, Spirit blest, our love revive;
   our failing prayer is made alive.

435

Come let us sing out our joy to
    the Lord!
Hail the rock of salvation,
come into his presence to give
    thanks,
singing psalms of triumph.

1. In his hands are the depths of the
       earth,
   the mountain peaks belong to him.
   His is the sea, he created it,
   His is the dry land, formed by his
       hands.

2. Bow down before him in prayer,
   kneel before the Lord and adore.
   He is the Lord our shepherd,
   we his people, the flock that he
       feeds.

3. Listen to the voice of the Lord,
   do not grow stubborn nor harden
       your hearts.
   Put not your God to the test,
   well you know how he cares for us.

4. Praise the Father who made all
       things,
   praise the Son who died for us.
   Praise the Spirit who gladdens
       our hearts,
   praise unceasing fill heaven and
       earth.

436

Come, Lord Jesus,
    come Lord, come!
Come, Lord Jesus,
    come Lord, come!
Open my eyes,
    open my mind,
open my heart to peace
    and love.

1. Like rain falling on the thirsty
       ground,
   like grass springing from the
       barren earth,
   like the sun rising over the land,
   heralds new life and a new rebirth.

2. So he comes bringing
       righteousness,
   bringing justice to all the land;
   so he comes as a man among men,
   Saviour and Lord of all mankind.

3. Wonder Counsellor and Prince
       of Peace,
   a man of such integrity!
   Come Lord Jesus, we plead to
       you,
   come and give us liberty.

437

1. Come, O divine Messiah!
   The world in silence waits the day
   when hope shall sing its triumph,
   and sadness flee away.

   Sweet Saviour, haste; come,
       come to earth:

dispel the night, and show Thy
    face,
and bid us hail the dawn of grace.
Come, O divine Messiah!
The world in silence waits the day
when hope shall sing its triumph,
and sadness flee away.

2. O Thou, whom nations sighed for,
    whom priests and prophets long
        foretold,
    wilt break the captive fetters,
    redeem the long-lost fold.

3. Shalt come in peace and meekness,
    and lowly will thy cradle be:
    all clothed in human weakness
    shall we thy Godhead see.

French 18th Century, tr Sr Mary of St Phillip

438

Come, O Lord, to my heart today
and stay with me all the day.
Come, O Lord, to my heart today
and stay with me all the day.

1. Your flesh is food and your
        blood is drink,
    and these you give to me your life.

2. This is the bread
        come down from heaven
    which, if a man eats, he'll live
        for ever.

3. He who takes my flesh and blood
    lives in me and I in him.

4. When you give your self to us,
    you bind us to yourself and each
        other.

Based on John 50, 55, 56, by Douglas Rowe
© 1980 Mayhew McCrimmon Ltd

439

1. Come, thou long-expected Jesus,
    born to set thy people free,
    from our fears and sins release us,
    let us find our rest in thee.

2. Israel's strength and consolation,
    hope of all the earth thou art;
    dear desire of every nation,
    joy of every longing heart.

3. Born thy people to deliver,
    born a child and yet a king,
    born to reign in us for ever,
    now thy gracious kingdom bring.

4. By thine own eternal Spirit
    rule in all our hearts alone;
    by thine all-sufficient merit
    raise us to thy glorious throne.

Charles Wesley (1707-88)

440

1. Day and night the heav'ns are
        telling
    the glory which with us is dwelling,
    the works of God to us made
        known.
    Dawn and dusk are still with
        wonder.
    The wind cries out, the waters
        thunder,
    displaying his almighty power.
    Our God is great indeed.
    He knows our constant need, our
        creator.
    So with creation we proclaim
    his goodness as we praise his
        name.

2. Lord, we stand in awe before you,
   your people coming to adore you,
   so cleanse our hearts, renew our
     minds.
   See us now in shadows dwelling,
   and come like sun, the clouds
     dispelling,
   enlighten, heal us, Lord of love.
   Your Spirit in us prays.
   He teaches us your ways,
   as we listen.
   Touch once again with living
     flame
   your people gathered in your
     name.

© Pamela Stotter

441

Day by day, dear Lord,
of thee three things I pray;
to see thee more clearly,
to love thee more dearly,
to follow thee more nearly,
day by day.

St Richard of Chichester, arr by D. Austin

442

1. Dear love of my heart,
     O heart of Christ, my Lord,
   what treasure you leave
     within my heart, O Guest!
   You come to my heart
     O heart on fire with love,
   and leave me your heart:
     O how my heart is blest!

2. My heart cannot tell,
     O King of angel hosts,
   how great was that pain
     you bore upon the cross:
   so small is my heart,
     so deep your wounds of love,
   so precious the crown
     of those you save from loss!

3. Your death has restored
     your likeness in my heart,
   your cross in my shield,
     your loving heart my gain!
   How sad is my heart
     when I recall my sins!
   How could I have loved
     what gave your heart such pain?

4. O King of all bliss,
     all glory set aside,
   what heart could have known
     the pain within your breast?
   The wound in your side
     laid bare your burning love,
   and opened for all
     the heart where all find rest!

Based on the Irish of Tadhg Gaelach O Suilleabhain,
by James Quinn, SJ © Geoffrey Chapman Ltd

443

Divided our pathways,
and heavy our guilt;
burden'd, unseeing,
we grope for the one way.
Far from our home,
O Father, we call out –
'Heal us, forgive us
bringing us together in Jesus your
     Son!
in Jesus your Son!'

1. Holy Father, keep those
   you have given me
   true to your name,
   so that they may all
   be as we are one.

2. Father, may they be one in us,
   as you are in me and I am in you,
   so that the world may come to
       believe
   it was you who sent me.

3. I have given them the glory
   that you gave to me,
   that they may all be one
   as we are one.

4. With me in them and you in me
   may they be so completely united,
   that the world may know
   that it was you who sent me,
   and that you love them
   as much as you love me.

From John 17:11-21-23 by Christopher Coelho
© 1974 Agapé

444

**Do not be afraid, for I have
redeemed you.
I have called you by your name;
you are mine.**

1. When you walk through the
       waters I'll be with you.
   You will never sink beneath the
       waves.

2. When the fire is burning all
       around you,
   you will never be consumed by
   the flames.

3. When the fear of loneliness is
       looming,
   then remember I am at your side.

4. When you dwell in the exile of the
       stranger,
   remember you are precious in my
       eyes.

5. You are mine, O my child, I am
       your Father,
   and I love you with a perfect love.

Gerald Markland, based on Isaiah 43:1-4
© 1978 Kevin Mayhew Ltd

445

1. 'Do you really love me?'
   Jesus said to Peter.
   'Do you really love me?'
   Jesus said again.
   'Lord, you know I love you!'
   Peter said with joy.
   'Then feed my lambs', he said,
   'Peter, feed my lambs.'

2. 'Do you really love me?'
   Jesus said to Peter.
   'Do you really love me?'
   Jesus said again.
   'Lord, you know I love you!'
   Peter said with joy.
   'Then feed my sheep,' he said,
   'Peter, feed my sheep.'

3. 'Do you really love me?'
   Jesus says to me.
   'Do you really love me?'
   Jesus says to you.
   'Yes, we really love you,
   we will follow you!'
   'Then feed my lambs,' he says,
   'people, feed my sheep.'

Do You Really Love Me? by Carey Landry
copyright © 1973 by Rev Carey Landry and North
American Liturgy Resources, 10802 N 23rd Ave, Pheonix,
AZ, 85029, USA. All rights reserved. Used with permission

446

1, Each morning with its new born
    light
    proclaims the Lord of life is great!
    His faithfulness will have no end;
    to him our songs of praise ascend.

2. The gift of light that fills the sky
    helps us to see and choose our
        way;
    then let us order our affairs
    in praise of him who for us cares.

3. Lord, let our eyes, the body's light,
    be drawn to what is good and right
    and to yourself, the source of life,
    our hope in fear, our peace in
        strife.

4. You, Lord of all creation, are
    as brilliant as the morning star;
    light in our hearts your holy flame
    and make us fit to bear your name.

5. Dispel the darkness from our days
    and free us from all bitterness,
    from haughty mind and blinded
        sight,
    and lead us forward day and night.

6. To walk as in the light of day,
    be steadfast always, come what
        may,
    we turn in faith to you, our Friend,
    and pray: sustain us to the end.

Johannes Zwick (1496-1542) tr by © Fred Kaan

447

Faith in God
    can move the mountains;
trust in him can calm the sea.
He's my fortress,
    he's my stronghold;
he's the rock who rescues me.

1. Lord, you are my refuge;
    never let me be ashamed.
    In your justice rescue me;
    turn to me and hear my prayer.

2. You are my salvation:
    from oppression set me free.
    Ever since my childhood
    you have been my only hope.

3. Bitter troubles burden me,
    but you fill me with new life.
    From the grave you raise me up,
    so my tongue will sing your praise.

Words para from Scripture by Aniceto Nazareth
© 1980 Aniceto Nazareth, St Pius College, Bombay 63

448

1. Fashion me a people,
    a people set apart;
    that I may be your God,
    and you will give me your heart.

2. Come together in community,
    a sign of my love here on earth,
    to share the life of Nazareth,
    and incarnate the myst'ry of my
        birth.

3. Be a fam'ly, humble and forgiving,
    who listen to my voice,
    who call upon my mercy,
    and at my coming rejoice.

4. Fashion me a people,
   a people set apart;
   that I may be your God,
   and I will give you my heart.

Carol Gordon © 1980 assigned to Mayhew McCrimmon Ltd

449

1. Father, hear the prayer we offer:
   not for ease that prayer shall be,
   but for strength that we may ever
   live our lives courageously.

2. Not for ever in green pastures
   do we ask our way to be;
   but the steep and rugged pathway
   may we tread rejoicingly.

3. Not for ever by still waters
   would we idly rest and stay;
   but would smite the living
      fountains
   from the rocks along the way.

4. Be our strength in hours of
      weakness,
   in our wanderings be our guide;
   through endeavour, failure,
      danger,
   Father, be there at our side.

Love Maria Willis (1824-1908) and others

450

1. Father, I place into your hands
   the things I cannot do.
   Father, I place into your hands
   the things that I've been through.
   Father, I place into your hands
   the way that I should go,
   For I know I always can trust you.

2. Father, I place into your hands
   my friends and family.
   Father, I place into your hands
   the things that trouble me.
   Father, I place into your hands
   the person I would be,
   for I know I always can trust you.

3. Father, we love to see your face,
   we love to hear your voice,
   Father, we love to sing your praise
   and in your name rejoice,
   Father, we love to walk with you
   and in your presence rest,
   for we know we always can trust
      you.

4. Father, I want to be with you
   and do the things you do.
   Father, I want to speak the words
   that you are speaking too.
   Father, I want to love the ones
   that you will draw to you,
   for I know that I am one with you.

*J. Hewer © 1975 Thankyou Music PO Box 75,
Eastbourne, BN23 6NW*

451

1. Father in heaven,
   grant to your children
   mercy and blessing,
   songs never ceasing,
   love to unite us,
   grace to redeem us,
   Father in heaven,
   Father our God.

2. Jesus, Redeemer,
   may we remember
   your gracious Passion,
   your resurrection.
   Worship we bring you,
   praise we shall sing you
   Jesus, Redeemer,
   Jesus our God.

3. Spirit descending
   whose is the blessing –
   strength for the weary,
   help for the needy,
   sealed in our sonship
   yours be our worship –
   Spirit unending,
   Spirit adored.

D. T. Niles © 1971 Christian Conference of Asia

452

1. Father, in my life I see,
   you are God, who walks with me.
   You hold my life in your hands:
   close beside you I will stand.
   I give all my life to you:
   help me, Father, to be true.

2. Jesus, in my life I see . . .

3. Spirit, in my life I see . . .

Frank Anderson, MSC, © Chevalier Press

453

1. Father, Lord of all creation,
   ground of being, life and love;
   height and depth beyond
      description
   only life in you can prove:

you are mortal life's dependence:
thought, speech, sight are ours by
   grace;
yours is every hour's existence,
Sovereign Lord of time and space.

2. Jesus Christ, the man for others,
   we, you people, make our prayer:
   give us grace to love as brothers
   all whose burdens we can share.
   Where your name binds us
      together
   you, Lord, Christ, will surely be;
   where no selfishness can sever
   there your love may all men see.

3. Holy Spirit, rushing, burning
   wind and flame of Pentecost,
   fire our hearts afresh with
      yearning
   to regain what we have lost.
   May your love unite our action,
   nevermore to speak alone:
   God, in us abolish faction,
   God, through us your love make
      known.

© Stewart Cross

454

1. Father of heaven, whose love
      profound
   a ransom for our souls hath found,
   before thy throne we sinners bend,
   to us thy pardoning love extend.

2. Almighty Son, incarnate Word,
   our prophet, priest, Redeemer,
      Lord,
   before thy throne we sinners bend,
   to us thy saving grace extend.

3. Eternal Spirit, by whose breath
   the soul is raised from sin and
      death,
   before thy throne we sinners bend,
   to us thy quickening power
      extend.

4. Thrice Holy Father, Spirit, Son;
   mysterious Godhead, Three in
      One,
   before thy throne we sinners bend,
   grace, pardon, life to us extend.

E. Cooper (1770-1833)

455

1. Father, we praise you,
      now the night is over;
   active and watchful,
      stand we all before you;
   singing, we offer pray'r
      and meditation:
      thus we adore you.

2. Monarch of all things,
      fit us for your kingdom;
   banish our weakness,
      health and wholeness sending;
   bring us to heaven,
      where your saints united
      joy without ending.

3. All holy Father, Son,
      and equal Spirit,
   Trinity blessed,
      send us your salvation;
   yours is the glory,
      gleaming and resounding
      through all creation.

St Gregory the Great (540-604) tr by Percy Dearmer
(1867-1936), slightly altered © OUP

456

Fear not, for I have redeemed you:
I have called you by name;
I have called you by name;
you are mine.

1. When you pass through the waters
   I will be with you;
   and through rivers,
   they will not overwhelm you.
   When you walk through the fire
   you will not be burned,
   the flames shall not consume you.

2. Because you are precious,
   and I love you;
   you whom I formed
   for my glory;
   you whom I called
   by my name,
   I will gather together.

3. You are my witness;
   I have chosen you
   that you may know
   and believe me.
   You are my servants
   for the world to see
   I am the Lord, I'm among you.

4. It's time now to lay aside
   the former things;
   a new day has dawned,
   do you see it
   I'm making a way
   in the wilderness
   and rivers to flow in the desert.

5. The rivers that flow
in the desert
give drink
to my chosen people;
to quench their thirst
and to strengthen them,
that they might show forth
my praise.

Based on Isaiah 43:2, 4, 10, 18-20, by Jodi Page
© 1975 Celebration Services International Ltd

457

**Fear not, rejoice and be glad,
the Lord hath done a great thing;
hath poured out his Spirit on all
mankind,
on those who confess his name.**

1. The fig tree is budding, the vine
beareth fruit,
the wheat fields are golden with
grain.
Thrust in the sickle, the harvest
is ripe,
the Lord has given us rain.

2. Ye shall eat in plenty and be
satisfied,
the mountains will drip with sweet
wine.
My children shall drink of the
fountain of life,
my children will know they are
mine.

3. My people shall know that I am
the Lord,
their shame I have taken away.
My Spirit will lead them together
again,
my Spirit will show them the way.

4. My children shall dwell in a body
of love,
a light to the world they will be.
Life shall come forth from the
Father above,
my body will set mankind free.

Priscilla Wright © 1971, 1975 Celebration Services
International Ltd

458

1. 'Feed my lambs, my son, feed
my sheep;
if you love me, do not sleep.
In the fields, my son, work and
weep;
feed my lambs, my son, feed
my sheep.'

2. To the servant girl first he lied:
'You were with him!' this she
cried.
But the Master he denied;
on the following day, Jesus died.

3. Someone questioned him quietly,
'Aren't you Peter of Galilee?
I can tell you by your speech,
you see.'
Peter swore and said, 'It's not me!'

4. Peter heard the cock when it crew;
as he left, he wept – and he knew!
Ev'ry one of us is guilty too;
yet Christ died for us, me and you.

5. Feed my lambs, my son, feed
my sheep;
if you love me, do not sleep.
In the fields, my son, work and
weep;
feed my lambs, my son, feed
my sheep.

Charles A. Buffham (altered) © 1969 Singspiration Inc

459

1. Firm is our faith in one true God,
   loving Father and King supreme,
   mighty creator, Lord of all,
   visible world and world unseen.

2. And we believe in God's own Son,
   one with him from eternal dawn,
   who by the Spirit was conceived,
   and of his Virgin Mother born.

3. Man he was made and man he
      lived,
   man he suffered in cruel strife
   when on the Cross he fought
      with death,
   conquered and rose to deathless
      life.

4. This is our faith in the Spirit too:
   Lord and giver of life is he,
   one with the Father and the Son,
   spirit of love and unity.

5. Faith we profess in one true
      Church,
   sin forgiven and grace restored,
   hope for the vict'ry over death,
   life without end in Christ the Lord.

Denis E. Hurley © Archdiocese of Durban

460

Follow me, follow me,
leave your home and family,
leave your fishing nets and boats
   upon the shore.
Leave the seed that you have sown,
leave the crops that you've grown,
leave the people you have known
and follow me.

1. The foxes have their holes
   and the swallows have their nests,
   but the Son of man has no place to
      lay down.
   I do not offer comfort,
   I do not offer wealth,
   but in me will all happiness be
      found.

2. If you would follow me,
   you must leave old ways behind.
   You must take my cross
   and follow on my path.
   You may be far from loved ones,
   you may be far from home
   but my Father will welcome you
      at last.

3. Although I go away
   you will never be alone,
   for the Spirit will be
   there to comfort you.
   Though all of you may scatter,
   each follow his own path,
   still the Spirit of love will lead
      you home.

Michael Cockett © 1978 Kevin Mayhew Ltd

461

1. For the fruits of his creation,
   thanks be to God;
   for his gifts to every nation,
   thanks be to God;
   for the ploughing, sowing,
      reaping,
   silent growth while men are
      sleeping,
   future needs in earth's safe
      keeping,
   thanks be to God.

2. In the just reward of labour,
   God's will is done;
   in the help we give our neighbour,
   God's will is done;
   in our world-wide task of caring
   for the hungry and despairing
   in the harvests men are sharing,
   God's will is done.

3. For the harvests of his Spirit,
   thanks be to God;
   for the good all men inherit,
   thanks be to God;
   for the wonders that astound us,
   for the truths that still confound
   us,
   most of all, that love has found us,
   thanks be to God.

   F. Pratt Green © *Stainer & Bell*

462

1. For the healing of the nations,
   Lord, we pray with one accord,
   for a just and equal sharing
   of the things that earth affords.
   To a life of love in action
   help us rise and pledge our word.

2. Lead us, father, into freedom,
   from despair your world release,
   that, redeemed from war and
   hatred,
   men may come and go in peace.
   Show us how through care and
   goodness
   fear will die and hope increase.

3. All that kills abundant living,
   let it from the earth be banned;
   pride of status, race or schooling,
   dogmas keeping man from man.
   In our common quest for justice
   may we hallow life's brief span.

4. You, creator-God, have written
   your great name on all mankind;
   for our growing in your likeness
   bring the life of Christ to mind;
   that by our response and service
   earth its destiny may find.

   Fred Kaan © *Stainer & Bell*

463

**For to those who love God,
who are called in his plan,
ev'rything works out for good.
And God himself chose them
to bear the likeness of his Son,
that he might be the first
of many, many brothers.**

1. Who is able to condemn?
   Only Christ who died for us;
   Christ who rose for us;
   Christ who prays for us.

2. In the face of all this
   what is there left to say?
   For if God is with us,
   who can be against us?

3. What can separate us
   from the love of Christ?
   Neither trouble, nor pain,
   nor persecution.

4. What can separate us
   from the love of Christ?
   Not the past, the present,
   nor the future.

   Based on Romans 8:29, 31-35 © *1970 Enrico Garzilli*

464

For unto us a child is born,
unto us a son is given;
and the government
shall be upon his shoulder
and his name shall be called
'wonderful-counsellor',
'the Mighty-God',
'the everlasting Father',
and 'the Prince of Peace' is he.

Based on Isaiah 9:6 © Centicle Publications Inc

465

**Freely I give to you the gift of
a child my own
in hope that you will receive the
life that he gives for your own . . .**

1. Call him Emmanuel for your God
   is with you this day
   he'll be by your side sharing your
   joy and pain . . .

2. Call him Jesus, for Yahweh gives
   his own
   for he is the shepherd who will
   guide his flock safely home . . .

3. Call him Lamb of God for he has
   died for your sins
   and all will be saved and truly
   belong to him . . .

© 1984 J. Garrity

466

1. From the depths of sin and
     sadness
   I have called unto the Lord;
   be not deaf to my poor pleading,
   in your mercy, hear my voice.
   Be not deaf to my poor pleading,
   in your mercy, hear my voice.

2. If you, Lord, record our sinning
   who could then before you stand?
   But with you there is forgiveness;
   you shall ever be revered.
   But with you there is forgiveness;
   you shall ever be revered.

3. For the Lord my heart is waiting,
   for his word I hope and wait.
   More than watchmen wait for
     sunrise
   I am waiting for the Lord.
   More than watchmen wait for
     sunrise
   I am waiting for the Lord.

4. Hope, O people, in your Saviour,
   he will save you from your sin.
   Jesus from his cross is praying,
   'Father, forgive them,
   they know not what they do.'
   Jesus from his cross is praying,
   'Father, forgive them,
   they know not what they do.'

Based on Psalm 129 (130) © Willard F. Jabusch

467

**Gather Christians, let's now
   celebrate;
gather Christians, the Lord we
   now await;
gather Christians, behold he comes;
rejoice and sing, for the Lord is
   King!**

1. To God the Father, let's give
   him praise;
   to God the Father, our voice we
   raise;
   to God the Father, who reigns
   above;
   praise the Lord for his mercy
   and his love.

2. As we stand here before our God,
   with Christ Jesus, our saving
   Lord,
   we'll hear his word now, and
   break the bread,
   as we proclaim: he's risen from
   the dead!

3. Let us all now, as one community,
   praise and honour the Trinity.
   Let us all now with one accord
   sing out our praise to the living
   Lord!

Garfield Rochard © 1980 Mayhew McCrimmon Ltd

468

1. Gathered here from many
   churches,*
   one in worship and intent,
   let us for the days that face us
   all our hopes to God present,
   that our life and work may be
   symbols of our unity.

2. May the spring of all our actions
   be, O Lord, your love for man;
   may your word be seen and
   spoken
   and your will be clearly done.
   Help us, who your image bear,
   for the good of each to care.

3. Give us grace to match our calling,
   faith to overcome the past;
   show us how to meet the future,

planning boldly, acting fast.
Let the servant-mind of Christ
in our life be manifest.

4. Now ourselves anew committing
   to each other and to you,
   Lord, we ask that you will train us
   for the truth we have to do;
   that the world may soon become
   your great city of shalom.

   * **or** Gathered here from many
   nations,

Fred Kaan © Stainer & Bell

469

1. Gifts of bread and wine, gifts
   we've offered,
   fruits of labour, fruits of love:
   taken, offered, sanctified,
   blessed and broken; words of one
   who died:
   'Take my body; take my saving
   blood.'
   Gifts of bread and wine: Christ
   our Lord.

2. Christ our Saviour, living presence
   here,
   as he promised while on earth:
   'I am with you for all time,
   I am with you in this bread and
   wine.
   Take my body, take my saving
   blood.'
   Gifts of bread and wine: Christ
   our Lord.

3. Through the Father, with the
    Spirit,
   one in union with the Son,
   for God's people, joined in prayer
   faith is strengthened by the food
    we share.
   'Take my body, take my saving
    blood.'
   Gifts of bread and wine: Christ
   our Lord.

Christine McCann © 1978 Kevin Mayhew Ltd

470

1. Give praise to the Lord, all you
    men, **alleluia!**
   O praise the name of the Lord,
    alleluia!
   Bless'd be the name of the Lord,
    alleluia, alleluia!

2. Now and evermore,
   from dawn to the close of the day,
   bless'd be the name of the Lord.

3. On high, above the earth is the
    Lord,
   his glory above the sky;
   there is none like the Lord our
    God.

4. Enthroned in heaven on high,
   he views the earth and the sky;
   to those in need he gives his help.

5. From the dust he raises the poor,
   he makes them sit among kings,
   among the kings of the earth.

6. Behold the barren wife,
   now abides in her home
   as the happy mother of sons.

7. Let us sing to the Lord,
   singing glory and praise,
   both now and evermore. Amen.

Based on Psalm 112 (113) Lucien Deiss
© World Library Publications Inc.
Reprinted with permission

471

1. Give us the will to listen
   to the message you impart:
   we thank you, Lord,
   for showing us your heart!

2. Give us the will to persevere
   though meaning disappears:
   we thank you, Lord,
   for calming all our fears.

3. Give us the will to work on
   at what we may like the least:
   we thank you, Lord,
   for ev'ry bird and beast.

4. Give us the will to work and serve
   where we are needed most:
   we thank you, Lord,
   for staying with us close.

5. Give us the will to seek you
   in the quiet and the calm:
   we thank you, Lord,
   for keeping us from harm.

6. Give us the will to see you
   as our God, as man, as friend:
   we thank you, Lord,
   for your love has no end.

Kurt Rommel, tr by Eileen M. Burzynska
© Burckaardthaus-Verlag GmbH. tr © 1980
Mayhew McCrimmon Ltd

472

1. Glorious things of you are spoken,
   Sion, city of our God:
   he whose word cannot be broken
   formed you for his own abode.
   On the Rock of Ages founded,
   what can shake your sure repose?
   With salvation's walls
     surrounded,
   you may smile at all your foes.

2. See, the streams of living waters,
   springing from eternal love,
   well supply your sons and
     daughters
   and all fear of want remove:
   who can faint while such a river
   ever flows their thirst to assuage –
   grace, which like the Lord the
     giver
   never fails from age to age?

3. Blest inhabitants of Sion,
   washed in their Redeemer's blood:
   Jesus, whom their souls rely on,
   makes them Kings and priests to
     God.
   'Tis his love his people raises
   over self to reign as kings,
   and as priests, his solemn praises
   each for a thank-offering brings.

4. Saviour, since of Sion's city
   I, through grace, a member am,
   let the world deride or pity,
   I will glory in your name:
   fading is the worldling's pleasure,
   all his boasted pomp and show;
   solid joys and lasting treasure
   none but Sion's children know.

   John Newton (1725-1807)

473

Glory and praise to our God,
who alone gives light to our days.
Many are the blessings He bears
to those who trust in his ways.

1. We, the daughters and sons of
     Him
   who built the valleys and plains,
   praise the wonders our God has
     done
   in ev'ry heart that sings.

2. In His wisdom He strengthens us,
   like gold that's tested in fire,
   though the power of sin prevails,
   our God is there to save.

3. Ev'ry moment of ev'ry day
   our God is waiting to save,
   always ready to seek the lost,
   to answer those who pray.

4. God has watered our barren land
   and spent His merciful rain.
   Now the rivers of life run full
   for anyone to drink.

474

Glory to God! Peace to all men,
joy to earth comes from heaven.

1. For all your wonders, O Lord
     God,
   your people come to thank you.
   Our gracious friend, we bless
     your name,

for your Kingdom which comes!
To you we bring our praises
through the love of the Son and
  of the Spirit.

2. The world's redeemer, Jesus
     Christ,
   receive the pray'r we bring you.
   O Lamb of God, you conquered
     death;
   now have mercy on us.
   Most holy Jesus, Son of God:
   living Lord of all worlds,
     our Lord God!

Tr by Erik Routley (1917-1982) © OUP

475

1. God, at creation's dawn,
   over a world unborn,
   your Spirit soared.
   By word and water deign
   that this same Spirit reign
   in those now born again,
   through Christ our Lord.

2. We, who in Adam fell,
   are, as the Scriptures tell,
   saved and restored.
   For, when these rites are done,
   dying we are made one,
   rising we overcome,
   with Christ our Lord.

3. Hear us, your Church, rejoice,
   singing with grateful voice,
   Father adored;
   telling our faith anew,
   greeting with welcome true
   children new born to you,
   in Christ our Lord.

Denis E. Hurley © Archdiocese of Durban

476

1. God be with you till we meet
     again;
   by his counsels guide, uphold you,
   with his sheep securely fold you:
   God be with you till we meet
     again.

2. God be with you till we meet
     again;
   'neath his wings protecting hide
     you,
   daily manna still provide you:
   God be with you till we meet
     again.

3. God be with you till we meet
     again;
   when life's perils thick confound
     you,
   put his arm unfailing round you:
   God be with you till we meet
     again.

4. God be with you till we meet
     again;
   keep love's banner floating o'er
     you,
   smite death's threatening wave
     before you:
   God be with you till we meet
     again.

J. E. Rankin (1828-1904)

477

1. God forgave my sin in Jesus'
     name;
   I've been born again, in Jesus'
     name;
   and in Jesus' name I come to you
   to share his love as he told me to.

He said:
'Freely, freely, you have received;
freely, freely give.
Go, in my name,
and because you believe,
others will know that I live.'

2. All pow'r is giv'n in Jesus' name,
in earth and heav'n in Jesus' name;
and in Jesus' name I come to you
to share his pow'r as he told me to.

3. God gives us life in Jesus' name,
he lives in us in Jesus' name;
and in Jesus' name I come to you
to share his peace as he told me to.

Carol Owens © 1972 Lexicon Music Inc
Word Music (UK) Ltd, Northbridge Road,
Berkhamsted, Herts, HP4 1EH, England

478

1. God gives us harvest from fields
we have sown,
bread that we bake has been
earned by our toil,
bread of our sadness we bring to
the Lord.

Praise to the Lord of the harvest.
Praise to the Lord of the harvest.
Lord of the vineyard be blest.
Lord of the vineyard be blest.

2. God has made fruitful the vines
we have grown,
wine that we make has been
pressed for our joy.
wine of our gladness we bring to
the Lord.

Patrick Lee © 1978 Kevin Mayhew Ltd

479

God has gladdened my heart with
joy, alleluia!
He has vested me with holiness,
alleluia!

1. Sing my soul of the glory of the
Lord;
with God's Spirit I'm full to
overflowing!

2. See the love that God showers on
the poor;
see the Lord overshadow those
who fear him.

3. All the world will join in this song
of praise,
for through me they now know the
Lord is with them.

4. To fulfill what he promised from
of old
God has chosen me! Bless his
name for ever.

5. Day by day, year by year, God's
love is sure;
Those who listen and keep his
word will know it.

6. See the pow'r of the Lord destroy
the strong!
Those who think themselves
strong, the Lord will humble.

7. Empty pride, self conceit, the Lord
ignores;
but he raises the poor who call
upon him.

8. No more thirst, no more hunger
with the Lord;
unsurpassed in his goodness to his
people.

9. See the care that the Lord shows to
   us all.
   Day by day, year by year, God's
   love's unending.

10. Praise the Father, the Son, the
   Spirit, praise!
   May the glory of God be sung
   for ever.

Words based on Luke 1: 46-55 Jean Paul Lecot.
W. R. Lawrence, R. B. Kelly © 1984 Kevin Mayhew Ltd

480

1. God is working his purpose out
   as year succeeds to year,
   God is working his purpose out
   and the time is drawing near;
   nearer and nearer draws the time,
   the time that shall surely be,
   when the earth shall be filled with
   the glory of God as the waters
   cover the sea.

2. From utmost east to utmost west
   where-e'er man's foot hath trod,
   by the mouth of many messengers
   goes forth the voice of God.
   'Give ear to me, ye continents, ye
   isles give ear to me,
   that the earth may be filled with
   the glory of God as the waters
   cover the sea.'

3. What can we do to work God's
   work, to prosper and increase
   the brotherhood of all mankind,
   the reign of the Prince of Peace?
   What can we do to hasten the time,
   the time that shall surely be,
   when the earth shall be filled with
   the glory of God as the waters
   cover the sea?

4. March we forth in the strength of
   God with the banner of Christ
   unfurled,
   that the light of the glorious
   Gospel of truth may shine
   throughout the world.
   Fight we the fight with sorrow and
   sin, to set their captives free,
   that the earth may be filled with
   the glory of God as the waters
   cover the sea.

5. All we can do is nothing worth
   unless God blesses the deed;
   vainly we hope for the harvest-tide
   till God gives life to the seed;
   yet nearer and nearer draws the
   time, the time that shall surely
   be,
   when the earth shall be filled with
   the glory of God as the waters
   cover the sea.

A. C. Ainger (1841-1919)

481

1. God made the birds, their home
   is the air;
   God made the beasts, each in its
   lair;
   God made the fish, their home
   is the sea;
   but God himself is home for me.

2. Birds find their food in their home
   of air;
   beasts find theirs too, 'most
   everywhere;
   the fish find theirs in the paths of
   the sea;
   but God himself is food for me.

3. God loves the birds, they answer
in song;
God loves the beasts, so
pow'rfully strong;
God loves the fish as they swim
in the sea;
but God himself is love for me.

Magnus Wenninger © 1980 Mayhew McCrimmon Ltd

482

1. God most high of all creation,
glory be to you!
Living God, we come before you,
glory be to you!
Hosts of Heav'n, your praises
are singing.
Shouts of joy and thanks are
ringing.
We on earth re-echo their praises;
glory be to you!

2. God of light, our darkness ending,
glory be to you!
God of truth, our doubts dispelling,
glory be to you!
Light of God on all men dawning,
Christ the rising sun brings
morning.
You have shed your light on our
pathway;
glory be to you!

3. Mighty God, who brings us
freedom,
glory be to you!
Faithful God who keeps his
promise,
glory be to you!
As your Church we gather before
you,

and with thanks, we sing and
adore you.
Now made one in Christ, let us
praise you;
glory be to you!

4. God of love, your ways are gentle,
glory be to you!
God of peace, you heal our sadness,
glory be to you!
Called by you, we hasten to meet
you,
and together pray as we greet you.
With your loving kindness surround
us,
glory be to you!

5. Sing your praise to God our
Father,
glory be to you!
Praise the Son and Holy Spirit,
glory be to you!
Abba, Father, Lord of creation,
Jesus Lord, who brought
salvation.
Holy Spirit, dwelling within us,
glory be to you!

French, tr and adapted by © Pamela Stotter

483

1. God, our maker, mighty Father,
all creation sings your praise,
sun and stars in all their
splendour,
moon in ev'ry changing phase,
earth with all its trees and grasses,
sparkling rivers, ocean blue,
all unite to pay you homage,
singing joyously to you.

2. Provident and wise creator,
   as your mighty plan unfurled,
   man you made to share your
       labour
   in the building of the world.
   Man and woman you created,
   that united, heart and home,
   they might work and strive
       together
   till your endless kingdom come.

3. God of truth and love unbounded,
   further still your mercy went,
   when uniting earth with heaven,
   your incarnate Son you sent:
   first-born of your vast creation,
   holding all in unity,
   leading all in power and wisdom
   to a glorious destiny.

Denis E. Hurley © Archdiocese of Durban

484

1. God rest you merry, gentlemen,
   let nothing you dismay,
   remember Christ our Saviour
   was born on Christmas Day,
   to save us all from Satan's pow'r
   when we were gone astray;
   O tidings of comfort and joy,
       comfort and joy,
   O tidings of comfort and joy.

2. In Bethelehem, in Jewry,
   this blessed Babe was born,
   and laid within a manger,
   upon this blessed morn;
   the which His Mother Mary,
   did nothing take in scorn.

3. From God our heavenly Father,
   a blessed Angel came;
   and unto certain Shepherds
   brought tidings of the same;
   how that in Bethlehem was born
   the Son of God by Name.

4. "Fear not then," said the Angel,
   "Let nothing you affright,
   this day is born a Saviour
   of a pure Virgin bright,
   to free all those who trust in Him
   from Satan's power and might."

5. The shepherds at those tidings
   rejoicéd much in mind,
   and left their flocks a-feeding,
   in tempest, storm, and wind;
   and went to Bethlehem
       straightway,
   the Son of God to find.

6. And when they came to Bethlehem
   where our dear Saviour lay,
   they found Him in a manger,
   where oxen feed on hay;
   His Mother Mary kneeling down,
   unto the Lord did pray.

7. Now to the Lord sing praises,
   all you within this place,
   and with true love and
       brotherhood
   each other now embrace;
   this holy tide of Christmas
   all other doth deface.

English Traditional Carol

485

God's Spirit precedes us,
guides and gently leads us.
Alleluia, alleluia!
God's Spirit precedes us,
guides and gently leads us.
Alleluia, alleluia!

1. Through mountains and valleys
   he journeys with us,
   all his work
   entrusts to our control;
   and those who know not
   what God wants from them
   must silently wait
   on the voice of our God.

2. In sorrow and gladness,
   he's always near us,
   and his love,
   he gives to everyone;
   and those who know not
   God's presence with them
   must just take a look
   at the life all around.

© tr from the Dutch by Bonaventure Hinwood
based on Psalms 65 (66) and 66 (67) © Bing Music

486

1. Good Christian men, rejoice
   and sing!
   Now is the triumph of our King!
   To all the world glad news we
   bring:
   Alleluia!

2. The Lord of Life is risen for ay:
   bring flowers of song to strew his
   way;
   let all mankind rejoice and say
   Alleluia!

3. Praise we in songs of victory
   that Love, that Life, which cannot
   die,
   and sing with hearts uplifted high
   Alleluia!

4. Thy name we bless, O risen Lord,
   and sing today with one accord
   the life laid down, the life restored:
   Alleluia!

C. A. Alington © Hymns Ancient and Modern

487

1. Good Lady Poverty,
   come be my bride;
   forever you and me,
   walk side by side.
   Teach me your wisdom,
   lead me your way.
   Show me the path you take
   and walk with Christ each day.

2. Good Lady Poverty,
   so filled with grace;
   such sweet humility
   shines from your face.
   You have no pride
   or vanity.
   Great daughter of the Lord,
   his love has made you free.

3. Good Lady Poverty,
   I sing your praise.
   St. Francis, blessed one,
   has walked your ways.
   He sang your virtues;
   you were his prize.
   Good Lady Poverty,
   an angel in disguise.

Sebastian Temple © 1967 Franciscan
Communications Centre

488

1. Grant us thy peace; for thou alone
   canst bend
   our faltering purpose to a nobler
   end;
   thy love alone can teach our hearts
   to see
   the fellowship that binds all lives
   in thee.

2. Grant us thy peace; for men have
   filled the years
   with greed and envy and with
   foolish fears,
   with squandered treasures and
   ignoble gain,
   and fruitless harvests that we
   reap in vain.

3. Grant us thy peace; till all our
   strife shall seem
   the hateful memory of some evil
   dream;
   till that new song ring out that
   shall not cease,
   'In heaven thy glory and on earth
   thy peace'.

J. H. B. Masterman (1867-1933)

489

**Greater love has no man than this:
that he give his life for his friends.**

1. Now I give you
   my new commandment:
   Love one another
   as I myself have loved you.

2. You will be my friends
   if you follow my precept:
   Love one another
   as I myself have loved you.

3. As the Father loves me always,
   so also have I loved you:
   Love one another
   as I myself have loved you.

4. Be constant in my love
   and follow my commandment.
   Love one another
   as I myself have loved you.

5. And approaching my Passover
   I have loved you to the end.
   Love one another
   as I myself have loved you.

6. By this shall men know
   that you are my disciples.
   Love one another
   as I myself have loved you.

From John 13, 14 and 15 arr by © Helena Scott

490

Hail Mary, full of grace,
the Lord is with you.
Blessed are you among women,
and blest is the fruit of your
womb, Jesus.
Holy Mary, Mother of God,
pray for us sinners
now and at the hour of death.
Amen.

**Gentle woman, quiet light,
morning star, so strong and bright,
gentle mother, peaceful dove,
teach us wisdom; teach us love.**

1. You were chosen by the Father;
   you were chosen for the Son.
   You were chosen from all women,
   and for women, shining one.

2. Blessed are you, among women.
   Blest in turn all women too.
   Blessed they with gentle spirits.
   Blessed they with gentle hearts.

491

1. Hail Mary, full of grace.
   The Lord is with thee.
   Blessed art thou among women,
   and blessed is the fruit of thy
   womb, Jesus.

2. Holy Mary, Mother of God,
   pray for us, sinners,
   now and at the hour of death;
   pray for us sinners now. Amen.

492

1. Hail Mary, mother of our God,
   a lamp that always burns;
   for you the angels keep a feast,
   from you all evil turns,
   from you all evil turns.

2. It's thanks to you God's only Son
   in darkness shed his light;
   it's thanks to you that sinful man

rejoiced to know what's right,
rejoiced to know what's right.

3. You gave a place within your
      womb
   to him who knows no bound;
   a virgin yet a mother too,
   in you his home he found,
   in you his home he found.

4. It's thanks to you creation came
   to know what's good and true;
   God calls his servant 'mother'
      now –
   no other maid but you,
   no other maid but you!

493

1. He is Lord, he is Lord.
   He is risen from the dead and he is
      Lord.
   Ev'ry knee shall bow, ev'ry tongue
      confess
   that Jesus Christ is Lord.

2. He is King, he is King.
   He is risen from the dead and he
      is King.
   Ev'ry knee shall bow, ev'ry tongue
      confess
   that Jesus Christ is King.

3. He is love, he is love.
   He is risen from the dead and he
      is love.
   Ev'ry knee shall bow, ev'ry tongue
      confess
   that Jesus Christ is love.

494

He is risen, alleluia, alleluia!
He is risen, alleluia, alleluia!

1. Cry out with joy the Lord, all the
   earth, **alleluia.**
   Serve the Lord with gladness,
   alleluia.
   Come before him, singing for joy,
   alleluia!

2. Know that he, the Lord, is God,
   alleluia.
   He made us, we belong to him,
   alleluia.
   We are his people, the sheep of his
   flock, **alleluia.**

3. Go within his gates giving
   thanks, **alleluia.**
   Enter his courts with songs of
   praise, **alleluia.**
   Give thanks to him and bless his
   name, **alleluia.**

4. Indeed, how good is the Lord,
   alleluia.
   Eternal his merciful love, **alleluia.**
   He is faithful from age to age,
   alleluia.

5. Glory to the Father and Son,
   alleluia.
   And to the Spirit with them one,
   alleluia.
   As it was and ever shall be one
   God for eternity.

Psalm 99 (100) (The Grail)

495

1. He is risen, tell the story
   to the nations of the night;
   from their sin and from their
   blindness,
   let them walk in Easter light.
   Now begins a new creation,
   now has come our true salvation.
   Jesus Christ, the Son of God!

2. Mary goes to tell the others
   of the wonders she has seen;
   John and Peter come a running
   what can all this truly mean?
   O Rabboni, Master holy,
   to appear to one so lowly!
   Jesus Christ, the Son of God!

3. He has cut down death and evil,
   he has conquered all despair;
   he has lifted from our shoulders,
   all the weight of anxious care.
   Risen Brother, now before you,
   we will worship and adore you.
   Jesus Christ, the Son of God!

4. Now get busy, bring the message,
   so that all may come to know
   there is hope for saint and sinner,
   for our God has loved us so.
   Ev'ry church bell is a'ringing,
   ev'ry Christian now is singing.
   Jesus Christ, the Son of God!

496

1. He's a most unusual man,
   he makes the crowds all stop and
      stare,
   he teaches people how to care,
   he teaches people how to share.
   He has no place to lay his head,
   his home is everywhere.
   Follow if you can,
   this most unusual man,
   follow if you can,
   this most unusual man.

2. He's a most unusual man,
   he makes the stormy days turn
      fine,
   he changes water into wine,
   he gives his body as a sign.
   And he died that we might live,
   his life is yours and mine.

3. He's a most unusual man,
   as rich and poor as a man can be,
   he came to set the prisoners free,
   he came to make the blind men
      see.
   And he gave the world this
      message,
   'Come and follow me.'

Wendy Poussard © 1978 Dove Communications Pty Ltd

497

1. Help us accept each other
   as Christ accepted us;
   teach us as sister, brother,
   each person to embrace.
   Be present, Lord among us
   and bring us to believe
   we are ourselves accepted
   and meant to love and live.

2. Teach us, O Lord, your lessons,
   as in our daily life
   we struggle to be human
   and search for hope and faith.
   Teach us to care for people,
   for all not just for some,
   to love them as we find them
   or as they may become.

3. Let your acceptance change us,
   so that we may be moved
   in living situations
   to do the truth in love;
   to practise your acceptance
   until we know by heart
   the table of forgiveness
   and laughter's healing art.

4. Lord, for today's encounters
   with all who are in need,
   who hunger for acceptance,
   for righteousness and bread,
   we need new eyes for seeing,
   new hands for holding on:
   renew us with your Spirit;
   Lord, free us, make us one!

Fred Kaan © 1975 Agapé

498

1. Hills of the north, rejoice;
   river and mountain-spring,
   hark to the advent voice;
   valley and lowland, sing:
   though absent long, your Lord is
      nigh;
   he judgement brings and victory.

2. Isles of the southern seas,
   deep in your coral caves
   pent be each warring breeze,
   lulled be your restless waves:
   he comes to reign with boundless
      sway,

and makes your wastes his great
   highway.

3. Lands of the east, awake,
   soon shall your sons be free;
   the sleep of ages break,
   and rise to liberty.
   On your far hills, long cold and
      grey,
   has dawned the everlasting day.

4. Shores of the utmost west,
   ye that have waited long,
   unvisited, unblest,
   break forth to swelling song;
   high raise the note, that Jesus died,
   yet lives and reigns, the Crucified.

5. Shout, while ye journey home;
   songs be in every mouth;
   lo, from the north we come,
   from east and west and south.
   City of God, the bond are free,
   we come to live and reign in thee!

C. E. Oakley (1832-65)

499

1. His light now shines in the
      darkness about us,
   his light now shines and the
      darkness has gone.

   **His name is love and he gives
      himself to us;
   his name is love, and he makes
      us his own.**

2. His love is warm like the sun
      of the morning,
   his love is warm like the promise
      of dawn.

3. His love surrounds like a
      mother's devotion,
   he meets our needs when awake
      and asleep.

4. How can we answer the love that
      he shows us,
   what can we do to respond to
      his care?

5. Receive his love and reflect it
      to others,
   do all for them as he does all for
      you.

6. For when we know him, we give
      ourselves to them,
   and when we love him, we give
      them out all.

Tom Colvin © 1969 Agapé

500

1. How lovely on the mountains
      are the feet of him
   who brings good news, good news,
   announcing peace, proclaiming
      news of happiness:
   Our God reigns . . .

2. You watchmen, lift your voices
      joyfully as one,
   shout for your king, your king!
   See eye to eye, the Lord restoring
      Sion:
   Our God reigns . . .

3. Wasteplaces of Jerusalem, break
      forth with joy!
   We are redeemed, redeemed,
   the Lord has saved and comforted
      his people.
   Our God reigns . . .

4. Ends of the earth, see the salvation
   of our God!
   Jesus, is Lord, is Lord!
   Before the nations, he has bared
   his holy arm.
   Our God reigns . . .

Based on Isaiah 52
Leonard J. Smith © 1974/78/L. E. Smith Jnr/Thankyou
Music, PO Box 75, Eastbourne, BN23 6NW.
Printed by permission

501

1. I am the Bread of life.
   He who comes to me shall not
   hunger;
   he who believes in me shall not
   thirst.
   No one can come to me
   unless the Father draw him.
   (Jn 6:35, 37)

   And I will raise him up,
   and I will raise him up,
   and I will raise him up
   on the last day.

2. The bread that I will give
   is my flesh for the life of the world,
   and he who eats of this bread,
   he shall live for ever,
   he shall live for ever.
   (Jn 6: 50-51)

3. Unless you eat
   of the flesh of the Son of Man,
   and drink of his blood,
   and drink of his blood,
   you shall not have life within you.
   (Jn 6:53)

4. For my flesh is food indeed,
   and my blood is drink indeed.
   He who eats of my flesh
   and drinks of my blood
   abides in me.
   (Jn 6: 55-56)

5. Yes, Lord, I/we believe,
   that you are the Christ,
   the Son of God,
   who have come
   into the world.
   (Jn 11:27)

Words arr by Suzanne Toolan © 1971
G.I.A. Publications Inc

502

1. I am the vine, you are the
   branches:
   no one can live apart from me.
   Cut off from me you can do
   nothing:
   yet joined with me, all things are
   yours.

2. You are the fruit borne by my
   Father,
   who tends and cares for every
   limb.
   Be not afraid: he will not harm
   you.
   Your fear he'll prune, and set you
   free.

3. Remain in me: keep my
   commandments.
   My love for you led me to die.
   Hold fast to me: I'll never leave
   you.
   in life, in death, I'll love you still.

Paraphrased from John 15 by John Glynn ©

503

1. I heard the Lord call my name;
   listen close, you'll hear the
      same! (3)
   Take his hand, we are glory
      bound!

2. His Word is love, love's his word,
   that's the message that I heard! (3)
   Take his hand; we are glory
      bound!
   Place your hand in his and you will
      know;
   he will show you where to go.

3. I felt his love from above
   settle on me like a dove. (3)
   Take his hand; we are glory
      bound!

4. And to the Father all your days
   with the Son and Spirit praise! (3)
   Take his hand, we are glory
      bound!
   Place your hand in his and you will
      know;
   he will show you where to go.

5. *Repeat verse 1.*

I heard the Lord
Jacob Krieger © 1973 The Word of God
All rights reserved

504

1. I lift my eyes to the mountains;
   from where shall come my help?
   My help shall come from the Lord,
      Yahweh;
   it is he who made heaven and
      earth.

2. May he never allow you to
      stumble,
   let him sleep not, your guard.
   No, he sleeps not, nor slumbers,
   the Lord, Israel's guard.

3. The Lord is your guard and your
      shade,
   at your right hand he stands.
   By day the sun shall not smite you,
   nor the moon in the night.

4. The Lord will guard you from evil,
   he will guard your soul.
   The Lord will guard your coming
      and going,
   both now and for evermore.
   The Lord will guard your going
      and coming,
   both now and for evermore.

Based on Psalm 120 (121) by Gregory Norbert
© The Benedictine Foundation

505

Antiphon:
   I lift up my eyes to the
      mountain,
   is anyone there to help me?
   Yes, my God comes to help me,
   the Lord who made both heaven
   and earth.

1. He will not allow you to stumble,
   he never sleeps but stands watch
      over you.
   The Lord who made both heaven
   and earth.
   No, he will not sleep nor slumber,
   he stands watch over all his people.
   Yes, my God comes to help me,
   the Lord who made both heaven and
   earth.

Our God keeps watch;
like a shadow he covers you.
**The Lord who made both heaven
and earth.**
In the daytime the sun shall not
strike you;
by night the moon shall not harm
you.
**Yes, my God comes to help me,
The Lord who made both heaven
and earth.**

3. He keeps all evil away from you;
he takes you under his protection.
**The Lord who made both heaven
and earth.**
Whether you are coming or going,
God looks after you for ever.
**Yes, my God comes to help me,
The Lord who made both heaven
and earth.**

Repeat Antiphon

*Psalm 120 (121) arr by Huub Oosterhuis tr by Tony Barr
and Jabulani Music*
© *Tony Barr*

506

1. I met you at the cross,
Jesus my Lord;
I heard you from that cross:
my name you called –
Asked me to follow you all of my
days,
asked me for evermore your name
to praise.

2. I saw you on the cross
dying for me;
I put you on that cross:

but your one plea –
Would I now follow you all of my
days,
and would I evermore your great
name praise?

3. Jesus, my Lord and King,
Saviour of all,
Jesus the King of kings,
you heard my call –
That I would follow you all of my
days,
and that for evermore your name
I'd praise.

© *Eric A. Thorn*

507

1. I saw a star up high above the
heavens.
I heard the angels singing in the
sky.
I watched the shepherds coming
from the sheepfold:
I even thought I heard a baby cry.

**No one there would listen to my
story,
and no one seemed to care about
the child;
but he was beautiful,
the baby born to save us,
as in his mother's arms he gently
lay.**

2. I saw the star shine down upon
the stable.
I watched the kings with gifts go
riding by.
I crept up close and looked into
the manger
and it was then I heard a baby cry.
But . . .

3. I hurried home and there I met
   the townsfolk.
   I wandered in the hills and all
   around.
   I tried to tell my friends about
   the story
   of angels, shepherds, kings and
   babe I'd found.

   But all alone I knelt before that
   manger,
   the sheeps and cows and oxen
   standing by;
   and he was beautiful —
   the baby born to save us,
   as in his mother's arms he gently
   lay.
   Yes, he was beautiful,
   the baby Jesus born on Christmas
   Day.

Joan McCrimmon © Mayhew McCrimmon Ltd

2. I, the Lord of snow and rain,
   I have borne my people's pain.
   I have wept for love of them.
   They turn away.
   I will break their hearts of stone,
   give them hearts for love alone.
   I will speak my word to them.
   Whom shall I send?

3. I, the Lord of wind and flame,
   I will send the poor and lame.
   I will set a feast for them.
   My hand will save.
   Finest bread I will provide
   till their hearts be satisfied.
   I will give my life to them.
   Whom shall I send?

509

1. I was born before creation,
   when the world was yet to be.
   From the dawn of time uncounted
   I have sung God's melody.

   I am Wisdom, his companion,
   ever at his side to be;
   I delight in his creating,
   never ending, ever free.

2. Ev'ry sea and ev'ry river
   I have seen them come to birth;
   for the hills and for the mountains
   seen him raise the virgin earth.

3. There were stars hung in the
   heavens,
   and the clouds were in his plan:
   but the time I'll ever cherish
   was the day he formed a man.

508

1. I, the Lord of sea and sky,
   I have heard my people cry.
   All who dwell in dark and sin
   my hand will save.
   I who made the stars of night,
   I will make their darkness bright.
   Who will bear my light to them?
   Whom shall I send?

   Here I am, Lord. Is it I, Lord?
   I have heard You calling in the
   night.
   I will go, Lord, if You lead me.
   I will hold Your people in my heart.

4. Never has he ceased creating,
   and I'm with him to this day;
   so I'm glad to see his image
   in the people of today.

Based on Proverbs 8: 22-31 © by John Glynn

510

**I will be with you wherever you go.
Go now throughout the world!
I will be with you in all that you say.
Go now and spread my word!**

1. Come, walk with me on stormy
   waters.
   Why fear? Reach out, and I'll be
   there.

2. And you, my friend, will you now
   leave me,
   or do you know me as your Lord?

3. Your life will be transformed with
   power
   by living truly in my name.

4. And if you say: 'Yes, Lord I love
   you,'
   then feed my lambs and feed my
   sheep.

Gerald Markland © 1978 Kevin Mayhew Ltd

511

1. I will never forget you,
   my people,
   I have carved you
   on the palm of my hand.
   I will never forget you;
   I will not leave you orphaned.
   I will never forget my own.

2. Does a mother
   forget her baby?
   Or a woman the child
   within her womb?
   Yet, even if these forget,
   yes, even if these forget,
   I will never forget my own.

Repeat Verse 1

512

1. I will sing, I will sing a song unto
   the Lord. (3)
   Alleluia, glory to the Lord.

   **Allelu alleluia, glory to the
   Lord (3)
   alleluia, glory to the Lord.**

2. We will come, we will come as one
   before the Lord. (3)
   Alleluia, glory to the Lord.

3. If the Son, if the Son shall make
   you free, (3)
   you shall be free indeed.

4. They that sow in tears shall reap
   in joy. (3)
   Alleluia, glory to the Lord.

5. Ev'ry knee shall bow and ev'ry
   tongue confess (3)
   that Jesus Christ is Lord.

6. In his name, in his name we have
   the victory. (3)
   Alleluia, glory to the Lord.

*Max Dyer © 1974, 75 Celebration Services
International Ltd*

513

I will tell of your love
for me always, Lord;
I will tell of your goodness to me.

1. Ev'ry morning the sun comes
      shining through
   to tell me a new day is born;
   and I feel a joy rising in my heart,
   the joy of life that comes from you.

2. Ev'ry mountain and hill that you
      have made
   tells me how strong you are;
   and I feel a pow'r rising in my
      heart,
   the pow'r of strength that comes
      from you.

3. Ev'ry flower that lifts its head to
      me
   tells me how gentle you are;
   and I feel a joy rising in my heart,
   the joy of love that comes from
      you.

4. As the darkness comes on at close
      of day
   it tells me you watch through the
      night;
   and I feel a longing rising in my
      heart,
   a longing to be one with you.

Sister Marie Lydia Pereira
© *1980 Mayhew McCrimmon Ltd*

514

I'll sing God's praises,
now and evermore.
I'll sing God's praises,
now and evermore.

1. He is my guide and my shepherd,
   now and evermore.
   He gives me rest in green pastures,
   now and evermore.

2. Near restful waters he leads me,
   now and evermore.
   Along the right path he keeps me,
   now and evermore.

3. His rod and crook are my comfort,
   now and evermore.
   With oil my head is anointed,
   now and evermore.

4. His loving favours pursue me,
   now and evermore.
   His house, my dwelling for ever,
   now and evermore.

Based on Psalm 22 (23) by Aniceto Nazareth
© *Aniceto Nazareth, St Pius College, Bombay 63*

515

If God is for us, who can be against,
if the Spirit of God has set us free?
If God is for us, who can be against,
if the Spirit of God has set us free?

1. I know that nothing in this world
   can ever take us from his love.

2. Nothing can take us from his love,
   poured out in Jesus, the Lord.

3. And nothing present or to come
   can ever take us from his love.

4. I know that neither death nor life
   can ever take us from his love.

*Based on Romans 8: 31-39 IF GOD IS FOR US
by John Foley, SJ Copyright* © *1975 by John B. Foley,
SJ and North American Liturgy Resources,
10802 N 23rd Ave, Phoenix, AZ 85029, USA.*

516

1. If God is our defender,
   who will th' accuser be?
   His only Son he spared not,
   but gave him graciously.
   When God himself grants pardon,
   who ventures to condemn?
   Will Jesus Christ, the Saviour,
   who died and rose for men?

2. Can anything divide us
   from that most loving Lord?
   Can pain, or tribulation?
   Can famine, peril, sword?
   No, none of these can cause us
   from his great love to fall;
   for by the strength he gave us,
   we triumph over all.

3. Of this we can be certain,
   and sing with every breath:
   that nought that is, or will be,
   and neither life nor death,
   and nothing in creation,
   below us or above,
   can tear us from Christ Jesus,
   and from his Father's love.

Based on Romans 8:31-39 by Denis E. Hurley
© Archdiocese of Durban

517

1. In God alone there is rest for
   my soul,
   from his care comes my safety
   in life.
   With him alone for my rock and
   my fortress,
   this I know I will never fall down.

So rest in God alone my soul,
he is the source of my hope.

2. In God I find my shelter, my
   strength
   all you people do rely on him.
   Unburden your hearts to the Lord
   your God,
   at all times he will listen to you.

3. Beware of those who will scoff
   at our God;
   their intent is to misguide your
   way.
   We trust alone in the rock of our
   safety
   and we know we will never lose
   hope.

Based on Psalm 70 (71) by Douglas Rowe
© Mayhew McCrimmon Ltd

518

In the beginning all was empty
   and void;
God's spirit moved above the
   water.
Our of the darkness came a word
   that brought new life:
'This is so good, let there be light.'

1. Then in the stillness of the night
   your Word
   leapt into our city of turmoil;
   a man was born, a man of peace
   and not of war,
   revealing hopes yet unfulfilled.

2. Jesus, his name and what a gift
   he was,
   inspired to know the Father's
   vision.

And he so loved us more than his
own life.
What greater gift could he have
shared?

3. So we are called to give flesh to
our word
and be creators with the Spirit.
Wonder will be the sign that we
are on the way,
sharing our hope, alive our word.

Gregory Norbert, OSB ©*The Benedictine Foundation*

519

1. It's a long hard journey,
and the road keeps turning
and we just keep travelling on;
the signs aren't clear enough,
the ends aren't near enough,
and half our time is gone.

**O, the Lord sends troubles,
the Lord sends trials,
the Lord sends a heavy load.
But he'll keep on leading us,
and keep on guiding us,
as long as we're trav'ling his road,
as long as we're trav'ling his road.**

2. With so many days to live,
it's hard for life to give
a meaning mile after mile.
The roads keep crossing,
and the coins we're tossing
choose the path in a visionless
style.

3. Though we walk as brothers,
still we hurt each other,
and our love turns acid and stone.
Though we're hand in hand
we don't understand
that no one's walking alone.

4. Well, he never told us
that the road before us
would be smooth or simple or
clear.
But he set us singing
and our hope keeps springing
and we're raised from hating and
fear.

5. Well, the road is ours
with its rocks and flowers
and mica gleams in the stone.
Well, there's joy awaiting
in the celebrating
that we're never walking alone.

© *Nick Hodson*

520

1. It's good to give thanks to the
Lord,
declare your love in the morning;
the lute will sound a new chord,
the melody adorning!

**And you, O Lord, have made me
glad;
for all your works I'll be singing;
the righteous flourishing like the
grass
which from the earth keeps
springing.**

2. They're planted in God's own
abode,
in God's own house they will
flourish;
they'll still bear fruit when they're
old,
for God will tend and nourish!

3. Sing glory to God up above,
the Son of God, our dear Saviour,
and to the Spirit of Love,
whose care will never waver!

Psalm 91 (92) paraphrased by John Ylvisaker ©

521

1. Jesus said: 'I am the bread.
Eat of my flesh, you will live for
ever.'
'How can this be?' the people said;
most of them went away.
So he said to the twelve, 'What of
you?'
And this is the answer they gave,
saying:

'Lord, to whom shall we go?
You have the words of eternal life.
Lord, to whom shall we go?
You have the message of life.'

2. Jesus said: 'I came from heaven.
I give my flesh for the life of the
world.'
'This man is mad!' the people said;
slowly, they went away.
So he said to the twelve, 'What of
you?'
And this is the answer they gave,
saying:

3. Jesus said: 'I have seen God.
Eat of my body and you too will
see him.'
'This is not true!' the people said;
angry, they went away.
So he said to the twelve, 'What of
you?'
And this is the answer they gave,
saying:

© *1984 Stephen Dean*

522

Jesus, the holy Lamb of God
carried the cross for me;
Jesus, the holy Lamb of God
died that I might be free.

1. He who is God made himself low:
a servant, and humbler yet,
He bowed his head
as he was led
obedient unto his death.

2. Therefore has God raised him on
high
and named him our saviour and
lord:
all knees will bend
in praise without end
to Jesus for ever adored.

Based on Philippians 2:6-11 by Briege O'Hare
© *1980 Mayhew McCrimmon Ltd*

523

1. Jesus the Lord said, 'I am the
bread,
the bread of life for mankind
am I.' (3)
Jesus the Lord said, 'I am the
bread,
the bread of life for mankind
am I.'

2. Jesus the Lord said, 'I am the door,
   the way and the door for the poor **am I.'** (3)
   Jesus the Lord said, 'I am the door,
   the way and the door for the poor am I.'

3. Jesus the Lord said, 'I am the light,
   the one true light of the world **am I.'** (3)
   Jesus the Lord said, 'I am the light,
   the one true light of the world am I.'

4. Jesus the Lord said, 'I am the shepherd,
   the one good shepherd of the **sheep am I.'** (3)
   Jesus the Lord said, 'I am the shepherd,
   the one good shepherd of the sheep am I.'

5. Jesus the Lord said, 'I am the life,
   the resurrection and the life **am I.'** (3)
   Jesus said, I am the life,
   the resurrection and the life am I.'

Anon, Urdu tr Dermott Monahan (1906-57)
© *The Methodist Church Division of Education and Youth*

524

1. Jesus the Word has lived among us,
   sharing his fullness, truth and grace,
   God's only Son, the Father's loved one
   reveals him to the human race.
   Jesus the Word has lived among us
   sharing his fullness, truth and grace.

2. He was with God from the beginning
   and through him all things came to be.
   He lightens darkness, conquers evil,
   gives life for living, glad and free.
   He was with God from the beginning
   and through him all things came to be.

3. Sing praise to God who sent Christ Jesus
   to be his sign of endless love;
   sent him to live his life among us,
   lifting our hearts to things above.
   Sing praise to God who sent Christ Jesus
   to be his sign of endless love!

John 1 and 3 paraphrased by Keith D. Pearson
© *1976 Joint Board of Christian Education of Australia
and New Zealand*

525

**Jesus, you are Lord.
You are risen from the dead
and you are Lord.
Ev'ry knee shall bow,
and ev'ry tongue confess
that Jesus, you are Lord.
You are the way.**

1. I am the Way.
   No one knows the Father but it be through me.
   I am in my Father, and my Father is in me,
   and we come in love to live within your hearts.

2. I am the Truth.
   And I set my spirit deep within
   your hearts,
   and you will know me, and love
   me,
   and the truth I give to you will set
   you free.

3. I am the Life.
   The living waters I pour out for
   you.
   Anyone who drinks of the waters
   that I give
   will have eternal life.

4. I am the Word,
   the true light that shines brightly
   in the dark,
   a light that darkness could not
   overpower,
   the Word made flesh, risen among
   you.

Based on St John: Mary Barrett © 1978 Kevin Mayhew Ltd

526

**Keep in mind that Jesus Christ has
died for us
and is risen from the dead.
He is our saving Lord,
he is joy for all ages.**

1. If we die with the Lord,
   we shall live with the Lord.

2. If we endure with the Lord,
   we shall reign with the Lord.

3. In him all our sorrow,
   in him all our joy.

4. In him hope of glory,
   in him all our love.

5. In him our redemption,
   in him all our grace.

6. In him our salvation,
   in him all our grace.

Lucien Deiss © 1965 World Library Publications Inc

527

Laudato sii, O mi Signore (4)

1. Yes, be praised in all your
   creatures,
   brother sun and sister moon;
   in the stars and in the wind,
   air and fire and flowing water.

2. For our sister, mother earth,
   she who feeds us and sustains us;
   for her fruits, her grass, her
   flowers,
   for the mountains and the oceans.

3. Praise for those who spread
   forgiveness,
   those who share your peace with
   others,
   bearing trials and sickness
   bravely!
   Even sister death won't harm
   them.

4. For our life is but a song,
   and the reason for our singing
   is to praise you for the music;
   join the dance of your creation.

5. Praise to you, Father most holy,
   praise and thanks to you, Lord
   Jesus,
   praise to you, most Holy Spirit,
   life and joy of all creation!

Based on St Francis of Assisi
Damian Lundy © 1981 Kevin Mayhew Ltd

528

**Lay your hands gently upon us,
let their touch render your peace;
let them bring your forgiveness
and healing,
lay your hands,
gently lay your hands.**

1. You were sent to free
   the broken hearted.
   You were sent to give sight
   to the blind.
   You desire to heal
   all our illness.
   Lay your hands,
   gently lay your hands.

2. Lord, we come to you
   through one another.
   Lord, we come to you
   in all our need.
   Lord, we come to you
   seeking wholeness.
   Lay your hands,
   gently lay your hands.

529

1. Lead me, guide me along life's
   way.
   If I should stumble, Lord, send a
   helping hand.
   Love me, lead me through the
   trials of life;
   and with my brothers, Lord,
   teach us to understand
   that you have all things in your
   mighty hands.

Take me and fold me in your
  loving arms,
on the day when I come home.
Take me and fold me in your
  loving arms
then I shall be yours for ever.

530

**Leave your country and your
  people,
leave your fam'ly and your friends.
Travel to the land he'll show you;
God will bless the ones he sends.**

1. Go like Abraham before you,
   when he heard the Father's call,
   walking forth in faith and trusting;
   God is master of us all.

2. Sometimes God's Word is
     demanding,
   leave security you know,
   breaking ties and bonds that
     hold you,
   when the voice of God says: "Go".

3. Take the path into the desert,
   barren seems the rock and sand.
   God will lead you through the
     desert
   when you follow his command.

4. Go with courage up the mountain,
   climb the narrow, rocky ledge,
   leave behind all things that hinder,
   go with only God as pledge.

531

1. Lest he be too far from us, he
   prepared his coming.
   He who longed to share our fate
   made with us his dwelling.

   **There among you stands the one
   you do not know. (2)**

2. He is everywhere at hand, every
   detail human.
   Yet he is not recognised, silent,
   never spoken.

3. God from God and light from
   light, all creation's keeper,
   has a human face and talks, man
   to man as brother.

4. So with patience as your guide,
   show all kinds of goodness:
   owe each other, for his sake,
   only love and kindness.

5. Now be carefree, full of joy:
   God, whom we do worship,
   brushes past us day by day, shares
   our home and kinship.

   Huub Oosterhuis, tr Tony Barr
   © Tony Barr and Jabulani Music

532

1. Let all who share one bread and
   cup remember
   the oneness of that host of
   countless number
   of those who are, as children
   of one Father,
   part of each other.

2. If only we would live as sisters,
   brothers,

put faith to practice, truly care
   for others,
   then we would do the will of him
   who sends us,
   whose love attends us.

3. Use for yourself our highest and
   profoundest,
   so that, O Lord, with all men
   who surround us,
   we may enjoy a world in Christ
   united,
   so long awaited.

   J. A. Cramer tr by Fred Kaan © 1972 Fred Kaan

533

Let it breathe on me, let it breathe
on me,
Let this breath of God now
breathe on me.
Let it breathe on me, let it breathe
on me,
Let this breath of God now breathe
on me.

   William E. Booth-Clibborn
   © William Booth-Clibborn

534

1. Let us praise our sovereign
   Saviour,
   Christ, our shepherd, and our
   leader,
   Till the ending of our days.
   Though we praise him all we're
   able,
   All our praise is all too feeble,
   he is far beyond all praise.

2. He, before he gave to others,
   Gave his little band of brothers
   Both his body and his blood —
   Not a mere symbolic token,
   Blood outpoured and body
      broken —
   As an everlasting food.

3. What a theme to baffle study –
   That mere bread becomes his
      body,
   Wine his blood! The King of kings
   Comes down on this altar duly
   To repeat the wonder daily,
   Quite outside the run of things.

Repeat verse 1

© *J. Gordon Nichols*

535

1. Let us talents and tongues employ,
   reaching out with a shout of joy:
   bread is broken, the wine is
      poured,
   Christ is spoken and seen and
      heard.

   Jesus lives again,
   earth can breath again,
   pass the Word around:
   loaves abound!

2. Christ is able to make us one,
   at his table he sets the tone,
   teaching people to live to bless,
   love in word and in deed express.

3. Jesus calls us in, sends us out
   bearing fruit in a world of doubt,
   gives us love to tell, bread to share:
   God-Immanuel everywhere!

Fred Kaan © *1975 Agapé*

536

1. Light the Advent candle one.
   Now the waiting has begun,
   we have started on our way:
   time to think of Christmas day.

   Candle, candle, burning bright,
   shining in the cold winter night.
   Candle, candle, burning bright,
   fill our hearts with Christmas light.

2. Light the Advent candle two.
   Think of humble shepherds who
   filled with wonder at the sight
   of the child on Christmas night.

3. Light the Advent candle three.
   Think of heav'nly harmony:
   angels singing 'Peace on earth'
   at the blessed Saviour's birth.

4. Light the Christmas candles now!
   Sing of donkey, sheep and cow.
   Birthday candles for the King –
   let the 'Alleluias' ring!

Mary Lu Walker © *The Missionary Society of St Paul*

537

1. Like a sea without a shore
   love divine is boundless.
   Time is now and evermore
   and his love surrounds us.

   Maranatha! Maranatha!
   Maranatha! Come, Lord Jesus,
      come!

2. So that mankind could be free
   he appeared among us,
   blest are those who have not seen,
   yet believe his promise.

3. All our visions, all our dreams,
   are but ghostly shadows
   of the radiant clarity
   waiting at life's close.

4. Death where is your victory?
   Death where is your sting?
   Closer than the air we breathe
   is our risen King.

Estelle White © *Kevin Mayhew Ltd*

538

**Like the deer that thirsts for water,
O God I long for you.**

1. Like the deer that thirsts for water,
   O God, I long for you.
   Weeping, I have heard them taunt
     me:
   'What help is in your God?'

2. Gladly I would lead your people
   rejoicing to your house.
   Trust in God, my soul, and praise
     him,
   and he will dry your tears.

3. Grief and pain, like roaring
     torrents,
   had swept my soul away.
   But his mercy is my rescue,
   I will praise him all my days.

4. Weeping, I have heard them
     taunt me:
   'What help is your God?'
   Rock of strength, do not forget
     me;
   in you alone I trust.

(5. To the Father, praise and honour;
   all glory to the Son;

honour to the Holy Spirit;
let God be glorified.)

Paraphrased from Psalm 41 (42) by Luke Connaughton
© *1972 Mayhew McCrimmon Ltd*

539

1. Look around, look around you
     and you will see,
   all the sunshine, the sky so blue
   and feel the breeze;
   they are saying: God's love is real.

2. Take a walk thru' the countryside
     and watch the trees,
   hear the birds singing sweetly
     and you will feel peace
   and joy you've never known.

   **If you doubt your Father loves you,
   stop and think for just a while:
   is it need or greed that drives you
   to be crying all the time?**

3. Cleanse your mind, open wide
     your heart,
   and call to him,
   and he'll fill you with wisdom
     so that you'll begin
   to realise God's love is real.

Ronald Gokool © *1980 Mayhew McCrimmon Ltd*

540

1. 'Look around you, can you see?
   Times are troubled, people grieve.
   See the violence, feel the hardness;
   all my people, weep with me.'

   **Kyrie eleison,
   Christe eleison,
   Kyrie eleison.**

2. 'Walk among them, I'll go with
   you.
   Reach out to them with my hands.
   Suffer with me, and together we
   will serve them,
   help them stand.'

3. Forgive us, Father; hear our
   prayer.
   We would walk with you
   anywhere,
   through your suff'ring, with
   forgiveness;
   take your life into the world.

*Jodi Page Clark © 1975 Celebration Services
International Ltd*

541

1. Looking at the sunrise
   heralding the dawn;
   list'ning to the birds sing
   hearing ev'ry sound.
   I'm at peace with nature,
   because, I suppose,
   all my cares and troubles
   are resting with the Lord.

2. Children playing round me,
   laughter's in my heart.
   People toiling sadly,
   comfort I impart.
   Joy is with me daily
   and it's all I know,
   because Jesus loves me,
   for he told me so.

3. Listen to me, brothers,
   heed to what I say;
   Place your trust in Jesus,
   let him guide your way.
   He will not forsake or
   from you turn away;

peace is yours, my brothers,
Jesus is the way.

Ronald Gokool © 1980 Mayhew McCrimmon Ltd

542

1. Lord, confronted with your might,
   with your purity and light
   we are made with shame to see
   all that we fail to be.

2. Conscious of our feeble will,
   wanting good, but choosing ill,
   we are sorry for our sin:
   Lord, make us clean within.

3. Steady, Lord, our stumbling feet,
   free our spirits from deceit.
   Give us openness for pride;
   we have no place to hide.

4. Lift us from despair and grief,
   help us in our unbelief.
   As we spread our hands to you,
   fill us with life anew.

5. For the sake of Christ, forgive,
   speak the Word, and we shall live.
   Send us forward on our way,
   Lord, with our heads held high.

Fred Kaan © 1975 Agapé

543

1. Lord, enthroned in heavenly
   splendour,
   first begotten from the dead,
   thou alone, our strong defender,
   liftest up thy people's head.
   Alleluia, alleluia,
   Jesus, true and living bread!

2. Prince of life, for us thou livest,
   by thy body souls are healed;
   Prince of peace, thy peace thou
       givest,
   by thy blood is pardon sealed;
   alleluia, alleluia,
   Word of God, in flesh revealed.

3. Paschal Lamb! Thine offering
       finished,
   once for all, when thou wast slain,
   in its fullness undiminished
   shall for evermore remain,
   alleluia, alleluia,
   cleansing souls from every stain.

4. Great high priest of our
       profession,
   through the veil thou enterest in;
   by thy mighty intercession
   grace and mercy thou canst win:
   alleluia, alleluia,
   only sacrifice for sin.

5. Life-imparting heavenly manna,
   stricken rock, with streaming side,
   heaven and earth, with loud
       hosanna,
   worship thee, the Lamb who died;
   alleluia, alleluia,
   risen, ascended, glorified!

G. H. Bourne (1840-1925)

544

1. Lord, graciously hear us,
   hear us as we call on you,
   we tried to be faithful, Lord,
   but we have sinned against you.

2. You gave us your message,
   you showed us the way to live;
   we tried to be faithful, Lord,
   but we have not understood.

3. Lord, show us your mercy,
   heal those we have wounded here;
   we wanted to love like you,
   but we have forgotten the way.

4. Speak, Lord, to your people,
   speak, now, in a million ways;
   we want to be true to you,
   help, Lord, and forgive us, we
       pray.

© *Anne Conway*

545

1. Lord, in everything I do
   let me always follow you;
   let the moments of my days
   overflow with endless praise;
   take my hands and let them move
   at the impulse of your love;
   every move that I shall make
   Lord, direct the steps I take.

2. Lord, with all your people here
   you invite me to draw near;
   Lord, accept the gifts I bring,
   Lord, accept the praise I sing.
   Take my lips and let them speak
   of your goodness through the
       week;
   let me echo this refrain
   till I come to you again.

3. As I listen to your call,
   Lord, I want to give my all;
   take my heart and mind and use
   every power you shall choose;
   all I have has come from you
   and I offer back to you
   only what was yours before:
   take my life for evermore.

Patrick Appleford © *Joseph Weinberger Ltd.*
Reproduced by permission

546

1. Lord Jesus Christ, be present now,
   and let your Holy Spirit bow
   all hearts in love and truth today
   to hear your Word and keep your
   way.

2. May your glad tidings always
   bring
   good news to men that they may
   sing
   of how you came to save all men.
   Instruct us till you come again.

3. To God the Father and the Son
   and Holy Spirit three in one,
   to you, O blessed Trinity,
   be praise throughout eternity.

Author unknown

547

1. Lord of Creation, to you be all
   praise!
   Most mighty your working, most
   wondrous your ways.
   Your glory and might are beyond
   us to tell,
   and yet in the heart of the humble
   you dwell.

2. Lord of all power, I give you my
   will,
   in joyful obedience your tasks to
   fulfil.
   Your bondage is freedom, your
   service is song,
   and, held in your keeping, my
   weakness is strong.

3. Lord of all wisdom, I give you
   my mind,
   rich truth that surpasses man's
   knowledge to find.
   What eye has not seen and what
   ear has not heard
   is taught by your Spirit and shines
   from your Word.

4. Lord of all bounty, I give you my
   heart;
   I praise and adore you for all
   you impart:
   your love to inspire me, your
   counsel to guide,
   your presence to cheer me,
   whatever betide.

5. Lord of all being, I give you my all;
   if e'er I disown you I stumble and
   fall;
   but, sworn in glad service your
   word to obey,
   I walk in your freedom to the end
   of the way.

This hymn may also start at Verse 2

Jack C. Winslow © United Reformed Church

548

1. Lord, this paschal time reminds us
   how you came back from the dead.
   Firm and true the faith that
   binds us
   to our glorious, risen Head.
   Alleluia, alleluia,
   you have risen as you said,
   alleluia, alleluia,
   you have risen as you said.

2. 'Neath the burden of our labour,
   mid our joy and pain and strife,
   in our trying to be neighbour,
   to be parent, husband, wife;
   alleluia, alleluia,
   be to us the source of life,
   alleluia, alleluia,
   be to us the source of life.

3. Make us true to our vocation
   with the strength that comes
       from you;
   make our life a dedication
   with the love that you imbue.
   Alleluia, alleluia,
   grace and peace in us renew,
   alleluia, alleluia,
   grace and peace in us renew.

4. Hold this vision, Lord, before us;
   in this hope our faith sustain:
   that to life you will restore us
   when at last you come again.
   Alleluia, alleluia,
   make us worthy of your reign,
   alleluia, alleluia,
   make us worthy of your reign.

Denis E. Hurley © Archdiocese of Durban

549

1. Lord, thy word abideth,
   and our footsteps guideth;
   who its truth believeth
   light and joy receiveth.

2. When our foes are near us,
   then thy word doth cheer us,
   word of consolation,
   message of salvation.

3. When the storms are o'er us,
   and dark clouds before us,
   then its light directeth,
   and our way protecteth.

4. Word of mercy, giving
   courage to the living;
   word of life, supplying
   comfort to the dying!

5. O that we discerning
   its most holy learning,
   Lord, may love and fear thee,
   evermore be near thee.

H. W. Baker (1875-1959)

550

1. Lord, you have come to the
       lakeside
   seeking neither wealthy nor wise
       men.
   You, only ask, Lord, that I should
   love you.

   **With love you have looked in my
       eyes, Lord,
   smiling gently. You called my
       name;
   and I left my boat by the lakeside,
   now with you I will seek other
       shores.**

2. Lord, you well know that I carry
   in my boat no treasure nor
       weapon.
   I bring you only my willing labour.

3. Lord, you have need of my hands;
   I shall labour that others may rest;
   and from my love, Lord, may
       others love you.

4. Lord, other seas call me onward;
   hope eternal for hearts that are
       searching;
   and love will bind us as friends
       for ever.

C. Gabarain © Ediciones Paulinas, Madrid.
Tr © Fr Edmund O'Shea

551

1. Love came down at Christmas,
   love all lovely, love divine:
   love was born at Christmas,
   star and angels gave the sign.

2. Worship we the Godhead,
   love incarnate, love divine;
   worship we our Jesus:
   but wherewith for sacred sign?

3. Love shall be our token,
   love be yours and love be mine,
   love to God and all men,
   love for plea and gift and sign.

Christina Rossetti (1830-94)

552

Lumen Christi! Alleluia! Amen!

1. I am the light of the world
   he who follows me
   will not walk in darkness.

2. You are the light of the world
   let your light
   shine before men.

3. Tell the wonderful deeds of the
   Lord
   He called you
   from darkness to light.

Jean Paul Lecot © 1984 assigned to Kevin Mayhew Ltd

553

**May the peace of the Lord be with
   you,
with your friends and your family
   too.
Let it be, let it grow, and**
**everywhere you go
may the peace of the Lord follow
   you.**

1. I leave you peace now, it's my
   peace I give to you:
   not as the world gives do I give
   to you.

2. Don't be afraid, let your hearts be
   untroubled:
   have faith in God and have faith
   in me.

554

1. Modern man has the city for his
   home
   where his life is walled by want
   and dread,
   pained by nights without sleep
   and days of grinding work,
   in the struggle to earn his daily
   bread.

2. In our cities, immense and
   growing out,
   there are millions from faith and
   love estranged,
   who need to recapture hope of
   better things,
   and whose hearts, by the grace of
   Christ, can change.

3. In the dark of our noisy city life,
   men and women are groping for
   the light,
   human beings who hunger to see
   right prevail,
   unaware of the liberating Christ.

4. In the great giant cities of our
      globe,
   hollowed out by the ways of greed
      and crime,
   we are set to reflect the likeness
      of our God
   and to act out renewal's great
      design.

5. Grow, then, cities to house the
      world of man,
   with your skyscrapers blotting
      out the sun.
   Let Christ be the light to shine
      from human homes
   in the high-rising blocks of steel
      and stone.

Words Joao Dias de Araujo, tr by Fred Kaan
© 1972 Fred Kaan

555

Mother of Jesus,
and mother of lowliness,
bearing the light of the world.
Radiant with glory,
the glory of Jesus,
conceived by the Spirit of God.

1. In the beginning of time
   God's Holy Spirit did shine,
   breathed on the deep
   and the darkness of night,
   bringing the promise of light.

2. Then in the fullness of time
   came the same Spirit sublime
   breathed on the womb
   of the Virgin of grace,
   called her the chosen of God.

3. Wond'rous the moment that
      heard
   you say 'Amen' to the Word;

Son of the Father,
and Light of his light,
face of the Godhead unveiled.

4. Mary, our Lady of light,
   you are the Father's delight:
   pray for us sinners
   to Jesus, your Son,
   show us the light of the world.

© John Glynn

556

My God, my God,
don't ever desert me,
my God, my God,
I need you beside me.
My life is so lonely,
my heart is so empty,
my God, only you
can comfort me.

1. In this cold, forbidding world
   where man seeks only himself,
   I can find no one who'll love
   or who'll help. There is only you.

2. In my joy I look for laughter,
   in my sorrow I seek a friend;
   but I see only fleeting shadows,
   and then I turn and find you there.

3. None but you know how I'm
      aching,
   you alone give the solace I seek.
   You alone give me kindness and
      care
   whenever I despair.

Ronald Gokool © 1980 Mayhew McCrimmon Ltd

557

My God, you fathom my heart and
you know me.

**My God, you fathom my heart and
you know me.**

Nothing in me lies concerned from
your eyes;
everything I do, you already know it.
You already know it.

How could I ever flee from your
spirit,
or where could I take refuge, you
see me everywhere.
You see me everywhere.

I climb to the heavens, you are in
the heavens:
in the depths of the earth I find you
even there.
I find you even there.

And should I flee away with the dawn
or
to the furthermost shores of the sea;
yes, even there shall your hand be
to help me.

**Yes, even there shall your hand be
to help me.**

How wond'rous are your plans
for me.
My God, how complete your designs.
My God, how complete your designs.

How can I count them, they are too
plenty,
as the sands of the sea even then . . .
then I shall know still nothing of
you.
**Then I shall know still nothing of
you.**

*From Psalm 138 (139) arr by Huub Oosterhuis,
tr by Tony Barr © Tony Barr and Jabulani Music*

558

**My soul is longing for your peace,
near to you, my God.**

1. Lord, you know
   that my heart is not proud,
   and my eyes are not
   lifted from earth.

2. Lofty thoughts
   have never filled my mind,
   far beyond my sight
   all ambitious deeds.

3. In your peace
   I have maintained my soul,
   I have kept my heart
   in your quiet peace.

4. As a child
   rests on his mother's knee,
   so I place my soul
   in your loving care.

5. Israel,
   put all your hope in God,
   place your trust in him,
   now and evermore.

*Based on Psalm 130 (131) by Lucien Deiss
© 1965 World Library Publications Inc.
Reprinted with permission*

559

**New life! New life!
You came to bring us new life.
New life! New life!
We find such joy in your abundant
life.**

1. You are the source of our great
   joy,
   the fountain of all life.
   You give us living water,
   you bid us come and drink.
   We come to you, we bless you,
   Lord,
   we glorify your name!
   We praise you, Lord,

we worship you,
we thank you for your gift
of new life!

2. You are the source of our new life;
in your light we see light.
You show us your goodness;
you bid us come and see.
We come to you, we bless you,
Lord,
we glorify your name!
We praise you, Lord
we worship you,
we thank you for your gift
of new life!

560

No one can give to me that peace
which my risen Lord,
my risen King can give.
No one can give to me that peace
which my risen Lord,
my risen King can give.

1. When I look around and see
all the things that trouble me
and I seem to lose my peace
in a world that's not at ease.

2. For I take Christ's word as true:
'My true peace I give to you,
but not as the world might give,
is my peace that makes you live.'

3. His true peace in me will stay,
as I live from day to day
and his joy will never end,
and in Heaven it will extend.

4. All the world's in search of peace,
but from sin they'll never cease
how can they expect to find
inner joys and peace of mind?

5. All injustice, hate and strife,
sins of malice, sex and pride,
stem from those who've never
known,
where the seeds of peace were
sown.

6. Christ has risen from the dead,
triumphed over sin and death
and he'll never die again,
but as Lord he'll live and reign.

561

1. Now let your people depart in
peace,
for we've partaken in this your
feast.
You are the Saviour of all the
earth,
a light to guide us from our birth.

Ev'ry time I feel the Spirit
moving in my heart I will pray!
Ev'ry time I feel the Spirit
moving in my heart, I will pray!

2. Sing glory to the Creator Lord,
and to the Spirit the comforter,
and unto Jesus the blessed Son,
forever three and ever one.

562

1. Now the tasks and toils are over
and another day at its end,
dear Lord, our drowsy spirits
into your hands we commend.
The day's familiar brightness
is lost in the pathless night;

you alone will be our refuge,
and only you our light.

2. The moonlight through the branches
by the evening wind is stirred,
the stars stand in their places
as faithful as your word:
although we shall not hear it,
though our eyes are held in sleep,
yet our wakeful hearts turn to you
their promises to keep.

3. Protect us from all evil,
from the terrors darkness brings
that we may rest securely
in the shadow of your wings.
O watchful Father, guide us,
our strength and life restore,
that we may wake at morning
to hear your voice once more.

Kevin Nichols © 1979 Mayhew McCrimmon Ltd

563

1. Now watch for God's coming,
be patient till then;
like sunshine at noontime he'll
brighten all men;
who hope in the Lord will possess
fertile land;
the poor he will welcome and
grasp by the hand.

2. Man's steps are directed, God
watches his path;
he guides him and holds him
and saves him from wrath,
and though he may fall he will not
go headlong,
for God gives sound footing and
keeps him from wrong.

3. So wait for his coming, be
patient till then;
the wicked are armed and would
kill honest men.
Their arms shall be broken, no
refuge they'll see,
but saved are the needy by God's
own decree.

4. Now those who do evil will wither
like grass,
like green of the springtime they
fade and they pass,
so trust in the Lord and to him
give your life,
he'll bring heart's desires and
peace in our strife.

© Willard F. Jabusch

564

1. Now with the fading light of day
Maker of all, to Thee we pray
that with Thy wonted care and
love,
Thou guard and protect us from
above.

2. Take far away each hideous
dream,
things in the night that monstrous
seem,
wiles of our old arch-foe restrain
lest faltering flesh contract a stain.

3. Father almighty, grace afford,
grant it through Jesus Christ
our Lord,
who with the Holy Ghost and
Thee
is reigning for all eternity.

Te lucis ante terminum, tr by Sebastian Bullough

565

O be joyful in the Lord!
O be joyful in the Lord!
Let us make a joyful noise,
let the whole earth rejoice!
O be joyful in the Lord,
all ye lands!

1. Know that the Lord he is God;
   he has made us, we are his.
   We are the sheep of his pasture,
   the people of his hand.

2. Enter his gates with thanksgiving:
   come into his courts with praise.
   Be thankful unto him,
   and speak good of his name.

3. Know that the Lord, he is good:
   his love lasts for ever.
   He's faithful and true,
   through ev'ry generation.

Psalm 99 (100) paraphrased by Jonathan Asprey
© 1975 Celebration Services International Ltd

566

1. O comfort my people
   and calm all their fear,
   and tell them the time of
   salvation draws near.
   O tell them I come to
   remove all their shame.
   Then they will forever
   give praise to my name.

2. Proclaim to the cities
   of Juda my word:
   that gentle yet strong is
   the hand of the Lord.
   I rescue the captives
   my people defend
   and bring them to justice
   and joy without end.

3. All mountains and hills shall
   become as a plain
   for vanished are mourning
   and hunger and pain.
   And never again shall
   these war against you.
   Behold I come quickly
   to make all things new.

Isaiah 40, paraphrased by © Chrysogonus Waddell

567

1. O food of travellers, angels' bread,
   manna wherewith the blest are fed,
   come nigh, and with thy sweetness fill
   the hungry hearts that seek thee still.

2. O fount of love, O well unpriced,
   outpouring from the heart of Christ,
   give us to drink of very thee,
   and all we pray shall answered be.

3. O Jesus Christ, we pray to thee
   that this presence which we see,
   though now in form of bread concealed,
   to us may be in heaven revealed.

Maintzisch Gesangbuch 1661,
tr by Walter H. Shewring and others

568

1. O lady, full of God's own grace,
   whose caring hands the child embraced,
   who listened to the Spirit's word,
   believed and trusted in the Lord.

   O virgin fair, star of the sea,
   my dearest mother, pray for me,

O virgin fair, star of the sea,
my dearest mother, pray for me.

2. O lady, who felt daily joy
in caring for the holy boy,
whose home was plain and shorn
   of wealth,
yet was enriched by God's own
   breath.

3. O lady, who bore living's pain
but still believed that love would
   reign,
who on a hill watched Jesus die
as on the cross they raised him
   high.

4. O lady, who, on Easter day,
had all your sorrow wiped away
as God the Father's will was done
when from death's hold he freed
   your Son.

Estelle White © Kevin Mayhew Ltd

569

1. O light forever dawning
beyond the darkest night;
O comfort of the mourning,
our strength and our delight;
receive our humble pleading
for those whose course is run,
lest pardon they be needing
for any evil done.

2. To him who like the eagle
arose on conqu'ring wing,
the cross his banner regal,
O death, where is your sting?
There's surely no rejection
for those who share his strife,
but hope and resurrection
and everlasting life.

Denis E. Hurley © Archdiocese of Durban

570

1. O raise your eyes on high and see
there stands our sovereign Lord,
his glory is this day revealed,
his Word a two-edged sword.

2. We glimpse the splendour and the
   power
of him who conquered death,
the Christ in whom the universe
knows God's creating breath.

3. Of every creed and nation King
in him all strife is stilled;
the promise made to Abraham
in him has been fulfilled.

4. The prophets stand and with great
   joy
give witness as they gaze;
the Father with a sign has sealed
our trust, our hope, our praise.

5. This glory that today our eyes
have glimpsed of God's own Son
will help us ever sing with love
of Three who are but One.

Ralph Wright, OSB, © Ampleforth Abbey Trustees

571

O, what a gift, what a wonderful
   gift;
who can tell the wonder of the Lord?
Let us open our eyes, our ears,
   and our hearts;
it is Christ the Lord, it is he!

1. In the stillness of the night, when
   the world was asleep,
the Lord made his message
   known.

It was then that his Word came
   down from on high,
from the Father's royal throne:
Christ our Lord and our King!

2. His mighty Word cuts quick and
      clean,
   far sharper than a two-edged
      sword:
   open your eyes, your ears,
      and your hearts,
   and hear the Word of the Lord:
   Christ our Lord and our King!

3. He came to his people, the chosen
      race,
   that his Father's will would be
      known;
   Lion of Judah, Light of the Word,
   our Redeemer came to his own,
   Christ our Lord and our King!

4. He lived here among us, he
      worked here among us,
   morning, night, and day;
   showed us his glory, gave us a
      promise,
   and then we turned away.
   Christ our Lord and our King!

5. At the Passover meal on the night
      before he died,
   he lifted up his eyes and prayed.
   Then he broke the bread,
      then he shared the wine
   the gift that God had made:
   Christ our Lord and our King!

6. On the hill of Calvary, the world
      held its breath;
   and there for the world to see,
   the Father gave his Son, his very
      own Son
   for the love of you and me.
   Christ our Lord and our King!

7. Early on that morning when the
      guards were asleep,
   the Father revealed his might;
   Christ in his glory arose from
      the dead,
   the Lord of Life and Light:
   Christ our Lord and our King!

8. On the road to Emmaus, the
      glory that is his,
   the disciples could never see.
   Then he broke the bread, then he
      shared the wine;
   it is the Lord, it is he:
   Christ our Lord and our King!

9. Now look around you
      and open your eyes;
   remember the Spirit is here.
   Here within his Church, his people
      are one.
   Look, the Lord is near:
   Christ our Lord and our King!

Pat Uhl and Michael Gilligan
© The American Catholic Press

572

1. Of one that is so fair and bright,
   velut maris stella,
   brighter than the day is light,
   parens et puella;
   I cry to thee to turn to me,
   lady, pray thy Son for me,
   tam pia,
   that I may come to thee,
   Maria.

2. In sorrow, counsel thou art best,
   felix fecundata:
   for all the weary thou art rest,
   mater honorata:
   beseech him in thy mildest mood,
   who for us did shed his blood

in cruce,
that we may come to him
in luce.

3. All this world was forlorn,
   Eva peccatrice,
   till our Saviour Lord was born
   de te genetrice;
   with thy ave sin went away,
   dark night went and in came day
   salutis.
   The well of healing sprang from
     thee,
   virtutis.

4. Lady, flower of everything,
   rosa sine spina,
   thou borest Jesus, heaven's king,
   gratia divina.
   Of all I say thou bore the prize,
   lady, queen of paradise,
   electa;
   maiden mild, mother
   es effecta.

Anon: medieval

573

1. Of the Father's love begotten,
   ere the worlds began to be,
   he is Alpha and Omega,
   he the source, the ending he,
   of all things that are and have been
   and that future years shall see:
   Evermore and evermore

2. By his word was all created;
   He commanded, it was done:
   heaven and earth and depth of
     ocean,
   universe of three in one,
   all that grows beneath the shining
   of the light of moon and sun:

3. Blessed was the day for ever
   when the virgin, full of grace,

by the Holy Ghost conceiving,
bore the Saviour of our race,
and the child, the world's
  Redeemer,
first revealed his sacred face:

4. O, ye heights of heaven, adore
     him,
   Angels and archangels sing!
   Every creature bow before him
   singing praise to God our King;
   let no earthly tongue be silent,
   all the world with homage ring:

5. He, by prophets sung, is here now,
   promised since the world began,
   now on earth in flesh descended
   to atone for sins of man.
   All creation praise its Master,
   see fulfilment of his plan:

6. Glory be to God the Father,
   glory be to God the Son,
   glory to the Holy Spirit,
   persons three, yet Godhead one.
   Glory be from all creation
   while eternal ages run:

Aurelius C. Prudentius (348-c 413) tr by
J. M. neale (1818-66), H. W. Baker (1821-77) and others

574

Oh the word of my Lord, deep
within my being,
oh the word of my Lord, you have
filled my mind.

1. Before I formed you in the womb
   I knew you through and through,
   I chose you to be mine.
   Before you left your mother's side
   I called to you, my child, to be
     my sign.

2. I know that you are very young,
   but I will make you strong
   – I'll fill you with my word;
   and you will travel through the
      land,
   fulfilling my command which you
      have heard.

3. And ev'rywhere you are to go
   my hand will follow you;
   you will not be alone.
   In all the danger that you fear
   you'll find me very near, your
      words my own.

4. With all my strength you will be
      filled:
   you will destroy and build,
   for that is my design.
   You will create and overthrow,
   reap harvests I will sow – your
      word is mine.

Based on Jeremiah 1. Damian Lundy
© *1978 Kevin Mayhew Ltd*

575

1. On a hill far away
   stood an old rugged cross,
   the emblem of suff'ring and
      shame;
   and I loved that old cross
   where the dearest and best
   for a world of lost sinners was
      slain.

   **So I'll cherish the old rugged cross
   'till my trophies at last I lay down;
   I will cling to the old rugged cross
   and exchange it someday for a
      crown.**

2. Oh that old rugged cross,
   so despised by the world,
   has a wondrous attraction for me:

for the dear Lamb of God
left his glory above
to bear it to dark Calvary.

3. In the old rugged cross,
   stained with blood so divine,
   a wondrous beauty I see.
   For 'twas on that old cross
   Jesus suffered and died
   to pardon and sanctify me.

4. To the old rugged cross
   I will ever be true,
   its shame and reproach gladly
      bear.
   Then he'll call me some day
   to my home far away
   there his glory for ever I'll share.

George Bennar

576

1. One day will come
   when this world which we roam
   will cease to produce sorrows
   from seeds which we have sown;
   that day there'll be such rejoicing,
   joy will banish all tears.
   One day when love conquers all
      our fears.

   **That day a glow will surround us,
   evil will be no more;
   no wars, nor hatred around us
   peace on earth will be sure.
   One day when man's heart
   returns to God;
   the day when all men acclaim him
   all pow'rful Lord;
   with radiant gowns he'll adorn us.
   'My true children', he'll say,
   one day when love teaches us how
      to pray.
   One day when love teaches us how
      to pray.**

2. Some day we'll learn
   how to control our lives.
   It's only then we'll be able
   to open our eyes
   to see the beauty around us,
   which God meant us to share.
   One day when love teaches us how
       to care.

Ronald Gokool © 1980 Mayhew McCrimmon Ltd

577

1. Our Father, we have wandered
   and hidden from your face,
   in foolishness have squandered
   your legacy of grace.
   But now, in exile dwelling,
   we rise with fear and shame,
   as distant but compelling,
   we hear you call our name.

2. And now at length discerning
   the evil that we do,
   behold us Lord, returning
   with hope and trust to you.
   In haste you come to meet us
   and home rejoicing bring.
   In gladness there to greet us
   with calf and robe and ring.

3. O Lord of all the living,
   both banished and restored,
   compassionate, forgiving
   and ever caring Lord,
   grant now that our transgressing,
   our faithlessness may cease.
   Stretch out your hand in blessing
   in pardon and in peace.

Kevin Nichols © 1974 ICEL

578

Antiphon:

   Our help is the name of the Lord
   who made the earth and the
       heavens.
   He is for us a most merciful
       Father,
   and his faithfulness has no end.
   Our help is in the name of the Lord
   and his faithfulness has no end.

1. He calls my life from out of the
       grave,
   he fills my days with happiness,
   and like an eagle my youth is
       restored.
   Our help is in the name of the Lord
   and his faithfulness has no end.
   Our help is in the name of the Lord
   and his faithfulness has no end.

2. This God of ours does not
       condemn us,
   never repays us evil for evil.
   For he is greater than our sins.
   Our help is in the name of the Lord
   and his faithfulness has no end.
   Our help is in the name of the Lord
   and his faithfulness has no end.

3. As any man shows mercy to his
       sons
   he is a merciful Father to us.
   He knows us through for he made
       us.

Repeat antiphon

   Our help is the name of the Lord
   who made the earth and the
       heavens.
   He is for us a most merciful
       Father,

and his faithfulness has no end.
**Our help is in the name of the Lord
and his faithfulness has no end.**

*From Psalm 102 (103):3-5, 8-10, 13-14.
Antiphon based on Psalm 120 (121): 2.
Versified by Huub Oosterhuis, tr by Tony Barr
© Tony Barr and Jabulani Music*

579

1. Our Saviour Jesus Christ
     proclaimed
   that when we gather in his name
   he would be there to love and
     guide,
   lead us towards the Father's side.

   **Our hearts are longing for you,
     Lord,
   give us the faith to trust your word.**

2. He told us, 'Ask, you will receive,
   seek and you'll find if you believe.
   Knock at the door of love and
     truth
   and we shall open it for you.'

3. His hands brought healing to the
     blind,
   his words brought ease to troubled
     minds.
   He said his friends could do the
     same
   by invocation of his name.

4. He came to earth in form of man
   to give to us his Father's plan.
   We are the branches, he the vine,
   we too can share his life divine.

Estelle White © Mayhew McCrimmon Ltd

580

1. Out of deep unordered water
   God created land and life;
   world of beast and bird and later
   twosome people, man and wife.

**There is water in the river
bringing life to tree and plant.
Let creation praise its giver:
there is water in the font.**

2. Water on the human forehead,
   birthmark of the love of God,
   is the sign of death and rising,
   through the sea there runs a road.

3. Standing round the font reminds
     us
   of the Hebrew's climb ashore.
   Life is hallowed by the knowledge
   God has been this way before.

Fred Kaan © Stainer & Bell

581

**'Peace is my parting gift to you,
my own peace.
Peace is my parting gift to you,'
says the Lord. (Jn 14:27)**

1. Set your troubled hearts at rest,
   and banish all your fears, for . . .
     (Jn 14:27)

2. I will give you peace such as
     the world,
   it cannot give, for . . .
     (Jn 14:27)

3. Come to me all who are weary
   and in need of rest, for . . .
     (Mk 11:28)

4. You will find my yoke is easy,
   and my burden light, for . . .
     (Mk 11:30)

5. As the Father sent me, so now
   I am sending you, for . . .
     (Jn 20:21)

6. In my Spirit's power
all your sins will be forgiven,
for . . .
(Jn 20:22-23)

7. Go and take my gift of peace
to all throughout the world, for . . .
(Mk 16:15 and Mt 28:18)

*Paraphrased from Scripture by Sr Gabriel
(verse 1 and response) and Robert B. Kelly
(verses 2-7) © 1980 Mayhew McCrimmon Ltd*

582

1. Peace, perfect peace,
in this dark world of sin?
The blood of Jesus whispers
peace within.

2. Peace, perfect peace,
by thronging duties pressed?
To do the will of Jesus, this is rest.

3. Peace, perfect peace,
with sorrows surging round?
On Jesus' bosom nought
but calm is found.

4. Peace, perfect peace,
with loved ones far away?
In Jesus' keeping we are safe,
and they.

5. Peace, perfect peace,
our future all unknown?
Jesus we know, and he is on
the throne.

6. Peace, perfect peace,
death shadowing us and ours?
Jesus has vanquished death
and all its powers.

7. It is enough; earth's troubles
soon shall cease,

and Jesus call us to heaven's
perfect peace.

E. H. Bickersteth (1823-1906)

583

**Peacetime, peacetime,
time for making peace.
Peacetime, peacetime,
time to say I forgive you,
time for saying 'I love you',
time to live as friends.**

1. Happy are they
who are makers of peace;
Happy are they
who forgive;
happy are they
who know how to love;
they're the sons
and daughters of God.

2. Happy are they
who are gentle of heart;
happy are those
who care;
happy are they
who seek the good of all;
they're the ones
so close to God's heart.

*PEACETIME by Carey Landry. Copyright © 1973 by
Rev Carey Landry and North American Liturgy
Resources, 10802 N 23rd Ave, Phoenix, AZ 85029, USA.
All rights reserved. Used with permission*

584

1. Praise the Lord for the heavens
above!
Praise the Lord for the sun and
the moon!
Praise the Lord for the stars
shining bright!
Yes praise, O praise the Lord!

2. Praise the Lord for the breezes
and the winds!
Praise the Lord for the cold and
heat!
Praise the Lord for the showers
so cool!
Yes praise, O praise the Lord!

3. Praise the Lord for the nights
and the days!
Praise the Lord for the weeks
and the months!
Praise the Lord for the years
as they pass!
Yes praise, O praise the Lord!

4. Praise the Lord for redemption
from sin!
Praise the Lord for salvation is
ours!
Praise the Lord for that glorious
day!
Yes praise, O praise the Lord!

5. Praise the Lord for his passion
and death!
Praise the Lord for his sufferings
so cruel!
Praise the Lord for arising
from death!
Yes praise, O praise the Lord!

Douglas Rowe, SJ. © 1980 Mayhew McCrimmon Ltd

585

1. Praise the Lord! Ye heavens,
adore him;
praise him, angels, in the height;
sun and moon, rejoice before him,
praise him, all ye stars of light.
Praise the Lord! for he hath
spoken;
worlds his mighty voice obeyed:

laws, which never shall be broken,
for their guidance he hath made.

2. Praise the Lord! for he is glorious;
never shall his promise fail:
God hath made his saints
victorious;
sin and death shall not prevail.
Praise the God of our salvation;
hosts on high, his power proclaim;
heaven and earth and all creation,
laud and magnify his name!

3. Worship, honour, glory, blessing,
Lord, we offer to thy name;
young and old, thy praise
expressing,
join their Saviour to proclaim.
As the saints in heaven adore thee,
we would bow before thy throne;
as thine angels serve before thee,
so on earth thy will be done.

*Verses 1-2 from the Foundling Hospital Collection
(1796); verse 3 by E. Osler (1798-1863)*

586

**Praise to the Lord! Praise him!
Praise to the Lord!**

1. Shout to God, all you heavens,
and clap your hands you on earth.
Enter into his presence
exulting and singing for joy!

2. Know that God is our Father;
he made us, we are his own.
Come to him with thanksgiving
extolling and blessing his name.

3. Merciful to us, sinners,
compassionate to his sons,
he has sent his beloved
to guide us in justice and peace!

4. Praise him, then, with full voices
   and sing to him from the heart!
   Gather, Christians, together,
   together, to joyfully sing.

5. Praise the Lord with trumpet.
   O praise his name with the dance;
   celebrate with the cymbal,
   exalt him with drum, pipe and
      string!

Paschal Jordan © 1980 Mayhew McCrimmon Ltd

587

Rain down justice,
you heavens, from above;
let the earth bring forth for us
the one who is to come.
(Isaiah 45:8)

1. Be not angry, O Lord,
   and remember no longer our
      sinfulness.
   Our city, the city of your Holy
      One,
   has become a desert.
   Sion is lying in the ruins;
   Jerusalem having fallen, lies
      desolate.
   Is this the House of your glory
      and your holiness,
   where our Fathers came to praise
      you?

2. We have sinned and stand before
      you unclean,
   we have chosen to walk our own
      ways.

We have fallen as the leaves of
   the autumn,
scattered by the wind.
Just as the ravage of earth
   by the winter storms,
we have blotted your memory
   from our sight.
You have hidden your face away
   from us,
you have crushed us with the
   weight of our evil.

3. See the sorrow of your People,
      O Lord;
   send the Saviour, the one who
      is to come.
   Send us the Lamb to take away
      the sins of the world,
   to take away our burdens.
   Send us a Lord to rule the earth,
   to this city built on your holy
      mountain.
   Then he shall free us from all
      that has enslaved us,
   the day he takes away the yoke
      of our captivity.

4. Be comforted, be comforted, my
      People,
   your salvation is very close at
      hand.
   Why are your hearts so full of
      sorrow,
   why does such grief so estrange
      you?
   Do not be afraid any more.
   I am the Promised One, the hope
      of ages.
   You are my People and soon I
      come to rescue you
   I am the Holy One, the Lord
      your Redeemer.

Based on Rorate, caeli, by Tony Barr © 1967
and 1979 by Tony Barr and Jabulani Music

588

Rejoice, and shout for joy
sing out in praise for what the
   Lord has done.
It's right to praise him and sing
   a new song.
Play it loudly. Sing so joyfully.
For his love it fills the earth.

1. O the words of the Lord are true
   and his works are worthy of trust.
   He loves what we do that's
      righteous
   and what we do that's just.
   He merely spoke and the world
      began
   the heav'ns were formed with
      moons and stars.
   He made the oceans by pouring
      them
   into vast reservoirs.

2. With one breath he can scatter
   the plans of a whole nation.
   His intentions are the same
   for ev'ry generation.
   Happy is the nation
   whose God is the Lord.
   Not the king whose army
   can boast a powerful sword.

3. O the Lord looks down from
      heaven
   and he knows ev'ry thing we do.
   He watches over those who obey
      him
   and trust in his love so true.
   O the Lord he saves and helps us
   and protects us like a shield.
   We depend on him. He is our
      hope.
   To him alone we yield.

From Psalm 32 (33) by Anne Seymour ©

589

Rejoice, rejoice, rejoice!
Come, let us praise the Lord! (3)
Praise the Lord! Praise the Lord!
   Praise the Lord!

1. Holy, holy, holy! (3)
   O, holy is the Lord!

2. Glory, glory, glory! (3)
   O, glory to the Lord!

Norbert Farrell © *1980 Mayhew McCrimmon Ltd*

590

1. 'Remember, man, that you are
      dust,
   and unto dust you shall return.'
   O who are we, mere creature clay,
   that we should dare to call you
      'Lord'?

2. 'Fear not, my child, I am your
      God.
   For you I came; for you I died.'
   What gift is this – a creature God!
   – And in return, what can we give?

3. 'O lift your heart, your heart of
      stone:
   no longer lost, you are my own.'
   O, we have sinned, deserve to die:
   how can our pride admit your love?

4. O Lord of love, we turn to you:
   forgive, and heal, and make us
      new.
   No eye can see, no ear can hear,
   no mind conceive what hope you
      bring,
   what hope you bring.

© *1980 John Glynn*

591

Return to the Lord, return,
   O Israel!
He calls to you.
For the Lord is full of love
   and tender mercy;
he waits for your heart.

1. What shall I do with you,
   O my people?
   This love of yours so quickly
   disappears. *(Hosea 6:4)*

2. When will you share your bread
   with the hungry?
   When will you welcome in the
   homeless poor? *(Isaiah 58:7)*

3. I do not take delight in burnt
   off'ring.
   Give me yourself, your crushed
   and broken heart. *(Psalm 51:17)*

4. And I will plant my law deep
   within you.
   Deep in your heart will I inscribe
   my name. *(Jeremiah 31:31)*

5. I love you with a love everlasting;
   I hold you constantly close to
   my heart. *(Jeremiah 31:31)*

Paschal Jordan © 1980 Mayhew McCrimmon Ltd

592

1. Rock of ages, cleft for me,
   let me hide myself in thee;
   let the water and the blood,
   from thy riven side which flowed,
   be of sin the double cure:
   cleanse me from its guilt and
   power.

2. Not the labours of my hands
   can fulfill thy law's demands;
   could my zeal no respite know,
   could my tears for ever flow,
   all for sin could not atone:
   thou must save, and thou alone.

3. Nothing in my hand I bring,
   simply to thy Cross I cling;
   naked, come to thee for dress;
   helpless, look to thee for grace;
   foul, I to the fountain fly;
   wash me, Saviour, or I die.

4. While I draw this fleeting breath,
   when my eyelids close in death,
   when I soar through tracts
     unknown,
   see thee on thy judgement throne;
   rock of ages, cleft for me,
   let me hide myself in thee.

A. M. Toplady (1740-1778)

593

1. Seek ye first the Kingdom of God,
   and his righteousness,
   and all these things shall be added
     unto you;
   allelu, alleluia.

Alleluia, alleluia, alleluia,
alleluia, alleluia.

2. Ask and it shall be given unto you,
   seek and ye shall find;
   knock and it shall be opened
     unto you;
   allelu, alleluia.

Karen Lafferty © 1972 Maranatha Music

594

1. Send forth your Spirit, God
     our Father,
   as you have sent him in the past:
   at Gabriel's word, by Jordan's
     water,
   as Jesus went to pray and fast.

2. In this same Spirit he proclaimed
     you
   on Juda's hills, by Galilee,
   he called us to your heav'nly
     kingdom,
   he died and rose triumphantly.

3. And now though seen by us no
     longer
   he rests not from the task begun,
   but breathes the Spirit of his
     sonship
   on men of ev'ry race and tongue.

4. May he be with us at this moment
   and give us of your Spirit still,
   that we may do the work that
     waits us
   and strive your purpose to fulfil.

At confirmation

5. May all who come for
     confirmation
   be richly with your Spirit sealed:
   to love and serve you in their
     brothers,
   until your glory is revealed.

Denis E. Hurley © *Archdiocese of Durban*

595

Send forth your Spirit, O Lord.
Send forth your Spirit
on these your chosen ones.
Send forth your Spirit of love.

1. To show the love of the Father,
   to show the love of the Son.
   To show the love of Jesus for all
     men;
   this is his new commandment.

Send forth your Spirit, O Lord.
Send forth your Spirit
on these your chosen ones.
Send forth your Spirit of truth.

2. To know the will of the Father,
   to know the will of the Son,
   to know the Gospel of Jesus the
     Lord,
   to proclaim to everyone.

Send forth your Spirit, O Lord.
Send forth your Spirit
on these your chosen ones.
**Send them to cast your fire on
   earth.**

Sung by Confirmation candidates

3. Come upon us, O Spirit of the
     living God!
   Come upon us, O Spirit of truth!
   Come upon us, O Spirit of love
     and life!
   Send us to cast your fire on earth!

Send forth your Spirit, O Lord.
Send forth your Spirit
on these your chosen ones.
**Send them to cast your fire on
   earth.**

Send forth your Spirit, O Lord.
Send forth your Spirit
on these your chosen ones.
Send forth your Spirit of love.

Garfield Rochard © *1980 Mayhew McCrimmon Ltd*

596

**Send forth your Spirit, O Lord,
that the face of the earth be
renewed.**

1. O my soul, arise and bless the
   Lord God,
   O Lord, in majesty,
   enrobed with pow'r and eternal
   might.

2. You are clothed with splendour
   and with beauty,
   O God, and heav'nly light
   is like a cloud that conceals your
   face.

3. You have built your palace on
   the waters;
   on wings of winds and fire
   you reign in heav'n, rule supreme
   on earth.

4. Like the winds your angels fly
   before you;
   as fire and flaming light,
   your ministers stand before your
   throne.

5. For the earth you fixed on its
   foundations;
   indeed, it shall stand firm,
   and not be moved for unending
   years.

6. On the earth the waters spread
   their mantle;
   and seas filled all the land;
   above the earth stood the
   rising flood.

7. When they heard on high your
   voice of thunder,
   in fear they took to flight;
   at your reproach, they dispersed
   and fled.

8. By your word, there sprang up
   hills and mountains;
   on earth the dry land rose,
   and in their place, rested glens
   and vales.

9. Your command sets bounds on
   all the waters,
   and they shall not return;
   they may not pass limits you
   have set.

10. Torrents fill the valleys at
    your order;
    while streams and rivers flow,
    refresh the beasts, slake the
    thirst of man.

11. From their nests, the birds give
    praise and glory
    to you, O Lord of hosts,
    from ev'ry branch, join in songs
    of praise.

12. In green fields you feed your
    sheep and cattle,
    and all your creatures, Lord;
    and yet to men, you have given
    more.

13. There is wine to cheer the heart
    of mankind;
    the wheat for man makes bread;
    and oil is used to anoint his head.

14. While I live, I sing the praise of
    Yahweh,
    O Lord, your glorious praise,
    my lips proclaim: Blessed be
    the Lord.

15. Praise to God, the author of
    these marvels,
    to God, the mighty One,
    who made the earth, glory to his
    name.

16. Praise to God, the Father, Son
    and Spirit,
    to God who gives us life,
    our thanks return, now and
    evermore.

Words from Psalm 103 (104) by Lucien Deiss
© 1965 World Library Publications

597

1. Shepherd of souls, in love come
   feed us.
   Life-giving bread for hungry
   hearts.
   To those refreshing waters lead us
   where dwells that grace your peace
   imparts.
   May we, the wayward in your fold,
   by your forgiveness rest consoled.

2. Life-giving vine, come, feed and
   nourish,
   strengthen each branch with life
   divine.
   Ever in you O may we flourish,
   fruitful the branches of the vine.
   Lord, may our souls be purified
   so that in Christ we may abide.

3. Sinful are we who stand before
   you
   worthy of you is Christ alone.
   So in Christ's name we do implore
   you;
   rich are the mercies you have
   shown.
   Say but the word, O Lord divine,
   then are our hearts made pure like
   thine.

4. Following you, O Lord, who led
   them,
   Multitudes thronged the
   mountainside;

Filled with compassion, Lord,
   you fed them,
Fed them with loaves you
   multiplied.
Come, feed us now, O Lord, we
   pray:
Lifegiving bread give us this day.

5. Help us, dear Lord, prepare a
   dwelling
   worthy of you who made us all;
   cleanse thou our hearts, our guilt
   dispelling,
   purify us who heed your call.
   'Take this and eat' were words
   you said,
   so we have gathered for this bread.

J. Clifford Evers © World Library Publications

598

1. Show me your ways that I may
   follow you,
   lead me, O master, on my way.
   Guide me in all the things that
   I must do,
   direct my steps that I don't go
   astray.

   **In you I place my confidence
   and trust,**
   **O Lord, have your way with me
   for I am yours.**

2. Guard me when temptation calls
   on me to sin.
   Protect me when the enemy is
   near.
   Strengthen me to turn to you
   that I may win,
   and bless me, Jesus, that I
   persevere.

The spirit's willing but the flesh
   is weak, O Lord.
But your support is all I'll ever need.

3. Show me your ways that I may
      follow you,
   lead me, O Master, on my way.
   Guide me in all the things that
      I must do,
   direct my steps that I don't go
      astray.

599

1. Sing a simple song unto the Lord;
   sing a simple song unto the Lord,
   sing it with your heart,
   sing it with your soul,
   sing a simple song unto the Lord.

   Oh Lord, I love you;
   O Lord, I see;
   Oh Lord, I love you,
   I see that you love me.

2. Say a simple prayer . . .

3. Give a simple gift . . .

600

1. Sing everyone
   a song to the Lord,
   a song to the Lord
   of all our hearts.
   He made us,
   we're the work of his hands,
   the work of his hands
   in all we are.

Lord, we offer you
everything we do,
sing everyone
a song to the Lord,
a song to the Lord
of all our hearts.

2. Come everyone
   who works for his life,
   who works for his life
   on this fair earth.
   He worked for
   us and left us himself,
   the gift of his life
   in bread and wine.
   Take our work and play,
   it's yours every day.
   Sing everyone
   a song to the Lord,
   a song to the Lord
   who makes us live.

3. Sing softly,
   for the Lord is around,
   he's there in the smallest
   summer breeze.
   Sing sweetly,
   for the Lord isn't harsh,
   he's gentle in voice,
   in giving, free.
   Lord, we love with you
   all those you give us now.
   Sing loudly,
   for the love of the Lord,
   the love of the Lord
   is all our joy.

601

1. Sing praises to the Lord; (3)
   alleluia, alleluia!

2. And holy be his Name; (3)
   alleluia, alleluia!

3. For he is kind and good, (3)
   alleluia, alleluia!

4. He died that we might live;
   he rose again to life;
   he lives no more to die,
   alleluia, alleluia!

Derick Clouden © 1980 Mayhew McCrimmon Ltd

602

**Sing to the Lord a song,
sing to the Lord a psalm.
Sing to the Lord, you nations!
Praise his name! (2)**

1. He made heaven, he made the
      earth;
   the sea, the sky and all there is,
   He made Adam out of naught,
   and told him these were his.

2. Now, Adam was a lonely man,
   and God decided he would give
   a helping-mate to this new man:
   created the woman Eve.

3. Then God told Adam what to do:
   'Go forth, good man, into the
      world,
   multiply and fill the earth
   and bless my holy name.'

Helena Warner © 1980 Mayhew McCrimmon Ltd

603

**Sing to the Lord, alleluia,
sing to the Lord.**

1. Bless his name,
   announce his salvation
   day after day,
   alleluia.

2. Give to him,
   you families of peoples
   glory and praise,
   alleluia.

3. Great is he,
   and worthy of praises
   day after day,
   alleluia.

4. He it is
   who gave us the heavens,
   glory to God,
   alleluia.

5. Tell his glories,
   tell all the nations,
   day after day,
   alleluia.

6. Bring your gifts
   and enter his temple,
   worship the Lord,
   alleluia.

*Psalm 95 (96) arr by John Foley, SJ. SING TO THE LORD
arr by John Foley. Copyright © 1970 by John Foley, SJ.
Published exclusively by North American Liturgy
Resources, 10802 N 23rd Ave, Phoenix, AZ 85029, USA.*

604

**Sing to the mountains, sing to the
   sea.
Raise your voices, lift your hearts.
This is the day the Lord has made.
Let all the earth rejoice.**

1. I will give thanks to you, my Lord.
   You have answered my plea.
   You have saved my soul from
      death.
   You are my strength and my song.

2. Holy, holy, holy Lord.
   Heaven and earth are full of your
      glory.

3. This is the day that the Lord has
made.
Let us be glad and rejoice.
He has turned all death to life.
Sing of the glory of God.

*Based on verses from Psalm 117 (118), Bob Dufford, SJ.
SING TO THE MOUNTAINS by Bob Dufford, SJ.
Copyright © 1975 by Bob Dufford, SJ and North American
Liturgy Resources, 10802, N 23rd Ave, Pheonix, AZ 85029,
USA. All rights reserved. Used with permission*

605

1. Sing to the world of Christ our
sov'reign Lord;
tell of his birth which brought
new life to all.
Speak of his life, his love, his
holy word;
let ev'ry nation hear and know his
call.
Sing to the World of Christ our
Sov'reign Lord.

2. Sing to the world of Christ the
Prince of peace,
showing to me the Father's loving
care,
pleading that love should reign
and wars might cease,
teaching we need the love of God
to share.
Sing to the world of Christ the
Prince of peace.

3. Sing to the world of Christ our
steadfast friend,
off'ring himself to live the
constant sign;
food for our souls until we meet
life's end,
gives us his flesh for bread, his
blood for wine.
Sing to the world of Christ our
steadfast friend.

4. Sing to the world of Christ our
Saviour King,
born that his death mankind's
release should win;
hung from a cross, forgiveness he
could bring;
buried, he rose to conquer death
and sin.
Sing to the world of Christ our
Saviour King.

5. Sing to the world of Christ at
God's right hand,
praise to the Spirit both have
sent to men,
living in us till earth shall reach
its span,
time be no more, and Christ shall
come again.
Sing to the world of Christ at
God's right hand.

Patrick Lee © 1978 Magnificat Music

606

1. Son of God and son of David,
priest devoid of dignity,
slave to ransom the enslaved,
butt of jibes and jealousy:
you were like us, struggling and
trying,
till your dying
for our liberty.

Every creature should, with
gladness,
kneel before your majesty;
every man, through joy and
sadness,
witness to your sanctity,
bring you a rich credit balance
from his talents
and activity.

3. Jesus' name in condemnation
   nailed to that torturing tree,
   'King of Jews' that provocation
   you forgave in agony.
   Hear, Lord, this sinner's petition
   for remission,
   life eternally.

Ds Willem Barnard, tr by © Bonaventure Hinwood

607

1. Son of the Father, Jesus,
      Lord and slave,
   born among the cattle in the
      squalor of a cave,
   one with God, you made yourself
   one with man, shunning wealth;
   Lord, we worship you with heart
      and mind.

2. Son of the Father, Jesus,
      workers' friend,
   you whom Joseph taught the skills
      of working with your hands,
   man, at home in builder's yard,
   one with man, toiling hard;
   Lord, we worship you with hand
      and mind.

3. Son of the Father, author of our
      faith,
   choosing men to follow you
      from every walk of life,
   who with them, in boats, on shore,
   troubles shared, burdens bore;
   Lord, we worship you with hand
      and mind.

4. See of the Father, from life's
      furrow born,
   teaching men in parables
      from agriculture drawn,
   Jesus, lover of the soil,

man of earth, son of toil;
Lord, we worship you with hand
   and mind.

5. Father and Spirit, Jesus, Lord
      and Man,
   bless us in the work you have
      appointed to be done.
   Lift our spirits, guide our wills,
   steer our hands, use our skills;
   Lord, we worship you with hand
      and mind.

© 1972 Fred Kaan

608

1. Take my life, and let it be
   consecrated, Lord, to thee;
   take my moments and my days,
   let them flow in ceaseless praise.

2. Take my hands, and let them move
   at the impulse of thy love.
   Take my feet, and let them be
   swift and purposeful for thee.

3. Take my voice, and let me sing
   always, only, for my King.
   Take my intellect, and use
   every power as thou shalt choose.

4. Take my will, and make it thine:
   it shall be no longer mine.
   Take my heart; it is thine own:
   it shall be thy royal throne.

5. Take my love; my Lord, I pour
   at thy feet its treasure-store.
   Take myself, and I will be
   ever, only, all for thee.

Frances R. Havergal (1836-1879)

609

1. Tell out, my soul, the greatness
     of the Lord!
   Unnumbered blessings, give my
     spirit voice;
   tender to me the promise of his
     word;
   in God my Saviour shall my heart
     rejoice.

2. Tell out, my soul, the greatness
     of his name!
   Make known his might, the deeds
     his arm has done;
   his mercy sure, from age to age
     the same;
   his holy name – the Lord, the
     Mighty One.

3. Tell out, my soul, the greatness
     of his might!
   Powers and dominions lay their
     glory by.
   Proud hearts and stubborn wills
     are put to flight,
   the hungry fed, the humble lifted
     high.

4. Tell out, my soul, the glories
     of his word!
   Firm is his promise, and his
     mercy sure.
   Tell out, my soul, the greatness
     of the Lord
   to children's children and for
     evermore!

© Timothy Dudley-Smith, based on Luke 1:46-55 in
The New English Bible

610

1. That which we have heard
   we have seen with our own eyes;
   that which we have felt and
     touched:

   The Word who is life,
   the Word who is life,
   the Word who is life for us.
   To him be glory,
   all honour and praise.
   To him be glory:
   Jesus, our Saviour and Lord.

2. He is the Light of lights;
   our redeemer King;
   he is the Lord of lords.

3. He is the bread of life;
   wonder-counsellor;
   he is Prince of peace.

Based on 1 John 1:1, THE WORD WHO IS LIFE, by Carey
   Landry. Copyright © 1975 by Rev Carey landry and
North American Liturgy Resources, 10802 N 23rd Ave,
   Phoenix, AZ 85029, USA. All rights reserved.
                        Used with permission

611

1. The angel Gabriel from heaven
     came,
   his wings as drifted snow, his eyes
     as flame;
   'All hail,' he said, 'thou lowly
     maiden Mary,
   most highly favoured lady.' *Gloria!*

2. 'For know, a blessed Mother thou
     shalt be,
   all generations laud and honour
     thee,
   thy Son shall be Emmanuel, by
     seers foretold;
   most highly favoured lady.'
     Gloria!

3. Then gentle Mary meekly bowed
     her head,
   'To me be as it pleaseth God,'
     she said,
   'my soul shall laud and magnify
     his holy name':
   most highly favoured lady. *Gloria!*

4. Of her, Emmanuel, the Christ
     was born
   in Bethlehem, all on a Christmas
     morn,
   and Christian folk throughout
     the world will ever say
   'most highly favoured lady.'
     Gloria!

Basque carol paraphrased by
Sabine Baring-Gould (1834-1924)

612

1. The Church is wherever God's
     people are easing
   burdens of others in love and
     good will.
   The Church is wherever the cross
     of the Saviour
   is borne by believers who follow
     him still.

2. The Church is wherever God's
     people are trusting;
   facing hard trials with hope,
     not despair.
   The Church is wherever a
     miracle follows
   beyond human power, in answer
     to prayer.

3. The Church is wherever his own
     come to Jesus,
   stirred by a longing and need
     to be whole.

The Church is wherever God's
     people adore him
in worship that rises from heart,
     mind and soul.

4. The Church is wherever disciples
     of Jesus
   turn to their Master each step
     of the way.
   The Church is wherever the love
     of the Saviour
   is seen in his followers' lives
     day by day.

Pet Regehr © 1980 Mayhew McCrimmon Ltd

613

1. The King shall come when
     morning dawns
   and light triumphant breaks,
   when beauty gilds the eastern hills
   and life to joy awakes.

2. Not as of old a little child,
   to bear and fight and die,
   but crowned with glory like the
     sun
   that lights the morning sky.

3. O brighter than the rising morn
   when he, victorious, rose,
   and left the lonesome place of
     death,
   despite the rage of foes.

4. O brighter than that glorious
     morn
   shall this fair morning be,
   when Christ our King in beauty
     comes,
   and we his face shall see!

5. The King shall come when
      morning dawns
   and light and beauty brings;
   "Hail, Christ the Lord!" your
      people pray,
   "Come quickly, King of kings!"

John Brownlie (1859-1925)

614

**The light of Christ
has come into the world,
the light of Christ
has come into the world.**

1. All men must be born again
   to see the kingdom of God;
   the water and the Spirit
   bring new life in God's love.

2. God gave up his only Son
   out of love for the world
   so that ev'ryone who believes in
      him
   will live for ever.

3. The Light of God has come to us
   so that we might have salvation,
   from the darkness of our sins, we
      walk
   into glory with Christ Jesus.

Donald Fishel © 1974 The Word of God

615

1. The Lord is my shepherd.
   He provides all I need
   in the rich grassland,
   where he lets me feed.
   He brings me to water
   my life to renew.

He guides me on true paths
because he is true.

2. I walk through the darkness,
   with nothing to fear;
   his right hand protects me
   when danger is near.
   He lays me a table
   in spite of my foes.
   He fills me with gladness,
   my cup overflows.

3. Each day he is goodness,
   each day he's my song.
   I live in his household
   the whole of life long.
   The Lord is my shepherd.
   He provides all I need
   in·the rich grassland,
   where he lets me feed.

*Based on Psalm 22 (23) by Hubert Richards
© 1970 Mayhew McCrimmon Ltd*

616

The seed is Christ's, the harvest his:
may we be stored within God's barn.
The sea is Christ's, the fish are his:
may we be caught within God's net.
From birth to age, from age to death,
enfold us, Christ, within your arms.
Until the end, the great re-birth,
Christ, be our joy in Paradise.

*Traditional Irish, tr by James Quinn. SJ
© Geoffrey Chapman Ltd*

617

**The Spirit is moving all over,
all over this land.**

1. People are gathering, the Church
   is born;

the Spirit is blowing on a world reborn.

2. Doors are opening as the Spirit comes;
his fire is burning in his people now.

3. Filled with his Spirit we are sent to serve;
we are called out as brothers, we are called to work.

4. The world, born once, is born again;
we recreate it in love and joy.

5. Old men are dreaming dreams;
and young men see the light.

6. Old walls are falling down;
and people are speaking with each other.

7. The Spirit fills us with his power to be his witnesses to all we meet.

8. The Spirit urges us to travel light to be people of courage who spread his fire.

9. God has poured out his Spirit on all; on all creation.

618

1. The Spirit lives to set us free,
walk, walk in the light.
He binds us all in unity,
walk, walk in the light.

**Walk in the light, (3)
walk in the light of the Lord.**

2. Jesus promised life to all,
The dead were wakened by his call.

3. He died in pain on Calvary,
to save the lost like you and me.

4. We know his death was not the end,
He gave his Spirit to be our friend.

5. By Jesus' love our wounds are healed,
The Father's kindness is revealed.

6. The Spirit lives in you and me,
His light will shine for all to see.

619

**The Spirit of God rests upon me,
the Spirit of God consecrates me,
the Spirit of God bids me go forth
to proclaim his peace his joy.**

1. The Spirit of God sends me forth,
called to witness the kingdom of Christ
among all the nations;
called to proclaim
the good news of Christ to the poor.
My spirit rejoices in God, my Saviour.

2. The Spirit of God sends me forth,
called to witness the kingdom of Christ
among all the nations;
called to console
the hearts overcome with great sorrow.
My spirit rejoices in God, my Saviour.

3. The Spirit of God sends me forth,
   called to witness the kingdom of
      Christ
   among to comfort
   the poor who mourn and who
      weep.
   My spirit rejoices in God, my
      Saviour.

4. The Spirit of God sends me forth,
   called to witness the kingdom of
      Christ
   among all the nations;
   called to announce
   the grace of salvation to men.
   My spirit rejoices in God, my
      Saviour.

5. The Spirit of God sends me forth,
   called to witness the kingdom of
      Christ
   among all the nations;
   called to reveal
   his glory among all the people
   My spirit rejoices in God, my
      Saviour.

Based on Isaiah 61:1-2 and Luke 4:18-19 by Lucien Deiss
© 1970 World Library Publications Inc

620

1. There is a river that flows from
      God above
   there is a fountain that's filled
   with his great love.

   **Come to the waters; there is a
   great supply;
   there is a river that never shall
   run dry.**

2. Wash me with water, and then
   I shall be clean;
   white as the new snow, if you
   remove my sin. *(Psalm 50)*

3. Plunged in the water, the tomb
   of our rebirth,
   so may we rise up to share in
   Christ's new life.

4. All who are thirsty, now hear
      God as he calls;
   come to the Lord's side, his life
   pours out for all. *(Jn 19: 33-35)*

5. Safe in the new Ark, the Church
   of Christ our Lord,
   praise God for water, his sign
   to save the world.

Verse 1 trad; verses 2-5 Robert B. Kelly
© 1980 Mayhew McCrimmon Ltd

621

**There is one Lord,
there is one faith,
there is one baptism,
one God, who is Father.**

1. We were called to be one in the
      Spirit of God,
   in the bond of peace, we sing
   and proclaim.

2. We were called to form one body
      in one spirit,
   we sing and proclaim.

3. We were called in the same hope
      in Christ the Lord,
   we sing and proclaim.

Based on Ephesians 4:5 by Lucien Deiss © 1965
World Library Publications Inc

622

1. Thine be the glory, risen,
      conquering Son,
   endless is the victory thou o'er
   death hast won;

angels in bright raiment rolled
the stone away,
kept the folded grave-clothes,
where thy body lay.

**Thine be the glory, risen,
conquering Son,
endless is the victory thou o'er
death hast won.**

2. Lo, Jesus meets us, risen from
the tomb;
lovingly he greets us, scatters
fear and gloom;
let the church with gladness,
hymns of triumph sing,
for her Lord is living, death has
lost its sting.

3. No more we doubt thee, glorious
Prince of life;
life is nought without thee: aid
us in our strife;
make us more than conquerors,
through thy deathless love:
bring us safe through Jordan to
thy home above.

*Edmond Louis Budry (1854-1932) tr Richard Birch
Hoyle (1875-1939) © World Student Christian Federation*

623

1. This is my body, broken for you,
bringing forgiveness, making you
free.
Take it and drink it, and when
you do,
do it in love for me.

2. This is my blood poured out for
you,
bringing forgiveness, making you
free.
Take it and drink it, and when
you do,
do it in love for me.

3. Back to my Father soon I shall go.
Do not forget me; then you will see
I am still with you, and you will
know
you're very close to me.

4. Filled with my Spirit, how you
will grow!
You are my branches; I am the
tree.
If you are faithful, others will
know
you are alive in me.

5. Love one another – I have loved
you,
and I have shown you how to be
free;
serve one another, and when you
do,
do it in love for me.

*Verses 1 and 2 Jimmy Owens © 1978 Lexicon Music Inc,
Word Music (UK) Ltd, Northbridge Road, Berkhamsted,
Herts, HP4 1EH, England. Verses 3-5 Damian Lundy
© Kevin Mayhew Ltd*

624

**This is the day
that the Lord has made,
let us rejoice and shout
"Alleluia!"**

1. We were asleep,
it seemed like death
but now the morning's broken.

2. The winter's past,
the grass is green
and Spring is life in our land.

3. The Lord of life
has passed through death
and still he lives among us.

*Based on Psalm 117 (118) by
Anne Conway © 1977 Anne Conway*

625

1. This is the day (2)
   that the Lord has made. (2)
   We will rejoice, (2)
   and be glad in it. (2)
   This is the day
   that the Lord has made.
   We will rejoice
   and be glad in it.
   This is the day
   that the Lord has made.

2. This is the day
   when he rose again . . .

3. This is the day
   when the Spirit came . . .

Author unknown © Mayhew McCrimmon Ltd

626

**This is the feast of vict'ry for
   our God**
**for the Lamb who was slain has
   begun his reign**
has begun his reign, alleluia!
**This is the feast of vict'ry for
   our God**
for the Lamb who was slain
has begun his reign, alleluia!

1. Worthy is Christ, the Lamb who
      was slain,
   whose blood set us free to be
      people of God.
   Power, riches, wisdom and
      strength
   and honour, blessing and glory
      are his.

2. Sing with all the people of God
   and join in the hymn of all
      creation:
   Blessing, honour, glory and might
   be to God and the Lamb for ever.
   Amen.

*Based on Revelation 4:9-14 by John Ylvsiker
© 1977 Augsburg Publishing House*

627

This is the night
when God delivered our forefathers
   from their chains,
led them dry shod through the sea,
   out of slavery.
Free your people once again.

This is the night
when Christ has ransomed us
   and paid the price of sin.
The Paschal Lamb was slain
   bringing peace through pain.
We will follow where he's been.

This is the night,
this is the night he rose triumphant
   from the grave,
opened what was sealed,
   forgave, and blessed, and healed
those he suffered death to save.

O happy fault!
O necessary sin!
A New Day rushes in!

This is the night
the pillar of fire becomes a beacon
   of belief
to lead the people on, when hope
   is nearly gone,
unwav'ring joy consuming grief.

This is the night,
this is the night of nights
   awaited since the Fall,
when death is our rebirth,

with heaven wed to earth,
reconciling one and all.

This is the night,
this is the night of joy,
of solemn songs of praise,
washing guilt away.
The night shall be as day,
mourning turned to dancing all
our days.

O happy fault!
O necessary sin!
A New Day rushes in!

Based on the Exsultet by Miriam Therese Winter
© The Medical Mission Sisters

628

That is what Yahweh asks of you,
only this:
that you act justly, that you
love tenderly,
that you walk humbly, with your
God.

1. 'My children, I am with you such
a little while,
and where I go now you cannot
come,
a new commandment I give to
you:
as I have loved you, so love each
other.'

2. 'Do not let your hearts be
troubled;
trust in God now, and trust in me.
I go to prepare a place for you,
and I shall come again to take
you home.'

3. 'Peace is the gift I leave with you,
a peace the world can never give.

If you keep my word, my Father
will love you,
and we will come to you to make
our home.'

Mary McGann, RSCJ © Ephpheta House

629

1. Thou whose almighty Word
chaos and darkness heard,
and took their flight;
hear us, we humbly pray,
and where the Gospel-day
sheds not its glorious ray
let there be light!

2. Thou who didst come to bring
on thy redeeming wing
healing and sight,
health to the sick in mind,
sight now to the inly blind,
ah! now to all mankind
let there be light!

3. Spirit of truth and love,
life-giving, holy dove,
speed forth thy flight!
Move on the waters' face,
bearing the lamp of grace,
and in earth's darkest place
let there be light!

4. Blessed and holy Three,
glorious Trinity,
wisdom, love, might;
boundless as ocean tide
rolling in fullest pride,
through the world far and wide
let there be light!

J. Marriott (1780-1825)

630

Though the mountains may fall,
and the hills turn to dust,
yet the love of the Lord will stand
as a shelter for all who will call on
his name.
Sing the praise and the glory of
God.

1. Could the Lord ever leave you?
Could the Lord forget his love?
Though the Mother forsake her
child,
he will not abandon you.

2. Should you turn and forsake him,
he will gently call your name.
Should you wander away from
him,
he will always take you back.

3. Go to him when you're weary;
he will give you eagle's wings.
You will run, never tire,
for your God will be your
strength.

4. As he swore to you Fathers,
when the flood destroyed the land.
He will never forsake you;
he will swear to you again.

631

1. Through all the changing scenes
of life,
in trouble and in joy,
the praises of my God shall still
my heart and tongue employ.

2. Of his deliverance I will boast,
till all that are distressed,
when learning this, will comfort
take
and calm their griefs to rest.

3. O magnify the Lord with me,
with me exalt his name;
when in distress to him I called
he to my rescue came.

4. The hosts of God encamp around
the dwellings of the just;
deliverance he affords to all
who on his succour trust.

5. O make but trial of his love;
experience will decide
how blest are they, and only they,
who in his truth confide.

6. Fear him, ye saints, and you will
then
having nothing else to fear;
make you his service your delight,
your wants shall be his care.

*Psalm 33 (34) 1-9, Nahum Tate (1625-1715) and
Nicholas Brady (1659-1726) alt*

632

To be the body of the Lord in
this world,
to have his Spirit coursing through
my soul,
to know the passion of my Jesus
in his love for every man,
to show his mercy in the shadows of
this land.

1. Come, walk with me; come, share
my life,
you must know the shadows
if you would know the light.

2. No eyes have I, no ears to hear,
you must be my Body and show
my Father's care.

3. Open your eyes, see what I see.
For this world how I suffer.
Share my destiny.

4. I am the vine, branches are you.
Life from me eternal to make
your world anew.

5. One bread, one cup; one heart
and mind.
One great human people
in fellowship divine.

Clyde Harvey © 1980 Mayhew McCrimmon Ltd

633

1. To God our Father be the praise,
be glory ever given,
for to this world he sent his Son
that we might be forgiven.

2. The world in sin and darkness lay;
goodness was put to flight;
and in the fulness of his time
God sent his Son, the Light.

3. 'In him was life' the Gospel says,
'this life was light of men.'
The darkness has been overcome,
the Light of God shines on.

4. The Light of God is in the world,
but shines not everywhere;
he shines alone in human lives
when he's invited there.

5. 'Behold at the door of your life I
stand
the Light, the Life, the Love;
I will come in,' he says 'and will
illuminate your soul.'

6. Rejoice then, you who sing this
hymn;
real life, real joy and light
shall be for you eternally,
if you will welcome him.

© *William Armitage*

634

**Together we journey on the
highway of God,
to the mountain of glory and grace;
and together we'll seek for the pearl
of great price
till we meet with the Lord face to
face.**

1. There's one on that journey
who's burdened with sorrow,
bitterness hidden by grief:
yet we shall bear it,
together we'll share it,
united in heart and in mind.

2. Another who travels is joyful
and trusting,
clothed with the garment of peace:
so we shall wear it, together we'll
share it,
united in heart and mind.

3. And all we who journey have
gladness and sorrow
somewhere on God's holy way:
so we shall bear them,
together we'll share them,
united in heart and in mind.

© *John Glynn*

635

**Trust in the Lord; you shall not tire.
Serve you the Lord; you shall not
weaken.
For the Lord's own strength will**

**uphold you.
You shall renew your life and live.**

1. The Lord is our eternal God.
   He neither faints nor grows weary.
   Our hearts he probes from afar,
   knowing our ways, knowing our
   ways.

2. Young hearts may grow faint and
   weak,
   youths may collapse, stumble and
   fall,
   they that hope in the Lord will
   renew their courage;
   they'll soar with eagle's might.

3. Old men shall dream new dreams;
   young men will find wisdom in
   visions.
   The Lord will speak in our
   lifetime,
   show his face to those who wait.

*Based on Isaiah 40:28-31 TRUST IN THE LORD by
Robert F. O'Connor, SJ. Copyright © 1976
by Robert F. O'Connor, SJ, and North American
Liturgy Resources, 10802 N 23rd Ave, Phoenix,
AZ 85029, USA. All rights reserved. Used with permission*

636

**Unite us, Lord, in peace
and uphold us with your love.**

1. Our faults divide and hinder;
   your grace can make us one;
   we wonder at your rising,
   your light is like the sun.

2. You are our expectation
   in loneliness and pain;
   your healing and your pardon
   are greater than our sin.

3. Lord, look upon the starving
   and set the captive free.

Share out among our brothers
the bread of unity.

4. How happy are the people
   who strive to be at one,
   who learn to live as brothers,
   who lay their hatred down.

5. O Lord, whose silent spirit
   enlightens and endows,
   make us in faith receptive
   and help us love your house.

6. Your cross will draw together
   the circle of mankind;
   in you shall all the people
   their true communion find.

7. Death can no longer hurt us,
   triumphant is your word.
   Let life now grow and blossom,
   O Jesus, risen Lord!

Dominique Ombrie, tr by Fred Kaan © 1972 Fred Kaan

637

1. Upon thy table, Lord, we place
   these symbols of our work and
   thine,
   life's food won only by thy grace,
   who giv'st to all the bread and
   wine.

2. Within these simple things there
   lie
   the height and depth of human
   life,
   the thought of man, his tears and
   toil,
   his hopes and fears, his joy and
   strife.

3. Accept them, Lord; from thee
   they come:

we take them humbly at thy hand.
these gifts of thine for higher use
we offer, as thou dost command.

M. F. C. Willson (1884-1944)

638

Veni Sancte Spiritus (4)

Some or all of these verses may be sung by a soloist.

1. Holy Spirit, Lord of light,
   radiance give from celestial height.
   Come thou Father of the poor,
   come now with treasures that
       endure:
   Light of all who live.

2. Thou of all consolers the best.
   Thou the soul's delightful guest;
   refreshing peace bestow.
   Thou in toil my comfort sweet,
   thou coolness in the heat.
   Thou my solace in time of woe.

3. Light immortal, light divine;
   fire of love, our hearts refine,
   our inmost being fill.
   Take thy grace away
   and nothing pure in man will stay,
   all his good is turned to ill.

4. Heal our wounds, our strength
       renew,
   on our dryness pour thy dew;
   wash guilt away, bend the
       stubborn heart
   melt the frozen, warm the chill
   and guide the steps that go astray.

5. Sevenfold gifts on us be pleased
       to pour,
   who thee confess and thee adore;
   bring us thy comfort when we die;

give us life with thee on high;
give us joys, give us joys that
   never end.

Attr to Stephen Langton (c1160-1228), altered by
Christopher Walker from the translation by
Edward Caswall (1814-1878)

639

1. 'Wake, awake! For night is dying,'
   the watchmen on the heights are
       crying,
   'Awake, Jerusalem, at last!'
   Midnight hears the welcome
       voices,
   and at the thrilling cry rejoices:
   'Come forth, you virgins, night is
       past;
   the bridegroom comes; awake,
   your lamps with gladness take,
   hallelujah!
   and for his marriage feast prepare,
   for you must go to meet him
       there.'

2. Sion hears the watchmen singing,
   and all her heart with joy is
       springing;
   she wakes, she rises from her
       gloom:
   for her Lord comes down
       all-glorious,
   the strong in grace, in truth
       victorious;
   her star is risen, her light is come.
   Now come, O blessed one,
   God's own beloved Son;
   hallelujah!
   we follow to the festal hall
   to sup with you, the Lord of all.

3. Now let earth and heaven adore
       you,
   as men and angels sing before you

with harp and cymbal's joyful
 tone;
of one pearl each shining portal,
where we join with the choirs
 immortal
of angels round your dazzling
 throne.
No eye has seen, nor ear
is yet attuned to hear,
such great glory;
hallelujah, as here we sing
our praise to you, eternal King!

Philipp Nicolai (1556-1608) tr Catherine Winkworth
(1827-78) alt

640

Wake up! the dawn is near;
no time for sleeping, this:
our God is sending us his gift,
his Son, the Lord of bliss.

1. Come, Lord of all the world,
 creation's source and sum;
 break through these barren,
  wintry skies
 and show your mercy – come!

2. Our sins are multiplied,
 yet yours alone we stand –
 you shaped us as the clay is shaped
 beneath the potter's hand.

3. See how we stray from you,
 so deeply have we sinned,
 swept on by wickedness; like
  leaves
 before the autumn wind.

4. Yet still we trust your word,
 your pardon precious-priced,
 your wisdom sweetly ruling all,
 the chosen one, your Christ.

Luke Connaughton © 1980 Mayhew McCrimmon Ltd

641

We are bound for the promised
 land,
we're bound for the promised land;
Oh, who will come and go with us?
We are bound for the promised
 land.

1. We seek you, Lord, and all your
  strength
 your presence constantly,
 rememb'ring all your marv'lous
  works,
 and all that you can be.

2. You are the Lord, you are the God
 whose judgements fill this earth;
 you're mindful of your covenant;
 we can trust you at your Word.

3. To Abraham you made a vow,
 a promise to his son:
 'I'll give to you the promised land!
 Your inheritance is won.'

4. Give glory to the Father, Son,
 and Spirit, One in Three;
 as it was in the beginning,
 it shall forever be.

From Psalm 104 (105) paraphrased by John C. Ylvisaker
© John C. Ylvisaker

642

We cry, 'Hosanna, Lord,' yes,
 'Hosanna, Lord,'
yes, 'Hosanna, Lord' to you.
We cry, 'Hosanna, Lord,' yes
 'Hosanna, Lord,'
yes, 'Hosanna, Lord,' to you.

1. Behold, our Saviour comes.
 Behold, the Son of our God.
 He offers himself and he comes
  among us,

a lowly servant to men.

2. Children wave their palms
as the King of all kings rides by.
Should we forget to praise our
     God,
the very stones would sing.

3. He comes to set us free.
He gives us liberty.
His vict'ry over death is
th'eternal sign of God's love for
     us.

Mimi Farra © *1975 Celebration Services
International Ltd*

643

1. We form one Church, one
     Christian folk,
redeemed by God's own Son;
refreshed by clear and saving
     streams,
we share in graces won.
We break the Bread of heaven
to feed us on our way,
we take the cup that holds his
     blood
to celebrate his day.

2. We know the kindness of his love;
we know his will to save;
we know he's won the victory
o'er sin and o'er the grave.
To each of us is given
the fullness of his grace,
to live in joy a life of love
until we see his face.

3. Our hope is based on Jesus Christ,
our faith is in his name;
we know he seeks the sinful one,
for that is why he came;
he cares for those who suffer,

he loves both young and old,
a man of sorrows, risen now,
as he himself foretold!

© *Willard F. Jabusch*

644

1. We gather together to ask the
     Lord's blessing,
he chastens and hastens his will
     to make known;
the wicked oppressing now cease
     from distressing,
sing praises to his Name; he
     forgets not his own.

2. Beside us to guide us, our God
     with us joining,
ordaining, maintaining his
     kingdom divine;
so from the beginning the fight
     we were winning:
thou, Lord, wast at our side: all
     glory be thine!

3. We all do extol thee, thou leader
     triumphant.
And pray that thou still our
     defender wilt be.
Let thy congregation escape
     tribulation:
thy Name be ever praised! O Lord,
     make us free!

Theodore Baker (1851-1934) by permission of
© *G. Schirmer, Inc*

645

1. We praise you and thank you
     our Father above,
who offer us peace in your
     kingdom of love.
Your people are saved by the

death of your Son
who leads us to glory
  where all will be one.
Accepting this Gospel we honour
  Saint Patrick,
who taught in our land what
  your kindness has done.

2. Your Word has revealed what
     our future will be,
   'Raised up from the earth
     I draw all men to me.'
   May we, like Saint Patrick,
     bear witness to you,
   reflecting your love in whatever
     we do.
   He came to our country which
     once had enslaved him,
   to preach the good news that
     God makes all things new.

646

1. We praise you, God, confessing
     you as Lord!
   Eternal Father, all earth worships
     you!
   Angelic choirs, high heavens,
     celestial powers,
   cherubs and seraphs praise you
     ceaselessly:
   'All-holy Lord, O God of heavenly
     hosts,
   your glorious majesty fills heaven
     and earth.'

2. Blessed apostles join in praise
     of you
   with prophets famed and martyrs
     clothed in white,
   singing with holy Church
     throughout the earth:
   'Father, we praise your boundless
     majesty!
   We praise your glorious, true
     and only Son!
   We praise you, Holy Spirit,
     Paraclete!'

3. You are the King of glory,
     Jesus Christ!
   You are the Father's everlasting
     Son!
   Born for mankind from lowly
     Virgin's womb,
   death you have conquered,
     opening heaven to faith;
   throned now in glory at the
     Father's side
   you shall return in glory as our
     judge.

4. We pray you, therefore, give
     your servants aid,
   whom you have ransomed with
     your precious blood,
   let them be ranked in glory
     with your saints;
   save, Lord, the people who are
     wholly yours,
   bless them, for they are your
     inheritance,
   and, as their ruler, ever raise
     them up.

5. Throughout each single day,
     we bless you Lord,
   for all eternity we praise your
     name.
   Keep us this day, Lord, free
     from every sin;
   have mercy on us, Lord;
     have mercy, Lord;
   show us your love, as we have
     hoped in you!
   You are my hope, Lord; you shall
     fail me not!

647

We thank you, Father, for the gift of
  faith
through Jesus Christ your son
and for the gift of life with each other
in this our family.
May your Good News be a constant
  source of strength and joy,
for all of us who share in your
  wonderful love each day.

To live in the Spirit is to grow in
  liberty.
Without love our freedom cannot be
  real.

Gregory Norbet, OSB, and Mary David Callahan,
OSB, © *The Benedictine Foundation of Vermont, Inc*

648

1. Welcome all ye noble saints of old,
   as now before your very eyes
     unfold
   the wonders all so long ago
     foretold.

   **God and man at table are sat
   down. (2)**

2. Elders, martyrs, all are falling
     down,
   prophets, patriarchs are gath'ring
     round;
   what angels longed to see, now
     man has found.

3. Who is this who spreads the vict'ry
     feast?
   Who is this who makes our waring
     cease?
   Jesus risen, Saviour, Prince of
     Peace.

4. Beggars lame, and harlots also
     here;

repentant publicans are drawing
  near;
wayward sons come home without
  a fear.

5. Worship in the presence of the
     Lord
   with joyful songs, and hearts in
     one accord,
   and let our host at table be adored.

6. When at last this earth shall pass
     away,
   when Jesus and his bride are one
     to stay,
   the feast of love is just begun that
     day.

© *Dawn Treader Music*

649

1. What child is this, who, laid to
     rest,
   on Mary's lap is sleeping?
   Whom angels greet
   with anthems sweet,
   while shepherds watch are
     keeping?
   This, this is Christ the King,
   whom shepherds guard and angels
     sing:
   come greet the infant Lord,
   the Babe, the Son of Mary!

2. Why lies he in such mean estate,
   where ox and ass are feeding?
   Good Christians, fear:
   for sinners here
   the silent Word is pleading.
   Nails, spear, shall pierce him
     through,
   the cross be born for me, for you:
   hail, hail the Word made flesh,
   the Babe, the Son of Mary!

3. So why bring him incense, gold
     and myrrh,
   come peasant, king, to own him.
   The King of kings
   salvation brings,
   let loving hearts enthrone him.
   Raise, raise the song on high,
   the Virgin sings her lullaby:
   joy, joy for Christ is born,
   the Babe, the Son of Mary!

W. C. Dix (1837-98)

650

1. What do you ask of me?
   What would you have me do?
   I give myself
   within these gifts I offer you.
   This bread is food for life.
   This wine is spirit of love for you.

2. What can I offer you?
   You've given life to me.
   You're part of all I am.
   What would you have me be?
   This bread is food for life,
   This wine is spirit of love for me.

Miriam Therese Winter © *The Medical Mission Sisters*

651

1. When Jesus comes to be baptised,
   he leaves the hidden years behind,
   The years of safety and of peace,
   to bear the sins of all mankind.

2. The Spirit of the Lord comes
     down,
   anoints the Christ to suffering,
   to preach the word, to free the
     bound,
   And to the mourner, comfort
     bring.

3. He will not quench the dying
     flame,
   and what is bruised he will not
     break,
   but heal the wound injustice dealt,
   and out of death his triumph
     make.

4. Our everlasting Father, praise,
   with Christ, his well-beloved Son,
   who with the Spirit reigns serene,
   untroubled Trinity in One.

© *The Benedictines of Stanbrook*

652

1. When morning gilds the skies,
   my heart awaking cries,
   may Jesus Christ be praised:
   alike at work and prayer
   to Jesus I repair;
   may Jesus Christ be praised.

2. To God, the word on high
   the hosts of angels cry:
   may Jesus Christ be praised!
   let mortals, too, upraise
   their voice in hymns of praise:
   May Jesus Christ be praised!

3. Let earth's wide circle round
   in joyful notes resound:
   May Jesus Christ be praised!
   let air, and sea, and sky,
   from depth to height, reply:
   May Jesus Christ be praised!

4. Does sadness fill my mind?
   A solace here I find,
   may Jesus Christ be praised:
   or fades my earthly bliss?
   My comfort still is this,
   may Jesus Christ be praised.

5. The night becomes as day,
   when from the heart we say,

may Jesus Christ be praised:
the powers of darkness fear,
when this sweet chant they hear,
may Jesus Christ be praised.

6. Be this, while life is mine,
my canticle divine,
may Jesus Christ be praised:
be this the eternal song
through ages all along,
may Jesus Christ be praised.

19th Century, tr E. Caswall (1814-78)

653

1. When the time came to stretch
out his arms,
and to lay down his life for his
friends
God's only Son in the breaking
of bread,
gave his own flesh as food for
mankind,
gave his own flesh as food for
mankind.

2. This is my flesh, O take it and eat.
This is my blood, O take it and
drink
and to proclaim my death for
mankind,
this must you do, until I return,
this must you do, until I return.

3. Hunger and thirst no longer we
fear,
Christ's holy flesh becomes now
our food.
And when we raise his chalice
to drink,
joy overflows, our hope is
renewed,
joy overflows, our hope is
renewed.

4. O bread of life, O Banquet Divine,
sign of the love that makes us all
one,
We who now share this gift from
above,
surely have seen the goodness of
God,
surely have seen the goodness of
God.

5. Through Jesus Christ, the perfect
high Priest,
and in the Spirit source of our
peace.
For this great feast which you have
prepared,
Father above, O praised be your
name,
Father above, O praised be your
name.

Words: Michel Scouarnec, Original French
© Sefim, © tr Margaret Daly

654

Whey he day? Whey he day?
Whey he day, mi Lard?
Whey he day? Whey he day?
Whey he day? mi Lard?
Whey he day? Whey he day?
Whey he day, mi Lard?
Ah cyant fine he, fine he at all.

1. Ah want to see de man from
Galalee,
Ah want to see de man who set
me free,
Ah want to see de man who died
for me,
Ah cyant fine he, fine he at all.

2. Ah want to see de man who bleed
for me,
Ah want to see de man dey scourge

for me,
Ah want to see dis man from
  Galalee,
Ah cyant fine he, fine he at all.

3. Whey de man who make de bline
    to see?
   Whey de man who set de captive
    free?
   Whey de man who make de lame
    to walk?
   An de li'l dumb boy to talk?

Anthony Pierre © 1980 Mayhew McCrimmon Ltd

bridegroom,
God is hers, his temple she.

3. Empires rise and sink like billows,
   vanish, and are seen no more;
   glorious as the star of morning
   she o'erlooks the wild uproar.
   Hers the household all-embracing,
   hers the vine that shadows earth:
   blest thy children, mighty mother;
   safe the stranger at thy hearth.

Aubrey de Vere (1814-1902)

655

1. Who is she that stands
    triumphant,
   rock in strength, upon the rock,
   like some city crowned with
    turrets,
   braving storm and earthquake
    shock?
   Who is she her arms extending,
   blessing thus a world restored,
   all the anthems of creation
   lifting to creation's Lord?

   Hers the kingdom, hers the sceptre;
   fall, ye nations, at her feet;
   hers that truth whose fruit is
   **   freedom;**
   light her yoke, her burden sweet.

2. As the moon its splendour
    borrows
   from a sun unseen at night,
   so from Christ, the sun of justice,
   evermore she draws her light.
   Touch'd by his, her hands have
    healing,
   bread of life, absolving key:
   Christ incarnate is her

656

1. Who wants to live as God here on
    this earth (2)
   must go the way of all seed,
   in doing so find mercy. (2)

2. Must go the way of all things
    born of earth, (2)
   must share the fate, with heart and
    soul,
   of all things bound for dying. (2)

3. Both sun and rain will touch each
    of his days: (2)
   the smallest seed, come rain or
    shine,
   must die so as to live. (2)

4. So people live to die for one
    another, (2)
   the smallest seed, as living bread,
   to feed, sustain each other. (2)

5. And that is how our Lord and
    God has shown himself, (2)
   and so becomes his living self
   for each of us on earth. (2)

Huub Oosterhuis © Tony Barr and Jabulani Music

657

A. Wind and fire, the signs of pow'r
   giv'n by God at Pentecost,
   to Apostles, full of joy,
   when their waiting days were past.

1. Wind, which at creation's start
   stirred dark waters into life;
   living Spirit, vital breath,
   breathing life through man and
      wife.

   Repeat Refrain A

2. Out they burst into the streets;
   stirred the people with their news;
   set explosive in men's minds
   then God's Spirit lit the fuse.

B. Wind and fire, the signs of pow'r
   giv'n by God to us today;
   fire, to set our hearts ablaze:
   wind, to blow our fears away.

3. Hearts ablaze and free from fear,
   we'll amaze the world again,
   and God's wind and fire will still
   surge into the minds of men.

   Repeat Refrain B

   © *Alan Gaunt and John Marsh*

658

Would you like to be happy?
Would you like to be good?
Then obey God's law of love,
obey as children should.

1. You should love the Lord your
      God,
   with your head and hand and
      heart;
   you should love the Lord your
      God,
   body, soul and ev'ry part.

2. When your head thinks, think
      with love;
   when your hand works, work
      with love;
   when your heart beats, beat
      with love;
   ev'ry part must work with love.

3. You should love the Lord your
      God,
   you should love him best of all.
   Love all people as yourself
   for he made and loves them all.

   Source unknown

659

Yahweh, I know you are near,
standing always at my side.
You guard me from the foe
and you lead me in ways
   everlasting.

1. Lord, you have searched my heart
   and you know when I sit and when
      I stand.
   Your hand is upon me, protecting
      me from death,
   keeping me from harm.

2. When can I run from your love?
   If I climb to the heavens, you are
      there.
   If I fly to the sunrise or sail beyond
      the sea
   still I'd find you there.

3. You know my heart and its ways,
   you who formed me before I was
      born,
   in secret of darkness, before I saw
      the sun,
   in my mother's womb.

4. Marvellous to me are your works;
   how profound are your thoughts,
      my Lord!

Even if I could count them, they
    number as the stars,
you would still be there.

660

1. You, Israel, return now;

   **return to God, your Father,
   your only great Creator;
   return to God, your Father.**

2. You won't be disappointed;

3. Although you have offended;

4. Although your sins are many;

5. He's sure to listen to you;

6. For he is calling to you;

7. Now seek your Lord's
   forgiveness;

8. He calls you all to hear him;

9. And give yourselves to him now;

10. For he is your redeemer;

11. The people's liberator;

12. Return now, O return now;

13. You lonely and you lost ones;

14. Now pray to him his people;

15. And he will quickly answer;

16. So come now all you people;

Tom Colvin. Based on a Tumbuka hymn by N. Z. Tembo
© 1976 Agapé

661

1. You must cry out the Word of
   the Lord!
   You must cry out the Word of
   the Lord!
   For you can heal a wounded man,
   or make a poor man rich,
   if you sing out the Word of the
   Lord!

2. You are called to the Word of
   the Lord!
   You are called to the Word of
   the Lord!
   For the Lord has come in power;
   if you believe, he lives in you,
   you must breathe out the Word of
   the Lord!

3. O my people, don't wait any
   longer!
   O my people, don't wait any
   longer!
   For my children are starving
   for my living water,
   you must cry out the Word of
   the Lord!

4. You must cry out the Word of
   the Lord!
   You must cry out the Word of
   the Lord!
   For you can heal a wounded man,
   or make a poor man rich,
   if you give out the Word of the
   Lord!

Carol Gordon
© Mayhew McCrimmon Ltd

662

1. You servants of God, now give
   him praise: alleluia!
   Sing out, for his goodness fills our
   days: alleluia!

His name let us praise now and
always: alleluia!

2. His name let us praise eternally:
   alleluia!
   Sing praise, night and day, on land
   and sea: alleluia!
   The Lord's name for ever blest will
   be: alleluia!

3. Above all creation is the Lord:
   alleluia!
   By all may he ever be adored:
   alleluia!
   For God has our fallen life
   restored: alleluia!

4. The weak, and the poor, and all in
   need: alleluia!
   The Lord without fail their pray'r
   will heed: alleluia!
   Above others they are blest
   indeed: alleluia!

5. Give praise to the Father, and the
   Son: alleluia!
   Give praise to the Spirit, three in
   one: alleluia!
   Whose reign is for evermore:
   alleluia!

*Based on Psalm 112 (113) © 1984
Assigned to Kevin Mayhew Ltd*

663

1. You shall cross the barren desert,
   but you shall not die of thirst.
   You shall wander far in safety
   though you do not know the way.
   You shall speak your words to
   foreign men
   and they will understand.
   You shall see the face of God
   and live.

**Be not afraid, I go before you
always.
Come, follow me, and I will give
you rest.**

2. If you pass through raging waters
   in the sea,
   you shall not drown.
   If you walk amid the burning
   flames,
   you shall not be harmed.
   If you stand before the pow'r of
   hell
   and death is at your side,
   know that I am with you through
   it all.

3. Blessed are your poor,
   for the kingdom shall be theirs
   blest are you that weep and
   mourn,
   for one day you shall laugh.
   And if wicked men insult and
   hate you
   all because of me,
   blessed, blessed are you!

*Based on Isaiah 43 and Luke 6 BE NOT AFRAID by
Robert J. Dufford, SJ. Copyright © 1975 by Robert
J. Dufford, SJ and North American Liturgy Resources,
10802 N 23rd Ave, Phoenix, AZ 85029, USA.
All rights reserved. Used with permission*

664

1. The eyes of the blind shall be
   opened,
   the ears of the deaf shall hear.
   The chains of the lame will be
   broken,
   streams will flow in deserts of fear.

**Your kingdom come, your will be
done,
now that we have become your sons.
Let the prayer of our hearts daily
be:**

'God, make us your family;
God make us your family.'

(Final time, add:)
God, make us your family.'

2. The ransomed of the Lord shall
   return,
   the islands will sing his songs at
   last.
   The chaff from the wheat shall be
   burned,
   his kingdom on earth it shall come
   to pass.

3. The nations will see their shame,
   the one true God will be adored.
   They turn from their fortune
   and shame,
   his holy mountain shall be
   restored.

*Based on Isaiah 35 by Tim Whipple © 1973, 1975
Celebration Services International Ltd*

THE PSALMS

665 *Psalm 8*

**How great is your name, O Lord our
God through all the earth!**

or

**What is mortal man that you care for
him?**

1. Your majesty is praised above the
   heavens;
   on the lips of children and of
   babes
   you have found praise to foil
   your enemy,
   to silence the foe and the rebel.

2. When I see the heavens, the work
   of your hands,
   the moon and stars which you
   arranged,
   what is man that you should keep
   him in mind,
   mortal man, that you care for
   him?

3. Yet you have made him little less
   than a god;
   with glory and honour you
   crowned him,
   gave him power over the works
   of your hand,
   put all things under his feet.

4. All of them, sheep and cattle,
   yes, even the savage beasts,
   birds of the air, and fish
   that make their way through the
   waters.

5. (Give glory to the Father almighty,
   to his Son, Jesus Christ, the Lord,
   to the Spirit who dwells in our
   hearts
   both now and for ever./Amen.)

© The Grail

666 *Psalm 18 (19) 8-15*

**You, O Lord, have the message of
eternal life.**

or

**Your words are spirit, Lord, and they
are life.**

1. The law of the Lord is perfect,
   it revives the soul.
   The rule of the Lord is to be
   trusted,
   it gives wisdom to the simple.

2. The **precepts** of the **Lord** are **right**,
   they **gladden** the **heart**.
   The com**mand** of the **Lord** is **clear**,
   it gives **light** to the **eyes**.

3. The **fear** of the Lord is **holy**,
   abiding for **ever**.
   The de**crees** of the **Lord** are **truth**,
   and **all** of them **just**.

4. They are **more** to be de**sired** than **gold**,
   than the **purest** of **gold**;
   and **sweeter** are **they** than **honey**,
   than **honey** from the **comb**.

5. So in **them** your **servant** finds in in**struction**,
   great **reward** is in their **keeping**.
   But **who** can de**tect** all his **errors**?
   From **hidden** faults ac**quit** me.

6. From pre**sumption** re**strain** your **servant**,
   and **let** it not **rule** me.
   Then shall **I** be **blameless**,
   clean from grave **sin**.

7. May the **spoken words** of my **mouth**,
   the **thoughts** of my **heart**,
   win **favour** in your **sight**, O **Lord**,
   my Rescuer, my **Rock**!

8. (Praise the **Father**, the **Son** and
   holy **Spirit**
   both **now** and for **ever**,
   the God who **is**, who **was** and who **will** be,
   world without **end**.)

© *The Grail*

667   *Psalm 22 (23)*

**My shepherd is the Lord, nothing
    indeed shall I want.**

or

**His goodness shall follow me always
    to the end of my days.**

or

The Lord himself will give me repose.

1. The **Lord** is my **shepherd**,
   there is **nothing** I shall **want**.
   Fresh and **green** are the **pastures**
   where he **gives** me re**pose**.
   near **restful** waters he **leads** me,
   to re**vive** my drooping **spirit**.

2. He **guides** me along the right **path**:
   he is **true** to **his name**.
   If **I** should **walk** in the valley of
   darkness
   no evil would I **fear**.
   You are **there** with your **crook**
   and your **staff**,
   with **these** you give me **comfort**.

3. You have prepared a **banquet**
   for **me**
   in the **sight** of my **foes**.
   My **head** you have **anointed**
   with **oil**;
   my **cup** is over**flowing**.

4. Surely **goodness** and **kindness** shall
   follow me
   all the **days** of my **life**.
   In the **Lord's** own **house** shall I
   dwell
   for **ever** and **ever**.

5. (Give **glory** to the **Father**
   Almighty,
   to his **Son**, Jesus **Christ**, our **Lord**,
   to the **Spirit** who **dwells** in our
   hearts.)

© *The Grail*

668

Psalm 23 (24)

**Seek the face of the Lord and yearn
for him.**

or

**Open wide, O you gates eternal, and
let the King of glory enter.**

or

Hosanna to the Son of David!

or

Hosanna in the highest heaven!

1. The **Lord's** is the **earth** and its
   fullness,
   the **world** and **all** its **peo**ples.
   It is **he** who **set** it on the **seas**;
   on the **wa**ters he **made** it **firm**.

2. Who shall **climb** the **moun**tain
   of the **Lord?**
   Who shall **stand** in his **ho**ly **place?**
   The **man** with clean **hands** and
   pure **heart**,
   who de**sires** not **worth**less **things**.

3. He shall re**ceive** **bless**ings from
   the **Lord**
   and re**ward** from the **God** who
   saves him.
   Such are the **men** who **seek** him,
   seek the **face** of the **God** of **Ja**cob.

4. O **gates**, lift **high** your **heads**;
   grow **high**er, **an**cient **doors**.
   let him **en**ter, the **king** of **glory**!

5. **Who** is the **king** of **glory?**
   The **Lord**, the **migh**ty, the **va**liant,
   the **Lord**, the **va**liant in **war**.

6. O **gates**, lift **high** your **heads**;
   grow **High**er, **an**cient **doors**,
   let him **en**ter, the **king** of **glory**!

7. **Who** is **he**, the **king** of **glory?**
   He, the **Lord** of **ar**mies,
   he is the **king** of **glory**.

8. (**Give** **glory** to **Fa**ther **Al**migh**ty**,
   to his **Son**, Jesus **Christ**, the **Lord**,
   to the **Spi**rit, who **dwells** in our
   hearts.)

   © *The Grail*

669

Psalm 24(25): 4-5, 6-7, 8-9, 10-11

To you, O Lord, I lift up my soul.

1. Lord, make me know your ways.
   Lord, teach me your paths.
   Make me walk in your truth, and
   teach me:
   for you are God my saviour.

2. Remember your mercy, Lord,
   and the love you have shown from
   of old.
   In your love remember me,
   because of your goodness, O Lord.

3. The Lord is good and upright.
   He shows the path to those who
   stray,
   he guides the humble in the right
   path;
   he teaches his way to the poor.

4. His ways are faithfulness and love
   for those who keep his covenant
   and will.
   The Lord's friendship is for those
   who revere him;
   to them he reveals his covenant.

5. (Glory be to the Father, and to
   the Son,
   and to the Holy Spirit,

as it was in the beginning, is now,
and ever shall be,
world without end. Amen.)

670 *Ps/26(27):1, 3-5, 7-9, 13-14*

Accents are for use with the
alternative (simple) setting

The Lord is my light and my help.

or

One thing I ask of the Lord,
for this I long,
to live in the house of the Lord,
all the days of my life.

or

I am sure I shall see the Lord's
goodness in the land of the living.

1. The Lórd is my líght and my hélp.
When shall I féar?
The Lórd is the strónghold of my
life,
before whóm shall I shrínk?

2. Though ármies do báttle agaínst
me,
my héart will not féar.
Though wár and destrúction
break fórth,
even thén would I trúst.

3. For thére in his hóuse I am sáfe,
in évil's dark hóur.
He hídes me and shélters my sóul,
my defénder, my róck.

4. There is óne thing I ásk of the
Lord,
for thís I lóng;
to live in the house of the Lord
all the dáys of my life,
to sávour the sweétness of the
Lórd,
to behóld his témple.

5. O Lórd, hear my voice when I cáll,
have mércy and ánswer.
Of yóu my héart has spóken:
'Seek his fáce'.

6. Your fáce, indeéd I seék it;
hide it nót from mé.
Dismiss not your sérvant in ánger,
for yóu are my hélp.

7. I knów I shall seé the Lord's
goódness,
in his prómised lánd.
Take héart and stand firm, O my
sóul,
put your hópe in the Lórd.

671 *Psalm 41 (42): 1-6*

My soul is thirsting for the Lord.
When shall I see him face to face?

or

I will pour clean water over you,
and cleanse you from all your sin.

1. **Like** the **deer** that **yearns**
for **running streams,**
so my **soul** is **yearning**
for **you,** my **God.**

2. My **soul** is **thirsting** for **God,**
the **God** of my **life;**
when can I **enter** and **see**
the **face** of **God**?

3. My **tears** have be**come** my **bread,**
by **night,** by **day;**
as I **hear** it **said** all day **long:**
'**Where** is your **God**?'

4. **These** things will **I remember**
as I **pour** out my **soul:**
how I would **lead** the **rejoicing**
crowd

into the **house** of **God.**

5. **Why** are you cast **down,** my **soul,**
   why **groan** within me?
   Hope in **God,** I will **praise** him
   still,
   my **Saviour** and my **God.**

6. (Praise the **Father,** the **Son** and
   Holy **Spirit,**
   both **now** and for ever,
   the God who **is,** who **was** and
   who **will** be,
   world without **end.)**

672   *Psalm 42 (43)*

**I will go to the altar of God, praise
the God of my joy.**

or

**Hope in God. I will praise him still,
my Saviour and my God.**

1. **Defend** me, O **God,** and plead my
   cause
   against a **god**less **na**tion:
   from de**ceit**ful and **cunning men**
   rescue me, O **God.**

2. Since **you,** O **God,** are my
   stronghold,
   why have you re**ject**ed me?
   Why do I go **mourn**ing,
   op**pressed** by the **foe?**

3. O **send** forth your **light** and your
   truth,
   let **these** be my **guide;**
   let them **bring** me to your **holy**
   mountain,
   to the **place** where you **dwell.**

4. And I will **come** to the **altar** of
   God,

the **God** of my **joy.**
My Redeemer, I will **thank** you
   on the **harp,**
O **God,** my **God!**

5. **Why** are you cast **down,** my **soul,**
   why **groan** within me?
   Hope in **God,** I will **praise him still,**
   my **Saviour** and my **God.**

6. (Praise the **Father,** the **Son** and
   Holy **Spirit,**
   both **now** and for ever,
   the God who **is,** who **was** and who
   will be,
   world without **end.)**

673   *Psalm 50 (51)*

**Have mercy on us, O Lord, for we have
sinned.**

or

A pure heart create for me, O God.

1. Have **mer**cy on me, **God,** in your
   kindness.
   In your com**pas**sion blot **out** my
   offence.
   O **wash** me more and **more** from
   my **guilt**
   and **cleanse** me **from** my **sin.**

2. My offences **truly** I **know** them;
   my **sin** is **al**ways be**fore** me.
   Against **you,** you **alone,** have I
   sinned;
   what is evil in your **sight** I have
   done.

3. That you may be **justified when**
   you give **sentence**
   and be without **reproach** when you

judge,
O **see**, in **guilt** I was **born**,
a sinner was I **conceived**.

4. **Indeed** you love **truth** in the **heart**;
then in the secret of my **heart**
teach me **wisdom**.
O **purify** me, **then** I shall be **clean**;
O **wash** me, I shall be **whiter** than
snow.

5. Make me **hear** rejoicing and ˙
gladness,
that the **bones** you have **crushed**
may **thrill**.
From my **sins** turn away your **face**
and **blot** out **all** my **guilt**.

6. A **pure** heart create for me,
O **God**,
put a **steadfast spirit within** me.
Do not **cast** me **away** from your
presence,
nor de**prive** me of your **holy spirit**.

7. Give me a**gain** the **joy** of your
help;
with a **spirit** of **fervour** su**stain** me,
that I may **teach** transgressors
your **ways**,
and **sinners** may return to **you**.

8. O **rescue** me, **God**, my **helper**,
and my **tongue** shall **ring** out your
goodness.
O **Lord**, **open** my **lips**,
and my **mouth** shall de**clare** your
praise.

9. For in **sacrifice** you **take** no
de**light**,
burnt offering from **me** you would
re**fuse**,
my **sacrifice**, a con**trite** spirit.
A humbled, contrite **heart** you will
not **spurn**.

10. (Give **glory** to the **Father**
al**mighty**,
to his **Son**, Jesus **Christ**, the **Lord**,
to the **Spirit** who **dwells** in our
hearts,
both **now** and for ever. **Amen**.)

674   *Psalm 62 (63): 1-6, 8-9*

O God, you are my God,
for you my soul is thirsting.

1. O God, you are my God, for <u>you</u>
I long;
for you my <u>soul</u> is thirsting.
My body <u>pines</u> for you
like a dry, weary land <u>without</u>
water. (R)

2. So I gaze on you <u>in</u> the sanctuary
to see your strength <u>and</u> your
glory.
For your love is bet<u>ter</u> than life,
my lips will <u>speak</u> your praise. (R)

3. So I will bless you <u>all</u> my life,
in your name I will lift <u>up</u> my
hands.
My mouth shall be filled as <u>with</u>
a banquet,
my mouth shall praise <u>you</u> with
joy. (R)

4. For you have <u>been</u> my help;
in the shadow of your wings <u>I</u>
rejoice.
My soul <u>clings</u> to you;
your right hand <u>holds</u> me fast. (R̄)

5. (Glory be to the Father, and <u>to</u>
the Son,
and to the <u>Holy</u> Spirit,
as it was in the beginning, is now,
and ev<u>er</u> shall be,
world without <u>end</u>. Amen.)

675

Psalm 83 (84)

**How lovely is your dwelling place,
Lord God of hosts.**

or

**Lord, God of hosts, happy the man
who trusts in you.**

1. My **soul** is **longing** and **yearning,**
   is **yearning** for the **courts** of the
   Lord.
   My **heart** and my **soul** ring out
   their **joy**
   to **God,** the **living God.**

2. The **sparrow** herself finds a **home**
   and the **swallow** a **nest** for her
   brood;
   she **lays** her **young** by your **altars.**
   Lord of **hosts,** my **King** and my
   God.

3. They are **happy** who **dwell** in your
   house,
   for ever **singing** your **praise.**
   They are **happy,** whose **strength**
   is in **you,**
   in whose **hearts** are the **roads** to
   Sion.

4. As they **go** through the **Bitter**
   Valley,
   they **make** it a **place** of **springs,**
   they **walk** with ever growing
   strength.
   They will **see** the God of **gods** in
   Sion.

5. O **Lord** God of **hosts,** hear my
   prayer,
   give **ear,** O **God** of Jacob.
   Turn your **eyes,** O **God** our **shield,**
   look on the **face** of your **anointed.**

6. One **day** within your **courts**

is **better** than a **thousand** elsewhere.
The **threshold** of the **house** of **God**
I **prefer** to the **dwellings** of the
wicked.

7. For the Lord **God** is a **rampart,** a
   shield;
   he will **give** us his **favour** and **glory.**
   The **Lord** will not **refuse** any **good**
   to **those** who **walk** without **blame.**

8. (Give **praise** to the **Father**
   Almighty,
   to his **Son,** Jesus **Christ,** the **Lord,**
   to the **Spirit** who **dwells** in our
   hearts,
   both **now** and for **ever. Amen.**)

© *The Grail*

676

Psalm 84 (85): 9-14

**Let us see O Lord, your mercy
and give us your saving help.**

or

Come, Lord, and save us (2)

1. I will **hear** what the Lord **God** has
   to **say,**
   a **voice** that **speaks** of **peace.**
   His **help** is **near** for **those** who **fear**
   him
   and his **glory** will **dwell** in our **land.**

2. **Mercy** and **faithfulness** have **met;**
   justice and **peace** have **embraced.**
   Faithfulness shall **spring** from the
   earth
   and **justice** look **down** from
   heaven.

3. The **Lord** will **make** us **prosper**
   and our **earth** shall **yield** its **fruit.**
   Justice shall **march** before him
   and **peace** shall **follow** his **steps.**

4. (Give glory to the Father
   almighty,
   to his Son, Jesus Christ, the Lord,
   to the Spirit who dwells in our
   hearts
   both now and for ever. Amen.)

677
Psalm 90 (91)

**Call upon the Lord and he will hear
you,**

or

Be with me, Lord, in my distress.

1. He who dwells in the shelter of
   the Most High
   and abides in the shade of the
   Almighty
   says to the Lord: 'My refuge,
   my stronghold, my God in whom
   I trust!'

2. It is he who will free you from
   the snare
   of the fowler who seeks to
   destroy you;
   he will conceal you with his
   pinions
   and under his wings you will find
   refuge.

3. You will not fear the terror of
   the night
   nor the arrow that flies by day,
   nor the plague that prowls in
   the darkness
   nor the scourge that lays waste
   at noon.

4. A thousand may fall at your side,
   ten thousand fall at your right,
   you, it will never approach;
   his faithfulness is buckler and
   shield.

5. Your eyes have only to look
   to see how the wicked are repaid,
   you who have said: 'Lord, my
   refuge!'
   and have made the Most High
   your dwelling.

6. Upon you no evil shall fall,
   no plague approach where you
   dwell.
   For you has he commanded his
   angels,
   to keep you in all your ways.

7. They shall bear you upon their
   hands
   lest you strike your foot against
   a stone.
   On the lion and the viper you will
   tread
   and trample the young lion and
   the dragon.

8. His love he set on me, so I will
   rescue him;
   protect him for he knows my name.
   When he calls I shall answer:
   'I am with you.'
   I will save him in distress and give
   him glory.

9. With length of life I will content
   him;
   I shall let him see my saving power.
   (To the Father, the Son and Holy
   Spirit
   give praise for ever./Amen.)

678
Psalm 92 (93)

The Lord is King for evermore.

or

Alleluia, alleluia, alleluia!

1. The Lord is king, with majesty

enrobed;
the Lord has robed himself with
  might,
he has girded himself with power.

2. The world you made firm,
    not to be moved;
  your throne has stood firm from
    of old;
  from all eternity, O Lord, you are.

3. The waters have lifted up, O Lord,
  the waters have lifted up their
    voice,
  the waters have lifted up their
    thunder.

4. Greater than the roar of mighty
    waters.
  more glorious than the surgings
    of the sea,
  the Lord is glorious on high.

5. Truly, your decrees are to be
    trusted.
  Holiness is fitting to your house,
  O Lord, until the end of time.

6. (Give glory to the Father
    Almighty,
  to his Son, Jesus Christ, the Lord,
  to the Spirit who dwells in our
    hearts.)

679   *Psalm 94 (95)*

O come, let us worship the Lord.

or

O that today you would listen to his
  voice:
harden not your hearts.

1. Come, ring out our joy to the Lord;
  hail the Rock who saves us.

Let us come before him, giving
  thanks,
with songs let us hail the Lord.

2. A mighty God is the Lord,
  a great king above all gods;
  in his hand are the depths of the
    earth;
  the heights of the mountains are
    his.
  To him belongs the sea, for he
    made it,
  and the dry land shaped by his
    hands.

3. Come in, let us bow and bend low;
  let us kneel before the God who
    made us,
  for he is our God and we
  the people who belong to his
    pasture,
  the flock that is led by his hand.

4. O that today you would listen to
    his voice!
  'Harden not your hearts as at
    Meribah,
  as on that day at Massah in the
    desert
  when your fathers put me to the
    test,
  when they tried me, though they
    saw my work.'

5. For forty years I was wearied of
    these people
  and I said: 'Their hearts are astray,
  these people do not know my ways.'
  Then I took an oath in my anger:
  'Never shall they enter my rest.'

6. Give glory to the Father
    Almighty,
  to his Son, Jesus Christ, the Lord,
  to the Spirit who dwells in our
    hearts,
  both now and for ever. Amen.

680

Psalm 99 (100)

Arise, come to your God, sing him your
    songs of rejoicing.

or

We are his people, the sheep of his
    flock.

or

Alleluia, alleluia, alleluia!

1. Cry out with **joy** to the **Lord**, all
    the **earth**.
    Serve the **Lord** with **gladness**.
    Come before him, singing for **joy**.

2. Know that **he**, the **Lord** is **God**.
    He **made** us, belong to **him**,
    we are his **people**, the **sheep** of his
    flock.

3. Go within his **gates**, giving **thanks**.
    Enter his **courts** with **songs** of
    praise.
    Give **thanks** to him and **bless** his
    name.

4. **Indeed**, how **good** is the **Lord**,
    eternal his **merciful love**;
    he is **faithful** from **age** to **age**.

5. (Give **glory** to the **Father**
    Almighty,
    to his **Son**, Jesus **Christ**, the **Lord**,
    to the **Spirit** who **dwells** in our
    hearts.)

                    © *The Grail*

681

Psalm 102 (103): 1-4, 8, 10, 12-13

The Lord is compassion and love,
alleluia, alleluia.

or

The Lord has set his sway in heaven,
alleluia, alleluia.

1. My **soul**, give **thanks** to the **Lord**,
    all my **being**, **bless** his holy **name**.
    My **soul**, give **thanks** to the **Lord**
    and **never** forget all his **blessings**.

2. It is **he** who **forgives** all your **guilt**,
    who **heals** every **one** of your **ills**,
    who re**deems** your **life** from the
      grave,
    who **crowns** you with **love** and
      compassion.

3. The **Lord** is compassion and **love**,
    slow to **anger** and **rich** in **mercy**.
    He does not **treat** us ac**cord**ing to
      our **sins**
    nor repay us ac**cord**ing to our
      faults.

4. As **far** as the **east** is from the **west**
    so **far** does he **remove** our **sins**.
    As a **father** has compassion on his
      sons,
    the Lord has **pity** on **those** who
      fear him.

5. (Give **glory** to the **Father**
    almighty,
    to his **Son**, Jesus **Christ**, the **Lord**,
    to the **Spirit** who **dwells** in our
      hearts
    both **now** and for **ever**./**Amen**.)

                    © *The Grail*

682

Psalm 103 (104) 1-2, 5-6,
24, 27-30, 10-14,

Send forth your Spirit, O Lord,
and renew the face of the earth.

1. **Bless** the **Lord**, my **soul**!
    Lord God, how **great** you **are**,

clothed in **majesty** and **glory**,
wrapped in **light** as in a **robe**!

2. You **founded** the **earth** on its **base**,
to stand **firm** from **age** to **age**.
You **wrapped** it **with** the ocean
like a **cloak**:
the waters stood **high**er than the
mountains.

3. You make **springs** gush **forth** in the
valleys:
they **flow** in be**tween** the **hills**.
On their **banks** dwell the **birds**
of **heaven**;
from the **branches** they **sing**
their **song**.

4. From your **dwel**ling you **water**
the **hills**;
earth drinks its **fill** of your **gift**.
You **make** the **grass** grow for the
cattle
and the **plants** to **serve** man's
needs.

5. How **many** are your **works**, O
Lord!
In **wis**dom you **made** them **all**.
The **earth** is **full** of your **riches**.
Bless the **Lord**, my **soul**!

6. All **creatures look** to **you**
to **give** them their **food** in due
season.
You **give** it, they **gather** it **up**:
you **open** your **hand**, they have
their **fill**.

7. You **take** back your **spirit**, they **die**,
re**turn**ing to the **dust** from which
they **came**.
You **send** forth your **spirit**, they
are created;
and you renew the **face** of the
earth.

8. May the **glory** of the **Lord** last for
ever!
May the **Lord** re**joice** in his **works**!
May my **thoughts** be **pleas**ing to
him.
I **find** my **joy** in the **Lord**.

9. (Give **glory** to the **Father**
al**migh**ty,
to his **Son**, Jesus **Christ**, the **Lord**,
to the **Spirit** who **dwells** in our
hearts
both **now** and for **ever**./**Amen**.)

© *The Grail*

683   *Psalms 114/115 (116)*

**I will walk in the presence of the Lord
in the land of the living.**

or

**How can I repay the Lord for his
goodness?**

1. I love the Lord for he has heard
the cry of my appeal;
for he turned his ear to me
in the day when I called him.

2. They surrounded me, the snares of
death,
with the anguish of the tomb;
they caught me, sorrow and
distress.
I called on the Lord's name.
O Lord my God, deliver me!

3. How gracious is the Lord, and
just;
our God has compassion.
The Lord protects the simple
hearts;
I was helpless so he saved me.

4. He has kept my soul from death,
   my eyes from tears
   and my feet from stumbling.
   I will walk in the presence of the
      Lord
   in the land of the living.

5. (Glory be to the Father, and to
      the Son,
   and to the Holy Spirit,
   as it was in the beginning, is now,
      and ever shall be,
   world without end. Amen.)

684   *Psalm 115*

1. My vows to the Lord I will fulfill
   before all his people.
   O precious in the eyes of the Lord
   is the death of his faithful.

2. Your servant, Lord, your servant
      am I;
   you have loosened my bonds.
   A thanksgiving sacrifice I make:
   I will call on the Lord's name.

3. My vows to the Lord I will fulfill
   before all his people,
   in the courts of the house of the
      Lord,
   in your midst, O Jerusalem.

4. I trusted, even when I said:
   'I am sorely afflicted,'
   and when I said in my alarm:
   'No man can be trusted.'

5. How can I repay the Lord
   for his goodness to me?
   The cup of salvation I will raise;
   I will call on the Lord's name.

6. (Glory be to the Father, and to
      the Son,

and to the Holy Spirit,
as it was in the beginning, is now,
   and ever shall be,
world without end. Amen.)

685   *Psalm 116 (117)*

Alleluia, alleluia.

Response is repeated throughout.

Meanwhile, choir/cantor sings:

O praise the Lord, all you nations,
acclaim him, all you peoples!
Strong is his love for us;
he is faithful for ever.

Repeat ad libitum.

Final time coda:

Alleluia!

686

Psalm 117 (118) 1-2, 16-17, 22-23

Alleluia, alleluia, alleluia!

or

**This day was made by the Lord;
we rejoice and we are glad.**

1. Give thanks to the Lord
   for he is good,
   for his love has no end.
   Let the sons of Israel say:
   'His love has no end
   his love has no end.'

2. The Lord's right hand
   has triumphed;
   his right hand raised me up.

I shall not die, I shall live
and recount his deeds,
recount his deeds.

3. The stone which the
      builders rejected
   has become the corner stone.
   This is the work of the Lord,
   a marvel in our eyes,
   a marvel in our eyes.

© *The Grail*

687
Psalm 121

**Give your peace, O Lord, to those
who count on you.**

or

**I rejoiced when I heard them say:
Let us go to God's house!**

or

Let us go to God's house, rejoicing.

1. I rejoic'd when I heard them say:
   'Let us go to God's house.
   And now our feet are standing
      within your gates,
   O Jerusalem.'

2. Jerusalem is built as a city
   strongly compact.
   It is there that the tribes go up,
      the tribes
   of the Lord.

3. For Israel's law it is
   there to praise the Lord's name.
   There were set the thrones of
      judgement, of the
   house of David.

4. For the peace of Jerusalem, pray:
   'Peace be to your homes!'
   May peace reign in your walls, in

your
palaces, peace!'

5. (Praise the Father, the Son and
      Holy Spirit,
   both now and forever:
   the God who is, who was and who
      will be,
   world without end.)

© *The Grail*

688
Psalm 125 (126)

**Those who sow in tears and sorrow,
one day will reap with joy.**

or

**What marvels the Lord worked for us!
Indeed we were glad.**

1. When the Lord delivered Sion
      from bondage,
   it seemed like a dream.
   Then was our mouth filled with
      laughter,
   on our lips there were songs.

2. The heathens themselves said:
      'What marvels
   the Lord worked for them!'
   What marvels the Lord worked
      for us!
   Indeed, we were glad.

3. Deliver us, O Lord, from our
      bondage,
   as streams in dry land.
   Those who sow in tears
   will sing when they reap.

4. They go out, they go out, full of
      tears,
   carrying seed for the sowing;
   they come back, they come back,
      full of song,
   carrying their sheaves.

5. (Praise the Father, the Son and
     Holy Spirit,
   both now and for ever,
   the God who is, who was and who
     will be,
   world without end.)

689 *Psalm 129 (130)*

**I place all my trust in you my God,
all my hope is in your saving word.**

or

I wait for the Lord; I count on his word.

or

**With the Lord there is mercy
and fullness of redemption.**

1. Out of the **depths I cry** to you,
     O **Lord,**
   Lord, hear my **voice!**
   O let your **ears** be attentive
   to the **voice** of my **pleading.**

2. If you, O **Lord,** should **mark**
     our **guilt,**
   Lord, who would survive?
   But with **you** is **found** forgiveness:
   for **this** we revere **you.**

3. My **soul** is **waiting** for the **Lord,**
   I **count** on his **word:**
   my **soul** is **longing** for the **Lord**
   more than **watch**man for
     day-break.

4. Because with the **Lord** there is
     mercy
   and **full**ness of redemption,
   Israel indeed he will **redeem**
   from **all** its in**iquity.**

5. (To the **Father** al**migh**ty give **glory,**
   give **glory** to his **Son,**

to the **Spirit** most **holy** give **praise,**
whose **reign** is for **ever.**)

690 *Psalm 135 (136)*

1. O give **thanks** to the **Lord** for he is
     good,
   great is his love, love without end.
   Give **thanks** to the **God** of **gods,**
   great is his love, love without end.
   Give **thanks** to the **Lord** of **lords,**
   great is his love, love without end.

2. Who **alone** has wrought
     marvellous **works,**
   great is his love, love without end;
   whose **wisdom** it **was** made the
     skies,
   great is his love, love without end;
   who **fixed** the **earth** on the **seas,**
   great is his love, love without end.

3. It was **he** who **made** the great
     lights,
   great is his love, love without end,
   the **sun** to **rule** in the **day,**
   great is his love, love without end,
   the **moon** and **stars** in the **night**
   great is his love, love without end.

4. The first-**born** of the Egyptians he
     smote,
   great is his love, love without end.
   He brought Israel **out** from their
     midst,
   great is his love, love without end;
   arm out**stretched,** with **power** in
     his **hand,**
   great is his love, love without end.

5. He divided the **Red** Sea in **two,**
   great is his love, love without end;
   he made Israel **pass** through the
     midst,

great is his love, love without end;
flung **Pharoah** and his **force** in the
sea,
great is his love, love without end.

6. Through the **desert** his **people** he
led,
great is his love, love without end.
Nations in their **great**ness he
struck,
great is his love, love without end.
Kings in their **splen**dour he **slew**,
great is his love, love without end.

7. He let Israel in**her**it their **land**,
great is his love, love without end.
On his **servant** their **land** he
bestowed,
great is his love, love without end.
He remembered us **in** our **distress**,
great is his love, love without end.

8. And he **snatched** us **away** from our
foes,
great is his love, love without end.
He gives **food** to **all** living **things**,
great is his love, love without end.
To the **God** of **heaven** give **thanks**,
great is his love, love without end.

691   *Psalm 144 (145) 1-2, 8-18*

I will bless your name for ever,
  O God my King.

or

You open wide your hand; O Lord,
  you grant our desires.

1. I will give you glory, O God my
King.
I will bless your name for ever.
I will bless you day after day
and praise your name for ever.

2. The Lord is kind and full of
compassion,
slow to anger, abounding in love.
How good is the Lord to all,
compassionate to all his creatures.

3. All your creatures shall thank you,
O Lord,
and your friends shall repeat their
blessing.
They shall speak of the glory of
your reign
and declare your might, O God.

4. To make known to men your
mighty deeds
and the glorious splendour of
your reign.
Yours is an everlasting kingdom;
your rule lasts from age to age.

5. The Lord is faithful in all his
words
and loving in all his deeds.
The Lord supports all who fall
and raises all who are bowed
down.

6. The eyes of all creatures look to
you
and give them their food in due
time.
You open wide your hand,
grant the desires of all who live.

7. The Lord is just in all his ways
and loving in all his deeds.
He is close to all who call him,
who call on him from their hearts.

8. (Glory be to the Father, and to
the Son,
and to the Holy Spirit,
as it was in the beginning, is now,
and ever shall be,
world without end. Amen.)

692

Alleluia, alleluia, alleluia.

1. Praise God for his holy dwelling;
   praise him on his mighty throne;
   praise him for his wonderful
     deeds;
   praise him for his sov'reign
     majesty.

2. Praise him with the blast of
     trumpet;
   praise him now with lyre and
     harps;
   praise him with the timbrel and
     dance;
   praise him with the sound of string
     and reed.

3. Praise him with resounding
     cymbals;
   with cymbals that crash give
     praise;
   O let everything that has breath,
   let all living creatures praise the
     Lord.

4. Praise God the almighty Father;
   praise Christ his beloved Son;
   give praise to the Spirit of love,
   for ever the triune God be praised.

© *World Library Publications*

693

The Benedictus

Blessed be the Lord, the God of
  Israel!
He has visited his people and
  redeemed them.

He has raised up for us a mighty
saviour
in the house of David his servant,
as he promised by the lips of holy
  men,
those who were his prophets from
  of old.

A saviour who would free us from
  our foes,
from the hands of all who hate us.
So his love for our fathers is fulfilled
and his holy covenant remembered.

He swore to Abraham our father to
  grant us,
that free from fear, and saved from
  the hands of our foes,
we might serve him in holiness and
  justice
all the days of our life in his presence.

As for you, little child,
you shall be called a prophet of God,
  the Most High.
You shall go ahead of the Lord
to prepare his ways before him.

To make known to his people their
  salvation
through forgiveness of all their sins,
the loving-kindness of the heart of
  our God
who visits us like the dawn from on
  high.

He will give light to those in darkness
those who dwell in the shadow of
  death,
and guide us into the way of peace.

Glory be to the Father, and to the
  Son,
and to the Holy Spirit,
as it was in the beginning, is now and
  ever shall be,
world without end, Amen.

© *The Grail*

694

The Magnificat (Luke 1: 46-55)

**The Lord has done marvels for me,
holy is his name.**

1. My **soul** glorifies the **Lord,**
my **spirit** rejoices in **God,** my
Saviour.

2. He **looks** on his **servant** in her
nothingness;
hence**forth** all ages will **call** me
blessed.

3. The Al**mighty** works **marvels** for
me.
Holy his **name!**

4. His **mercy** is from **age** to **age,**
on **those** who **fear** him.

5. He **puts** forth his **arm** in **strength**
and **scatters** the proud-**hearted.**

6. He **casts** the **migh**ty from their
thrones
and **raises** the **lowly.**

7. He **fills** the **starving** with good
things,
sends the **rich** away **empty.**

8. He pro**tects** Israel, his **servant,**
remem**bering** his **mercy.**

9. The **mercy pro**mised to our
fathers,
for **Abraham** and his **sons** for ever.

10. (Praise the Father, the **Son,** and
Holy **Spirit,**
both **now** and forever, **world**
without **end.)**

© *The Grail*

*Other settings of the Magnificat
are numbers: 414 and 479*

695

Nunc Dimittis (Luke 2- 29-32)

**Guard us, O Lord, while we sleep
and keep us in peace.**

or

**My eyes have seen your salvation:
the light of all peoples.**

1. At **last,** all **powerful** Master,
you give **leave** to your **servant** to
go
in **peace,** according to your
promise.

2. For my **eyes** have **seen** your
salvation
which **you** have **prepared** for all
nations
the **light** to enligh**ten** the **Gentiles**
and give **glory** to Israel, your
people.

3. Give **praise** to the **Father** al**mighty,**
to his **Son,** Jesus **Christ,** the **Lord.**
to the **Spirit,** who **dwells** in our
hearts,
both **now** and forever. **Amen.**

© *The Grail*

*Another setting of the Nunc Dimittis
is number 561*

ROUNDS, CANONS
AND REFRAINS

696

Adoramus te Domine.

697
698

These are settings of the Alleluia which are found in the melody line and full music editions.

699

The Beatitudes (Mt 5:3-10)

**Blessed are they who follow God's law
and walk in his way:
the Kingdom is theirs.**

1. Blest the poor in spirit,
   for theirs is the kingdom of Heaven.

2. Blest the gentle,
   for they shall inherit the earth.

3. Blest those who mourn,
   for they shall be comforted.

4. Blest those who hunger and thirst for justice,
   for they shall be satisfied.

5. Blest the merciful
   for they shall have mercy shown them.

6. Blest the pure in heart,
   for they shall see God.

7. Blest the peacemakers
   for they shall be called sons of God.

8. Blest those who suffer for righteousness,
   for theirs is the kingdom of Heaven.

The chorus is sung continuously. The cantor sings verses as required. When the cantor is singing, the people hum with closed lips.

700

1. Breath of life overflow in us, crying:
   at last we are born again.

2. Breath of life overflow in us, laughing:
   at last we are born again.

3. Breath of life overflow in us, knowing:
   at last we are born again.

701

1. Dona nobis pacem, pacem.
   Dona nobis pacem.

2. Dona nobis pacem.
   Dona nobis pacem.

3. Dona nobis pacem.
   Dona nobis pacem.

702

Glory be to God the Father, God
  the Father,
God the Son and Holy Spirit, Holy
  Spirit,
as it was and shall be evermore.

703

[1]Go out to the [2] whole world,
 [3] proclaim the [4] Good News.

(Mark 16: 15)

704

[1]I rejoiced[2] when [3]I heard them say
'Let us go to God's house.'
Alleluia!

Psalm 121 (122):1

705

1. Jesus Christ, little Lord,
  God and Saviour he,
  born into this sinful world
  to set the people free.

2. Sing, Jesus come to us
  and teach us how to pray,
  we will share your joy and love,
  and peace this Christmas Day.

Roger Humphrey © *Mayhew McCrimmon Ltd*

706

Jubilate Deo, jubilate Deo, alleluia.

707

[1]Jubilate Deo [2]omnis terra.
Servite Domino in laetitia.
Alleluia, alleluia, in laetitia.
Alleluia, alleluia, in laetitia!

708

[1]Let us go forth into the world
[2]with the good news, spreading his
  word, for we're
[3]Easter people, saved by Christ.

© *1984 Mayhew McCrimmon Ltd*

709

**Misericordias Domini in aeternum
cantabo.**

1. From age to age through all
  generations,
  my mouth shall proclaim your
  truth, O Lord.

2. Who, O God, who in the universe
  can compare with you?

3. Blest be the Lord for ever,
  throughout eternity. Amen!
  Amen!

From Psalm 88 (89)
© *Les Presses de Taizé*

710

O Lord, hear my prayer,
O Lord, hear my prayer:
when I call, answer me.
O Lord, hear my prayer,
O Lord, hear my prayer.
Come and listen to me.

© *Les Presses de Taizé*

711

Ostende nobis Domine,
 misericordiam tuam. Amen!
Amen!
Maranatha! Maranatha!

© Les Presses de Taizé

712

1. Sing alleluia to the Lord.
2. Sing alleluia to the Lord.
1. Sing alleluia to the Lord.
2. Sing alleluia.
1. Sing alleluia, sing alleluia,
2. Alleluia.
1 & 2. Sing alleluia to the Lord.

© Linda Stassen

713

¹Sing and rejoice in the
²Lord in your hearts with
 thanksgiving,
³sing and rejoice in him.

Hermann Stern © Verlag Merseburger Berlin

714

¹Stand and stare not at what used to
 be
²and remain not in the past. For
³I, says he, make new beginnings.
 Look,
⁴all things are new now, do you not
 see?

*Huub Oosterhuis. English arr by © Tony Barr and
Jubulani Music*

LATIN HYMNS

715 Christus Vincit

Christus vincit: Christus regnat:
 Christus imperat.
Christus vincit: Christus regnat:
 Christus imperat.
Exaudi Christe.
Exaudi Christe.
Summo Pontifici et universali Papae
 vita.
Salvator mundi:
tu illum adjuva.
Sancta Maria:
tu illum adjuva.
Sancte Petre:
tu illum adjuva.
Sancte Paule:
tu illum adjuva.
Sancte Gregori:
tu illum adjuva.
Christus vincit: Christus regnat:
 Christus imperat.
Rex regnum!
Christus vincit.
Rex noster!
Christus regnat.
Gloria nostra!
Christus imperat.
Ipsi soli imperium
gloria et potestas,
per immortalia saecula saeculorum.
 Amen.
Christus vincit: Christus regnat:
 Christus imperat.

716 Pange Lingua

1. Pange, lingua, gloriosi
   corporis mysterium,
   sanguinisque pretiosi,
   quem in mundi pretium
   fructus ventris generosi
   Rex effudit gentium.

2. Nobis datus, nobis natus
   ex inacta Virgine;
   et in mundo conversatus,
   sparso verbi semine,
   sui moras incolatus
   miro clausit ordine.

3. In supremae nocte coenae
   recumbens cum fratribus,
   observata lege plene
   cibis in legalibus:
   cibum turbae duodenae
   se dat suis manibus.

4. Verbum caro, panem verum
   Verbo carnem efficit:
   fitque sanguis Christi merum;
   et si sensus deficit,
   ad firmandum cor sincerum
   sola fides sufficit.

5. Tantum ergo Sacramentum
   veneremur cernui:
   et antiquum documentum
   novo cedat ritui:
   præstet fides supplementum
   sensuum defectui.

6. Genitori, genitoque
   laus, et jubilatio,
   salus, honor, virtus quoque
   sit et benedictio:
   procendenti ab utroque
   compar sit laudatio. Amen.

St Thomas Aquinas (1227-74)

717 Regina cæli

Regina cæli, lætare, alleluia,
quia quem meruisti portare, alleluia,
resurrexit sicut dixit, alleluia.
Ora pro nobis Deum, alleluia.

Trad anthem
© *Les Presses de Taizé*

718 Salve Regina

Salve Regina, Mater misericordiæ:
vita dulcedo, et spes nostra, salve.
Ad te clamamus, exules filii hevæ.
Ad te suspiramus, gementes et
   flentes,
in hac lacrimarum vale.
Eja ergo, Advocata nostra,
illos tuos misericordes oculos
ad nos converte.
Et Jesum benedictum fructum
   ventris tui,
nobis post hoc exsilium ostende.
O clemens, O pia, O dulcis Virgo
Maria.

719 Te Deum Laudamus

Te Deum laudamus: te Dominum
   confitemur.
Te æternum Patrem omnis terra
   veneratur.
Tibi omnes Angeli, tibi cæli et
   universæ potestates:
tibi Cherubim et Seraphim
   incessabili voce proclaimant:
Sanctus: Sanctus: Sanctus
   Dominus Deus Sabaoth.
Pleni sunt cæli et terra majestatis

gloriæ.
Te gloriosus Apostolorum chorus:
Te Prophetatum laudabilis numerus:
Te Martyrum candidatus laudat
exercitus.
Te per orbem terrarum sancta
confitetur Ecclesia:
Patrem immensæ majestatis:
Venerandum tuum verum et unicum
Filium:
Sanctum quoque Paraclitum
Spiritum.
Tu Rex gloriæ, Christe.
Tu Patris sempiternus es Filius.
Tu ad liberandum suscepturus
hominem,
non horruisti Virginis uterum.
Tu devicto mortis aculeo,
aperuisti credentibus regna cælorum.
Tu ad dexteram Dei sedes, in gloria
Patris.
Judex crederis esse venturus.
Te ergo quæsumus, tuis famulis
subveni,
quos pretioso sanguine redemisti.
Æterna fac cum sanctis tuis in gloria
numerari.
Salvum fac populum tuum Domine,
et benedic hære ditate tuæ.
Et rege eos, et extolle illos usque in
æternum.
Per singulos dies, benedicimus te.
Et laudamus nomen tuum in
sæculum, et in sæculum sæculi.
Dignare Domine die isto
sine peccato nos custodire.
Miserere nostri Domine, miserere
nostri.
Fiat misericordia tua Domine super
nos,
quem admodum speravimus in te.
In te Domine speravi:
non confundar in æternum.

720 Veni, Creator Spiritus

1. Veni, Creator Spiritus,
   mentes tuorum visita,
   imple superna gratia,
   quae tu creasti pectora.

2. Qui diceris Paraclitus,
   Altissimi donum Dei,
   fons vivus, ignis, caritas,
   et spiritalis unctio.

3. Tu septiformis munere,
   digitus paternae dexterae,
   Tu rite promissum Patris,
   sermone ditans guttura.

4. Accende lumen sensibus,
   infunde amorem codibus,
   infirma nostri corporis
   virtute firmans perpeti.

5. Hostem repellas longius,
   pacemque dones protinus:
   ductore sic te praevio,
   vitemus omne noxium.

6. Per te sciamus, da, Patrem,
   noscamus atque Filium,
   teque utriusque Spiritum
   credamus omni Tempore.

Attr to Rabanus Maurus (766-856)

721 Victimae paschali laudes

Victimae paschali laudes
immolent Christiani.
Agnus redemit oves:
Christus innocens Patri
reconciliavit peccatores.
Mors et vita duello
conflixere mirando:
dux vitae mortuus
regnat vivus.

Dic nobis Maria
quid vidisti in via?
Sepulchrum Christi viventis
et gloriam vidi resurgentis:
Angelicos testes
sudarium et vestes.

Surrexit Christus spes mea:
praecedit suos in Galilaeam.
Scimus Christum surrexisse
a mortuis vere:
tu nobis, victor Rex, miserere.
Amen. (Alleluia.)

THE DIVINE OFFICE

The basic order of Morning and Evening Prayer is as follows:
INTRODUCTION
HYMN
PSALMODY (including a biblical canticle)
SCRIPTURE
RESPONSORY
GOSPEL CANTICLE
INTERCESSIONS AND PRAYER
BLESSING

The full texts will be found in the books containing the Divine Office. A election is given here which will allow a parish or group to celebrate a form of morning, evening or night prayer according to their needs.

1. INTRODUCTION

O God, come to our aid.
O Lord, make haste to help us.
Glory be to the Father, the Son and the Holy Spirit,
as it was in the beginning, is now and ever shall be
world without end, amen, alleluia.
Alternative introductions
I rejoiced when I heard them say
Jubilate Deo
Jubilate Servite

2. HYMN

A hymn may be chosen from any appropriate section of the book.

3. PSALMODY

First given below are the psalms used in the four-week cycle of Sunday Evening Prayer. (The Antiphons to the Psalms are not given.) Below is a list of all the psalms contained in the book. One of the items in the psalmody is usually a Canticle; these are listed after the Psalms.

PSALM 109(110) Weeks 1-4

1. The Lord's revelation to my
      Master:
   'Sit on my right:
   your foes I will put beneath your
      feet.'

2. The Lord will wield from Sion
   your sceptre of power:
   rule in the midst of all your foes.

3. A prince from the day of your
      birth
   on the holy mountains;
   from the womb before the dawn I
      begot you.

4. The Lord has sworn an oath he
      will not change.
   'You are a priest for ever,
   a priest like Melchizedek of old.'

5. The master standing at your right
      hand
   will shatter kings in the day of his
      wrath.

6. He shall drink from the stream by
      the wayside
   and therefore he shall lift up his
      head.

7. Glory be to the Father, and to the
      Son
   and to the Holy Spirit.

8. As it was in the beginning, is now,
      and ever shall be,
   world without end, amen.

Psalm 113A(114) Week 1

1. When Israel came forth from
      Egypt,
   Jacob's sons from an alien people,
   Judah became the Lord's temple,
   Israel became his kingdom.

2. The sea fled at the sight:
   the Jordan turned back on its
      course,
   the mountains leapt like rams
   and the hills like yearling sheep.

3. Why was it sea, that you fled,
   that you turned back, Jordan, on
      your course?
   Mountains, that you leapt like
      rams,
   hills, like yearling sheep?

4. Tremble, O earth, before the Lord,
   in the presence of the God of
      Jacob,
   who turns the rock into a pool
   and flint into a spring of water.

5. Glory be to the Father, and to the
      Son
   and to the Holy Spirit,
   as it was in the beginning, is now
      and ever shall be,
   world without end. Amen.

Psalm 113B(115) Week 2

1. Not to us, Lord, not to us,
   but to your name give the glory
   for the sake of your love and your
      truth,

lest the heathen say: 'Where _is_
   their God?'

2. But our God is _in_ the heavens;
   he does whatev_er_ he wills.
   Their idols are sil_ver_ and gold,
   the work of _human_ hands.

3. They have mouths but they _cannot_
   speak;
   they have eyes but they _cannot_ see;
   they have ears but they _cannot_
   hear;
   they have nostrils but they _cannot_
   smell.

4. With their hands they cannot feel;|
   with their feet they _cannot_ walk.
   No sound comes _from_ their
   throats.
   Their makers will come _to_ be like
   them,
   and so will _all_ who trust in them

5. Sons of Israel, trust _in_ the Lord;
   he is their help _and_ their shield.
   Sons of Aaron, trust _in_ the Lord;
   he is their help _and_ their shield.

6. You who fear him, trust _in_ the
   Lord;
   he is their help _and_ their shield.
   He remembers us, and _he_ will bless
   us:
   he will bless the sons of Israel.|
   He will bless the _sons_ of Aaron.

7. The Lord will bless _those_ who fear
   him,
   the little no less _than_ the great:
   to you may the Lord _grant_
   increase,
   to you and _all_ your children.

8. May you be blessed _by_ the Lord
   the maker of hea_ven_ and earth.
   The heavens belong _to_ the Lord

but the earth he has gi_ven_ to men.

9. The dead shall not _praise_ the Lord,
   nor those who go _down_ in_to_ the
   silence.
   But we who live _bless_ the Lord
   now and for e_ver._ Amen.

10. Glory be to the Father, and _to_ the
    Son
    and to the _Holy_ Spirit,
    as it was in the beginning, is now
    and _ever_ shall be
    world without _end._ Amen.

Psalm 110(111)   *Week 3*

1. I will thank the Lord with _all_ my
   heart
   in the meeting of the just and _their_
   assembly.
   Great are the works _of_ the Lord;
   to be pondered by _all_ who love
   them.

2. Majestic and glori_ous_ his work,
   his justice stands _firm_ for ever.
   He makes us remem_ber_ his
   wonders.
   The Lord is compas_sion_ and love.

3. He gives food to _those_ who fear
   him;
   keeps his covenant _ever_ in mind.
   He has shown his might _to_ his
   people
   by giving them the lands _of_ the
   nations.

4. His works are just_ice_ and truth:
   his precepts are all _of_ them sure,
   standing firm for _ever_ and ever:
   they are made in upright_ness_ and
   truth.

5. He has sent deliverance to his
   people|
   and established his covenant for
   ever.
   Holy his name, to be feared.
   To fear the Lord is the first stage of
   wisdom;|
   all who do so prove themselves
   wise.
   His praise shall last for ever!

6. Glory be to the Father, and to the
   Son,
   and to the Holy Spirit,
   as it was in the beginning, is now|
   and ever shall be,
   world without end. Amen.

Psalm 111(112)   Week 4

1. Happy the man who fears the
   Lord,
   who takes delight in all his
   commands.
   His sons will be powerful on earth;
   the children of the upright are
   blessed.

2. Riches and wealth are in his house;
   his justice stands firm for ever.

He is a light in the darkness for the
   upright:
   he is generous, merciful and just.

3. The good man takes pity and
   lends,
   he conducts his affairs with
   honour.
   The just man will never waver:
   he will be remembered for ever.

4. He has no fear of evil news;
   with a firm heart he trusts in the
   Lord.
   With a steadfast heart he will not
   fear;
   he will see the downfall of his foes.

5. Open-handed, he gives to the
   poor;
   his justice stands firm for ever.
   His head will be raised in glory.
   The wicked man sees and is angry,|
   grinds his teeth and fades away;
   the desire of the wicked leads to
   doom.

6. Glory be to the Father, and to the
   Son
   and to the Holy Spirit,
   as it was in the beginning, is now|
   and ever shall be
   world without end. Amen.

Other Psalms in Volumes 1 & 2 (including paraphrases and hymns):
Grail Psalms are in bold type.'

Ps.8	Sing people of God, sing
Ps.8	**Your majesty is praised**
Ps.18(19)8-15	**The law of the Lord is perfect**
Ps.22(23)	**The Lord is my Shepherd**
	The King of love
	The Lord is my Shepherd
	The Lord is my Shepherd
	The Lord's my Shepherd

Ps.23(24)	**The Lord's is the earth**
Ps.24(25)	
Ps.26(27)	The Lord is my light and my help
Ps.32(33)1-7.10-12.16.	
18-22	Rejoice and shout for joy
Ps.33(34)2-5,9,17	Through all the changing scenes
Ps.41(42)1-6	**Like the deer that yearns**
3-6,11-12	Like the deer that thirsts
Ps.42(43)	**Defend me, O God**
Ps.50(51)3-19	**Have mercy on me, Lord**
Ps.62(63)	**O God, you are my God**
Ps.65(66)1-7.10.12	All you nations
Ps.83(84)	**How lovely is your dwelling place**
Ps.84(85)9-14	**I will hear what the Lord God has to say**
Ps.89(90)1-6	O God, our help in ages past
Ps.90(91) complete	**He who dwells**
Ps.90(91)3-7	Blest be the Lord
Ps.91(92)1,2,14,15	It is good to give thanks
Ps.94(95) complete	**Come, ring out our joy**
1-2,4-7,9	Come, sing out our joy
Ps.99(100)	**Cry out with joy**
	All people that on earth do dwell
	All the earth, proclaim the Lord
	He is risen, alleluia
	O be joyful in the Lord
Ps.102(103)1-4,8,10,12,13	**My soul, give thanks**
4-5,8,10,13,14	Our help is the name of the Lord
Ps.103(104)1-2,5-6,10-14,	
24,27-30	**Bless the Lord**
1-15	Send forth your Spirit
1,24,30,31	Alleluia (Bless the Lord)
Ps.104(105)4-5,7-8,9-11	We are bound for the promised land
Ps.112(113)1-2,4-7,9	Alleluia (O servants)
	Give praise to the Lord
Ps.114(115)	**I love the Lord for he has heard**
Ps.115(116)	**I trusted, even when I said**
Ps.116(117)	**Alleluia (O praise the Lord)**
	Come, praise the Lord
Ps.117(118)1-2,16-17,22-23	**Alleluia (Give thanks)**
1,16,23,27	Alleluia (Praise the Lord)
Ps.120(121)	I lift up my eyes (575)
	I lift up my eyes (565)
Ps.121(122)	**I rejoiced when I heard them say**
Ps.125(126)	**When the Lord delivered Zion**

Ps.129(130)	**Out of the depths**
	From the deep
	From the depths of sin and sadness
Ps.130(131)	My soul is longing for the Lord
Ps.135(136)	**O give thanks to the Lord**
1-2,7-9,25	Let us with a gladsome mind
Ps.138(139)1-3,7-8,13-14,	
17-18	Yahweh, I know you are near
1-2,7-10,17-18	My God, you fathom my heart
Ps.144(145)	**I will give you glory**
Ps.150	Alleluia (Praise God)

CANTICLES AND HYMNS BASED ON SCRIPTURE

Old Testament:

    All creation, bless the Lord (Daniel 3:35ff)
    All nations of the earth   (″   ″   )

Though the mountains may fall (Is.54:6-10,49:15,40:31-32)
Trust in the Lord (Is.40:28-31)
You shall cross the barren desert (Is:43:2-3 and Luke 6:20ff)
Greater love has no man (Jn.13,14,15)

New Testament:

    Rejoice in the Lord always (Phil:4:4-5)
    Alleluia! Salvation and glory (Rev.19)
    Christ suffered for you (1 Peter 2)
    For to those who love God (Rom.8:29-35)
    If God is for us (Rom.8:22-31)
    Greater love has no man (Ju.13,14,15)
    Jesus, the Holy Lamb of God (Phil.2:6-11)
    That which we have heard (1 Jn 1)
    There is one Lord (Eph.4:5)
    This is the feast of victory (Rev.4:9-14)

4. SCRIPTURE READING
5. RESPONSORY
This has the function of a response or comment on the Reading.
A. Texts of the short responsories of Sunday evening prayer in ordinary time:

Weeks 1 and 3
Blessed are you in the vault of heaven. (*Repeat*)
You are exalted and glorified above all else for ever. **Blessed...**
Glory be to the Father and to the Son, and to the Holy Spirit. **Blessed...**
Weeks 2 and 4

Great is our Lord: great is his might. (*Repeat*)
His wisdom can never be measured. **Great is our Lord...**

Glory be to the Father, and to the Son, and to the Holy Spirit. **Great is our Lord...**

B. *Other pieces suitable to be used as responsories:*

Adoramus te Domine
Breath of life
Dona nobis pacem
Glory be to the Father
Misericordias Domini
Sing and rejoice

Any other meditative piece may be chosen.

6. GOSPEL CANTICLE
   At Morning Prayer: The Benedictus
   At Evening Prayer: The Magnificat
   At Night Prayer: The Nunc Dimittis

7. INTERCESSIONS
   OUR FATHER
   CONCLUDING PRAYER

8. BLESSING

NATIONAL SONGS

722

1. I vow to thee, my country,
   all earthly things above,
   entire and whole and perfect,
   the service of my love;
   the love that asks no question,
   the love that stands the test,
   that lays upon the altar,
   the dearest and the best;
   the love that never falters,
   the love that pays the price,
   the love that makes undaunted
   the final sacrifice.

2. And there's another country,
   I've heard of long ago,
   most dear to them that love her,
   most great to them that know;
   we may not count her armies,
   we may not see her King;
   her fortress is a faithful heart,
   her pride is suffering;
   and soul by soul and silently
   her shining bounds increase,
   and her ways are ways of
      gentleness
   and all her paths are peace.

Words and music: G. Holst (1874-1934)

723

THE NATIONAL ANTHEM
GOD SAVE THE QUEEN

God save our gracious Queen,
Long live our noble Queen,
God save the Queen.
Send her victorious,
Happy and glorious,
Long to reign over us:
God save the Queen.

Thy choicest gifts in store
On her be pleased to pour,
Long may she reign.
May she defend our laws,
And ever give us cause
To sing with heart and voice,
God save the Queen.

Index of First Lines

*Hymns recorded or † in preparation for Mayhew McCrimmon's Hymn Cassette series.

HYMNS

A certain traveller on his way	376
A child is born for us today*	377
A child is born in Bethlehem	378
A mighty stronghold is our God	379
A new commandment I give	380
A noble flow'r of Juda*	381
A sign is seen in heaven	382
Abba, Abba, Father	383
Abba, Father, send your spirit	384
Across the years there echoes*	385
Again the Lord's own day†	386
Alabaré, a mi Señor	387
All for Jesus	388
All my hope on God is founded*	389
All the earth proclaim the Lord	390
All you nations*	391
Alleluia (X3), Jesus is alive	392
Alleluia (X3), May God's spirit come	393
Alleluia (X3), Sons of God arise†	394
Alleluia (X2), give thanks*	395
Alleluia (X2), salvation and glory	396
Almighty Father, who for us	397
Angel voices ever singing	398
An upper room	399
As earth that is dry	400
As I kneel before you*	401
As long as men	402
As one body	403
As the bridegroom†	404
Awake, awake	405
Bartimaeus, Bartimaeus	406
Be like your Father (See 417)	
Be still, my soul†	407
Before Christ died	408
Bind us together*	409
Blest are you, Lord	410
Blest be the Lord	411
Bread of the world	412
Break not the circle*	413
Breathing the words	414
Bright star of morning	415
Brother Sun and Sister Moon*	416
But I say unto you	417
By his wounds	418
By the cross	419
Called to be servants*	420
Child in the manger*	421
Christ be my way*	422
Christ has arisen, Alleluia!	423
Christ is alive	424
Christ is arisen	425
Christ is coming*	426
Christ is made the sure foundation†	427
Christ is the world's light	428
Christ is the world's redeemer	429
Christ our Lord has come	430
Christ our Pasch	431
Christ suffered for you (See 418)	
City of God	432
Come, God's people	433
Come, Holy Lord	434
Come let us sing out our joy	435
Come, Lord Jesus*	436
Come, O divine Messiah!	437
Come, O Lord, to my heart today	438
Come, thou long-expected Jesus	439
Day and night the heav'ns	440
Day by day	441
Dear love of my heart	442
Divided our pathways	443
Do not be afraid*	444
'Do you really love me?'	445
Each morning with its new born light	446
Faith in God*	447
Fashion me a people	448
Father, hear the prayer we offer	449
Father, I place into your hands	450
Father in heaven	451
Father, in my life I see*	452
Father, Lord of all creation	453

Father of heaven, whose love profound 454
Father, we praise you† 455
Fear not, for I have redeemed you 456
Fear not, rejoice and be glad 457
'Feed my lambs, my son'* 458
Firm is our faith 459
Follow me, follow me 460
For the fruits of his creation 461
For the healing of the nations 462
For to those who love God 463
For unto us a child is born† 464
Freely I give to you* 465
From the depths of sin and sadness 466
Gather Christians 467
Gathered here from many churches 468
Gifts of bread and wine 469
Give praise to the Lord 470
Give us the will to listen 471
Glorious things of you are spoken 472
Glory and praise to our God 473
Glory to God! Peace to all men 474
God, at creation's dawn* 475
God be with you 476
God forgave my sin* 477
God gives us harvest* 478
God has gladdened my heart 479
God is working his purpose out 480
God made the birds* 481
God most high of all creation 482
God, our maker 483
God rest you merry, gentlemen* 484
God's spirit precedes us 485
Good Christian men 486
Good Lady Poverty 487
Grant us thy peace 488
Greater love has no man 489
Hail Mary, full of grace (Landry)* 490
Hail Mary, full of grace (Walker)* 491
Hail Mary, mother of our God 492
He is Lord, he is Lord† 493
He is risen, alleluia, alleluia!* 494
He is risen, tell the story 495
He's a most unusual man 496
Help us accept each other 497

Here I am Lord (See 508)

Hills of the north, rejoice 498
His light now shines 499

Holy Spirit, Lord of light (See 638)
How lovely on the mountains* 500
I am the bread of life* 501
I am the vine 502

I am the way (See 525)

I heard the Lord call my name 503
I lift my eyes to the mountains 504
I lift up my eyes 505
I met you at the cross 506
I saw a star up high* 507
I, the Lord (Here I am, Lord)* 508
I was born before creation 509
I will be with you 510
I will never forget you 511
I will sing, I will sing 512
I will tell of your love 513
I'll sing God's praises 514
If God is for us 515
If God is our defender 516
In God alone there is rest 517
In the beginning all was empty 518
It's a long hard journey* 519
It's good to give thanks 520
Jesus said: 'I am the bread' 521
Jesus, the holy Lamb of God 522
Jesus the Lord said 523
Jesus the Word 524
Jesus, you are Lord 525
Keep in mind 526
Laudato sii 527
Lay your hands gently upon us* 528
Lead me, guide me 529
Leave your country 530
Lest he be too far from us 531
Let all who share one bread 532
Let it breathe on me 533
Let us praise our sovereign Saviour 534
Let us talents and tongues employ 535
Light the Advent candle one* 536
Like a sea without a shore 537
Like the deer that thirsts* 538
Look around, look around you 539
Look around you, can you see?† 540
Looking at the sunrise 541
Lord, confronted with your might 542
Lord, enthroned 543
Lord, graciously hear us 544
Lord, in everything I do 545

Lord Jesus Christ, be present now 546
Lord of creation (Lord of all power) 547
Lord, this paschal time 548
Lord thy word abideth 549
Lord, you have come to the lakeside 550
Love came down at Christmas 551
Lumen Christi! 552
May the peace of the Lord 553
Modern man has the city 554
Mother of Jesus 555
My God, my God 556
My God, you fathom my heart 557
My soul is longing for your peace 558
New life! New life! 559
No one can give to me that peace 560
Now let your people depart in peace 561
Now the tasks and toils are over 562
Now watch for God's coming 563
Now with the fading light 564
O be joyful in the Lord* 565
O comfort my people 566
O food of travellers 567
O Lady, full of God's own grace 568
O light forever dawning* 569
O raise your eyes on high 570
O what a gift 571
Of one that is so fair 572
Of the Father's love begotten 573
Oh the word of my Lord* 574
On a hill far away* 575
One day will come* 576
Our Father, we have wandered† 577

Our God reigns (See 500)

Our help is the name of the Lord 578
Our Saviour Jesus Christ proclaimed 579
Out of the deep unordered waters* 580

Pasch of the New Law (See 431)

Peace is my parting gift 581
Peace, perfect peace 582
Peacetime, peacetime* 583
Praise the Lord for the heavens 584
Praise the Lord! Ye heavens adore* 585
Praise to the Lord! Praise him! 586
Rain down justice 587
Rejoice, and shout for joy 588
Rejoice, rejoice, rejoice! 589
Remember, man, that you are dust 590
Return to the Lord 591

Rock of ages 592
Seek ye first the kingdom of God* 593
Send forth your Spirit, God 594
Send forth your Spirit, O Lord
  (Rochard)* 595
Send forth your Spirit, O Lord
  (Deiss) 596
Shepherd of Souls 597
Show me your ways* 598
Sing a simple song 599
Sing everyone 600
Sing praises to the Lord 601
Sing to the Lord a song 602
Sing to the Lord, alleluia 603
Sing to the mountains 604
Sing to the world of Christ 605
Son of God and son of David 606
Son of the Father 607
Take my life 608
Tell out, my soul* 609
That which we have heard 610
The angel Gabriel from heaven came 611
The Church is wherever 612

The eyes of the blind (See 664)

The King shall come 613
The light of Christ* 614
The Lord is my shepherd* 615
The seed is Christ's 616
The Spirit is moving 617
The Spirit lives to set us free† 618
The Spirit of God rests upon me 619
There is a river that flows* 620
There is one Lord 621
Thine be the glory* 622
This is my body 623
This is the day 624
This is the day, this is the day 625
This is the feast of vict'ry 626
This is the night 627
This is what Yahweh asks 628
Thou whose almighty Word 629
Though the mountains may fall 630
Through all the changing scenes* 631
To be the body of the Lord* 632
To God our Father 633
Together we journey 634
Trust in the Lord 635
Unite us, Lord 636

Upon thy table 637
Veni Sancte Spiritus 638
Wake, awake! For night is dying 639
Wake up! The dawn is near 640
We are bound for the promised land 641
We cry 'Hosanna, Lord'* 642
We form one Church 643
We gather together 644
We praise you and thank you 645
We praise you, God 646
We thank you, Father 647
Welcome all ye noble saints 648
What child is this 649
What do you ask of me? 650
When Jesus comes to be baptised 651
When morning gilds the skies 652
When the time came 653
Whey he day? Whey he day? 654
Who is she that stands triumphant 655
Who wants to live as God 656
Wind and fire, the signs of pow'r 657
Would you like to be happy? 658
Yahweh, I know you are near* 659
You, Israel, return now 660
You must cry out the word† 661
You servants of God 662
You shall come the barren desert* 663
Your Kingdom come 664

THE PSALMS

Ps 8 Your majesty is praised 665
Ps 18 (19) The law of the Lord 666
Ps 22 (23) The Lord is my shepherd 667
Ps 23(24) The Lord's is the earth 668
Ps 24(25) Lord make me know your
ways 669
Ps 26(27) The Lord is my light 670
Ps 41(42) Like the deer that yearns 671
Ps 42(43) Defend me, O God 672
Ps 50(51) Have mercy on me, God 673
Ps 62(63) O God, you are my God 674
Ps 83(84) My soul is longing 675
Ps 84(85) I will hear 676
Ps 90(91) He who dwells 677
Ps 92(93) The Lord is King 678
Ps 94(95) Come, ring out our joy 679
Ps 99(100) Cry out with joy 680
Ps 102(103) My soul give thanks 681

Ps 103(104) Bless the Lord, my soul 682
Ps 114/115(116) I love the Lord 683
Ps 115 My vows to the Lord 684
Ps 116(117) O praise the Lord 685
Ps 117(118) Give thanks to the Lord 686
Ps 121(122) I rejoiced when I heard 687
Ps 125(126) When the Lord delivered
Sion 688
Ps 129(130) Out of the depths 689
Ps 135(136) O give thanks to the Lord 690
Ps 144(145) I will give you glory 691
Ps 150 Praise God in his holy dwelling 692

The Benedictus. Blessed be the Lord 693
The Magnificat. My soul glorifies
the Lord 694
Nunc Dimittus. At last, all powerful
Master 695

ROUNDS, CANONS AND REFRAINS

Adoramus te Domine 696
Alleluia (Walker) 697
Alleluia (Boyce) 698
Blessed are they (The Beatitudes) 699
Breath of life 700
Dona nobis pacem 701
Glory be to God the Father 702
Go out to the whole world 703
I rejoiced when I heard them say 704
Jesus Christ, little Lord 705
Jubilate Deo 706
Jubilate Deo omnis terra 707
Let us go forth into the world 708
Misericordias Domini 709
O Lord, hear my prayer 710
Ostende nobis Domine 711
Sing alleluia to the Lord 712
Sing and rejoice in the Lord 713
Stand and stare not 714

LATIN HYMNS

Christus vincit† 715
Pange lingua† 716
Regina caeli† 717
Salve Regina† 718
Te Deum laudamus† 719
Veni, Creator Spiritus† 720
Victimae paschali laudes† 721

THE DIVINE OFFICE

O God, come to our aid
Ps 109(110) The Lord's revelation
Ps 111(112) Happy the man
Ps 110(111) I will thank the Lord
Ps 113A(114) When Israel came forth
Ps 113B(115) Not to us Lord

Responsories:
  Blessed are you in the vault of heaven
  Great is our Lord: great is his might

NATIONAL SONGS

I vow to thee my country   722
The National Anthem (God Save
  the Queen)   723

Index of Uses

Volume 1 and Volume 2

*Hymns recorded or † in preparation
for Mayhew McCrimmon cassettes.*

1. THE MASS
ENTRANCE

Vol. 1

All creation, bless the Lord*   3
All people that on earth do dwell*   10
All the nations of the earth*   12
At the name of Jesus*   28
Come my brothers   52
Come to the Lord   54
Father most holy   70
Holy God, we praise thy name*   121
Holy, holy, holy, Lord God
  almighty*   122
Immortal, invisible, God only wise*   134
Jesus is God! The solid earth   156
O holy Lord, by all adored   228
Open your ears   242
O worship the King*   253
This day God gives me   325
We celebrate this festive day   344
We gather together   345

****

Vol. 2

Again the Lord's own day is here†   386
All the earth proclaim the Lord   390
All you nations*   391
Awake, awake: fling off the night!   405
Christ is coming to set the
  captives free*   426
Come, holy Lord, our faith renew   434
Come, let us sing out our joy to
  the Lord   435
Father, we praise you†   455
Gather Christians   467
He is risen, alleluia*   494
Our help is the name of the Lord   578
Praise to the Lord, praise him   586
The light of Christ*   614
This is the day, this is the day   625
We gather together to ask the Lord's
  blessing   644
Jubilate Deo   706
Jubilate Deo omnis terra   707

RITE OF BLESSING OF WATER:
see Baptism, Lent

GLORY TO GOD

Glory to God (Peruvian Gloria)*   89

****

Glory to God, peace to all men   474
God most high of all creation   482

PSALMS: A full list is given in the Divine Office section

GOSPEL ACCLAMATION

Alleluia*   5

****

Alleluia (rounds)   697, 698
Alleluia! give thanks to the risen
   Lord*   395
Lumen Christi!   552
Sing alleluia to the Lord   712

PREPARATION OF THE GIFTS

Accept, O Father   2
All that I am*   11
Almighty Father Lord most high   17
Almighty Father take this bread   18
Come Lord Jesus*   51
Father and life giver   69
Fill my house   74
In bread we bring you Lord*   135
Lord accept the gifts we offer*   177
O God, we give ourselves today   224
O king of might and splendour   234
Praise to the Lord, the almighty*   264
Reap me the earth†   268
Take my hands*   296
Take our bread we ask you*   297
We are gathering together   341
We bring our gifts   343
What can we offer you?   351

****

Blest are you   410
Father, I place into your hands   450
God gives us harvest*   478
Lord of creation (Lord of all power)   547
Show me your ways*   598
Sing everyone   600
Son of the Father   607
Take my life and let it be   608
Upon thy table, Lord   637
Welcome, all ye noble saints   648
  Ps 83(84): My soul is longing   675
  Ps 121(122): I rejoiced   687

MEMORIAL ACCLAMATIONS

He is Lord†   493
Jesus, you are Lord   525

COMMUNION

Alleluia, sing to Jesus   7
Draw nigh and take the body   65
Fill my house†   74
Give me yourself   85
Godhead here in hiding   95
I am the bread of life*   128
In Christ there is no east or west   136
Into one we all are gathered*   139
In the earth the small seed   138
I saw the grass*   140
I watch the sunrise*   145
Jesus, thou art coming   158
Let all mortal flesh†   166
Lord Jesus Christ*   179
O thou who art thy Eucharist†   249
This is my will   327
Where is love and loving kindness?   358

****

An upper room   399
As one body   403
Before Christ died   408
Bread of the world   412
Come, O Lord   438
I am the bread of life†   501
Jesus the Lord said: I am the bread   523
Let all who share one Bread   532
Let us talents and tongues employ†   535
Lord, enthroned in heavenly
   splendour   543
O food of travellers   567
Shepherd of souls   597
This is my body   623
When the time came   653

RECESSIONAL

Colours of day*   45
Forth in the peace of Christ   78
Forth in thy name, O Lord†   79
Glory to thee, Lord God   90
God's spirit is in my heart*   99
Go, the Mass is ended*   102
Peace, perfect peace*   257
Praise him   259
Shalom   276
The Mass is ended   313
Walk with me, Oh my Lord*   340

With a song in our hearts 361
****
Alleluia, sons of God arise 394
Almighty Father, who for us 397
God be with you till we meet again 476
I will be with you 510
Lord, in everything I do 545
Now let your people depart in peace 561
Peace is my parting gift 581
Praise the Lord! Ye heavens,
  adore him* 585
The Spirit lives to set us free† 618
Go out to the whole world
Jubilate Deo 706
Jubilate Deo omnis terra 707
Let us go forth 708
Stand and stare not 714

THE SACRAMENTS
BAPTISM

Colours of day* 45
Come down, O love divine* 49
Come, Holy Ghost, Creator, come* 50
Firmly I believe and truly* 75
Here's a child for you, O Lord 116
Immortal, invisible, God only wise* 134
Love is his word, love is his way* 185
Oh living water† 225
****
Alleluia, sons of God arise 394
Called to be servants* 420
Christ our Lord has come to save 430
God, at creation's dawn* 475
New life, new life 559
Out of deep unordered water* 580
The light of Christ* 614
There is a river* 620
There is one Lord
  Ps 41(42) Like the deer that yearns 671
  Ps 62(63) O God, you are my God 674

CONFIRMATION (See also
Commitment, Ordination)

Breathe on me, breath of God 37
God's spirit is in my heart 99
Spirit of the living God 289
****
Follow me 460

I will be with you 510
Lord, in everything I do 545
O the word of my Lord* 574
Send forth your Spirit 594
Send forth your Spirit, O Lord 595
Send forth your Spirit, O Lord 596
Take my life, and let it be 608
The Spirit is moving 617
The Spirit of God 619

PENANCE AND RECONCILIATION

From the deep I lift my voice 81
God of mercy and compassion* 98
It's me O Lord 144
Many times I have turned 191
O God of earth and altar 221
O God, thy people gather* 223
Oh Lord My God* 227
O sacred head sore wounded* 247
Seasons come, seasons go 273
Thou wilt keep him in perfect peace 330
Walk with me* 340
We will walk 350
Yahweh, you are my strength 362
****
As earth that is dry 400
Come, Lord Jesus* 436
Divided our pathways 443
Father of heaven, whose love
  profound 454
Father we praise you 455
God forgave my sin* 477
Lord, confronted with your might 542
Lord, graciously hear us 544
Our Father, we have wandered† 577
Return to the Lord 591
You, Israel, return now 660
  Ps 50(51) Have mercy on me, God 673

MARRIAGE

Father, within thy house today 71
O perfect love* 243
Sing of the bride† 280
The Lord's my shepherd* 312
The Lord is my Shepherd 615

ORDINATION, PROFESSION
(See also Confirmation, Commitment)

Be thou my vision* 35
God's spirit is in my heart* 99
Happy the man* 111
He who would valiant be* 119
This is my will 327
****
As the bridegroom to his chosen† 404
Do you really love me? 445
Follow me 460
Good lady poverty 487
How lovely on the mountains* 500
I, the Lord of earth and sky
(Here I am, Lord) 508
Leave your country 530
Lord of creation (Lord of all power)† 547
Lord, you have come to the lakeside 550
O the word of my Lord 574
Take my life 608
Thou whose almighty word 629

ANOINTING (See also Trust)

Abide with me* 1
All ye who seek a comfort sure 15
Be still and know I am with you* 32
Be still and know that I am God* 33
Jesu, lover of my soul 150
Lead, kindly light† 164
****
Bartimaeus 406
Be still, my soul† 407
Father, I place into your hands 450
In God alone is my soul at rest 517
Lay your hands* 528
My soul is longing 558
Our Saviour Jesus Christ proclaimed 579

FUNERALS

For all the saints* 77
From the deep I lift my voice 81
Going Home 100
Jerusalem the golden† 149
Lead, kindly light 164
Now come to me 208
Oh Lord, my God* 227
Steal away 291
The Lord's my shepherd* 312

We will walk through the valley 350
****
I am the bread of life* 501
In God alone is my soul at rest 517
Lead me, guide me 529
Like the deer that thirsts* 538
O light forever dawning* 569
Ps 22(23) The Lord is my shepherd 667
Ps 26(27) The Lord is my light and
my life 670
Ps 41(42) Like the deer that yearns 671
Ps 62(63) O God, you are my God 674
Ps 83(84) My soul is longing and
yearning 675

DEDICATION OF A CHURCH
(See also Church)

On this house your blessing, Lord 240
****
Christ is made the sure foundation 427
Ps 83(84) My soul is longing and
yearning 675
Ps 121(122) I rejoiced when I heard
them say 687

2. TIMES AND SEASONS

ADVENT

Hail to the Lord's anointed* 110
Hark! a herald voice is calling 112
O come, O come Emmanuel* 216
O Jesus Christ, remember* 233
On Jordan's bank the Baptist's cry 239
Promised Lord and Christ is he* 267
The coming of our God 301
****
A noble flower of Judah* 381
Across the years there echoes still* 385
Christ is coming* 426
Come, Lord Jesus* 436
Come, O divine Messiah* 437
Come, thou long-expected Jesus 439
God is working his purpose out 480
Hills of the north, rejoice 498
Lest he be too far from us 531
Light the Advent candle one* 536
O comfort my people 566
Rains down justice 587

The angel Gabriel 611
The king shall come when morning
  dawns 613
Wake, awake 639
Wake up, the dawn is near 640
  Ps 23(24) The Lord's is the earth 668
  Ps 84(85) I will hear 676
  Ps 121(122) I rejoiced 687

CHRISTMAS

Angels we have heard in heaven 21
Angels we have heard on high* 22
As with gladness men of old 24
Away in a manger* 30
Come Christian people* 47
Come, come, come to the manger* 48
Ding dong merrily on high 62
Go tell it on the mountain 92
Hark, the herald angels sing* 113
How dark was the stable 127
In the bleak midwinter 137
It came upon the midnight clear* 143
I wonder as I wander 147
Little Jesus, sweetly sleep* 174
Long ago in Bethlehem* 175
O come all ye faithful* 214
O little town of Bethlehem* 235
Once in Royal David's city* 238
See, amid the winter's snow 274
Silent night* 277
Sleep, holy babe* 285
The first Nowell* 305
The Virgin Mary had a baby boy* 321
Unto us is born a Son 337
While shepherds watched 360
       ****
A child is born for us today* 377
A child is born in Bethlehem 378
A noble flower of Judah* 381
Child in the manger* 421
Freely, I give to you* 465
God rest you merry, gentlemen* 484
I saw a star up high* 507
Love came down at Christmas 551
Of the Father's love begotten 573
What child is this, who laid to rest 649

THE HOLY FAMILY

Away in a manger* 30
In the bleak midwinter 137
O little town of Bethlehem* 235
Once in Royal David's city* 238
On this house your blessing, Lord* 240
Sing of Mary 281
       ****
Child in the manger* 421
O Lady, full of God's own grace 568
What child is this, who laid to rest 649

EPIPHANY

Bethlehem! of noblest cities 34
Songs of thankfulness and praise 286
The first Nowell* 305
The race that long in darkness 315
We three kings of Orient are* 349
       ****
A child is born for us today* 377
A child is born in Bethlehem 378
I saw a star* 507

BAPTISM OF THE LORD

Hail to the Lord's anointed* 110
Open your ears 242
Songs of thankfulness and praise 286
The race that long in darkness pined 315
       ****
Christ through the waters
For unto us a child is born† 464
The Spirit of God rests upon me 619
When Jesus comes to be baptised 651

THE PRESENTATION OF THE
LORD (Feb 2)

At last, all-powerful Master
  (Nunc Dimittis) 695
Christ is the world's light 428
Lumen Christi! 552
Now let your people (Nunc Dimittis)
The light of Christ* 614

LENT

Attend and keep this happy fast 25
At the cross her station keeping* 26

Crown him with many crowns	56
Forty days and forty nights	80
From the deep I lift my voice	81
From the depths we cry to thee	82
God of mercy and compassion*	98
Keep we the fast that men of old	160
Lord, who throughout these forty days	183
O come and mourn*	215
O sacred head sore wounded*	247

****

As earth that is dry	400
Christ suffered for you (By his wounds)	418
Divided our pathways	443
Father of heaven, whose love profound	454
God forgave my sin (Freely, freely)*	477
Like the deer that thirsts*	538
O raise your eyes on high (2nd Sunday)	570
Our Father, we have wandered	577
Remember, man, that you are dust	590
You, Israel, return now	660
Ps 41(42) Like the deer that yearns	671
Ps 50(51) Have mercy on me, God	673
Ps 90(91) He who dwells	677
Ps 129(130) Out of the depths	689

HOLY WEEK

Palm Sunday

All glory, laud and honour	8
Ride on, ride on in majesty*	271

****

We cry Hosanna, Lord	642

Maundy Thursday

Into one we all are gathered*	139
Love is his word*	185
Of the glorious body telling*	219
O thou who at thy Eucharist	249
The heavenly word	309
This is my will	327
Where is love and loving kindness	358

****

An upper room	399
As one body, We are one	403
Greater love has no man	489

This is my body, broken for you	623
This is what Yahweh asks of you	628
Though so many, we are one	
When the time came	653
Pange lingua†	716

Good Friday, the Passion

All ye who seek a comfort sure	15
By the blood that flowed from thee	40
Glory be to Jesus*	88
I met you at the Cross*	
O come and mourn*	215
O sacred head	247
Praise to the holiest*	262
Sing my tongue, the glorious battle*	279
There is a green hill far away*	316
The royal banners forward go	318
They hung him on a cross	323
Were you there*	347
When I survey the wondrous cross*	355

****

By the cross which did to death	419
Jesus the holy Lamb of God	522

Easter Vigil

Now the green blade†	S.3
Oh living water†	225
This joyful Eastertide*	328

****

Alleluia! Sons of God arise†	394
As earth that is dry	400
Called to be servants*	420
Christ is arisen, alleluia	425
Christ the Lord has come to save his people	430
Christ our Pasch (Pasch of the new law)	431
God at creation's dawn*	475
Good Christian men	486
Keep in mind	526
Like the deer that thirsts*	538
Lumen Christi!	552
There is a river*	620
This is the night	627

EASTERTIDE

At the lamb's high feast we sing	27
Battle is o'er, hell's armies flee*	31
Bring, all you dear-bought nations	38

Christ the Lord is risen today*	44
Dust, dust and ashes	66
He was born like you and I	118
Jesus Christ is risen today*	153
Now Jesus said	209
Now the green blade riseth†	S.3
The bakerwoman	299
The day of resurrection	302
They hung him on a cross	323
This joyful Eastertide*	328
Were you there?*	347
We will walk through the valley	350
Ye choirs of New Jerusalem	363
Ye sons and daughters of the Lord	364

****

Alleluia, alleluia, give thanks to the risen Lord*	395
Christ has arisen, alleluia	423
Christ is alive, with joy we sing	424
Christ is arisen	425
Christ our Pasch	431
Come God's people, sing for joy	433
Good Christian men	486
He is risen, alleluia*	494
He is risen, tell the story	495
Keep in mind	526
Lord, enthroned in heavenly splendour	543
Lord, this paschal time reminds us	548
New life, new life	559
Pasch of the new law	
Sing to the mountains	604
The light of Christ*	614
There is a river*	620
There is one Lord	621
Thine be the glory*	622
This is the day	625
Victimae paschali†	721

ASCENSION

At the name of Jesus*	28
Hail the day that sees him rise	108
New praises be given	207
Rejoice! the Lord is King*	270
The head that once was crowned with thorns	308

****

Christ is the world's redeemer	429
He is Lord†	493
Jesus, you are Lord	525
Stand and stare not	714

PENTECOST, THE HOLY SPIRIT

Breathe on me breath of God*	37
Colours of day*	45
Come down, O love divine*	49
Come Holy Ghost, Creator, come*	50
God's Spirit is in my heart*	99
Holy spirit Lord of light	124
Holy Spirit of fire	125
Love is his word, love is his way*	185
Oh living water	225
Out and away	252
Spirit of the living God*	289
Where does the wind come from?	357

****

Send forth your Spirit, O Lord	595
Send forth your Spirit, O Lord	596
The Spirit is moving	617
Veni, sancte Spiritus†	638
Wind and fire, the signs of power	657
Ps 102(103) My soul, give thanks	681
Veni Creator Spiritus†	720

TRINITY

Father most holy	70
Holy God, we praise thy name*	121
Holy, holy, holy, Lord God*	123
Lead us heavenly Father, lead us†	165
Merrily on	193
Most ancient of all mysteries	198
O Trinity, most blessed light	250
Sing praises to the living God	284

****

Father in heaven	451
Father, in my life I see†	452
Father, Lord of all creation	453

CORPUS CHRISTI: See Communion, Holy Week (Maundy Thursday)

CHRIST THE KING

All hail the power of Jesus' name†	9
At the name of Jesus*	28
Christ is king	42

Christ is our king	43
Crown him with many crowns	56
Hail, Redeemer, King divine!*	107
King of glory, king of peace*	161
Praise we now the Lord our God	265
Rejoice! the Lord is King*	270
To Christ the Lord of worlds	332

****

How lovely on the mountains†	500
Sing to the world of Christ	605
This is the feast of victory	626
Ps 23(24) The Lord's is the earth	668
Ps 92(93) The Lord is King	678
Christus vincit	715

BLESSED VIRGIN

Ave Maria, O Maiden, O Mother*	29
Bring flowers of the rarest*	39
Daily, daily sing to Mary*	57
Hail, Queen of heaven*	106
Hail, thou star of ocean	109
Holy Virgin, by God's decree†	126
I'll sing a hymn to Mary*	132
Immaculate Mary!*	133
Look down, O Mother Mary*	176
Maiden, yet a mother	188
Mary immaculate	192
Mother of mercy, day by day	199
O Mother blest*	236
O purest of creatures!*	246
Sing of Mary, pure and lowly	281
Star of ocean, lead us	290
The bakerwoman	299
The God whom earth and sea	306
This is the image of the Queen	326
Virgin wholly marvellous	339
Where are you bound, Mary?	356
Ye who own the faith of Jesus	365

****

As I kneel before you†	401
Hail Mary (Landry)*	490
Hail Mary (Walker)*	491
Hail Mary, mother of our God	492
Mother of Jesus	555
O lady, full of God's own grace	568
Of one that is so fair and bright	572
Tell out, my soul (The Magnificat)*	609
My soul glorifies the Lord (The Magnificat)†	694

Regina caeli†	717
Salve regina†	718

SAINTS (See also Commitment, Love of others)

Be thou my vision*	35
Blest are the pure in heart*	36
Faith of our fathers*	68
For all the saints*	77
Great St Andrew*	103
Hail glorious St Patrick*	105
Hail, holy Joseph, hail	S.6
Happy the man*	111
Jerusalem the golden†	149
Leader now on earth (St George)	163
O great St David*	S.4
St Andrew, called to follow Christ*	S.5
The hand, O God, has guided	331

****

Across the years (St John the Baptist)	385
As the bridegroom to his chosen	404
How lovely on the mountains†	500
We praise you and thank you (St Patrick)	645

HOLY SOULS

Help, Lord, the souls	115

****

O light, forever dawning	569
Ps 26(27) The Lord is my light	670
Ps 41(42) Like the deer that yearns	671
Ps 62(63) O God, you are my God	674
Ps 83(84) My soul is longing	675

3. TOPICAL INDEX

COMMITMENT, DISCIPLESHIP

All that I am*	11
Fight the good fight	73
Follow Christ	76
Forth in the peace of Christ	78
Forth in thy name, O Lord	79
God's Spirit is in my heart*	99
He who would valiant be*	119
My God, accept my heart*	201
Onward, Christian soldiers*	241

Take my hands*   296
          ****
Christ be my way   422
Fear not   456
Follow me   460
Give us the will to listen   471
Good lady poverty   487
He's a most unusual man   496
I, the Lord of sea and sky
    (Here I am)*   508
I will be with you   510
Leave your country and your people 530
Lord, in everything I do   545
Lord of creation (Lord of all power)† 547
Lord, you have come to the lakeside 550
Lord of all power
Oh the word of my Lord*   574
Seek ye first the kingdom of God* 593
Take my life   608
Together we journey   634
The Spirit is moving   617
Trust in the Lord   635
Wake up! The dawn is near   640
Who wants to live the life   656
Go out to the whole world   703
Let us go forth   708
Stand and stare not   714

CHURCH: CHURCH UNITY

Colours of day*   45
Come to the Lord   54
Do you know that the Lord?   64
Follow Christ   76
He's got the whole world   117
In Christ there is no east or west 136
Let's make peace   170
Lord, make me an instrument   S.7
Lord, we pray for golden peace   182
Make me a channel of your peace*   189
Moses, I know you're the man   197
Open your ears   242
Peace is the gift of heaven   255
Sons of God*   287
The Church's one foundation*   300
Thy hand, O God, has guided†   331
We are one in the spirit*   342
We gather together   345
We shall overcome   348

When Israel was in Egypt's Land   354
          ****
Bind us together*   409
Called to be servants*   420
City of God   432
Divided our pathways   443
Fashion me a people   448
Gathered here from many churches 468
Glorious things of thee are spoken 472
I am the vine   502
The Church is wherever   612
There is one Lord   621
To be the body of the Lord*   632
We thank you, Father   647
Who is she that stands triumphant 655

CREATION

All creation, bless the Lord*   3
All creatures of our God and King   4
All the nations of the earth*   12
Glory be to God, the King of kings 87
          ****
All you nations   391
Day and night the heavens are telling 440
God made the birds*   481
God our maker, mighty Father   483
I was born before creation   509
In the beginning   518
Send forth your Spirit (Deiss)   596
  Ps 103(104) Bless the Lord   682

EVENING NIGHT

Day is done   59
Glory to thee, my God, this night   91
I watch the sunrise*   145
Round me falls the night   272
Sweet Saviour bless us*   295
The day thou gavest*   303
          ****
My soul is longing for your peace 558
Now the tasks and toils are over   562
Now with the fading light of day   564

EVANGELISATION (See also
Ordination, Commitment, Church)

Colours of day*   45
Do you really love me?   445

Feed my lambs*	458
For the healing of the nations	462
Lord, thy word abideth†	549
Thou, whose almighty word	629
Go out to the whole world	703

FAITH

Firmly I believe and truly*	75
I believe in God almighty	129
I believe in God the Father	130

****

Faith in God can move the mountains*	447
Father, hear the prayer we offer	449
Firm is our faith	459
Jesus said, I am the bread	521
We thank you, Father	647

GOD'S LOVE AND CARE

Ask and you shall receive	23
Be still and know I am with you*	32
Day by day in the market place	58
God is love	96
God is love: his the care	97
Jesu, meek and lowly	151
Let us with a gladsome mind	171
Love divine, all loves excelling	184
Love is his word	185
My God loves me	205
Now come to me	208
Now thank we all our God	211
Oh Lord, all the world	226
Oh the love of my Lord is the essence*	231
O worship the King†	253
Praise my soul the king of heaven	260
Praise we our God	266
Sing my soul	278
The prophet in his hunger	314

****

Do not be afraid†	444
Fear not, for I have redeemed you	456
Fear not, rejoice and be glad	457
His light now shines in the darkness	499
I heard the Lord	503
I, the Lord of sea and sky (Here I am)*	508
I will never forget you	511

I will tell of your love	513
Jesus the Lord said	523
Like a sea without a shore	537
Look around you†	540
My God, you fathom my heart	557
Son of the Father	607
The love of God made me	
Yahweh, I know you are near*	659
Ps 135(136) O give thanks to the Lord	690
Ps 138(139)	
Ps 144(145) I will give you glory	691

HARVEST

In the earth the small seed	138
Reap we the earth	268
We plough the fields†	346

****

For the fruits of his creation	461
God gives us harvest†	478

JESUS' MINISTRY AND MIRACLES

Christ is our King*	43
Day by day in the market place	58
Feed us now	72
Follow Christ	76
I saw the grass*	140
Man of Galilee	190
Now come to me	208
Songs of thankfulness	286
The King of glory comes	310
The prophet in his hunger	314
The spirit of the Lord	319
Walk with me*	340

****

Bartimaeus	406
Come, Lord Jesus*	436
Lay your hands*	528
The spirit of God rests upon me	619

LAW OF GOD

Blest are the pure in heart*	36
God be in my head	93
Happy the man*	111
Many times have I turned	191
O God of earth and altar	221

O God, thy people gather*   223
****

Lord, confronted with your might   542
Lord, graciously hear us   544
Lord, in everything I do   545
Our Father, we have wandered   577
Ps 18(19) The law of the Lord   666

LOVE OF OTHERS

Do you know that the Lord   64
Follow Christ   76
In Christ there is no east or west   136
Into one we all are gathered   139
Man of Galilee   190
Now Jesus said   210
Sons of God*   287
This is my will   327
Whatsoever you do   352
Where is love and loving kindness   358
****

A certain traveller   376
A new commandment   380
Almighty Father   397
Be like your Father   417
Bind us together*   409
Break not the circle*   413
For the healing of the nations   462
Greater love has no man   489
Help us accept each other   497
Look around you†   540
The Church is wherever   612
This is what Yahweh asks   628
Would you like to be happy   658

MORNING

Morning has broken*   196
This day God gives me   325
****

Awake, awake   405
Bright star of morning   415
Each morning with its newborn light   446
Father, we praise you   455
When morning gilds the skies   652

OUR LOVE OF GOD

Be thou my vision*   35
Christ be beside me*   41

Jesu, the very thought of thee   152
King of glory, king of peace*   161
Lord of all hopefulness*   181
My God, how wonderful thou art   203
My God, I love thee   204
Oh Lord, my God*   227
Seasons come, seasons go   273
****

Abba, Abba, Father   383
As long as man on earth   402
As the bridegroom to his chosen†   404
Bright star of morning   415
Day by day   441
Dear love of my heart   442
Do you really love me?   445

•

PEACE AND JUSTICE

Christ is our king*   43
Do you know   64
Feed us now   72
Follow Christ   76
I sing the Lord God's praises   142
Lord, make me an instrument   S.7
Lord, we pray for golden peace   182
Make me a channel of your peace*   189
There is a world   317
Whatsoever you do   352
****

For the healing of the nations   462
Grant us thy peace   488
Help us accept each other   497
Let all who share one bread   532
Look around you†   540
My soul is longing for your peace   558
Peace is my parting gift to you   581
Peacetime, peacetime*   583
Tell out, my soul   609
The eyes of the blind   663
The Spirit of God   619
The spirit of the living God
To be the body of the Lord*   632
Unite us, Lord, in peace   636
You must cry out the word   661
Ps 84(85) I will hear   676
Ps 121(122) I rejoiced   687
Dona nobis pacem   701

PRAISE

Come, my brothers 52
Come, praise the Lord 53
Immortal, invisible* 134
I sing a song to you, Lord* 141
I will give you glory 146
Let all that is within me* 167
Let all the world 168

****

Alabare a mi señor 387
All the earth, proclaim the Lord 390
Christ is alive, with joy we sing 424
Give praise to the Lord all you men 470
God most high of all creation 482
He is Lord, he is Lord† 493
I will sing, I will sing 512
I'll sing God's praises 514
O be joyful in the Lord* 565
O praise ye the Lord*
Praise the Lord for the heavens 584
Praise the Lord, ye heavens
    adore him 585
Sing praises to the Lord 601
Sing to the Lord, alleluia 603
When morning gilds the skies 652
    Ps 102(103) My soul, give thanks 681
    Ps 112(113)
    Ps 135(136) O give thanks 690
    Ps 150 Alleluia 692
Jubilate Deo†
Jubilate, servite†
Te Deum laudamus† 719

THANKSGIVING

Amazing grace* 19
God everlasting 94
Now thank we all our God* 211
Praise, my soul, the King of heaven* 260

****

As long as men on earth 402
Fear not, rejoice and be glad 457
Glory and praise to our God 473
For the fruits of his creation 461
It is good to give thanks 520
O what a gift 571
Tell out, my soul* 609

TRUST IN GOD, GUIDANCE

All ye who seek 15

Dear Lord and Father* 60
Guide me, O thou great Redeemer* 104
I watch the sunrise* 145
Jesu, lover of my soul 150
Just a closer walk 159
Lead us, heavenly Father† 165
Loving shepherd 187
O God, our help in ages past 222
O my Lord, within my heart 237
This day God gives me 325
Walk with me* 340
We will walk through the valley 350
Yahweh, you are my strength 362

****

A mighty stronghold is our God 379
All my hope on God is founded* 389
Be still, my soul 407
Bright star of morning 415
Christ be my way* 422
Father, I place into your hands 450
For to those who love God 463
God made the birds* 481
God our maker, mighty Father 483
Grant us thy peace 488
I lift my eyes 504
I lift up my eyes 505
If God is for us 515
If God is our defender 516
In God alone is there rest 517
Into you hands, O Lord 518
It's a long hard journey* 519
Lay your hands gently upon me* 528
Lest he be too far from us 531
Like a sea without a shore 537
Lord, thy word abideth 549
Lord, you have come to the lakeside 550
My God, my God 556
No one can give to me that peace 560
One day will come* 576
Our Saviour Jesus Christ proclaimed 579
Peace, perfect peace 582
Rock of ages 592
Show me your ways* 598
Sing a simple song 599
The Lord is my shepherd 615
This is what Yahweh asks 628
Though the mountains may fall 630
Through all the changing scenes* 631

Whey he day	654	WORD OF GOD		
You will cross the barren desert*	663	In the beginning		518
Ps 22(23) The Lord is my shepherd	667	Jesus the Word has lived among us		524
Ps 90(91) He who dwells	677	Lord, thy word abideth		549
		That which we have heard		610
		Thou, whose almighty word		629
UNITY		You must cry out the word of the		
		Lord†		661
See Church, Love of Others				

Acknowledgements

The publishers wish to express their gratitude to the following for the use of their copyright material in this book:

Agapé, Carol Stream, IL 60188, USA, for *Break not the circle* © 1975; *Divided our pathways* © 1974; *Help us accept each other* © 1975; *His light now shines in the darkness* © 1969; *Let us talents and tongues employ* © 1975; *Lord , confronted with your might* © 1975; *You, Israel, return now* © 1976. International copyright secured. All rights reserved. Used with permission.

John Ainslie, 76 Great Bushey Drive, Totteridge, London, N20 8QL, for the tune 'Ellenborough' *(Grant us thy peace)*. Used by permission.

The American Catholic Press, 1223 Rossell Oak Park, Illinois 60302, USA for the words and music of *O what a gift* © 1967, 1970. Used by permission. All rights reserved.

Ampleforth Abbey Trustees, Ampleforth Abbey, York, YO6 4EN, for the words of *O raise your eyes on high and see*. Used by permission.

The Archdiocese of Durban, 408 Innes Road, Durban 4001, South Africa, for the words of *Across the years; God at creation's dawn; God, our maker; If God is our defender; Lord, this paschaltime; O light forever dawning; Send forth your Spirit;* and for the words and music of *Firm is our faith*. All used by permission.

William Armitage, Canada, for the words of *To God Our Father* © 1977.

Augsburg Publishing House, 426 South Fifth Street, Box 1209, Minneapolis MN 55440, USA for *This is the feast*, reprinted from *Contemporary Worship 2: The Holy Communion,* © 1970; *Christ has arisen, Alleluia!* reprinted by permission from *Lead Us, Lord,* ed by Howard S. Olson, © 1977. Used by permission.

Tony Barr, 9 Patmore Road, Colchester, Essex for the words and music of *Rain down justice*. Tony Barr and Jabulani Music, 9 Patmore Road, Colchester, Essex, for *My God you fathom my heart, The song of God among us (Lest he be too far from us), I lift up my eyes, Our help is the name of the Lord, Who wants to live as God (The song of all seed), Breath of life* and *Stand and stare not*. Text © Huub Oosterhuis; translation © Tony Barr. Used with permission.

The Benedictine Foundation of the State of Vermont, Inc, Weston Priory, Weston, Vermont 05161, USA, for *A child is born for us today* © 1971; *I lift my eyes to the mountains* © 1975; In the beginning © 1974, 1975; *We thank you, Father* © 1971, 1980. All used with permission.

The Benedictines of Stanbrook, Stanbrook Abbey Press, Callow End, Worcester WR2 4TD, for the words and music of *When Jesus comes to be baptised*. Used with permission.

Laurence Bevenot, OSB, St Mary's, 67 Talbot Street, Canton, Cardiff, CF1 9BX, for *Christus Vincit*. Used with permission.

Mrs William Booth-Clibbon for the words and music of *Let it breathe on me*.

Burckhardthaus Verlag GmbH, 6460 Gelnhausen 1, Germany, for the original words and music of *Give us the will to listen*. Used with permission.

Celebration Services (International) Limited, Cathedral of the Isles, Millport, Isle of Cumbrae, KA28 0HE, Scotland, for the words and music of *Alleluia! Sons of God arise!* © 1971, 1975; *Be like your Father* © 1979; *Fear not, rejoice and be glad* © 1971, 1975; *Fear not, for I have redeemed you* © 1975; *I will sing, I will sing* © 1974, 1975; *Look around you (Kyrie Eleison); O be joyful in the Lord!* © 1975; *The eyes of the blind (God make us your family)* © 1973, 1975; *We cry 'Hosanna, Lord'* © 1975. All used with permission.